**Emotions Across Languages and Cultures:
Diversity and Universals**

In this ground-breaking new book, Anna Wierzbicka brings psychological, anthropological and linguistic insights to bear on our understanding of the way emotions are expressed and experienced in different cultures, languages and culturally shaped social relations. The expression of emotion in the face, body and modes of speech are all explored and Wierzbicka shows how the bodily expression of emotion varies across cultures and challenges traditional approaches to the study of facial expressions. As well as offering a new perspective on human emotions based on the analysis of language and ways of talking about emotion, this fascinating and controversial book attempts to identify universals of human emotion by analysing empirical evidence from different languages and cultures. This book will be invaluable to academics and students of emotion across the Social Sciences.

**Anna Wierzbicka** is Professor in the Department of Linguistics at the Australian National University in Canberra. A Fellow of the Australian Academy of the Humanities and of the Academy of Social Sciences of Australia, and a Foreign Member of the Russian Academy of Sciences, she has lectured extensively in Europe, America and Japan and published twenty books in the fields of linguistics, anthropology and psychology.

D1291805

# STUDIES IN EMOTION AND SOCIAL INTERACTION
Second Series

Series Editors

Keith Oatley
*University of Toronto*

Antony Manstead
*University of Amsterdam*

This series is jointly published by the Cambridge University Press and the Editions de la Maison des Sciences de l'Homme, as part of the joint publishing agreement established in 1977 between the Fondation de la Maison des Sciences de l'Homme and the Syndics of the Cambridge University Press.

Cette publication est publiée co-édition par Cambridge University Press et les Éditions de la Maison des Sciences de l'Homme. Elle s'intègre dans le programme de co-édition établi en 1977 par la Fondation de la Maison des Sciences de l'Homme et les Syndics de Cambridge University Press.

*Titles published in the Second Series:*

*The Psychology of Facial Expression*
0 521 496675 Hardback and 0 521 58796 4 Paperback
Edited by James A. Russell and José Miguel Fernández-Dols

*Emotions, the Social Bond, and Human Reality: Part/Whole Analysis*
0 521 58491 4 Hardback and 0 521 58545 7 Paperback
Thomas J. Scheff

*Intersubjective Communication and Emotion in Early Ontogeny*
0 521 622573 Hardback and 2 7351 0772 8 Hardback (France only)
Edited by Stein Bråten

# Emotions Across Languages and Cultures: Diversity and Universals

Anna Wierzbicka

CAMBRIDGE
UNIVERSITY PRESS

Editions de la Maison des Sciences de l'Homme
*Paris*

PUBLISHED BY THE PRESS SYNDICATE OF THE UNIVERSITY OF CAMBRIDGE
The Pitt Building, Trumpington Street, Cambridge United Kingdom
Editions de la Maison des Sciences de l'Homme
54 Boulevard Raspail, 75270 Paris Cedes 06, France

CAMBRIDGE UNIVERSITY PRESS
The Edinburgh Building, Cambridge, CB2 2RU, UK http://www.cup.cam.ac.uk
40 West 20th Street, New York, NY 10011–4211, USA http://www.cup.org
10 Stamford Road, Oakleigh, Melbourne 3166, Australia

© Anna Wierzbicka 1999

First published 1999

Printed in the United Kingdom at the University Press, Cambridge

Typeset in Palatino 10/12pt [vN]

*A catalogue record for this book is available from the British Library*

ISBN 0 521 59042 6 hardback
ISBN 0 521 59971 7 paperback

# Contents

v

# Figures

# Acknowledgments

Work on this book was supported by the Australian Research Council which funded valuable research assistance. I am extremely grateful to both my research assistants, Lea Brown, who has worked with me throughout, and Helen O'Loghlin, who joined us at a late but still crucial stage. Their competence, dedication, and acumen were essential to the successful completion of the project. I would also like to express my thanks and appreciation to Ellalene Seymour for her expert, thoughtful, and good-humoured typing and editing of the successive drafts of the manuscript. Cliff Goddard has read, critically and attentively, the first draft of the entire manuscript, discussed it with me almost page by page, and made innumerable helpful suggestions. Individual chapters were also read and extensively commented on by Nick Enflield, Jean Harkins, and – last but not least – by my daughters Mary and Clare Besemeres. It is a pleasure to acknowledge my debt and express my gratitude to all these people.

Some portions of the book first appeared, in a different form, as articles in journals or chapters in edited volumes. I thank the publishers for permission to include revised and expanded versions of the following publications or their parts:

Anna Wierzbicka (1994) Emotion, language, and "cultural scripts", in Shinobu Kitayama and Hazel Rose Markus (eds.), *Emotion and Culture: Empirical studies of mutual influence*, Washington: American Psychological Association, 130–98; Anna Wierzbicka (1998) Angst, *Culture and Psychology* 4(2):161–88; Anna Wierzbicka (1998) Russian Emotional Expression, *Ethos*, 26(4): 456–83 (Copyright American Anthropological Association).

I also thank Prof. Paul Ekman, Prof. Carroll Izard, and Prof. James Russell for permission to reprint the photographs included here as figures 2, 3, 4, and 6, which previously appeared in the following publications: Paul Ekman (1975) The universal smile: face muscles talk in every language, *Psychology Today*, September 34: 35–9 (figure 4);

Carroll E. Izard (1971) *The Face of Emotion*, New York: Appleton-Centruy-Croft (figure 6); James A. Russell (1997) Reading emotions from and into faces: resurrecting a dimentional – contextual perspective, in J. A. Russell and J. M. Fernandez-Dols (eds.) *The Psychology of Facial Expression*, Cambridge: Cambridge University Presss (figures 2 and 3).

# Abbreviations

| | |
|---|---|
| ACC | accusative |
| DAT | dative |
| IMP | imperfect |
| NOM | nominative |
| 1s | first person singular |
| 3s | third person singular |
| NEUT | neuter |
| MASC | masculine |
| ADV | adverb |
| ADJ | adjective |
| REFL | reflexive |
| PSR | possessor |
| NMZ | nominalizer |
| LOC | locative |

# CHAPTER 1

# Introduction: feelings, languages, and cultures

## 1 Emotions or feelings?

According to the biologist Charles Birch (1995: ix), "Feelings are what matter most in life"[1]. While it is debatable whether they really matter "most", they certainly matter a great deal; and it is good to see that after a long period of scholarly neglect, feelings are now at the forefront of interdisciplinary investigations, spanning the humanities, social sciences, and biological sciences.

Some would say: not "feelings", but "emotions" – and the question "which of the two (feelings or emotions)?" plunges us straight into the heart of the central controversy concerning the relationship between human biology on the one hand and language and culture on the other.

Many psychologists appear to be more comfortable with the term "emotion" than "feeling" because "emotions" seem to be somehow "objective". It is often assumed that only the "objective" is real and amenable to rigorous study, and that "emotions" have a biological foundation and can therefore be studied "objectively", whereas feelings cannot be studied at all. (Birch (1995: v) calls this attitude "the flight from subjectivity"; see also Gaylin 1979).

Seventy years ago the founder of behaviourism John Watson proposed the following definition (quoted in Plutchik 1994: 3): "An emotion is an hereditary 'pattern-reaction' involving profound changes of the bodily mechanisms as a whole, but particularly of the visceral and glandular systems". While such purely behaviouristic conceptions of "emotions" have now been repudiated, "emotions" are still often seen as something that, for example, can be measured. Plutchik (1994: 139) himself writes: "Because emotions are complex states of the organism involving feelings, behaviour, impulses, physiological changes and efforts at control, the measurement of emotions is also a complex process".

Many anthropologists, too, prefer to talk about "emotions" rather than "feelings" – in their case not because of the former's "objective" biological foundation but because of their interpersonal, social basis. (See e.g. Lutz 1988; White 1993.)

1

But the word *emotion* is not as unproblematic as it seems; and by taking the notion of "emotion" as our starting point we may be committing ourselves, at the outset, to a perspective which is shaped by our own native language, or by the language currently predominant in some academic disciplines rather than taking a maximally "neutral" and culture-independent point of view. (Some will say, no doubt: "nothing is neutral, nothing is culture-independent". To avoid getting bogged down in this particular controversy at the outset, I repeat: *maximally* neutral, *maximally* culture-independent.)

The English word *emotion* combines in its meaning a reference to "feeling", a reference to "thinking", and a reference to a person's body. For example, one can talk about a "feeling of hunger", or a "feeling of heartburn", but not about an "emotion of hunger" or an "emotion of heartburn", because the feelings in question are not thought-related. One can also talk about a "feeling of loneliness" or a "feeling of alienation", but not an "emotion of loneliness" or an "emotion of alienation", because while these feelings are clearly related to thoughts (such as "I am all alone", "I don't belong" etc.), they do not suggest any associated bodily events or processes (such as rising blood pressure, a rush of blood to the head, tears, and so on).

In the anthropological literature on "emotions", "feelings" and "body" are often confused, and the word *feelings* is sometimes treated as interchangeable with the expression *bodily feelings*. In fact, some writers try to vindicate the importance of feelings for "human emotions" by arguing for the importance of the body. For example, Michelle Rosaldo (1984: 143) in her ground-breaking work on "emotions" has written, inter alia: "Emotions are thoughts somehow 'felt' in flushes, pulses, 'movements' of our livers, minds, hearts, stomachs, skin. They are *embodied* thoughts, thoughts seeped with the apprehension that 'I am involved'". Quoting this passage with approval, Leavitt (1996: 524) comments: "This apprehension, then, is clearly not simply a cognition, judgment, or model, but is as bodily, as felt, as the stab of a pin or the stroke of a feather". I agree with Rosaldo and Leavitt that some thoughts are linked with feelings and with bodily events, and that in all cultures people are aware of such links and interested in them (to a varying degree). But I do not agree that "feelings" equals "bodily feelings". For example, if one says that one feels "abandoned", or "lost", one is referring to a feeling without referring to anything that happens in the body. Precisely for this reason, one would normally not call such feelings "emotions", because the English word *emotion* requires a combination of all three elements (thoughts, feelings, and bodily events/processes).

In the hypothetical set of universal human concepts, evolved by the author and colleagues over many years' cross-linguistic investigations (see below, section 8), "feel" is indeed one of the elements, but "emotion" is not. If words such as *emotion* (or, for that matter, *sensation*) are taken for granted as analytical tools, and if their English-based character is not kept in mind, they can reify (for English speakers and English writers) inherently fluid phenomena which could be conceptualized and categorized in many different ways. Phrases such as "the psychology of emotion", or "psychobiological theory of emotion", or "operational definition of emotion" (such as galvanic skin response, GSR) create the impression that "emotion" is an objectively existing category, delimited from other categories by nature itself, and that the concept of "emotion" carves nature at its joints. But even languages culturally (as well as genetically) closely related to English provide evidence of different ways of conceptualizing and categorizing human experience.

For example, in ordinary German there is no word for "emotion" at all. The word usually used as the translation equivalent of the English *emotion*, *Gefühl* (from *fühlen* "to feel") makes no distinction between mental and physical feelings, although contemporary scientific German uses increasingly the word *Emotion*, borrowed from scientific English, while in older academic German the compound *Gemütsbewegung*, roughly "movement of the mind", was often used in a similar sense. (It is interesting to note, for example, that in the bilingual German–English editions of Ludwig Wittgenstein's writings, the word *emotion* used in the English translation stands for Wittgenstein's word *Gemütsbewegung*, not *Emotion*; see e.g. Wittgenstein 1967: 86.) At the same time, the plural form – *Gefühle* – is restricted to thought-related feelings, although – unlike the English *emotion* – it doesn't imply any "bodily disturbances" or processes of any kind. The same is true of Russian, where there is no word corresponding to *emotion*, and where the noun *čuvstvo* (from *čuvstvovat'* "to feel") corresponds to *feeling* whereas the plural form *čuvstva* suggests cognitively based feelings. To take a non-European example, Gerber (1985) notes that Samoan has no word corresponding to the English term *emotion* and relies, instead, on the notion of *lagona* "feeling" (see also Ochs 1986: 258). The French word *sentiment* (unlike the Russian *čuvstvo* and the German *Gefühl*) includes only two of these elements (a feeling and a thought). This is why one can speak in Russian of both a *čuvstvo styda* "a feeling of shame" and a *čuvstvo goloda* "a feeling of hunger", and in German of both a *Schamgefühl* and a *Hungergefühl*, whereas in French one can speak of a *sentiment de honte* (a "mental feeling" of shame) but not a *sentiment de faim* (a "mental feeling of hunger"); and also, why one can speak (in French) of *le sentiment de sa valeur* (a feeling of one's own worth) but not (in English) of the "emotion of one's own worth": one does not expect a feeling of one's own worth to be associated with any bodily events or processes. (As for the relations between the French word *émotion*, the Italian *emozione*, and the Spanish *emoción*, see Wierzbicka 1995c.)

Thus, while the concept of "feeling" is universal and can be safely used in the investigation of human experience and human nature[2] (see below, section 8; see also chapter 7), the concept of "emotion" is culture-bound and cannot be similarly relied on.

Of course scholars who debate the nature of "emotions" are interested in something other than just "feelings". In fact, the notion that "emotions" must not be reduced to "feelings" is one of the few ideas that advocates of different approaches to "emotion" (biological, cognitive, and socio-cultural) tend to strongly agree on (cf. e.g. Schachter and Singer 1962; Solomon 1984: 248; Lutz 1986: 295). Since, however, it is the concept of "feel" (rather than the concept of "emotion") which is universal and untinted by our own culture, it is preferable to take it as the starting point for any exploration of the area under consideration. This need not preclude us from investigating other phenomena at the same time. We can ask, for example: When people feel something, what happens in their bodies? What do they do? What do they think? What do they say? Do they think they know what they feel? Can they identify their feelings for themselves and others? Does their interpretation of what they feel depend on what they think they *should* feel, or on what they think people around them think they should feel? How are people's reported or presumed feelings related to what is thought of, in a given society, as "good" or "bad"? How are they related to social interaction? And so on.

Nothing illustrates the confusion surrounding the term *emotion* better than the combination of claims that emotions are not cognitively based with the practice of including in the category of "emotions" only those feelings which in fact *are* related to thoughts (and excluding those which are not). For example, Izard (1984: 24) explicitly states that "emotion has no cognitive component. I maintain that the emotion process is bounded by the feeling that derives *directly* from the activity of the neurochemical substrates". Yet as examples of "emotions" Izard mentions "shame", "anger", "sadness", and so on – not, for example, "pain", "hunger", "thirst", "itch", or "heartburn". In practice, then, Izard, too, distinguishes cognitively based (i.e. thought-related) feelings (such as "shame" or "sadness") from purely bodily feelings (such as "hunger" or "itch") and calls only the former "emotions". While denying that "emotions" are cognitively based he doesn't go so far as to include among them "hunger" or "thirst". On what basis, then, does he distinguish his "emotions" from hunger, thirst, or pain? The very meanings of words such as *shame, anger,* or *sadness* on the one hand, and *hunger* or *thirst* on the other draw a distinction between feelings based on thoughts and purely bodily feelings; and the word *emotion*, too, is in practice only used with respect to thought-related feelings, never with respect to bodily feelings such as hunger or thirst. Thus, in drawing a line between feelings such as "shame" or "sadness" on the one hand and "hunger" or "thirst" on the other, even "anti-cognitivist" scholars like Izard accept in practice the distinction drawn in everyday conceptions. Yet, at the same time, they reject this distinction at a theoretical level!

A hundred years after the publication of William James' famous paper "What is an emotion?" some scholars still argue about the "right" answer to James' question, instead of rephrasing the question itself. For example, Marks (1995: 3) writes: "What, then, is (an) emotion? The most obvious answer is 'A feeling'", and then he goes on to discuss "the apparent inadequacy of the feeling view of emotion", citing, among others, the philosopher Robert Solomon's celebrated statement that "an emotion *is* a judgement" (1976: 185). At the end, Marks rejects both the "feeling view of emotions" and what he calls "the New View of Emotions [as Judgement]" in favour of what he calls "an even Newer View . . . that emotions are not just things in the head but essentially involve culture" (p. 5).

But there is absolutely no reason why we should have to make such choices, linking "emotion" either with bodily processes, or with feelings, or with thoughts, or with culture. The very meaning of the English word *emotion* includes both a reference to feelings and a reference to thoughts (as well as a reference to the body), and culture often shapes both ways of thinking and ways of feeling. All these things can be and need to be studied: ways of thinking, ways of feeling, ways of living, the links between ways of living and ways of thinking, the links between thoughts and feelings, the links between what people feel and what happens inside their bodies, and so on. But to study all these, we need a clear and reliable conceptual framework, and the English word *emotion* cannot serve as the cornerstone of such a framework. It is good to see, therefore, that even within psychology the practice of taking the word *emotion* for granted is now increasingly being questioned. George Mandler, who first tried to draw attention to the problem more than twenty years ago (see Mandler 1975), has recently expressed surprise at the fact that "something as vague and intellectually slippery as emotion" could have been used for so long, by so many scholars, as a seemingly unproblematic notion (Mandler 1997: vii). Speaking specifically of what is often referred to as the "facial expression of emotions", Mandler (1997: xii) asks rhetorically: "Are *expression* and *emotion* even the right concepts, or has our everyday language frozen in place ideas that were only half-baked and prescientific?"

In a similar vein, Russell (1997: 19) writes: "'Emotion' is an ordinary, everyday word understood by all, rather than a precise concept honed through scientific analysis. Perhaps 'emotion' is a concept that could be dispensed with in scientific discourse (except as a folk concept requiring rather than providing explanation)". Referring, in particular, to the "facial expression of emotion", Russell (ibid.) concludes: "we have probably reached the point where further usefulness of thinking of facial expressions in terms of emotion requires a clarification of the concept of emotion itself". (Cf. also Ginsburg 1997.) As many writers on "emotion" have begun to agree, the point can be generalized: progress of research into "human emotions" requires clarification of the concept of "emotion" itself. For example, Lisa Feldman-Barrett (1998: v) in her recent article entitled "The future of emotion research" notes that "there is still little consensus on what emotion is or is not", and states: "The future of affective science will be determined by our ability to establish the fundamental nature of what we are studying".

But calls for clarification and explanation of the concept of "emotion" raise some crucial methodological questions. To explain the concept of "emotion" (or any other concept) we have to render it in terms of some other concepts, and our proposed explanations will only be clear if those other concepts are themselves clear; if they are not, they, in turn, will also need to be explained, and this can involve us in infinite regress. It is essential, therefore, that our explanation of "emotion" be couched in terms which are not equally problematic and obscure. If we do not anchor our explanations in something that is self-explanatory, or at least more self-explanatory than the concept we are trying to explain, they can only be pseudo-explanations (as "explanations" in scholarly literature often are). To quote Leibniz:

> If nothing could be understood in itself nothing at all could ever be understood. Because what can only be understood via something else can be understood only to the extent to which that other thing can be understood, and so on; accordingly, we can say that we have understood something only when we have broken it down into parts which can be understood in themselves. (Couturat 1903: 430; my translation)

This basic point, which in modern times has often been lost sight of, was made repeatedly in the writings on language by the great French thinkers of the seventeenth century such as Descartes, Pascal, and Arnauld. For example, Descartes wrote:

> I declare that there are certain things which we render more obscure by trying to define them, because, since they are very simple and clear, we cannot know and perceive them better than by themselves. Nay, we must place in the number of those chief errors that can be commit-

ted in the sciences, the mistakes committed by those who would try to define what ought only to be conceived, and who cannot distinguish the clear from the obscure, nor discriminate between what, in order to be known, requires and deserves to be defined, from what can be best known by itself. (1931[1701]: 324)

In my 1996 book *Semantics: Primes and Universals* I illustrated this point with a recent discussion of the concept IF by two prominent researchers into child language who start by saying that "it is difficult to provide a precise definition of the word *if*", and at the end conclude that "The fundamental meaning of *if*, in both logic and ordinary language, is one of implication" (French and Nelson 1985: 38). These statements reflect two common assumptions: first, that it is possible to define all words – including *if*; and second, that if a word seems difficult to define, one can always reach for a scientific-sounding word of Latin origin (such as *implication)* to "define" it with. These assumptions are not merely false; jointly, they constitute a major stumbling block for the semantic analysis of any domain. One cannot define all words, because the very idea of "defining" implies that there is not only something to be defined but also something to define it with.

What applies to *if* and *implication*, applies also to *feel* and *emotion*: one can define *implication* via *if*, and *emotion* via *feel*, but not the other way around, as was attempted, for example, in the following explanation: "'feeling' is our subjective awareness of our own emotional state" (Gaylin 1979: 2). If someone doesn't know what *feel* means then they wouldn't know what an *emotional state* means either.

## 2 Breaking the "hermeneutical circle"

There are of course many scholars who claim that nothing is truly self-explanatory and who appear to accept and even to rejoice in the idea that there is no way out of "the hermeneutic circle". Charles Taylor (1979[1971]: 34) applied this idea specifically to emotions when he wrote:

> The vocabulary defining meaning – words like "terrifying", "attractive" – is linked with that describing feeling – "fear", "desire" – and that describing goals – "safety", "possession".
>
> Moreover, our understanding of these terms moves inescapably in a hermeneutical circle. An emotion term like "shame", for instance, essentially refers us to a certain kind of situation, the "shameful", or "humiliating" . . . But this situation in its turn can only be identified in relation to the feelings which it provokes . . . We have to be within the circle.
>
> An emotion term like "shame" can only be explained by reference to other concepts which in turn cannot be understood without

reference to shame. To understand these concepts we have to be in on a certain experience, we have to understand a certain language, not just of words, but also a certain language of mutual action and communication, by which we blame, exhort, admire, esteem each other. In the end we are in on this because we grow up in the ambit of certain common meanings. But we can often experience what it is like to be on the outside when we encounter the feeling, action and experiential meaning language of another civilization. Here there is no translation, no way of explaining in other, more accessible concepts. We can only catch on by getting somehow into their way of life, if only in imagination.

There is an important truth in what Taylor is saying here, but it is a partial truth, and it is distorted by being presented as the whole truth. It is true that there are "communities of meaning" sharing the familiarity with certain common meanings, such as, for example, the meaning of the Russian words *toska* (roughly, "melancholy-cum-yearning") or *žalet'* (roughly, "to lovingly pity someone"; for detailed discussion, see Wierzbicka 1992a), or the Ifaluk concept *fago* (roughly, "sadness / compassion / love", cf. Lutz 1995). It is also true that verbal explanations of such concepts cannot replace experiential familiarity with them and with their functioning within the local "stream of life" (to use Wittgenstein's phrase; cf. Malcolm 1966: 93). But it is not true that no verbal explanations illuminating to outsiders are possible at all.

The crucial point is that while most concepts (including *toska*, *žalet'*, *fago*, *shame*, *emotion*, *implication*) are complex (decomposable) and culture-specific, others are simple (non-decomposable) and universal (e.g. FEEL, WANT, KNOW, THINK, SAY, DO, HAPPEN, IF); and that the former can be explained in terms of the latter. For example, while there is no word in English matching the Russian word *toska*, one can still explain to a native speaker of English what *toska* means, relying on concepts shared by these two languages (as well as all other languages of the world): it is how one feels when one wants some things to happen and knows that they cannot happen (for detailed discussion, see Wierzbicka 1992a).[3] Crucially, this (simplified) definition can be translated word for word into Russian, and tested with "ordinary" native speakers.

Shared, universal concepts such as FEEL, WANT, KNOW, THINK, SAY, DO, HAPPEN, and IF (in Russian ČUVSTVOVAT', XOTET', ZNAT', DUMAT', SKAZAT', SDELAT', SLUČIT'SJA, ESLI) constitute the bedrock of intercultural understanding. These concepts are the stepping stones by which we can escape the "hermeneutical circle".

Needless to say, not everything worth knowing can be explained in words. But as Wittgenstein (1988[1922]: 27) put it, "what can be said at all can be said clearly". And even if someone wished to insist that concepts such as FEEL, WANT, SAY, THINK, DO, or IF are not entirely clear to them either, they would have to admit that they are clearer and more intelligible than *emotion, sensation, volition, locution, cognition, agency,* or *implication.* And it is indisputably more intelligible to say, for example, that "I want to do something and can't do it" than to say that I experience "a lack of goal conductiveness" (cf. chapter 4).

This doesn't mean that complex and technical words should always be *replaced* by simple and easily comprehensible ones. For example, Izard (1977, 1991) may have good reasons for describing "emotions" as "consisting of neuro-physiological, behavioural, and subjective components" (cf. Russell and Fernández-Dols 1997a: 19) rather than in terms of "feeling something, doing something, and having something happen inside one's body". But complex and technical concepts such as "neuro-physiological", "behavioural", and "subjective" have to be introduced and explained, at some stage, via intuitively intelligible concepts such as "body", "happen", "do", and "feel", rather than the other way around.

Generally speaking, scientific discourse – and in particular scientific discourse about "human emotions", "human subjectivity", "human emotional experience", or "human communication" – has to build on ordinary discourse, and on words intelligible to those ordinary mortals whose "subjectivity" it seeks to investigate and explain.

*Emotion* shouldn't be taken for granted in scientific discourse, not so much because it is "an ordinary, everyday word understood by all" (and not "a precise concept honed through scientific analysis") but rather because it is a fairly complex and culture-specific word which does require explanation. It is not "understood by all" because, as mentioned earlier, it doesn't have exact equivalents in other languages (not even in other European languages such as German, Russian, or French); and it is not "understood by all" because children have to learn it on the basis of a prior understanding of words such as *feel, think, know, want,* and *body.*

One can imagine a child asking an adult: "What does the word *emotion* mean?" or "What does the word *sensation* mean?" but not "What does the word *feel* mean?" or "What does the word *want* mean?" And the answer to the questions about the meanings of *emotion* and *sensation* would have to be based on the concept "feel". For example, one might say to the child: "*Sensation* means that you feel something in some part of your body, e.g. you feel cold or itchy, and *emotion* means that you feel sad, or happy, or angry – something to do with what you think".

"Precise concepts honed through scientific analysis" are of course necessary, too; but to have any explanatory power they have to build on simple and intuitively clear concepts such as FEEL and WANT, which a child picks up in social interaction *before* any verbal explanations can be offered and understood.

Scientific discourse about "humans" can have an explanatory value only if it can address questions which arise on the basis of people's fundamental conceptual models, models which cannot be reduced to anything else. Semantic investigations into English and a great many other languages suggest that "ordinary people" conceive of a human individual as someone who can think, feel, want, and know something; and who can also say things and do things. The universal availability of words expressing precisely these concepts (e.g., not "believe" but "think"; not "intention" or "volition" but "want"; not "emotion", "sensation", or "experience", but "feel") allows us to say that these particular concepts (THINK, KNOW, FEEL, WANT, SAY, and DO) represent different and irreducible aspects of a universal "folk model of a person" (cf. Bruner 1990; D'Andrade 1987).

Complex and language-specific notions such as, for example, *belief*, *intention*, *emotion*, *sensation*, or *mood* have to be defined on the basis of those fundamental, universal, and presumably innate "indefinables". Even concepts as central to the traditional scientific pursuits carried out through the medium of the English language as "mind" have to be acknowledged for what they are – cultural artifacts of one particular language and tradition, no more scientifically valid than the German *Geist*, the Russian *duša*, or the Samoan *loto* (cf. Wierzbicka 1992a and 1993a; Mandler 1975). All such concepts can of course be retained in scientific discourse if they are found to be useful – but they can only be truly useful if they are previously anchored in something more fundamental and more self-explanatory (also to children, and to speakers of other languages).

## 3 "Experience-near" and "experience-distant" concepts

The distinction between "experience-near" and "experience-distant" concepts was introduced into human sciences by Clifford Geertz (1984[1976]: 227–8) (who credited it to the psychoanalyst Heinz Kohut). To quote:

> An experience-near concept is, roughly, one which an individual – a patient, a subject, in our case an informant – might himself naturally and effortlessly use to define what he and his fellows see, feel, think, imagine, and so on, and which he would readily understand when similarly applied by others. An experience-distant concept is one which various types of specialist – an analyst, an experimenter, an ethnographer, even a priest or an ideologist – employ to forward their scientific, philosophical, or practical aims. "Love" is an experience-near concept; "object cathesis" is an experience-distant one.

As Geertz (ibid.) points out, the distinction is not absolute but a matter of degree; for example, "'fear' is experience-nearer than 'phobia', and 'phobia' experience-nearer than 'ego-dissontic'".

On the face of it, it would seem obvious that "experience-near" concepts like "love" or "fear" throw more light on human "emotional" experience than "experience-distant" ones like "object cathexis" or "ego-dissontic". But the catch is that experience-near concepts like "love" and "fear" are language-specific and so cannot give us a handle on human experience in general. To quote Geertz (1984[1976]: 124) again:

> Confinement to experience-near concepts leaves an ethnographer awash in immediacies as well as entangled in vernacular. Confinement to experience-distant ones leaves him stranded in abstractions and smothered in jargon. The real question . . . is what roles the two kinds of concepts play in anthropological analysis. To be more exact: How, in each case, should they be deployed so as to produce an interpretation of the way a people live which is neither imprisoned within their mental horizons, an ethnography of witchcraft as written by a witch, nor systematically deaf to the distinctive tonalities of witchcraft as written by a geometer?

Fortunately, it is not the case that *all* experience-near concepts are language-specific and that their use has to "entangle us in the vernacular". For example, concepts like FEEL, WANT, and THINK are experience-near (unlike *affect*, *volition*, or *cognition*), and yet using them in our explanations or definitions we do not get "entangled in the vernacular", because "lexical exponents" of these concepts can be readily found in every language.

Thus, we are not forced to choose in our discussions of "human emotions" between, on the one hand, experience-near but language-specific concepts such as the Russian *toska*, the Ifaluk *fago*, the German *Schadenfreude*, or the English *embarrassment* (see chapter 2, section 6) and on the other, language-independent but experience-distant expressions such as "object cathexis" or "ego-dissontic". By explaining concepts like *toska*, *fago*, *Schadenfreude*, or *embarrassment* in terms of universal concepts such as FEEL, THINK, WANT, and HAPPEN (as illustrated earlier) we can have our cake and eat it too, for concepts of this kind are both experience-near and readily translatable into any other language (as are also their combinations like the one illustrated in the definition of *toska*).

What applies to particular "emotion concepts" such as *toska*, *Schadenfreude*, or *embarrassment*, applies also to the concept of *emotion* in general. While *emotion* is not as experience-distant as its more technical (and somewhat dated) substitute *affect*, it is not as experience-near as *feel*. At the same time, it is not the experience-near concept *feel* which would entangle us in the idiosyncrasies of the English vernacular, but the (relatively) experience-distant concept *emotion*. As Russell (1997: 19) has put it, *emotion* is a "folk concept requiring rather than providing explanations"; and to be truly explanatory, our explanation of this concept has to be phrased in terms of concepts which themselves do not require any further explanation (because there is nothing simpler or clearer to explain them with).

In this book I will, nonetheless, use the word *emotion* (generally either in italics or in inverted commas), because the book is written in English and *emotion* is an important and convenient English word; I will not, however, *rely* on this word and treat it as an unproblematic analytical tool; and I will be using it as an abbreviation for, roughly speaking, "feelings based on thoughts". On the other hand, I *will* use as unproblematic analytical tools words like *feel*, *want*, and *happen* (in their basic and indefinable meanings), which stand for concepts that are both experience-near and – as linguistic evidence suggests – universal.

## 4 Describing feelings through prototypes

In literature, feelings are frequently described by means of comparisons: the hero felt as a person might feel in the following situation (description follows). Some examples from Tolstoy's novel *Anna Karenina* (for more detailed discussion see Wierzbicka 1973; the quotes below are from Louise and Aylmer Maude's translation, see Tolstoy 1970[1918]):

> [At the station, Vronsky, who is in love with Anna, catches sight of Anna's husband]
> Vronsky . . . had such a disagreeable sensation as a man tortured by thirst might feel on reaching a spring and finding a dog, sheep, or pig in it, drinking the water and making it muddy. (p. 97)
>
> He [Anna's husband] now felt like a man who on coming home finds his house locked against him. "But perhaps the key can still be found", thought Karenin. (p. 132)
>
> [Anna has finally left her husband]
> He felt like a man who has just had a tooth drawn which has been hurting him a long time. (p. 254)

The same mode of description is also often used in everyday discourse, as well as in popular songs and other similar texts. A simple example comes from a blues song: "I feel like a motherless child". Much could of course be written about "what it means to feel like a motherless child", but the expression "I feel like . . . " itself cannot be defined or explained any further: it is as simple and clear as anything can be. There is no point in trying to define or explain the meaning of "I", "feel", "like", or the combination "I feel like (this)". The understanding of the whole line depends not only on the assumption that one knows (or can imagine) how "motherless children" feel, but also that the meaning of the expression "I feel like (this)" is intuitively clear.

But while "feeling" cannot be defined, "ordinary people" generally assume that the way one feels *can* be described and that one *can* tell other people how one feels. There are many ways of describing to other people how one feels but most of them can be reduced to two basic modes (a third mode will be discussed later): (1) one can tell other people that one "feels good" or that one "feels bad", and (2) one can tell other people that one feels like a person feels in a certain situation and then identify, in one way or another, that prototypical situation. If I tell someone that I "feel wonderful", or that I "feel awful", I am following the first mode of describing feelings. If I tell them that I "feel like a motherless child", or that I "feel lost", or that I "feel abandoned", I am following the second mode.

In addition to "feeling good", "feeling bad", and "feeling like this" (with some reference point for "this" provided) other ways of describing "how I feel" are of course also open to us: one can say, for example, that one "feels sad" or "feels angry"; and also, that one "feels hungry", "feels hot", "feels itchy", "feels tired", or "feels sleepy". But ready-made labels for describing feelings are usually based on the same two basic modes.

For example, the expression "to feel hungry" is a conventional abbreviation (encoded as such in the English language) for saying, roughly speaking, that one feels like a person does if he or she hasn't eaten anything for a long time and wants to eat something because of that. Using a standardized (but still intuitively intelligible) mode of semantic representation, we can portray the meaning of expressions like "feel hungry" as follows:

> I felt hungry. =
> I felt something
>> sometimes a person doesn't eat anything for a long time
>> afterwards this person feels something bad because of this
>> this person wants to eat something
> I felt like this

> I felt tired. =
> I felt something
>> sometimes a person does many things for a long time

        afterwards this person feels something bad because of this
        this person doesn't want to do anything for some time
I felt like this

I felt sleepy. =
I felt something
        sometimes a person doesn't sleep for a long time
        afterwards this person feels something because of this
        this person wants to sleep
I felt like this

Descriptive labels like *sad, angry, afraid,* or *guilty* differ, of course, from those like *hungry, tired,* or *sleepy* in some important respects (to be discussed below), but they, too, rely on the two basic modes of describing feelings, that is, the "feel good/bad" mode, and the "feel like this" mode. For example, to "feel guilty" means, roughly, to "feel bad, like a person does who thinks: I have done something (bad), something bad happened because of this". Using, again, the standardized mode of semantic description we could represent this as follows:

I felt guilty. =
I felt something because I thought something
        sometimes a person thinks:
        "I did something
        something bad happened because of this"
        because this person thinks this, this person feels some-
            thing bad
I felt (something) like this because I thought something like this

I felt afraid. =
I felt something because I thought something
        sometimes a person thinks:
        "something bad can happen to me now
        I don't want this to happen
        because of this I want to do something
        I don't know what I can do"
        because this person thinks this, this person feels
            something bad
I felt (something) like this because I thought something like this

As these formulae illustrate, expressions like *feel guilty* or *feel afraid* can be defined via a "prototype", describing, in very general terms, a kind of situation (or a "scenario"), associated in people's minds with a recognizable kind of feeling.[4]

The main difference between words like *guilty* and *afraid* on the one hand and words like *hungry* or *sleepy* on the other has to do, roughly speaking, with the "cognitive" character of the former and the "non-cognitive" character of the latter. What this means is that the prototypical scenario serving as a reference point for the phrase "feel like this" (e.g. in "I felt like this") is formulated in the case of words like *guilty* or *afraid* in terms of somebody's thoughts ("sometimes a person thinks: . . ."), whereas in the case of words like *hungry, sleepy,* or *tired* there is no reference to thoughts. (Cf. Wittgenstein (1967: 88e): "A thought rouses emotions [*Gemütsbewegungen*] in me (fear, sorrow etc.), not bodily pain".) In addition, in the case of *hungry* or *sleepy* (but not *tired*) there are also references to somebody's body (implicit in the meaning of the words *eat* and *sleep*).

The very fact that besides words with bodily references like *hungry* and *sleepy* and words with references to thoughts such as *afraid* or *guilty* there are also words like *tired*, which refer neither to the body nor to thoughts but which nonetheless do refer to a kind of feeling, highlights the futility of attempts (cf. e.g. Coulter 1986) to ascribe two different meanings to *feel*, a physical one (as in *hungry*) and a mental one (as in *guilty*): *tired* is neither necessarily "physical" nor necessarily "mental", yet it does imply that one "feels" something (in the basic and undifferentiated sense of the word *feel*, which we find in every language).

The distinction between "thought-based" feelings and other kinds of feelings is of course a valid and an important one. It has to be recognized, however, that this distinction is based not on two allegedly different meanings of the word *feel* (or its equivalents in other languages) but on the kind of prototypical scenario implied by a given "feeling word": some words, e.g. *afraid* and *guilty* in English, imply a thought-related scenario, whereas others, e.g., *hungry* and *tired* in English, imply a scenario not based on thoughts; and *hungry*, though not *tired*, implies, in addition, a scenario related specifically to a person's body.

As I will discuss in detail in chapter 7, the remarkable facts are that, first, all languages have a general, undifferentiated word for FEEL (covering both thought-related and not-thought-related kinds of feelings), and that, second, all languages have some words for some particular kinds of thought-related feelings (e.g. *afraid* and *guilty* in English and *toska* in Russian). The meanings of such words are language-specific and, generally speaking, do not match across languages and cultures. Every language, however, has lexically encoded some scenarios involving both thoughts and feelings and serving as a reference point for the identification of what the speakers of this language see as distinct kinds of feelings. For example, Russian has no word for *guilt,*[5] and of course English has no word for *toska*; but both *guilt* and *toska* identify what the speakers of the language see as a specific kind of feeling, associated with an identifiable cognitive scenario.

Since the cognitive scenarios linked with *guilty* and *toska* can be stated in the same, universal human concepts (such as FEEL, WANT, BAD, DO, and so on), these scenarios can be understood by cultural outsiders, and the kinds of feeling associated with them can be identified, explained, and compared; and both the similarities and differences between scenarios lexicalized in different languages can be pinpointed. But the very possibility of comparisons rests on the availability of a universal *tertium comparationis*, provided by universal concepts like FEEL, WANT, BAD, GOOD, or DO, and universally available configurations of concepts such as, for example, "I feel like this".

Importantly, the same *tertium comparationis* can also be used for comparing feelings described in a third mode available in many languages and cultures, linking thought-related feelings and "felt" bodily processes. This mode can be illustrated with Charlotte Brontë's (1971[1847]: 14) description of what happened to Jane Eyre when she was locked in a room believed to be haunted and when she saw a beam of light that she thought was a ghost:

> My heart beat thick, my head grew hot; a sound filled my ears, which I deemed the rushing of wings; something seemed near me; I was oppressed, suffocated; endurance broke down; I rushed to the door and shook the lock in desperate effort.

Gaylin (1979: 47), who quotes this description, seems to have no doubt that there is an accurate label to describe it: "it is horror that she is experiencing", but even if Jane's thought-related feelings can indeed be loosely described as "horror" (for a detailed analysis of "horror" and related concepts see chapter 2) the passage implies also that those thought-related feelings were associated with some bodily events, and that these bodily events could be felt, too (as we feel, for example, our movements; cf. Wittgenstein 1967: 85e). Schematically (the first person reflects Jane's point of view):

(a) I felt something because I thought something
(b) when I felt this some things were happening inside my body
(c) I could feel these things happening

Since the bodily feelings in component (c) co-occur with the thought-related ones, the two can be perceived by the experiencer as a global experience and the description of the bodily events may be used as a way of characterizing one's state of mind.

It is possible, and indeed likely, that such a "global" way of describing a person's thought-related feelings is used (to a varying degree) in all cultures. But it is of course not the only way, and not necessarily the dominant one. (For another major mode of describing feelings, based on "bodily images" such as "heart-broken", "blood-boiling", or "a heavy heart", see chapter 7.)

## 5. "Emotions": disruptive episodes or vital forces that mould our lives?

There is a tradition within Anglo academic psychology which tends to be hostile to "emotions". Fehr and Russell (1984: 473) have illustrated this culture-specific attitude with the following characteristic sentences from an English-language introductory psychology textbook:

> A state of emotion is recognized by its holder as a departure from his or her normal state of composure; at the same time there are physical changes that can be detected objectively.

> When sufficiently intense, emotion can seriously impair the processes that control organized behavior.

> Sometimes emotion is hard to control.

> Emotion accompanies motivated behavior; the effect can be facilitating or interfering.

Sentences of this kind, seemingly objective and scientific, are in fact loaded with unconscious cultural assumptions and saturated with the values of a powerful stream within Anglo-American culture (arguably, the dominant stream), and reading them it is hard not to think of Catherine Lutz's (1988) provocative title "Ethnopsychology compared to what?" The basic assumption is that a person's "normal state" is a state of "composure", and that an emotion constitutes a departure from a "normal state".

It would be difficult, however, to find evidence for such assumptions in, for example, mainstream Russian, Italian, or German culture. Similar *attitudes* could no doubt be found anywhere, but the cultural premiss taking such attitudes for granted and treating them as background assumptions, is culture-specific, and, as I will illustrate below, it is reflected in the English language. On the other hand, there is ample evidence showing that, for example, from the point of view of traditional Russian culture, states such as "joy", "worry", "sadness", "sorrow", "grief", "delight", and so on constitute most people's normal state, and that an absence of "emotions" would be seen as indicating a deadening of a person's *duša* ("heart/soul"). In fact, experiences comparable to "joy", "sadness", or "anger" are often conceptualized in Russian as inner activities in which one engages rather than as states which one passively undergoes, and so they are often designated by verbs rather than adjectives. Some examples: *radovat'sja* "to rejoice" (in English archaic), *grustit'* (from *grust'*, roughly "sadness"), *toskovat'* (from *toska* "melancholy-cum-longing"), *serdit'sja* (roughly, "to be angry", but a verb, like *to rage* in English), *stydit'sja* (roughly "to be ashamed"), and so on (for detailed discussion see Wierzbicka 1992a and 1995a). The cultural ideal of "composure" as a person's "normal state" is alien to mainstream Russian culture (cf. Wierzbicka 1989, 1990a, and 1992a and the references cited there; see also chapter 5).

It is also interesting to compare the characteristic "Anglo" attitude to "emotions" reflected in the sentences quoted from the psychology textbooks with that reflected, for example, in Goethe's reference to "glorious feelings":

> Die uns das Leben gaben, herrliche Gefühle
> Erstarren in dem irdischen Gewühle.
>
> The fine emotions whence our lives we mold
> Lie in the earthly tumult dumb and cold.
> (Faust, Pt.1, sc.1, 1.286, quoted in Stevenson 1949: 661)

From Goethe's point of view, *herrliche Gefühle* ("glorious feelings") are not something that has to be controlled or something that threatens to impair, or interfere with, "organized behavior"; rather, they are positive forces that "give us life".

Of course "Anglo" culture in general, and "Anglo emotionology" in particular, is heterogeneous and changeable (cf. e.g. P. Stearns 1994; Stearns and Stearns 1986), and in any case, individual scholars are free to side with Goethe rather than with the psychology textbooks quoted above, as the following passage written by (the American philosopher) Robert Solomon (1995: 257) illustrates: "Emotions are not just disruptions of our otherwise calm and reasonable experience; they are at the very heart of that experience, determining our focus, influencing our interests, defining the dimensions of our world . . . Emotions . . . lie at the very heart of ethics, determining our values, focusing our vision, influencing our every judgement, giving meaning to our lives." But in any culture, in any epoch, the prevailing "emotionology" finds its reflection in language, and any counter-emotionology must define itself with reference to the prevailing one (cf. e.g. Lutz 1990). For example, while feminist thought in America has challenged the dominant Anglo attitudes to feelings and sought to place more value on them, it has had to define itself with reference to those traditional attitudes; and, moreover, it is easier to challenge overt ideologies than the implicit ones which have found their reflection even in some terms of everyday discourse, and have become imperceptible (as the air we breathe).

For example, there is a certain unconscious "ideology" written into the English word *emotional* – an "ideology" which assumes that showing feelings over which one has no control is a departure from "normal" behaviour. The word has pejorative overtones, and even when it is used in a "tolerant" tone it still implies that there is something there, in the "emotional outburst", which needs to be excused (the loss of "control" over one's feelings and over their display). There are no words analogous to *emotional* in German, French, Italian, or Russian. An individual speaker of English may feel out of sympathy with the perspective reflected in this word and may not use it herself, but she cannot erase it at will from the English lexicon.

The perspective on feelings and their manifestation which is reflected in psychology textbook phrases like "departure from the normal state of composure" is also reflected, in a more subtle way, in the ordinary English word *upset*, which, unlike *sad*, doesn't have equivalents in other European languages. The hidden metaphor of an "upset" position of normal equilibrium (as in an upset vase) is highly suggestive: it implies that the "bad feeling", over which the experiencer has no control, is viewed as a temporary departure from a "normal" state. To quote Gaylin (1979: 175):

> The central image in the feeling of upset is one of disorder and disarray. The synonyms for feeling upset all include a sense of confusion, and an interruption of the normal control and orderliness of life . . . We tend to feel upset when we have a sense that our normal orderly control over our lives is threatened. The feeling of upset suggests a thinness of our defense mechanisms, so that we perceive ourselves as particularly vulnerable to a shake-up, an explosion, or an eruption of emotion. Whatever initiated the feeling of being at sixes and sevens, the risk perceived is not from the original stimulus but from our sense that we are losing control.

Gaylin's comments are perceptive, and yet he misses one important point: that the very idea of "feeling upset" is a cultural creation, and that the central concern with "losing control" reflects preoccupations which are anything but universal. The point is all the more instructive in that the main thrust of Gaylin's book is anti-behaviourist, denouncing the widespread preoccupation with "the orderly charts, statistics, and physiological measurements that have come to represent the academic world of emotion" (p. 425).[6]

The perspective on human feelings which sees them as "disruptive episodes" is also reflected in Paul Ekman's (1992a: 186) suggestion (based partly on the distinction between "emotions" and "moods") that "emotions are typically a matter of seconds, not minutes, hours or days". It also appears to reify the distinction drawn by the English lexicon between *emotion* and *mood*, for which French and Italian, for example, have no equivalent.[7] Ekman comments: "It may be that under exceptional circumstances a single emotion endures for more than seconds or minutes, but I think it more likely that close inspection would reveal that the same emotion is being repeatedly evoked." But whose "close inspection" does Ekman have in mind, the experiencer's or the psychologist's? The following quote provides an answer to this question:

> My proposal that emotions are typically a matter of seconds, not minutes or hours, is supported by some preliminary evidence. Examining the duration of both expressive and physiological changes during spontaneous emotional events suggests a short time span. When subjects have reported experiencing an emotion for 15 or 20 minutes, and I have had access to a videotaped record of their preceding behaviour, I found that they showed multiple expression of that emotion. My interpretation of such incidents is that people summate in their verbal report what was actually a series of repeated but discrete emotion episodes.

Thus, when the person experiencing an "emotion" reports a 15 or 20 minutes' duration, Ekman assumes that the report is inaccurate and that in fact a series of very brief, discrete "emotion episodes" took place. But while an outsider (in this case, a scientist) may be able to gather data about my facial behaviour, or about the physiological changes in my body which accompany the feeling, this will not give him access to the feelings as such, let alone privileged access more reliable than that of the person directly involved.

There is no reason to assume, then, that feelings (rather than muscle contractions or physiological changes in the body) are a matter of seconds (rather than minutes or hours). The idea that – despite people's introspective reports – their feelings must have a very brief duration, reflects a strong behaviourist bias, assisted, so to speak, by the (culturally shaped) semantics of the English word *emotion*: were Ekman using the English word *feelings*, or the German word *Gefühle*, or the Russian word *čuvstva*, he would probably be less likely to restrict the duration of the phenomena in question to "seconds": even if it were true that human feelings are associated with repeated episodes of muscular or other physiological changes, there would not be the same temptation to assume that what applies to the muscles must also apply to feelings. There would also be less temptation to speak of feelings as discrete entities, as in the case of Ekman's phrase "a single emotion". (Of course Ekman doesn't say that "feelings" are typically a matter of seconds, only that "emotions" are; but in doing so he unwittingly identifies "emotions" with muscular changes and leaves the feelings out of account altogether.) Take, for example, a German Jew, Victor Klemperer's (1996: 420), record of his feelings noted in his diary during the Nazi era:

> Immer hat man den Druck und das Ekelgefühl auf der Seele und entgeht ihn nur noch auf Minuten.
> "One has constantly an oppressive feeling and a feeling of disgust/ revulsion [lit. 'on the heart / soul'], which one can only escape for minutes."

Why should Klemperer's personal testimony, based on the German concept of *Gefühl* "feeling", be any less valid than Ekman's speculative theory, based on the English notion of *emotion*?

Wittgenstein, whose philosophy of psychology was coloured by the German folk model, thought about human feelings in terms of the distinction between *Gemütsbewegungen* (literally, movements of the *Gemüt*) and *Empfindungen* (roughly, "sensations"). *Gemüt* stands for a folk construct which can be described, loosely, as a kind of cross between "mind" and "inner disposition". As examples of *Gemütsbewegungen* Wittgenstein cited *Freude* (roughly, "joy"), *Trauer* (roughly, "sorrow") and *Depression* ("depression"). He saw *Empfindungen* (in Elizabeth Anscombe's English translation, *sensations*) and *Gemütsbewegungen* (in Anscombe's translation , *emotions*) as both having genuine duration and having "a course", but unlike *Empfindungen*, he observed, *Gemütsbewegungen* are not localized in the body, though not "diffuse" either.

While Wittgenstein's *Gemütsbewegungen* (in contrast to his *Gemütsdispositionen*, "dispositions of the *Gemüt*", such as *Liebe* "love" and *Haß* "hate") are characterized by duration, they are *not* characterized – as Ekman's "emotions" are – by *brief* duration. This is hardly surprising given that the category of *Gemütsbewegung*, suggested to Wittgenstein by the ordinary German, can include *Depression* "depression" and *Trauer* "sorrow" as well as *Freude* "joy". What all this illustrates is that, for example, Ekman's theory of "emotions" (having extremely brief duration) is coloured by the ordinary English word *emotion*. More generally, it shows that language-specific interpretive categories such as *emotion, mood, mind, anxiety,* or *contempt* (the latest alleged "basic emotion"; cf. e.g. Ekman and Friesen 1986; Matsumoto 1996), should not be treated as "neutral" analytical tools.

To deny the universality of "emotion" as a conceptual (and lexical) category does not mean, of course, denying the reality of the links between thoughts, feelings, and bodily processes, or the universality of the human awareness of, and interest in, such links. In fact, linguistic evidence tends to confirm the universality of the perception that thoughts, feelings, and bodily processes are often interrelated. First, all languages appear to have expressions presenting thought-related feelings in terms of bodily images, such as the English *heart-broken, heavy heart,* or *getting cold feet;* and second, all languages appear to have some words or expressions referring, in a non-figurative way, to the interrelation between thoughts, feelings, and bodily events, such as, for example, the English words *laugh* and *cry* (cf. Plessner 1970[1961]). To illustrate, here is a tentative (prototype-based) explication of the English word *cry*:

> Person X was crying. =
> something was happening to person X
>> sometimes a person thinks:
>> "something bad is happening to me now
>> I don't want this to be happening
>> I want to do something because of this
>> I can't do anything"
>> when this person thinks this this person feels something bad
>> because of this something is happening in this person's body
>> because of this people can hear something in this place
>> like people can hear something when someone is saying something
>> at the same time other people can see something like water in this person's eyes
> something like this was happening to person X

As this explication shows, the concept of *crying* is based on a prototype (indented) involving fairly complex thoughts, feelings, and some audible and visible bodily events.

I am not suggesting, then, that there is anything "ethnocentric" in studying links between thoughts, feelings, and bodily events in research seeking to gain knowledge about "humans" in general. It is necessary to remember, however, that these aspects are conceptually dissociable, and that the word *emotion,* which links them in one overarching category, is a culture-specific conceptual artifact. When we want to talk about "humans", we are always on firmer ground if we refer to what people think, what they feel, what happens in their bodies, and what they do and say to one another, than if we speak about their "emotions".

Another point which needs to be made here has to do with the relationship between the concept *emotion* and concepts like *sadness, anger,* or *relief*. In the literature on "emotions", words of this kind are commonly referred to as "emotion terms", and in ordinary language, too, "sadness", "anger", or "relief" can be described as "emotions". This doesn't mean, however, that the concept of *emotion* is included in the very meaning of *sadness, anger,* or *relief.*[8] *Sadness* or *relief* could be classified ad hoc as "kinds of emotion", just as *knives* could be classified ad hoc as "a kind of weapon" or "a kind of cutlery" (especially in a "forced choice" task); but just as both *weapon* and *cutlery* include semantic components absent from *knife*, so *emotion* contains components (or a component) absent from *sadness* or *relief*. The missing component is that referring to "bodily events". So-called "emotion terms" like *sadness* or *relief* do not imply by virtue of their very meaning that something is happening in a person's body, and so they are comparable in meaning to words like *tristesse* and *soulagement* in French, *Traurigheit* and *Erleichterung* in German, or *grust'* and *oblegčenie* in Russian, that is to words that clearly do not embody the English concept of *emotion* (which has no equivalent in those languages).[9]

To sum up, then, *emotion* is an English classificatory term which has been borrowed from "folk English" into the language of scholarly literature, where it is now used in a variety of non-defined ways coloured by the folk concept and where it has contributed to a culturally shaped view of "human psychology". It is not really well suited for cross-linguistic and cross-cultural comparisons or for discussions of "human nature" or "human psychology" in general. It is a word, however, which is so firmly entrenched in the scholarly literature written in English, and even in non-scholarly "educated" English discourse, that it seems unrealistic at this stage to give it up altogether (as, for example, Leavitt 1996 appears to recommend, although he doesn't do it himself). Ideally, it should be used in scholarly work in inverted commas, and in any case the argument should not depend on it at all, but should rely, instead, on solid, "experience-near" and yet universal, concepts like FEEL, THINK, WANT, BODY, DO, and HAPPEN.

The psychologist Panksepp (1982: 449) has written: "The semantic controversies that routinely arise in the discussion of emotion have long hindered the progress of research in this area" (quoted in Fehr and Russell 1984: 483), and "it is unlikely that we can resolve disagreements concerning the meanings of terms such as *emotions* and *feelings*" (Panksepp 1982: 453). But given a coherent semantic theory and well-developed semantic methodology, the meaning of words such as *feelings* and *emotions can* be stated in a non-arbitrary way open to intersubjective assessment; and it is the absence of serious investigation of the semantics of "emotions", rather than its exaggerated pursuit, which has long hindered the progress of research in this area.

In particular, by clarifying the issues from a semantic point of view, we can go beyond the debates on whether "emotions" are "biologically based" or "culturally constituted", "private" and "internal", or "public" and "social" (as if they couldn't be all these things at the same time; cf. Leavitt 1996), and move on to investigate clearly formulated questions focussing on what people think, feel, want, know, say, and do; what happens in their bodies; how the thoughts, feelings, wants, and bodily events are linked (temporarily and/or causally); and also, how those links are perceived, and spoken about, by the "actors" and experiencers themselves, and what role the feelings (linked with culturally shaped thoughts and biologically based bodily events) play in the stream of life.

### 6 Why words matter

Human beings are "classifying animals": they categorize both the "contents of the world" and events into categories and put labels on them. Among other things, they categorize feelings, including "thought-related" ones (which I will call, for convenience, "emotions"), and they do so differently in different speech communities. Generally speaking, the labels do not match across language boundaries. For example, speakers of English use categories such as *sad, angry, disgusted,* and *happy,* whereas the speakers of Ifaluk use different, non-matching categories such as *fago, song, waires,* and *ker* (cf. Lutz 1988; Wierzbicka 1992a), whilst speakers of Malay use categories such as *sedih, marah, jijik* and *gembira,* which are different again.[10]

Until recently many scholars refused to believe that the categorization of "emotions" can differ from language to language and insisted that at least some "emotions" must be linguistically recognized in all languages. There can no longer be any doubt, however, that this is not the case. Although much more is known about this diversity now than twenty or thirty years ago, the basic fact that in principle "emotion words" don't match was known at that time too. Even an extreme "universalist" like Paul Ekman, who has claimed for decades that the same "basic emotions" (i.e. happiness, sadness, anger, fear, disgust, and surprise, cf. e.g. Ekman 1973: 219–20; see also Ekman 1993, 1994a and b) are recognized in all cultures, acknowledged more than twenty years ago that the Dani people of the New Guinea Highlands, whose faces and "emotions" he had studied in the field, "don't even have words for the six emotions" (Ekman 1975: 39).

Undoubtedly, the "emotion lexicons" of different languages show similarities as well as differences (I will discuss these similarities in detail in chapter 7). But it is essential to recognize the diversity, too, and to abandon the idea that all languages must have words for something as "basic" and as "natural" as "sadness", "anger", "fear", "happiness", "disgust", and "surprise".

It might seem that once the basic fact of lexical diversity has been recognized the battle against ethnocentrism in the study of "emotions" has been won, but this is not the case either. For even when this fact is acknowledged, many scholars feel free to dismiss its importance and to affirm that behind or beneath this lexical diversity there lies cross-cultural uniformity. For example, the psychologist Paul Harris (1995: 355) writes: "what is in dispute is whether we can draw any conclusions – other than lexical conclusions – about the emotional universe of a culture by examining its emotion lexicon". If one takes this attitude, one feels free to dismiss the lexical categories of any distant culture in favour of one's own – and to fall back, once again (as Harris does), on English lexical categories such as *sadness*, *anger*, and so on, to identify what really matters to people in that other culture.

Ekman (1993: 384) has claimed that "no one to date has obtained strong evidence of cross-cultural disagreement about the interpretation of fear, anger, disgust, sadness, or enjoyment expressions". But how *could* anyone obtain such evidence if the key interpretive categories "fear", "anger", "enjoyment", etc. are taken for granted from the outset and built into the research project itself?

I, for example, as a native speaker of Polish, would never interpret Ekman's smiling faces in terms of "enjoyment", because there is no such category in the Polish lexicon. I agree with Ekman and Izard that smiling faces do convey a universal, culture-independent message, but I would argue that this message can only be represented accurately in terms of universal, culture-independent concepts; and I would propose as the core of this message the formula "I feel something good now" (see chapter 4).

Speaking of the "uncritical presumption that in their emotional lives human beings anywhere are by and large essentially alike", Needham (1981: 99) remarked that "it calls for very little acquaintance with history or ethnography to provoke the serious doubt that this view can be correct", and he added: "For a comparativist, the prime field of evidence is presented by vocabularies of emotion in different linguistic traditions; and the first lesson is that simply in the numbers of emotions discriminated they diverge very greatly". But many influential recent writers on "emotions" have simply ignored such warnings, and some continue to do so.

As William James noted, we know from introspection that, on the one hand, we are capable of a great variety of feelings, and on the other, that these different feelings are not clearly separated from one another and cannot be counted. James pointed out that upon this largely nebulous world of feelings every language imposes its own interpretive grid.

> if one should seek to name each particular one [of the emotions] of which the human heart is the seat, it is plain that the limit to their number would lie in the introspective vocabulary of the seeker, each race of men having found names for some shade of feeling which other races have left undiscriminated. If we should seek to break the emotions, thus enumerated, into groups, according to their affinities, it is again plain that all sorts of groupings would be possible, according as we chose this character or that as a basis, and that all groupings would be equally real and true. (1890: 485)

Thus, the way people interpret their own emotions depends, to some extent at least, on the lexical grid provided by their native language. To take an example from ethnobiology, two different creatures (e.g. a large nocturnal moth attracted by lights and a clothes moth) may be classified as 'the same kind of creature" in one language (e.g. in English) and as "two different kinds of creature" in another language (e.g. in Polish *ćma* and *mól* respectively), and conversely, two different animals (e.g. a mouse and a rat) may be classified as "two different kinds of animal" in one language (e.g. *mouse* and *rat* in English) and as 'the same kind of animal" in another language (e.g. *nezumi* in Japanese). The same applies to "emotions": whether or not two feelings are interpreted as two different instances of, essentially, "the same emotion" or as instances of "two different emotions" depends largely on the language through the prism of which these feelings are interpreted; and that prism depends on culture.

It is ethnocentric to think that if the Tahitians don't have a word corresponding to the English word *sad* (Levy 1973), they must nonetheless have an innate conceptual category of "sadness"; or to assume that in their emotional experience "sadness" – for which they have no name – is nonetheless more salient and more relevant to their "emotional universe" than, for example, the feelings of *tōiaha* or *pe'ape'a*, for which they do have a name (although English does not). Ekman (1994b: 147) dismisses Levy's report "that the Tahitians do not have a word for sadness, and do not recognize the constellation of sad behaviour as caused by the loss of a loved person" with the following characteristic comment: "this is not sufficient to assert that the relationship between the sadness Antecedent and sadness responses is absent in that culture . . .

The Tahitians did show sad behaviours in response to loss even though they did not label it as sadness, and attributed those responses to illness rather than to loss". Ekman doesn't consider the possibility that the Tahitians' interpretation of their own experience might be just as valid as his (i.e. an outsider's) interpretation of it. He is convinced that what the Tahitians, unbeknown to themselves, "really feel" is "sadness".

Obviously, there is no reason to think that Tahitians are incapable of feeling "sad"; but neither is there any reason to believe that the speakers of English are incapable of feeling "tōiaha" or "pe'ape'a". Above all, there is no reason to think that "sadness" is more important or more "universal" than "tōiaha" or "pe'ape'a". The conceptual categories of "sadness" or "anger" are highly relevant to the speakers of English, and also to the speakers of other languages which have words corresponding in meaning to the English words *sad* and *angry* or *sadness* and *anger*. In many other cultures, however, the conceptual grid provided by language is different. To quote Russell (1994: 14): "We speakers of English find it plausible that our concepts of *anger, fear, contempt* and the like are universal categories, exposing nature at its joints. One way to overcome the influence of such implicit assumptions is to emphasize alternative conceptualizations."

The unselfconscious use of English emotion terms in the study of human emotions illustrates well what Smedslund (1992: 454) calls the empiricist *Zeitgeist* of contemporary psychology. He writes:

> There appears to be no awareness of the conceptual grid *through which* our experiences are filtered and in terms of which our descriptions *must* be made. The . . . metaphor of a distinction between the study of the world as seen through lenses and the study of the lenses through which the world is seen, is helpful here. Both are necessary for the process of achieving scientific knowledge. However, empiricism is exclusively focused on what is experienced and ignores the study of what is presupposed in, or structures, that experience.

As in other areas of research, investigation of "emotion" vocabulary is a necessary first step for identifying the object of our inquiry. We cannot say anything about "anger" if we don't know what we are talking about, and to know what we are talking about we must first analyse the meaning of the word *anger*. As Shweder (1994: 32) puts it, "anger" is just an "interpretive scheme" imposed by speakers of English on raw emotional experience. There are countless other interpretive schemes which can be imposed on similar experiences, and the one associated with the English word *anger* can hardly be regarded as providing privileged access to some language-independent psychological reality. (I say "similar" rather than "the same" because as Harré (1986a) and others have pointed out, the interpretive scheme may well become part of the experience itself.)

The idea that there may be an infinite variety of "emotion" categories operating across cultures is not incompatible with the view that there may also be some universal patterns of emotional organization. The crucial point is that if there are universal patterns they cannot be captured by means of English folk categories such as *anger, sadness,* or *disgust,* but only in terms of *universal* human concepts.

Linguistics can contribute to the cross-disciplinary study of "emotions" by describing and analysing "data" from the world's languages, and a great deal has been done in this area in recent years. (Cf. e.g. Athanasiadou and Tabakowska 1998; Goddard 1996a; Harkins 1996; Hasada 1998; Iordanskaja 1970, 1974, 1986; Iordanskaja and Mel'čuk 1990; Levontina and Zaliznjak (forthcoming); Travis 1998; Zaliznjak 1992; papers in Apresjan 1997; and Mel'čuk et al. 1984, 1988, 1992). But perhaps the most important role for linguistics in "emotion research" is to emphasize the "non-transparency" of the language of description and the trap waiting for those who declare that they want to study "emotions as such" and "are not interested in language". For language stands between the researchers and the "emotions" that they wish to investigate and it cannot be ignored.

Some psychologists are reluctant to concede that there may be a problem here. To quote from a recent rejoinder by the distinguished psychologist Richard Lazarus (1995) directed, amongst others, at myself:

> Wierzbicka suggests that I underestimate the depth of cultural variation in emotion concepts as well as the problem of language. (p. 255)

> Words have power to influence, yet – as in the Whorfian hypotheses writ large – they cannot override the life conditions that make people sad or angry, which they can sense to some extent without words . . .
> I am suggesting, in effect, that all people experience anger, sadness, and so forth, regardless of what they call it . . . Words are important, but we must not deify them. (p. 250)

But by refusing to pay attention to differences between different languages, scholars who take this position end up doing precisely what they wished to avoid, that is, "deifying" some words from their own native language and reifying the concepts encapsulated in them.

Words matter for at least two different but equally important reasons. First, words provide clues to other people's conceptualizations. Pace Harris, Ekman, Lazarus, Pinker, and many others, it is words, more than anything, which allow us access to the "emotional universe" of people from another culture. Second, it is only by studying words that we can go *beyond* words. For example, if we are interested in "emotions" and uninterested in words (as for example Ekman (1994a) professes to be), we still have to take enough interest in words to notice that English words such as *sadness, enjoyment,* or *anger* are no more than the cultural artifacts of one particular language. As Edward Sapir warned, "the philosopher needs to understand language if only to protect himself against his own language habits" (Sapir 1949[1929]: 165).

"Emotion" is "expressed" or communicated at every level of language, including grammar and intonation; it is also expressed in facial gestures such as frowns and raised eyebrows or in bodily gestures such as kisses or foot-stamping. All these facets of "emotion" need to be studied cross-culturally. None of them, however, can be studied effectively if the researcher doesn't "protect himself against his own language habits".

To insist that words matter is not the same as "to define emotions as emotion words" or to "reduce emotion to a kind of meaning" (cf. Leavitt 1996: 552). Of course an "emotion" is no more an "emotion word" than an illness is an illness word. Nor is an emotion or an illness reducible to a "meaning". But one can't discuss either "emotions" or illnesses without using *some* words, and if we don't want to mistake our own folk-taxonomies for "natural", objectively valid categories (a practice spectacularly illustrated recently by Stephen Pinker's discussion of "human emotions" in his *How the Mind Works*)[11] we had better pay some attention to words.

A good example of the consequences of failing to do this is provided by Ernest Becker (1962: 39) in his *The Birth and Death of Meaning*:

> The question "What fact is the most basic to an understanding of human motivation?" can be answered with just one word: anxiety. Anxiety is a prime mover of human behaviour, and many will do anything to avoid it . . . In fact, one is tempted to coin still another definition, and call man "the anxiety-avoiding animal" . . . Freud, who spent a lifetime trying to uncover the mainsprings of motivation, devoted an entire work to the problem of anxiety.

What is most striking about this passage is Becker's substitution of the English word *anxiety* for the German word *Angst* employed by Freud. Clearly, Becker believed that he was in full agreement with Freud, and indeed that he was only developing Freud's ideas. In fact he was talking about something else: anxiety, not Angst (for a discussion of the differences between the two concepts see chapter 3). As a result, Becker's theory of human motivation and human nature misrepresented Freud (cf. Gaylin 1979: 49–51).

Curiously, research into the meanings of "emotion terms" in different languages is occasionally attacked even by linguists, who are sometimes so eager to emphasize the importance of non-lexical manifestations of "emotions" in language that they seem to deny the value of lexical research altogether. For example, Taylor and Mbense (1998: 221) conclude their valuable study of metaphors in Zulu talk about "emotions" with an attack on the present writer as someone interested in lexical semantics:

> In spite of a number of uncertainties in the interpretation of our data, we would like, nevertheless, to stress the methodological point that the issues discussed in this paper would simply not have arisen (and so could not have been addressed at all) if we had restricted our attention merely to the lexical semantics of the noun *ulaka* and the verb *thukuthela*, in the style of Wierzbicka's studies.

Although the phrase "Wierzbicka's studies" is in the plural, the only reference to my work on "emotions" is to an article entitled" 'Sadness' and 'Anger' in Russian" in the same volume (Athanasiadou and Tabakowska 1998). This paucity of references suggests that the authors are unaware of my numerous non-lexical studies of "emotions", such as, for example, the extensive study of Russian and Polish expressive derivation in Wierzbicka 1992a; the studies of different attitudes to feelings associated with different grammatical frames (Wierzbicka 1988a and 1995a); the study of emotive interjections (Wierzbicka 1991); the study of emotions in discourse (Wierzbicka 1994d); or indeed my study of similes as a means for describing feelings, published at a time when most present-day cognitive linguists were still faithful practitioners of Chomsky's anti-semantic transformational grammar (Wierzbicka 1973). (See also the numerous non-lexical studies included in the volume on emotions which I edited a decade ago, Wierzbicka 1990e.)

But while I fully agree with Taylor and Mbense (1998) that the linguistic study of "emotions" should include not only lexicon but also grammar, phraseology, similes, metaphors, and so on (as my studies over a quarter of a century demonstrate), I believe that the lexicon is also very important. The insouciant way in which Taylor and Mbense are prepared to use the English word *anger* in talking about the Zulu ways of speaking suggests that they still haven't grasped the danger of ethnocentrism inherent in such practice. The very title of their paper "Red dogs and rotten mealies: how Zulus talk about anger" is misleading, to say the least: it is "Anglos" who speak about "anger", not Zulus. Much as Taylor and Mbense despise lexical studies, the Zulus speak not about *anger* but about *ulaka*, and so if we want to understand the Zulu perspective as feelings we should indeed take an interest in what *ulaka* means, rather than imposing on them the perspective encoded in the English word *anger*.

I am not suggesting that everybody who wants to study the Zulu perspective must engage in lexical research. For example, the study of Zulu metaphors presented by Taylor and Mbense is, in my view, valuable and informative as it is (despite the misleading title and glosses). It is a pity, however, that these and other cognitive linguists who don't engage in lexical semantic investigations themselves find it necessary to try to underscore the value of their own work with attacks on lexical research (cf. e.g. Lakoff and Johnson 1980; Lakoff 1987; for discussion see Wierzbicka 1986b), without which the multiple perspectives on human experience reflected in "emotion" terms in different languages would never be revealed and the perspective reflected in twentieth-century English would continue to be mistaken for one which is universal, innate, and simply "human".

## 7 Emotion and culture

The literature on "emotions" often contrasts "biology" with "culture", as if the two were mutually exclusive. It is worth remembering, therefore, that it was actually a psychologist (William James), not an anthropologist or linguist, who said that the categorization of feelings depends on "the introspective vocabulary of the seeker", which in turn depends on his or her language and culture (James 1890: 485). James held that feelings represented the subjective experience of biological (physiological) events, but he recognized that feelings can be categorized in a variety of ways, and that they *are* differently categorized in different cultures. This is not to say that there are no common threads (I will discuss some of these in chapter 7). But the diversity is very considerable indeed.

The meaning of English "emotion words" has actually changed a great deal in the course of history. Had Shakespeare been interested in proposing a basic "emotional keyboard" (cf. Shweder 1985: 200) it would have been different from that proposed by twentieth-century psychologists – even if it contained some of the same words, for example *angry*. The view of *anger* as something that can be manipulated – "controlled", "vented", "released", left "unresolved", "directed" at this or that target, "stirred up", "repressed", "expressed", "suppressed", and so on (for examples see, e.g. Pendergrast 1998: 23, 24, 219, 242, 243, 364) – is entirely modern and goes far beyond the semantic range of the Shakespearian *anger* (cf. Logan 1998; also Stearns and Stearns 1986). It also goes beyond the range of the supposed equivalents of *anger* in other languages (for example, Polish). In fact, the Polish

words closest to the English *anger* and *angry* are so different from them
in meaning that it would be virtually impossible to translate into Polish
perfectly "normal" sentences in twentieth-century English such as the
following one (for detailed discussion, see chapter 2, section 4): "Dying
people may feel angry . . . Some people feel angry at God for allowing
them to get sick, at their doctors for not being able to find a cure, at the
government for putting money into weapons instead of medical research, or at the world in general" (Callanan and Kelley 1993: 44).

The two closest Polish counterparts of the English *anger* are *złość* and
*gniew*, with the corresponding verbs *złościć się* and *gniewać się*, and the
adjectives *zły* (literally, "bad") and *gniewny*. The verb *złościć się* (often
used about children) has pejorative connotations and suggests something like a temper tantrum; the adjective *zły* (with the object in the
accusative and the preposition *na*) means something like "cross (with
someone)"; the adjective *gniewny* refers to outward expression, not an
inner feeling, and the verb *gniewać się* (which takes an object in the
accusative case with the preposition *na*) suggests a position of authority
and an exercise of some power (for example, a mother can *gniewać się na*
a child, typically, by scolding the child). Clearly, none of these words is
compatible with the situation of the dying person who feels *angry* at
God, at the doctors, and at the world; to say that someone is *zły na Pana
Boga* or *gniewa się na Pana Boga* or *złości się na Pana Boga* ("is angry at
God", literally "at Lord God") would sound humorous. The nouns
*złość* and *gniew* are not really applicable to this situation either; *gniew* is
analogous to *wrath* and it could only be directed at someone who (in the
experiencer's view) "has done something bad", not at doctors who
were not able to find a cure and not at "the world" or any other
impersonal force, phenomenon, or thing.

What this example shows is that an apparently basic and innocent
concept like *anger* is in fact linked with a certain cultural model and so
cannot be taken for granted as a "culture-free" analytical tool or as a
universal standard for describing "human emotions".

Examples of this kind provide an answer for those who, like Paul
Harris, ask "whether we can draw any conclusions – other than lexical
conclusions – about the emotional universe of a culture by examining
its emotion lexicon". The answer is that by examining the meaning and
the use of words like *anger* and *angry* in contemporary English we can
indeed learn a great deal about the "emotional universe" of the
speakers of contemporary English. "Emotion words" such as *anger*
reflect, and pass on, certain cultural models; and these models, in turn,
reflect and pass on values, preoccupations, and frames of reference of
the society (or speech community) within which they have evolved.
They reflect its "habits of the heart" (Bellah et al. 1985) and the con-

comitant "habits of the mind". The English *anger* and *angry* (with their current range of meanings) both reflect and reinforce what Bellah et al. 1985 call the "therapeutic culture" in modern Anglo society; and the shift from the Shakespearian *wrath* to modern *anger* both reflects and constitutes an aspect of the democratization of society and the passing of the feudal order (cf. de Tocqueville 1953[1835–40]; Stearns and Stearns 1986).

Let me adduce here two more Polish examples: the word of *tęsknota* (noun) and *tęsknić* (verb) and the adverb *przykro*.

*Tęsknota* is cognate with the Russian *toska* and with words like *tesknost* or *teskoba* in other Slavic languages. In the course of the nineteenth century, however, *tęsknota*, which had previously had a more general meaning of something like *malaise*, developed a meaning focussed specifically on pain associated with separation from loved people and places. In this new meaning, it acquired the status of one of Polish culture's key words (for detailed discussion see Wierzbicka 1986a and 1992a; see also Hoffman 1989). Both the semantic change and the cultural salience of *tęsknota* were clearly associated with the partitions of Poland by the neighbouring powers at the end of the eighteenth century, the national uprisings (especially that of 1830) which followed them, and the resulting "Great Emigration". For those forced into exile, and among them the political, literary, and artistic elite of the nation including the poet Adam Mickiewicz and the composer Fryderyk Szopen (Frédéric Chopin), the pain of exile became one of the dominant themes. The increasingly frequent use of the words *tęsknota* and *tęsknić* in Polish emigré poetry and prose no doubt contributed to the emergence of this new "emotional key concept", which can be roughly described as a combination of nostalgia, painfully missing someone, and a longing to be reunited with them. It would be hard to find a clearer example of a culturally constructed and historically based "emotion concept".

The word *przykro*, to which I have devoted a separate study (cf. Wierzbicka forthcoming a) can also be seen as one of Polish culture's key concepts. Roughly speaking, it describes a kind of "bad feeling" arising in interpersonal relations when someone fails to show us the warmth or affection or, more generally, "good feelings" that we expect from them. The causer of the bad feeling doesn't have to "hurt our feelings" in any way, it is enough that he or she doesn't show us affection. The cultural implications of this key concept seem quite clear: it points to the great value that Polish culture places on showing people warmth, or, as one says in Polish, *serdeczność* (from *serce* "heart"). The importance of the value of "serdeczność" in Polish culture, reflected both in the word *serdeczność* and in the semantically related word *przykro* (roughly, pain caused by lack of *serdeczność*), is also supported by other evidence, linguistic and non-linguistic (for detailed discussion see Chapter 6).

Naturally it is not only the lexicon which provides clues to the "emotional universe of a culture". Grammar does too, as do phraseology, discourse structure, gestures, intonation, interjections, swearwords, forms of address, culture-specific facial expressions and bodily postures, gestures, and so on. For example, it is clearly significant that "active" verbs like *rejoice* have all but disappeared from modern English usage, giving way to "passive" adjectives like *happy* or *pleased*; or that those "emotion verbs" which remain tend to have pejorative or humorous connotations (cf. e.g. *fume, fret, sulk, pine, enthuse, rage,* and so on; for detailed discussion see Wierzbicka 1988a, 1995a)

Similarly, the Russian "emotional universe" is reflected in Russian expressive derivation, including notably the numerous "diminutive" suffixes with different emotional shadings encoded in each of them (for detailed discussion see Wierzbicka 1992a; see also Friedrich 1997). It is also reflected in the culture-specific phraseology centred on the human body and expressive bodily (and facial) behaviour (cf. Iordanskaja and Paperno 1996; for detailed discussion see chapter 5).

All these aspects of both verbal and non-verbal communication need to be studied, and to be studied across cultures. We also need to study different cultures' "cultural scripts", which implicitly (and sometimes explicitly) tell people what to feel, and what not to feel, and what to say and do, or not say and do, when they feel something (see chapter 6). To study all this, however, we need reliable analytical tools and a reliable methodology. I believe that such a methodology can be provided by the Natural Semantic Metalanguage, to which I will now turn.

## 8 The Natural Semantic Metalanguage (NSM) as a tool for cross-cultural analysis

This book proposes a new perspective on "human emotions". The basic idea is that language is a key issue in "emotion research" and that progress in the understanding of "emotions" requires that this issue be squarely addressed. "Human emotions" vary a great deal across languages and cultures, but they also share a great deal. Neither the diversity nor the universal aspects of "emotions", however, can be studied without an appropriate metalanguage. All attempts to study "human emotions" in terms of ordinary English (or any other natural language) are bound to lead to distortions, because every natural language contains its own "naive picture of the world" (cf. Apresjan 1992[1974]), including its own "ethnopsychology". By relying, uncritically, on ordinary English words we unwittingly fall prey to the "naive picture" that is reflected in them.

Nor can we transcend this "naive picture" by adopting the conventional technical language of traditional psychology, because this conventional language has developed on the basis of ordinary language and is coloured by the naive picture embedded in it. The reliance of many psychologists on folk-English distinctions such as that between *emotion* and *mood* is a good case in point. (Cf. Mandler 1975.)

The approach to "emotions" adopted in this book (and in earlier publications by the author and colleagues)[12] seeks to break the dependence on any one natural language as the source of "common sense insights" by anchoring the analysis in universal human concepts and their "universal grammar". Both the universal concepts and their rules of combination (i.e. their "grammar") have been arrived at by empirical cross-linguistic investigations carried out by several linguists over many years and based on work with typologically diverse and genetically unrelated languages, including Chinese (Chappell 1986, 1991, 1994), Japanese (Hasada 1996, 1997; Onishi 1994, 1997; Travis 1997), Malay (Goddard 1995, 1996a), Lao (Enfield forthcoming), Mbula (Bugenhagen 1994), Ewe (Ameka 1990a and b, 1994), French (Peeters 1994, 1997), several Australian Aboriginal languages (Goddard 1991b; Harkins 1995, 1996; Harkins and Wilkins 1994; Wilkins 1986), and many others.

Most words in any language are specific to this particular language or to a group of languages, and are not universal. For example, neither English nor Spanish nor Malay has a word with a meaning corresponding exactly to the meaning of the German word *Angst* (see chapter 3). At the same time, evidence suggests that all languages have words with meanings corresponding exactly to the meanings of the English words *good* and *bad*, or *know* and *want*. This suggests that the concepts of "good" and "bad" (or "know" and "want") are universal, and can, therefore, be used as elements of a culture-independent semantic metalanguage.

To reflect the special status of such words as exponents of universal human concepts, I will render them in capital letters, as GOOD and BAD, or BUENO and MALO (Spanish), or BAIK and BURUK (Malay), thus indicating that they are being used as elements of a special semantic metalanguage. At the same time we can identify them with the meanings of ordinary English, Spanish, and Malay words (*good* and *bad*, *bueno* and *malo*, *baik* and *buruk*), and require that semantic formulae including these words be testable via natural language.

Since the words of ordinary language are often polysemous, we need to identify the meanings in question by means of certain "canonical" sentences such as, for example, "this person did something bad", "esta persona ha hecho algo malo" (Spanish), and "orang ini buat sesuatu yang buruk" (Malay), or "something good happened to me", "algo bueno me ha sucedido" (Spanish), "sesuatu yang baik terjadi kepada aku" (Malay). Proceeding in this way, we can overcome both the incomprehensibility and unverifiability of a technical language relying on "experience-distant" concepts and the ethnocentrism of descriptions using a full-blown natural language such as ordinary English, in all its culture-specific richness.

Whether or not all languages do share a minimum of basic concepts is an empirical question, and one which colleagues and I have been pursuing on an empirical basis for many years. The results of these investigations have been reported in two collective volumes *Semantic and Lexical Universals – Theory and empirical findings* (Goddard and Wierzbicka 1994) and *Meaning and Universal Grammar: Theory and empirical findings* (Goddard and Wierzbicka forthcoming), as well as in my *Semantics: Primes and Universals* (Wierzbicka 1996a) and in Goddard's (1998) *Semantic Analysis: A practical introduction*.

These results tend to confirm the thrust of centuries of philosophical speculations about "innate ideas" (Descartes, e.g. 1931[1701]), "the alphabet of human thoughts" (Leibniz, cf. Couturat 1903), the "mid-point around which all languages revolve" (Humboldt 1903–36, v.4: 21–3) and the "psychic unity of mankind" (Boas 1966[1911]). The main conclusion is that all languages do indeed appear to share a common core, both in their lexical repertoire and in their grammar, and that this common core can be used as a basis for a non-arbitrary and non-ethnocentric metalanguage for the description of languages and for the study of human cognition and emotion. This shared lexical core derived from empirical cross-linguistic investigations, is summarized in the following table:

*Conceptual primitives and lexical universals*[13]

| Substantives | I, YOU, SOMEONE(PERSON), SOMETHING(THING), PEOPLE, BODY |
|---|---|
| Determiners | THIS, THE SAME, OTHER |
| Quantifiers | ONE, TWO, SOME, MANY/MUCH, ALL |
| Attributes | GOOD, BAD, BIG, SMALL |
| Mental predicates | THINK, KNOW, WANT, FEEL, SEE, HEAR |
| Speech | SAY, WORD, TRUE |
| Actions, events, movements | DO, HAPPEN, MOVE |
| Existence and possession | THERE IS, HAVE |

| Life and death | LIVE, DIE |
| Logical concepts | NOT, MAYBE, CAN, BECAUSE, IF |
| Time | WHEN(TIME), NOW, AFTER, BEFORE, A LONG TIME, A SHORT TIME, FOR SOME TIME |
| Space | WHERE(PLACE), HERE, ABOVE, BELOW, FAR, NEAR; SIDE, INSIDE |
| Intensifier, augmentor | VERY, MORE |
| Taxonomy, partonomy | KIND OF, PART OF |
| Similarity | LIKE |

*Spanish Version*

| Substantives | YO, TÚ; ALGUÉN, ALGO; GENTE; CUERPO |
| Determiners | ESTE, EL MISMO, OTRO |
| Quantifiers | UNO, DOS, ALGUNOS, MUCHOS, TODOS |
| Attributes | BUENO, MALO, GRANDE, PEQUENO |
| Mental predicates | PENSAR, SABER/CONOCER, QUERER, SENTIR, VER, OÍR |
| Speech | DECIR, PALABRA, VERDAD |
| Actions, events, and movements | HACER, SUCEDER, MOVERSE |
| Existence and possession | HAY (EXISTIR), TENER |
| Life and death | VIVIR, MORIR |
| Logical concepts | NO, QUIZÁS, PODER, PORQUE, SÍ |
| Time | CUANDO, AHORA, ANTES, DESPUÉS, MUCHO TIEMPO, POCO TIEMPO, POR UN TIEMPO |
| Space | DÓNDE, ACQUÍ, SOBRE, DEBAJO, LEJOS, CERCA, LADO, DENTRO |
| Intensifier, augmentor | MUY, MÁS |
| Taxonomy, partonomy | GÉNERO, PARTE |
| Similarity | COMO |

*Malay Version*

| Substantives | AKU, KAU, SESEORANG, SESUATU, ORANG, BADAN |
| Determiners | INI, (YANG) SAMA, LAIN |
| Quantifiers | SATU, DUA, BEBERAPA, BANYAK, SEMUA |
| Attributes | BAIK, BURUK, BESAR, KECIL |
| Mental predicates | FIKIR, TAHU, MAHU, RASA, LIHAT, DENGAR |
| Speech | KATA, PERKATAAN, BENAR |
| Actions, events, movements | BUAT, TERJADI, BERGERAK |
| Existence and possession | ADA$_1$, ADA$_2$ |
| Life and death | HIDUP, MATI |
| Logical concepts | TIDAK, MUNGKIN, BOLEH, SEBAB, KALAU |
| Time | BILA(MASA), SEKARANG, SELEPAS, SEBELUM, LAMA, SEKEJAP, SEBENTAR |

| Space | MANA(TEMPAT), (DI) SINI, (DI) ATAS, (DI) BAWAH, JAUH, DEKAT; SEBELAH, DALAM |
| Intensifier, augmentor | SANGAT, LAGI |
| Taxonomy, partonomy | JENIS, BAHAGIAN |
| Similarity | MACAM |

This, then, is what the "alphabet of human thoughts" appears to look like. All complex meanings, in all conceptual domains, can be represented and explained as configurations of these sixty or so fundamental conceptual building blocks.[14] (For fuller discussion and justification of this set see the references given above.)

What applies to the universal "lexicon of human thoughts" applies also to the universal "grammar of human thoughts" manifested in universal syntactic patterns. Empirical evidence suggests that despite the colossal variation in language structures there is also a common core of shared or matching grammatical patterns in which the shared lexical items can be used. This common core defines a set of "basic sentences" which can be said in any language and matched across language boundaries and it can be used as a natural semantic metalanguage for the description and comparison of meanings.

Thus, a configuration of conceptual primes such as "I feel (something) good now" appears to be universally possible and can therefore be plausibly proposed as the meaning of a smile, in preference to culture-specific English words like *enjoyment* or *happy* (see chapter 4). Similarly, configurations such as "I want to do something", "I know I can't do anything", or "I know: something bad happened" also appear to be universally present and can be assigned as plausible semantic components to "emotion words" such as, for example, the English *sadness* and the Russian *grust'*, helping to map the similarities and differences between them.

## 9 An illustration: "sadness" in English and in Russian

Like other so-called "emotion terms" (e.g. *fear, joy, surprise, disgust, shame*, and so on), the English word *sadness* has a meaning which purports to link a particular kind (or range) of feeling with a particular cognitive scenario. Typically, the feeling of "sadness" is triggered (according to the folk-psychology reflected in the word *sad*) by a combination of thoughts which can be represented as follows:

(a) I know: something bad happened
(b) I don't want things like this to happen
(c) I can't think now: "I will do something because of this"
(d) I know that I can't do anything

For example, if I say that I feel sad because my dog died I mean (a) that something bad happened (my dog died); (b) that I don't want things like this to happen; and (c) that I am not planning to do anything because of this because (d) I realize I can't do anything about it. In addition, I imply that while I think those thoughts I feel something – something "bad".

This cognitive scenario (which is readily translatable into any other language) is presented in the meaning of this English word as typical rather than necessary, for one can say in English, for example, "I feel sad – I don't know why" (cf. Johnson-Laird and Oatley 1989). What this shows is that by describing my feeling as "sadness" I would be saying, in effect, that I feel LIKE a person does who actually thinks some such thoughts.

The full meaning of *sadness* can be presented as follows:

> *sadness* (e.g. X feels sad)
> (a) X feels something
> (b)　　sometimes a person thinks:
> (c)　　"I know: something bad happened
> (d)　　I don't want things like this to happen
> (e)　　I can't think now: I will do something because of this
> (f)　　I know that I can't do anything"
> (g)　　because of this, this person feels something bad
> (h) X feels something like this

This, then, is one of the cognitive scenarios "singled out" by the English lexicon and encoded in the word *sad*. Other languages single out other cognitive scenarios, and draw different conceptual distinctions.

While the explication of *sadness* proposed above includes a prototypical scenario (shown here as the indented middle part), this type of prototypical scenario differs considerably from those proposed in current psychological literature, where no attempt is usually made to capture the *invariant* of a given "emotion concept", or to analyse this concept via simpler and more universal concepts. As an illustration of these differences in approach, I reproduce below (in a slightly abbreviated form) the "prototype of sadness" proposed by Shaver et al. (1987: 1077).

*The prototype of sadness*
An undesirable outcome; getting what was not wanted . . .
Discovering that one is powerless, helpless, impotent
Empathy with someone who is sad, hurt, etc.
Sitting or lying around; being inactive, lethargic, listless
Tired, rundown, low in energy; slow shuffling movements; slumped, drooping posture
Withdrawing from social contact; talking little or not at all
Low, quiet, slow, monotonous voice; saying sad things
Frowning, not smiling; crying, tears, whimpering
Irritable, touchy, grouchy; moping, brooding, being moody
Negative outlook; thinking only about the negative side of things
Giving up; no longer trying to improve or control the situation
Blaming, criticizing oneself
Talking to someone about the sad feelings or events
Taking action, becoming active . . . suppressing the negative feelings

A "prototypical scenario" of this kind includes lots of ideas which may come to mind in connection with the concept of "sadness", but it does not separate essential features from more or less accidental ones. For example, something like "an undesirable outcome" may indeed be a necessary part of the "sadness scenario", but "withdrawing from social contact" or "slumped, drooping posture" is not. (Listing various possible ways of behaving which may be associated with "sadness" is no substitute for defining *sadness*: on the contrary, in order to be able to say meaningfully that a sad person is likely to cry or to assume a slumped, drooping posture we must first be able to define *sad* independently.)

The NSM approach seeks above all to distinguish the essential from the optional, to capture the invariant, and to break complex concepts into maximally simple ones, relying exclusively on independently established conceptual primes and lexico-grammatical universals.

English–Russian dictionaries usually offer two Russian words as equivalents of the English word *sad*: *grustnyj* and *pečal'nyj* (cf. e.g. Falla et al. 1992). The noun *sadness* is usually given two glosses: *grust'* and *pečal'*, although sometimes a third Russian word, *toska*, is also added (cf. e.g. Falla et al. 1992). This implies that *grustnyj* and *grust'* mean the same as *pečal'nyj* and *pečal'* (as well as *sad* and *sadness*). In fact, however, this is not the case.

Both *grust'* and *pečal'* are common, everyday words in Russian (unlike, for example, *melancholy* in English). In fact, they are both much more common in Russian speech than *sadness* is in English. *Toska*, glossed sometimes as "sadness", also has an extremely high frequency in Russian speech (cf. Wierzbicka 1992a).

Although figures that can be found in frequency dictionaries are only broadly indicative (if only because they differ from one frequency dictionary to another) the differences between the Russian and the English data are, nonetheless, too marked to be ignored. At the very least they show that neither *pečal'* nor *grust'* is marginal in Russian speech, the way *melancholy* is marginal in English. They also show that Russian has three common everyday words (or families of words) in the domain in which English has only one.

Given, then, that both *pečal'* and *grust'* are conceptual categories of great salience in Russian culture, and that they both correspond, to some degree, to the English *sadness*, how exactly are they related to one another (and to *sadness*)?

If one asks native speakers of Russian what the difference between *grust'* and *pečal'* is, they usually reply, somewhat vaguely, that one of these emotions is "more concrete" than the other, or "more serious", "more definite", "more general", and so on. But a systematic study of the differences in collocations and grammatical frames of the two words and their derivational families allows us to capture the semantic differences in question in more precise terms.

To begin with, *pečal'* is much more readily described as "deep" than *grust'* is (*glubokaja pečal'*, ?*glubokaja grust'*). Similarly, the adjective *pečal'nyj* – in contrast to *grustnyj* – co-occurs readily with the adverb *gluboko* "deeply", as the following example illustrates:

> Duxovnaja bezkrylost', bezdarnost' russkoj revolucii možet dostavljat' zloradnoe udovolstvie vsem ee vragam. No éto fakt gluboko pečal'nyj (*grustnyj) dlja russkogo naroda i ego buduščego. (Fedotov 1981[1938]:103)
> "The spiritual squalor of the Russian revolution can be a source of Schadenfreude for its enemies. But it is a tragic [lit. deeply *pečal'nyj*] fact for the Russian nation and its future."

In the literature on human "emotions", the situation often adduced as the prototypical situation of "sadness" is that of one's child (or other beloved person) dying. In Russian, *grust'* (described by Uryson (1997: 442) as a "not deep and not very intensive feeling") would not be normally linked with such a situation. *Pečal'* might; although given Russian cultural attitudes more dramatic emotions such as *gore* (grief/sorrow) or *otčajanie* (despair) would probably be regarded as more natural.

Just as *pečal'* is more readily described as "deep" (*glubokaja*) than *grust'*, so *grust'* is more readily described as "light" (in weight) or "passing" than *pečal'* (*mimoletnaja grust'*, ?*mimoletnaja pečal'*, *legkaja grust'*, ?*legkaja pečal'*). This is consistent with the fact that an expression such as *pečalnoe lico* (roughly, "a sad face") implies a permanent characteristic, whereas *grustnoe lico* ("a sad face") is more likely to refer to a passing emotion. It is also consistent with the fact that one can say *pogruzit'sja v pečal'* "to sink into *pečal'*" but not *\*pogruzit'sja v grust'* (cf. Mostovaja 1998).

The adverb *grustno* can occur in the so-called dative construction, which indicates a purely subjective perspective (the feeling may be inexplicable, and not externally manifested); but the corresponding adverb *pečal'no* cannot occur in this construction:

> Mne   grustno.
> to-me   sad-ADV
> "I feel sad."
> \*Mne pečal'no.

*Grust'*, like *sadness*, may not have any clearly identified cause, but *pečal'* is more similar in this respect to the English words *sorrow* and *grief*. One cannot feel *sorrow*, *grief*, or *pečal'* without being aware of the cause of the feeling. The dative construction with the adverb *grustno*, on the other hand, is particularly suitable for referring to a feeling with no identifiable cause:

> Emu    bylo   grustno,  on   sam      ne     znal   počemu.
> to-him  was    sad-ADV   he   (himself)  didn't  know   why
> "He felt sad, he himself didn't know why."

This difference in the grammatical behaviour of the two alleged synonyms suggests that *pečal'* – but not *grust'* – is based on a conscious judgment: "this is bad". *Grust'* implies that one feels LIKE a person who is making some such judgment, but *pečal'* implies that one is actually making the judgment. The dative construction implies that the feeling is, as it were, involuntary and inexplicable, whereas *pečal'* implies that the feeling is due to a conscious and as it were intentional thought. Presumably, this is why the dative construction *\*mne pečal'no* ("I feel sad", literally, "to me it is sad") is unacceptable, whereas the corresponding version with *grustno* is perfectly natural.

Though the dative construction is particularly suited to the expression of "vague sadness", the noun *grust'* can also refer to such a situation, whereas the noun *pečal'* cannot.

> On čuvstvoval kakuju-to grust', on sam ne znal počemu.
> ?On čuvstvoval kakuju-to pečal', on sam ne znal počemu.
> "He felt some sadness, he himself didn't know why."

While the *Oxford Russian Dictionary* (Falla et al. 1992) glosses *sad* as "grustnyj, pečal'nyj", the corresponding Russian nouns are glossed differently: *"grust'* – sadness, melancholy", *"pečal'* – grief, sorrow". These glosses are in keeping with the fact that *melancholy* needs no identifiable cause, whereas *grief* and *sorrow* do.

On the other hand, one might say that *grief* and *sorrow* are both "more personal" than *pečal'*: they refer to "something bad that happened TO ME", whereas *pečal'* implies that "something bad happened" (not necessarily to me), and also, more generally, that what happened results in a situation which is seen as "bad", too. In particular, the adjective *pečal'nyj* is frequently used to describe objective situations, and to imply a negative evaluation of such situations, as in the following examples:

> vmeste s nimi sudili ix mašinistku Veru Laškovu i Alekseja Dobrovol'skogo, sygravšego pečal'nuju (*grustnuju) rol' provokatora. (Amal'rik 1982: 41)

> "Together with them, they put on trial their typist, Vera Laškova, and Aleksej Dobrovol'ski, who had played the pitiful (pečal'nuju) role of agent provocateur."

Consider also the following line from a poem by Lermontov:

> Pečal'no ja smotrju na éto pokolenie.
> sadly   I   look-1s   on   this   generation
> "I look with sadness on this generation."

The phrase *pečal'no smotrju* clearly implies an evaluation ("I think the state of this generation is bad"). The use of the adverb *grustno* would imply "a sad look" (i.e. a sad facial expression) rather than a negative evaluation.

The *Oxford Russian Dictionary* also cites the phrases *pečal'nyj konec* "dismal end" and *pečal'nye resul'taty* "unfortunate results". Although the dictionary assigns both *pečal'nyj* and *grustnyj* a second meaning glossed as "grievous", no similar phrases are offered for *grustnyj* and the second sense of *grustnyj* is glossed in fact as "grievous, distressing", whereas the second sense of *pečal'nyj* is glossed simply as "grievous" (without "distressing"). Though a little confusing, these choices are consistent with the idea that *pečal'nyj* implies an objective evaluation, whereas *grustnyj* refers to a personal reaction to a situation.

All these considerations bring us to the following explications (the contrasting parts are shown in capitals):

> *pečal'*
> (a)  X felt something BECAUSE X THOUGHT SOMETHING
> (b)  sometimes a person thinks:

(c)    "I know: something bad happened
(d)    THIS IS BAD
(e)    I don't want things like this to happen
(f)    I can't think now: I will do something because of this
(g)    I know that I can't do anything"
(h)    because this person thinks this, this person feels some-
         thing BAD
(i)  X felt something like this
(j)  BECAUSE X THOUGHT SOMETHING LIKE THIS
(k) X THOUGHT ABOUT IT FOR A LONG TIME
(l)  X FELT SOMETHING BECAUSE OF THIS FOR A LONG TIME

*grust'*
(a)  X felt something
(b)  sometimes a person thinks:
(c)  "I know: something bad happened NOW
(d)  ————————————————
(e)  I don't want things like this to happen
(f)  I can't think now: I will do something because of this
(g)  I know that I can't do anything"
(h)  because this person thinks this, this person feels some-
         thing FOR A SHORT TIME
(i)  X felt something like this

The differences between the two explications can be summarized as
follows.

First, the feeling of *grust'* is described only via a prototype ("X felt
something like this"); no actual thoughts are attributed to the experiencer. In the case of *pečal'*, however, a thought ("something bad happened") is in fact attributed to him/her (component (j)). This difference
accounts for the possibility of using *grust'*, in contrast to *pečal'*, in the
case of an unidentifiable cause.

Second, in the case of *pečal'* the negative evaluation of the event
("something bad happened") is generalized and extended beyond this
event as such: "this is bad" (component (d)).

Third, in the case of *pečal'* the feeling (as well as the underlying
thought) is portrayed as extended in time (components (k) and (l)). In
the case of *grust'*, time is left unspecified. This accounts for the fact that
*mimoletnaja grust'* "a passing sadness" sounds better than ?*mimoletnaja
pečal'* (cf. Uryson 1997).

Fourth, the feeling associated with *grust'* is not presented in the
explication as a "bad feeling". Since the underlying thought (in the
prototypical scenario) refers to a "bad" event ("something bad hap-

pened"), the explication invites the inference that the feeling caused by it is a "bad" feeling, but the explication does not state this explicitly. In the explication of *pečal'*, however, the feeling is specified as "bad" (component (h)). This difference accounts for the fact that *grust'* can be sometimes described as *svetlaja* "luminous", whereas *pečal'* normally cannot (except in poetry).

Fifth, the triggering event is presented in the explication of *grust'* as current or recent ("now", component (c)), where no such reference to the present is included in the explication of *pečal'*.

It will be clear from the foregoing discussion that while both *grust'* and *pečal'* have a great deal in common with the English *sadness*, they both differ from it in some respects. Unlike *sadness, pečal'* has to have a definite cause, it has to imply a negative evaluation of some event or state of affairs, as well as a "bad feeling", and it has to extend in time; and *grust'* differs from *sadness* in implying (prototypically at least) a short term feeling and not necessarily a "bad one". (The death of a child, frequently mentioned in the literature as a "prototypical anteced-ent" of "sadness", could hardly be linked with *grust'*.) Thus, each of the three words considered here (*sadness, grust', pečal'*) has its own distinct meaning. There is of course no reason to think that one of these words corresponds to some universal cognitive scenario (let alone a distinctive universal pattern of autonomic nervous system activity, cf. Ekman 1994b: 17), whereas the others do not.

It could be said that the differences between *grust', pečal'*, and *sadness* are relatively minor. As noted earlier, however, there are languages (like Tahitian; cf. Levy 1973) where the closest counterpart of *sadness* differs from it so much that the language can be said to have no counterpart of *sadness* at all (not even an approximate one). The main point of this section was not to claim that Russian, like Tahitian, "has no word for sadness", but rather to demonstrate the methodology which can be used for comparing any "emotion concepts", no matter how different, both within a given language and across languages and cultures.

## 10 The scope of this book

The main theoretical themes of the book have been introduced in this chapter, but they will reappear in various contexts in other chapters as well. Throughout the book, the focus is on both cultural diversity and "emotional universals". The unity of the analysis lies in its methodol-ogy: looking at the phenomena discussed through the prism of the same universal human concepts.

Chapter 2 presents a systematic account of several dozen "emotion concepts", studying in detail similarities and differences within each group. The groups discussed are based on distinctions such as that between "good feelings" (e.g. *joy*) and "bad feelings" (e.g. *frustration)*, between feelings based on the thought that "something bad happened" (e.g. *sadness*) and those based on the thought "something bad can happen" (e.g. *fear*), and between "thinking about someone else" (e.g. *envy*) and "thinking about ourselves" (e.g. *shame*).

While in discussing "joy", "frustration", "sadness", "fear", "envy", and "shame" one must look in detail at the meaning of the corresponding English words, the chapter is not intended to be just a study in lexical semantics. By uncovering the cognitive scenarios encoded in such words and discussing them in a cross-cultural and often historical perspective, I hope to identify many cognitive components which play a role in "emotional universes" other than that encoded in the contemporary English lexicon, and thus prepare the ground for the study of "emotional universals" in chapters 4 and 7. Throughout chapter 2, I have engaged with the existing literature on "individual emotions" – psychological, anthropological, philosophical, historical, and so on. Each "emotion" is the subject of a mini-study, and an exercise in multifaceted cross-disciplinary analysis, within a clear methodological framework.

Chapter 3 is a case study devoted to the German key concept *Angst*. While showing how the uses of *Angst* in German psychology, philosophy, and theology are rooted in the everyday use of the word, it explores its cultural underpinnings, tracing the origins of this unique German concept to the spiritual, cultural, and linguistic legacy of Martin Luther.

Chapter 4 explores human facial expressions. Rejecting analyses carried out in terms of language-specific English words such as *sad*, *happy*, *angry*, or *disgusted*, it proposes a radically new approach, shifting the perspective from the "psychology of the human face" to the "semantics of the human face". Arguing that meaningful facial components such as "raised eyebrows" or "drawn-together eyebrows" can be identified on an experiential semiotic basis, it isolates eight such meaningful facial gestures and assigns to them invariant (context-independent) meanings formulated in the Natural Semantic Metalanguage. The chapter's main hypothesis is that if there is a universal biologically based "emotional keyboard", it can be identified on the basis of universal, experientially recognizable facial gestures, and that its keys include, for example, the following ones: the "raised-eyebrows feelings", the "wrinkled-nose feelings", the "corners-of-the-mouth-up feelings", and so on. As demonstrated in chapter 7, these universals of feelings based on facial expressions are not necessarily the same as the common themes which can be detected through the study of the lexicons of the world's languages.

Whereas chapter 4 studies human faces from a universal point of view and seeks to establish a set of "facial universals", chapter 5 views the human body from the point of view of one particular culture – Russian – and does so by analysing Russian phraseology related to the body. The chapter discusses the differences between Russian and English ethnophraseology to do with the human body, and demonstrates, using linguistic evidence, how the human body seen through the prism of the Russian language is culturally constructed.

Chapter 6 introduces the notion of "cultural script" (developed by the author and colleagues in a number of earlier publications, see in particular Goddard 1997a, Wierzbicka 1990b, 1994b, c, and d, 1996b and c, 1998a), applying it to the comparison of two cultures, Polish and Anglo-American. The chapter shows how the theory of "cultural scripts" can be applied to cross-cultural study of "emotions" and proposes a number of contrasting Polish and Anglo-American "emotional scripts". The "scripts" discussed have to do with "feeling good feelings", "showing good feelings", "not showing any feelings that one doesn't feel", "showing good feelings towards other people", and so on. The chapter uses linguistic evidence of various kinds, as well as observations made by bilingual writers, and discusses both verbal and non-verbal behaviour.

Chapter 7 puts forward a number of hypotheses concerning "emotional universals". It discusses the evidence for the universality of the concept FEEL (undifferentiated between "mental" and "physical" feelings and distinct from the concept THINK), the universal tendency that people have to talk about "good feelings" and "bad feelings", the universal phenomenon of expressive words linking feelings with thoughts, i.e., interjections (e.g. *Gee!*, *Wow!*, or *Yuk!* in English), the existence in all languages of *descriptive* words linking feelings with thoughts (such as *sadness* or *grust'*), the universal phenomenon of using images of internal bodily events and processes to describe thought-related feelings (e.g. *heart-broken* in English), and the apparently universal recognition of some links between thoughts, feelings, and bodily processes (e.g. *blush* in English). The discussion raises again the question of "facial universals" (such as the "raised eyebrows" feeling or the "corners-of-the-mouth-up" feeling). The chapter tries to show how the study of "human emotions" can be freed from a dependence on language-specific English words such as *sad, angry, disgusted,* or *happy*; and how the study of linguistic and cultural diversity can be reconciled with a search for genuine universals.

Ekman and Davidson (1994: 46) unjustifiably attributed to the present writer a position of extreme relativity when they wrote: "In challenging Ekman and also Johnson-Laird and Oatley, Shweder cites Wierzbicka's arguments about language differences. Even Scherer would not accept Wierzbicka's position about the total variability in the lexicon of emotions."

But first, given Ekman's clearly declared lack of interest in "words" (see in particular Ekman 1994a: 282) and his frequent insistence that he is talking about "emotions", not about "words", it is difficult to see why he should have any problems with "total variability in the lexicon of emotion". Second, if by "position of total variability" Ekman and Davidson mean the claim that words like *anger, sadness,* or *surprise* do not have exact equivalents in many other languages, then the evidence in favour of this position would seem to be by now overwhelming. And third, if the authors are claiming that I deny the existence of any common themes running through the "emotion lexicons" of different languages then they are mistaken. I have in fact never denied this, and in chapter 7 of this book I try to identify some such common themes in precise ways, with reference to cross-linguistic evidence. Indeed, as chapter 7 illustrates, I, too, believe in the existence of "emotional universals", and I am as interested in these as I am in cultural diversity. I believe, however, that to be able to compare languages, cultures, and conceptual systems at all we need a reliable *tertium comparationis*, and that to study "human mind", "human cognition", or "human emotions" we must reach beyond the conventional English lexicon and anchor our investigations in conceptual universals.

# CHAPTER 2

# Defining emotion concepts: discovering "cognitive scenarios"

## Introduction

Ten years ago Ortony, Clore, and Collins (1988: 12) argued that "an analysis of emotion must go beyond differentiating positive from negative emotions to give a systematic account of the qualitative differences among individual emotions such as fear, envy, anger, pride, relief, and admiration". While a great deal of work has been done during the intervening decade I believe no such systematic account has as yet emerged.

This chapter makes an attempt at such a systematic account, anchored in an independently established and justified set of universal semantic primes. While no exhaustive discussion of all the emotion concepts encoded in the English lexicon has been attempted, the account given here does include detailed analysis of some fifty emotion concepts such as *fear, pride, relief,* and *admiration,* which constitute the core of the English emotion lexicon. Most of the emotion concepts which have been written about in the extensive cross-disciplinary literature on "emotions" have in fact been covered here, and while it was impossible to discuss the literature on individual "emotions" fully, all sections of this chapter include some critical discussion of their earlier treatment – by psychologists, philosophers, anthropologists, sociologists, and historians.

Like any other set of complex entities, emotion concepts can be classified in many different ways. For the purposes of this chapter, I have divided them into six groups based on the following general themes: (1) "something good happened" (e.g. *joy* or being *happy*); (2) "something bad happened" (e.g. *sadness* or *grief*); (3) "something bad can/will happen (e.g. *fear* or *anxiety*); (4) "I don't want things like this to happen" (e.g. *anger* or *indignation*); (5) "thinking about other people" (e.g. *envy* or *Schadenfreude*); and (6) "thinking about ourselves" (e.g. *shame* or *remorse*). Each of these themes is linked with some aspect of the cognitive scenarios which underlie the emotion concepts included in a given group.

# 1 "Something good happened" and related concepts

Like other languages, English has a relatively small set of emotion terms referring to "good events" (cf. Averill 1980) and not all such words are linked with "good feelings". For example, *envy* implies that "something good happened", but alas, it happened to someone else, and the experiencer feels "something bad", not "something good". We assure other people that we feel something good because something good happened to them when we *congratulate* them; but *congratulate* is a speech act verb, and there is no corresponding emotion term (while there *is* a term – at least a loan word – for feeling something good because something bad happened to someone else; see section 5).

In this section I will discuss several common English words which are linked with thoughts about "good things" that happened, are happening, or will/can happen, and which imply "good feelings". These words include *joy*, *happy* (and *happiness*), *contented*, *pleased* (and *pleasure*), *delighted* (*delight*), *relieved* (*relief*), *excited* (*excitement*), and *hope*. (As the nouns do not always mean the same as the corresponding adjectives I will not attempt to standardize the part of speech used to identify a given emotion concept.) For comparison, I will also include here the word *relief*, which refers to "good feelings" but not to "good events".

## 1.1 Joy

*Joy* is not a very common everyday word in modern English, and its frequency is much lower than that of the adjective *happy*. One could say that the concept of being *happy* has expanded in the history of English emotions, at the expense of *joy*. For example, in Shakespeare's writings (Spevack 1968) *joy* and *happy* have the same frequency of 215, whereas in Bernard Shaw's works (Bevan 1971) *happy* is seven times more common than *joy* (339: 52). The reasons for this decline of *joy* and expansion of *happy* will be discussed later.

Nonetheless, the cognitive scenario of *joy* is simpler than that of *happy* or *happiness*, and partly for this reason *joy* is a better starting point for the analysis of "positive emotion terms". There are two crucial cognitive components in the *joy* scenario, an evaluative one: "something very good is happening", and a volitive one: "I want this to be happening":

A full explication of *joy* follows:

> *Joy* (X felt joy)
> (a) X felt something because X thought something
> (b)    sometimes a person thinks:

(c) "something very good is happening
(d) I want this to be happening"
(e) when this person thinks this this person feels something very good
(f) X felt something like this
(g) because X thought something like this

Instead of commenting on the individual components of this explication directly, I will discuss them in relation to the explication of the related and culturally more salient concept of *happy*.

### 1.2 Happy and happiness

> I have at last got the little room I have wanted so long, and am very happy about it. (Louise May Alcott, 1975[1846]: 32)

As this quote illustrates, we are *happy* when something good has happened to us that we have wanted to happen (e.g. when we get, at last, a room of our own). One clear difference between *happy* and *joy*, then, has to do with the personal character of the former (highlighted by expressions such as *pursuit of happiness* or *personal happiness*), and the non-personal, "selfless" character of *joy*. Unlike being *happy*, *joy* can be shared with other people and can be seen as open to everyone (cf. expressions like *the joy of Christmas* or *the joy of knowledge*). If *joy* implies that "something very good is happening", *happy* implies that "some good things happened TO ME". (Of course people can pursue happiness *en deux*, as a couple, but this doesn't make it non-personal or selfless.)

As the phrasing of these two components suggests, the "TO ME" aspect of being *happy* defines only one dimension of the contrast with *joy*. There is also the temporal dimension and, so to speak, the quantitative one. Unlike *joy*, being *happy* can be understood as a long-term state (as well as an emotion), and as an emotion, it can be seen as a more "settled" one than *joy*. In some ways, *joy* can be seen as more intense, more thrilling than being *happy* – and more likely to be a short-term emotion. To quote J. D. Salinger (1964: 155): "the most singular difference between happiness and joy is that happiness is a solid and joy a liquid. Mine started to seep through its container as early as the next morning."

Being *happy* is more consistent, then, with goals achieved and dreams fulfilled than with unexpected and undreamed-of good events. (One is more likely to be, in C. S. Lewis' and Wordsworth's phrases, "surprised by joy" than "surprised by being happy"; and one can hardly *seek joy*, as one can *seek happiness*.) This is consistent with the past tense of the evaluative component in *happy*: "some good things happened to me" (vs. "something very good is happening" in *joy*) and also with the past tense of the volitive component: "I wanted things like this to happen to me" (vs. "I want this to be happening" in *joy*). It is also consistent with a broader range of causes: "some good things" vs. "something very good" in *joy*. Since being *happy* can be a long-term state it may seem to be better portrayed in terms of present rather than past events ("some good things are happening to me" rather than "some good things happened to me"). But in fact, an expression like *a happy end* implies that some good things have already happened (to the protagonists), while inviting the inference that after that, no change in their fortunes is to be expected. Of course more good things can happen to them in the future, but *happy* doesn't depend on that; rather, it implies a state based on some good things which have already happened. A hypothetical *"joyous end"* wouldn't have a similarly backward-looking perspective, and would suggest, rather, that the end itself was a joyous moment.

But there is one further important difference between being *happy* and *joy*, which (as we will see) links the former with *contentedness*: the implication that one doesn't want anything else, that one has all one wanted. This leads us to the following explication:

> *Happy* (X was happy).
> (a)  X felt something (because X thought something)
> (b)    sometimes a person thinks:
> (c)    "some good things happened to me
> (d)    I wanted things like this to happen
> (e)    I don't want anything else now"
> (f)    when this person thinks this this person feels something
>        good
> (g)  X felt something like this

The differences between *happy* and *joy*, then, can be summed up in the form of the following contrasts: (1) the presence vs. absence of "to me"; (2) "happened" vs. "is happening"; (3) "some things" vs. "something"; (4) "good" vs. "very good"; in components (c) and (f); (5) "I wanted" vs. "I want"; and (6) the presence vs. absence of the component "don't want anything else".

It must be emphasized, however, that the adjective *happy* differs in meaning from the noun *happiness* and is, so to speak, weaker. For example, if one says

I am happy with the present arrangements.

one is not implying that one feels happiness. The fact that one can combine *happy* with *quite*, as in the following exchange:

A: Are you thinking of applying for a transfer?
B. No, I am quite happy (*joyful, *joyous) where I am.

suggests that to feel *happy* one doesn't even have to feel "something very good" – it can be simply "something good". Nor does one have to think that "some very good things" have happened to one – it can be simply "some good things".

Finally, there is the question of the possibility of feeling unaccountably *happy*:

I feel happy today, I don't know why.

The noun *happiness* appears to be more dependent on some basic cognitive appraisal ("some very good things happened to me"), as does also the noun *joy* ("something very good is happening"). But the adjective *happy* (like the adjective *sad*) can be also used to describe, so to speak, a certain mood, not necessarily linked with any thoughts, no matter how diffuse or less than fully conscious.

The noun *happiness*, whose implications far exceed those of the adjective *happy*, can be compared with similarly "superlative" words in other European languages, such as *Glück* in German, *bonheur* in French, *felicità* in Italian, or *sčast'e* in Russian (e.g. when I say that "I'm happy with the present arrangements" I don't mean that I experience "happiness"). By contrast, the English adjective *happy* is much "weaker" in meaning than the corresponding adjectives in German *(glücklich)*, French *(heureux)*, Italian *( felice)*, or Russian *(sčastlivyj)*, which do imply a feeling of happiness. One consequence of this difference is that, for example, human faces described by Ekman (1975: 36) and others as evidently "happy" ("everyone agrees on what the faces say", according to the caption) would not normally be described in the other languages mentioned as *glücklich, heureux, felice*, or *sčastlivyj*. The meaning of *happiness* can be explicated as follows:

*Happiness* (X felt happiness)
(a)  X felt something (because X thought something)
(b)    sometimes a person thinks:
(c)    "some very good things happened to me
(d)    I wanted things like this to happen
(e)    I can't want anything else"
(f)    when this person thinks this this person feels something
        very good
(g)  X felt something like this (because X thought something
        like this)

The main differences between *happiness* and *happy* lie in the contrast between "very good" and "good" (components (c) and (f)) and between "I can't want anything else" vs. "I don't want anything else" (component (e)). In *happiness* (as in *Glück, bonheur, felicità* and *sčast'e*) one's heart is, so to speak, filled to overflowing, and there is no room left for any further (unfulfilled) desires or wishes.

This difference in "intensity" between *happy* and *happiness* appears to be the result of a historical process in the course of which *happy* "weakened" and expanded in use at the same time (at the expense of more "intense" concepts like *joy* and *rejoice*). In support of this conjecture I would point out that the frame "happy with" (e.g. "I'm happy with the present arrangements") appears to be a modern innovation. For example, there are no such cases among the 215 occurrences of *happy* in Shakespeare's writings (Spevack 1968), whereas the concordance of Bernard Shaw's works (Bevan 1971) shows twelve such examples and in the OED (1993[1933]) the earliest quote for "happy with" is dated 1947. *Happy with* doesn't imply *happiness* but something less intense than that (rather like *satisfied*). It could be suggested, therefore, that both the decline of *joy* (as well as of the verb *rejoice*) and the semantic weakening of *happy* are manifestations of an overall process of the "dampening of the emotions", the trend against emotional intensity, characteristic of modern Anglo emotional culture (cf. P. Stearns 1994).

At the same time, the remarkable expansion of the concept *happy* (in its less intense and more pragmatic persona) is consistent with the spread of the emotional culture of "positive thinking", "optimism", "cheerfulness", "fun", and so on. (See chapter 6.)

Considerations of this kind make one sceptical about the reliability of questionnaires trying to find out the proportion of people who regard themselves as "happy" in different societies (cf. e.g. Myers and Diener 1995; Pinker 1997). First, cross-cultural investigations of this kind are misleading because the words supposedly corresponding to *happy* (e.g. *glücklich, heureux, felice, sčastlivyj*) in fact differ from *happy* considerably; and second, in a culture where "positive thinking" and "feeling good" are valued and seen as signs of success and indeed achievements in themselves, any self-reports about "being happy" are bound to reflect in some (unknown) measure the pressure of the prevailing emotional ideology.

### 1.3 Contented

The word *contented* could apply to the (presumed) feelings of a cat lying comfortably in a warm spot. Its meaning can be stated as follows:

*Contented* (X was contented)
(a) X felt something because X thought something
(b)     sometimes a person thinks:
(c)     "some good things happened to me before now
(d)     I feel something good because of this now
(e)     I don't want other things now"
(f)     when this person thinks this this person feels something
          good
(g) X felt something like this
(h) because X thought something like this

Like *happy*, *contented* can combine with the modifier *quite*: "She is quite contented (quite happy) here", but unlike *happy*, it doesn't easily combine with *very*: "She is very happy (?very contented) here". This difference in combinability highlights the fact that *contented* is "weaker" and more pragmatic than *happy* (while *happy* is "weaker" and more "pragmatic" than *happiness* or *joy*). *Contented* is also more focussed on the present well-being ("I feel something good now") based on past good events ("some good events happened to me before now"), and on the lack of present desires ("I don't want other things now"). It is therefore more limited in scope than *happy*, which is based on past events ("some good things happened to me") matching past wanting ("I wanted something like this to happen") and therefore is more compatible with the achievement of goals and fulfilment of long-term wishes.

### 1.4 Pleased and pleasure

> Mr Butler, who is highly pleased with Mr King's past administration
> of his property, wished . . . to give him some token of his satisfaction
> (Kemble 1975[1839]: 263).

The quote above is 160 years old, but it fits the current use of the word *pleased* well: one is *pleased* with something that has – in one's estimation – gone well and in accordance with one's wishes.

To begin with, then, *pleased* – unlike *happy* – requires a thought. It would be odd to say "?I feel pleased, I don't know why", as one can say "I feel happy, I don't know why". One is *pleased* "with something" or "about something", that is, one thinks about something and one feels *pleased* because of this.

If *happy* is compatible with the achievement of goals and with the fulfilment of wishes, so is *pleased*; but *pleased* is less personal and has, so to speak, a sharper focus. For example, if a colleague gets a promotion, and I say that I am *pleased*, this implies that I think that something good happened and that I wanted it (this particular event) to happen. If I say to the colleague, however, that I am *happy* (about her promotion) I imply that I identify with the colleague ("something good happened to me"), and also, that I wanted good things (in general) to happen to her.

*Pleased* seems also to be more "focussed" than *happy* because it refers (prototypically) to one particular event rather than to "some events" in the plural. For this reason, no doubt, *pleased* cannot be linked with open-ended and diffused causes implied by references to place or time:

> I am happy here.
> ?I am pleased here.
> I feel happy today.
> ?I feel pleased today

Neither does *pleased* refer to "not wanting other things"; it is focussed (prototypically) on one particular event ("something good happened") and implies nothing about other things, whether desired or not desired.

> *Pleased* (X was pleased)
> (a)  X felt something because X thought something
> (b)     sometimes a person thinks:
> (c)     "something good happened
> (d)     I wanted this to happen"
> (e)     when this person thinks this this person feels something
>            good
> (f)  X felt something like this
> (g)  because X thought something like this

Finally, a "warning" about *pleasure*. Despite the morphological kinship with *pleased*, *pleasure* is semantically only a distant cousin; when one is *contented*, *delighted*, *relieved*, or *excited*, one feels *contentedness*, *delight*, *relief*, or *excitement*, but when one is *pleased* one doesn't necessarily feel *pleasure*. In fact, *pleasure* is usually not regarded as an "emotion" at all, and with good reason, for it doesn't imply any cognitive scenario at all, not even a prototypical one. Rather, it implies only that a person feels something good because of something that is happening to him or her at the same time – not necessarily something seen as "something good". It is only the feeling which is (feels) "good", no cognitive evaluation needs to be involved.

In their theory of emotions, Ortony, Clore, and Collins (1988) decided to use the terms *pleased* and *displeased* as indefinable semantic primitives, analysing all other emotion terms with the help of these two. The authors defended their decision by emphasizing that these terms "simply represent the best we can do to find relatively intensity-neutral English words that refer (only) to the undifferentiated affective reactions one can have to events and their consequences" (p. 20). In fact, however, *pleased* and *displeased* are as complex as any other emotion terms and need to be analysed themselves, and the perfect primitives which can be found for this purpose are the extremely versatile universal human concepts GOOD and BAD.

## 1.5 Delight

A person who feels *delighted* has just discovered that something unexpected and very good has happened, as the birthday girl did in the following example:

> She arrived to candlelight and twenty five presents – from trinkets to treasures – hidden Easter-egg style throughout the apartment . . . After the fourth or fifth gift, and all the way up to her birthday number, she would look at me incredulously each time or squeal with childlike delight as she eagerly set out to find the next surprise." (Feinstein and Mayo 1993: 56)

Roughly speaking, *delighted* could be compared to a mixture of being surprised and very pleased at the same time, but as the proposed explications of *delighted* and *pleased* show, *pleased* is more compatible with achievements of goals and with a sense of control over events ("I wanted this to happen"). In addition, *delighted* implies also that what happened is not just "good" but "very good", and that one feels something "very good" because of this. In politeness routines, therefore, "I'm delighted to hear it" sounds more enthusiastic (sometimes gushing) than "I'm pleased to hear it".

> *Delighted* (X was delighted)
> (a)  X felt something because X thought something
> (b)   sometimes a person thinks:
> (c)   "I know now: something very good happened
> (d)   I didn't know that this would happen"
> (e)   when this person thinks this this person feels something very good
> (f)  X felt something like this
> (g)  because X thought something like this

## 1.6 Relief

Johnson-Laird and Oatley (1989) have defined *relief* as "happiness as a result of something that brings to an end fear or sadness". But of course one can feel *relief* without feeling *happiness*; and it can follow not only *fear* or *sadness* but also some other oppressive feeling (e.g. *anxiety* or *nervousness*). In addition, concepts like *happiness*, *fear*, and *sadness* are just as complex as *relief* itself, so analysing *relief* via those three concepts constitutes a case of explaining unknowns via unknowns.

The definition of *relief* proposed by Ortony, Clore, and Collins (1988) is somewhat more satisfactory in this respect (although it uses one emotion term, too, *pleased*): "(pleased about) the disconfirmation of the prospect of an undesirable event". But this analysis, too, relies on concepts which are complex and highly language-specific (*disconfirmation*, *prospect*, *undesirable*). Avoiding concepts of this kind we can say that if *delighted* implies that something unexpected – and very good – has happened, *relieved* implies that something expected – and bad – is not going to happen. More precisely:

> Relieved (X was relieved)
> (a) X felt something because X thought something
> (b) sometimes a person thinks:
> (c) "I thought that something bad would happen
> (d) I felt something bad because of this
> (e) I know now: this bad thing will not happen"
> (f) when this person thinks this this person feels something good
> (g) X felt something like this
> (h) because X thought something like this

(As will be argued in more detail later, this is directly antithetical to *disappointment*.)

### 1.7 Excitement

> There is a wonderful kind of excitement in modern neuroscience, a romantic, moon-walk sense of exploring and setting out for new frontiers. (Jamison 1997: 196)

*Excitement* – like *hope* – is linked with future rather than present or past events: it implies that "something very good will happen"; it also implies, like *hope*, that "I want this to happen". In *excitement*, this is often linked with an active attitude ("I want to do something"). This active attitude, however, is not linked with a sense of control; on the contrary, there is an element of "out-of-controlness" here, in so far as one cannot fully control one's thoughts ("I can't think about other things now").

Like *delight* and *relief*, *excitement* (as well as *surprise*) is also linked with a recent discovery or realization ("I know now"). Unlike *delight* (or *surprise*), however, it doesn't imply anything contrary to expectations

("I didn't think that this would happen"). Like *joy*, *excitement* refers to current rather than past desires ("I want this to happen"), and this combined with the certainty that the desired event will happen creates an impression of vividness, "arousal", and something like thrill.

> *Excited* (X was excited)
> (a) X felt something because X thought something
> (b)   sometimes a person thinks:
> (c)   "I know now: something very good will happen
> (d)   I want it to happen
> (e)   I can't think about other things now"
> (f)   when this person thinks this this person feels something good
> (g) X felt something like this
> (h) because X thought something like this

## 1.8 Hope

Like *excitement*, *hope* refers to desired future events. But unlike in *excitement*, these desired future events are seen as "good" rather than "very good", and they are seen as possible rather than certain ("I think good things can happen" vs. "I know now: something very good will happen"). As the phrasing of the two components just mentioned suggests, prototypically *hope* is also less focussed than *excitement* ("some good things" vs. "something very good"). Finally, *hope* implies a lack of knowledge about the future ("I don't know what will happen"), and in this (as well as in some other respects) it is parallel to *fear*:

> *Hope* (X felt hope)
> (a) X felt something because X thought something
> (b)   sometimes a person thinks:
> (c)   "I don't know what will happen
> (d)   some good things can happen (some time after now)
> (e)   I want these things to happen"
> (f)   when this person thinks this this person feels something good
> (g) X felt something like this
> (h) because X thought something like this

*Fear* will be discussed later, but it will be useful to outline its explication here for comparison:

> *Fear* (X felt fear)
> (a) X felt something because X thought something

(b)    sometimes a person thinks:
(c)    "I don't know what will happen
(d)    some bad things can happen
(e)    I don't want these things to happen
(f)    I want to do something because of this if I can
(g)    I don't know if I can do anything"
(h)    when this person thinks this this person feels something bad
(i)    X felt something like this
(j)    because X thought something like this

Apart from the "good vs. bad" contrast, the main difference between *fear* and *hope* lies in components (f) and (g) of *fear*, which suggest a desire to do something as well as a sense of helplessness. No parallel components are included in *hope*, which may seem, as a result, a more placid, less involved, attitude. In addition, however, *hope* seems to be focussed on more distant events than *fear*: in *fear*, the threat can extend to any time from now to a distant future, whereas in *hope*, the good events to come seem to be separated (at least notionally) from the present time. *Hope* is different in this respect not only from *fear* but also from *excitement*, which can also refer to imminent events (and also from *confidence*, which will not be discussed here). Hence the subcomponent "some time after now" in component (d) of *hope*.

## 2 "Something bad happened" and related concepts

In English, as in many other languages, there are many emotion terms associated with cognitive scenarios in which something bad happened, is happening, or will happen. In this chapter, words of this kind are divided into two broad categories, one including real events (past or present), and the other hypothetical (essentially, future) events. The first category, discussed in this section, includes the words *sadness*, *unhappiness*, *distress*, *sorrow*, *grief*, and *despair* (for comparison I will also discuss here *disappointment* and *frustration*), and the second (section 3), words like *fear*, *fright*, *dread*, and *anxiety*.

### 2.1 Sadness

The concept of "sadness" has often been discussed in the literature, and various interpretations have been proposed. For example, Paul Harris (1989: 103) linked "sadness" with the situation "when desirable goals are lost", Richard Lazarus (1991: 122) assigned to it (as its "core relational theme") "having experienced an irrevocable loss", whereas

Philip Johnson-Laird and Keith Oatley (1989: 91) have suggested that it should be treated as an unanalysable semantic primitive.

To begin with Johnson-Laird and Oatley's suggestion, *sad* is a complex concept, related to other complex concepts (such as, for example, *disappointed, distressed, worried,* etc.) and sharing with them certain components; it cannot, therefore, be a semantic primitive. Furthermore, it is certainly not a universal concept: there are languages (e.g. Tahitian) which have no word corresponding to anything like it (cf. Levy 1973: 305), and other languages which have various words roughly comparable but none corresponding to it exactly. (See, for example, my discussion of the closest counterparts of *sadness* in the Australian language Pitjantjatjara in Wierzbicka 1992c and in Russian in Wierzbicka 1998b.) Levy (1984) himself has put forward a hypothesis that "sadness" is "hypocognized" in Tahitian. The idea of "hypocognition" has been readily accepted by many other scholars – in my view, too readily, both because the hypothesis is essentially unverifiable, and because it gives an unduly privileged position to the English lexicon (as a standard for what is "hypocognized" elsewhere). What *is* verifiable (on the basis of lexical evidence) is that the Anglo concept of *sadness* is just as language- and culture-specific as are the Russian concepts of *toska, grust',* or *pečal'* or the Pitjantjatjara concept of *tjituru-tjituru.* (For detailed discussion, see Wierzbicka 1992c; for other arguments against *sadness* as a supposedly universal human emotion, see C. Stearns, 1993.)

Returning to English, Harris' analysis allows him to capture some relationships between *sadness* ("desirable goals lost") and certain other emotion concepts, notably *anger* ("desirable goals blocked") and *joy* ("desirable goals achieved"). But it does not capture the similarities and differences between *sadness* and, for example, *unhappiness, distress,* or *disappointment.* It is also inconsistent with empirical linguistic evidence. The word *goal* implies that one is doing something because one wants something to happen. But the word *sad* can also be applied to situations where no "goals" are involved at all. For example, I may feel sad when I hear that my friend's dog died, but this has nothing to do with any goals that I may have had.

Lazarus' (1991) suggestion that *sadness* is linked with an "irrevocable loss" is not sustainable either. If there is an emotion concept in English which can be characterized in these terms, it is *grief,* not *sadness.* For example, if the death of a friend or a relative causes us *grief,* this implies indeed that we construe this death as, roughly speaking, an "irrevocable loss" (see section 2.5). *Sadness,* however, doesn't have to be linked with personal losses at all. Consider, for example, the following statement by a woman visiting in hospital a colleague dying of cancer (Callanan and Kelley 1993: 50):

I miss you a lot at work . . . I feel so sad about what's happening to you.

The "theme" of the visitor's sadness is not the fact that she is losing a colleague (although she misses her at work) but rather the "bad thing" that has happened (the colleague's illness) and the awareness that she can't do anything about it.

Thus, the prototypical cognitive scenario associated with the concept *sad* involves an awareness that "something bad has happened" (not necessarily to me) and an acceptance of the fact that one can't do anything about it. More precisely, this scenario can be represented as follows (cf. chapter 1, section 9):

> *Sad* (X was sad)
> (a)  X felt something
> (b)     sometimes a person thinks:
> (c)     "I know: something bad happened
> (d)     I don't want things like this to happen
> (e)     I can't think: I will do something because of it now
> (f)     I know I can't do anything"
> (g)   when this person thinks this this person feels something bad
> (h)  X felt something like this

Consider, for example, the following passage from a wife's account of the last stages of her husband's illness:

> Sometimes we'd talk about the early years of our marriage, and his hopes for the boys, and how awful it was that he'd gotten sick. We'd cry because we didn't know how we'd manage without one another. It sounds sad, and it was, but it was a lot better than yelling at each other, as we'd been doing. (Callanan and Kelley 1993: 47)

The wife acknowledges that something bad has happened, she expresses something like regret at what has happened, but she accepts that she can't do anything about it (unlike at an earlier stage when both she and her husband were angry and unaccepting).

As has often been pointed out, a person who feels *sad* may not be conscious of the reason for the sadness, and one can say:

I feel sad today, I don't know why.

For this reason, component (a) of the explication has been formulated as "X felt something", not as "X felt something because X thought something" (the person who is said to feel *sad* doesn't have to think about anything in particular: "something bad happened"). Nonetheless, the feeling of sadness – to the extent to which it can be identified at all – can only be identified with reference to a prototypical cognitive scenario ("X feels like people usually do when they think . . .").

Comparing *sadness* with *distress*, Ekman and Friesen (1975: 117) argued that "sadness is a passive, not an active feeling", and that while "in distress there is more of a protest against the loss, in sadness you are resigned to the loss". Again, the word *loss* is not well chosen, for it implies that "something bad happened to me", and yet if my friend's dog dies I may be sad although no personal loss is involved. But the idea of something like resignation and of a passive rather than active attitude is, I think, correct, and consistent with the explication proposed here (cf. components (d), (e), and (f)).

## 2.2 Unhappiness

*Unhappiness* differs from *sadness* in a number of ways. Firstly, it does require some underlying thoughts (i.e. some known reason), for while one can say "I feel sad, I don't know why", it would be a little odd to say "I feel unhappy, I don't know why".

Secondly, *unhappy* implies a more "intense" feeling and a "stronger" negative evaluation (one can be crushed by unhappiness, but not by sadness), and it is less readily combinable with minimizing qualifiers like *a little* or *slightly*:

> She felt a little (slightly) sad.
> ?She felt a little (slightly) unhappy.

Thirdly, *unhappy* has a more personal character than *sad*: I can be saddened by bad things that have happened to other people, but if I am unhappy, I am unhappy because of bad things that have happened to me personally.

Fourthly, *unhappy* – in contrast to *sad* – does not suggest a resigned state of mind. If in the case of *sadness* the experiencer focusses on the thought "I can't do anything about it", in the case of *unhappiness* he/she focusses on some thwarted desires ("I wanted things like this not to happen to me"), and hence it is more closely associated semantically with *happy*. The attitude is not exactly "active" because one doesn't necessarily want anything to happen, but it is not "passive" either, for one doesn't take the perspective "I can't do anything about it".

Finally, *unhappy* seems to suggest, prototypically, a state extended in time rather than a momentary occurrence (cf. "a moment of sadness" vs. "?a moment of unhappiness"). It seems also (like *happy*) to refer, prototypically, to "some things" (in the plural) rather than simply "something".

> *Unhappy* (X was unhappy)
> (a) X felt something because X thought something
> (b)    sometimes a person thinks for some time:
> (c)    "some very bad things happened to me
> (d)    I wanted things like this not to happen to me
> (e)    I can't not think about it"
> (f)    when this person thinks this this person feels something
>        bad for some time
> (g) X felt something like this
> (h) because X thought something like this

### 2.3 Distress

The key differences between *distress* and *sadness* lie in the present orientation of *distress* ("something bad is happening NOW" vs. "something bad happened"); in its personal character ("something bad is happening TO ME"); in its "active and less resigned" attitude, noted by Ekman and Friesen ("I don't want this to be happening to me", "because of this I want to do something"). The overall meaning of *distress* can be represented as follows:

> *Distressed* (X was distressed)
> (a) X felt something because X thought something
> (b)    sometimes a person thinks:
> (c)    "something bad is happening to me now
> (d)    I don't want this to be happening
> (e)    because of this I want to do something if I can
> (f)    I don't know what I can do
> (g)    I want someone to do something"
> (h)    when this person thinks this this person feels something
>        bad
> (i) X felt something like this
> (j) because X thought something like this

In various works on facial expression of emotions (see e.g. Ekman 1973) the words *distress* or *distressed* are often used to refer to crying infants, whereas the word *sad* is used in connection with photographs showing adults who neither cry nor scream (one can imagine "tears of sadness", but only tears, not loud crying or screaming). This contrast in the choice of labels is consistent with the definitions proposed here. The state of mind of a crying infant is no doubt more consistent with a present tense personal concern ("something bad IS HAPPENING TO ME now"), posited here for *distressed*, than with the past tense impersonal thought posited for *sad* ("something bad HAPPENED").

Furthermore, a crying infant is not quietly accepting the situation but actively opposing it ("I don't want this to be happening"). The infant may feel helpless and unable to cope with that situation ("I don't know what I can do"), but he or she is not passive; rather, he or she is trying to signal his or her feelings to the outside world, thus implicitly calling for help ("I want someone to do something"). The phrases *cry of distress* and *damsel in distress* point in the same direction, as does also the common phrase *distress signals*, used with reference to ships. The ship's crew may well wish to signal a message along the following lines: "something bad is happening to us", "we don't want this to be happening", "because of this we want to do something", "we don't know what we can do" (and, by implication: "we want someone (else) to do something"). But there would be no point in any ship sending out "signals of sadness", or, for that matter, "signals of unhappiness".

Consider also the following passage from a newspaper article, reporting Australian academics' *distress* at what was happening to Australian education as a result of the then Government's policies (*The Australian*, 3 July 1991, p. 11):

> What we are saying to the Government is: "ignore this at your peril".
> We are really doing them a favour, 18 months before an election, by showing how deeply academics feel.
> We want a result. We aren't interested in the Coalition or the Government, we are doing this for higher education. The bottom line is that people are distressed at what is happening to the higher education system.

If the academics said they were *sad* rather than *distressed* they would be implying that something bad had already happened and that they couldn't do anything about. (Consequently, they would not be sad AT something, but BECAUSE of something; cf. Osmond 1997.) The choice of *distressed* implies here a current situation ("something bad is happening to us now"), an opposition to this situation ("we don't want this to be happening"), a desire to do something ("we want to do something because of this if we can"), uncertainty as to what one can do ("we don't know what we can do"), and a call for action by someone else, the Government ("we want someone to do something").

## 2.4 Sorrow

*Sorrow* (which is very different in meaning from the adjective *sorry*) is personal, like *distress* and *unhappiness*, not impersonal like *sadness* ("something very bad happened TO ME"). It is more "intense" than *sadness* ("something VERY bad happened to me"). It can be caused by a past event (somebody's death, some other great loss), but if so then it is not focussed on that past event as such. Rather, it implies a long term state (possibly resulting from a past event, or from a past discovery of a long-term condition (e.g. childlessness or an incurable disease of one's child or spouse). If the experiencer focusses on the past event as such, however, then one would speak of a *tragedy* rather than of a *sorrow*. *Sorrow* may have its roots in the past, but the stress is on the on-going, long-term state. This aspect of *sorrow* is highlighted in the following (admittedly archaic) examples from Stevenson (1949:1886):

> The longest sorrow finds at last relief.
> (William Rowley)

> Eighty odd years of sorrow have I seen.
> (Shakespeare)

In terms of attitude, *sorrow* can be said to be half way between *sadness* (accepting) and *distress* (not accepting). Since the "bad thing" is perceived as still happening ("something very bad is happening to me") the experiencer's attitude can be one of "not wanting" ("I don't want this to be happening"). At the same time, however, the realization that one "can't do anything" encourages a more accepting attitude ("I can't think: I will do something because of this" – but not "I want to do something because of this", as in the case of *distress*).

It is also interesting to compare *sorrow* with *unhappiness*, since the two concepts are often applicable to the same situation, depending on the speaker's construal of it. In both cases, the event is seen as very bad for the experiencer, and in both cases this event looms large in the experiencer's thoughts ("I can't not think about this"). One clear difference between the two has to do with the temporal perspective: an *unhappy* person thinks "some very bad things happened to me", whereas *sorrow* is associated with the thought "something very bad is happening to me". In addition, *sorrow* – but not *unhappiness* – suggests a degree of resignation ("I can't do anything about it"), whereas *unhappiness* – but not *sorrow* – suggests thwarted desires ("I wanted things like this not to happen"). Presumably, it is this semi-accepting, or at least semi-resigned attitude to long-term intense adversity or pain ("something very bad is happening to me") which lends *sorrow* its peculiar air of dignity, which commands not only compassion but also respect. To quote Oscar Wilde's "De profundis": "Where there is sorrow, there is holy ground" (Stevenson 1949: 1884).

The fact that there is something irreparable about *sorrow* links it with *grief*, to which we will turn shortly. *Sorrow* and *grief* are also linked by the experiencer's dwelling on the painful subject; but in the case of *grief* and *grieving* the experiencer intentionally focusses on the painful subject ("I want to think about this"), whereas in the case of *sorrow* there is, rather, an inability to forget ("I can't not think about this").

> *Sorrow* (X felt sorrow)
> (a) X felt something because X thought something
> (b)   sometimes a person thinks for a long time:
> (c)   "something very bad is happening to me
> (d)   I don't want this to be happening
> (e)   I can't think: I will do something because of this
> (f)   I can't do anything
> (g)   I can't not think about this"
> (h)   when this person thinks this this person feels something very bad
> (i) X felt something like this
> (j) because X thought something like this

The combination of intensity, long-term suffering, and a semi-accepting attitude, makes *sorrow* a somewhat old-fashioned emotion. In the modern Anglo emotional culture, characterized by the "dampening of the emotions" in general and avoidance of long-term "unpleasant emotions" in particular (cf. P. Stearns 1994), *sorrow* has largely given way to the milder, less painful, and more transient *sadness*.

## 2.5 Grief

> The beloved is [. . .] part of ourselves.
> (C. S. Lewis 1989: 8)
>
> The death of a beloved is an amputation.
> (L'Engle 1989: 6)

*Grief* is prototypically linked with death, although it can also be extended to other situations when one "loses" a person who was "like a part of me". By a further extension, *grief* can be attributed to a person who "loses" *something* (rather than *someone*) that was "like a part of me": one's capacity for work, physical mobility, sight, and so on.

Although it is often said in the literature on emotions that *sadness* is caused by a "loss", in fact the metaphor of "loss" is much more appropriate for *grief*. As pointed out earlier, *sadness* can be caused by events which don't affect us personally and which don't make us "lose" anyone or anything. *Grief*, however, can indeed be said (metaphorically) to be occasioned by a "loss", more specifically, by the "loss" of a person ("someone was like a part of me", "something happened to this person", "because of this this person can't be like a part of me any more"). At the moment, the experiencer is absorbed by thoughts of the painful event ("I want to think about this"), almost to the exclusion of everything else ("I can't think about other things now"). The fact that *grief* has an (intransitive) verbal counterpart (*to grieve*) is consistent with the presence of a volitive component in its meaning (*grieving* can almost be seen as something that one does, like *rejoicing* or *worrying*). One is fully absorbed by the thoughts of one's bereavement, and one is neither able nor willing to direct one's thoughts to anything else. To quote C. S. Lewis again:

> There is a sort of invisible blanket between the world and me. I find it hard to take in what anyone says. Or perhaps, hard to want to take it in. It is so uninteresting. (1989: 15)

*Grief* (X felt grief)
(a)  X felt something because X thought something
(b)  sometimes a person thinks:
(c)  "something very bad happened to me (a short time before now)
(d)  someone was like a part of me
(e)  something happened to this person
(f)  because of this this person cannot be like a part of me any more
(h)  I want to think about this
(i)  I can't think about other things now"
(j)  when this person thinks this this person feels something very bad
(k)  X felt something like this
(l)  because X thought something like this

The first cognitive component of this definition ("something very bad happened to me") is similar to that of *sorrow* in being "personal" (TO ME), intense (VERY bad), and past (HAPPENED). Unlike *sorrow*, however, *grief* is not (prototypically) a long-term state. Typically, it is caused by a recent event ("something happened a short time before now"), it is more likely to express itself in actions (if only crying), and, unlike *sorrow*, it is not associated with the thoughts "I can't think: I will do something because of this", "I can't do anything", which may lead in the direction of resignation. In this lack of any signs of resignation or acceptance *grief* is closer to *despair* than to *sorrow*.

As the above explication illustrates, *grief* is a very intense emotion, painful, dramatic, and absorbing. It is therefore hardly surprising that the twentieth century trend against emotional intensity (what P. Stearns (1994) calls "the dampening of the passions") has also had its impact on *grief*, and that in America many psychotherapists have "castigated the old idea of grief as heartbreak" (P. Stearns 1994: 153). "A bit of grief", Stearns summarizes this trend, might be tolerable, but weeks of tears suggested "something morbid, either mental or physical" (p. 153). "By the 1970s even counselling with older widows encouraged the development of new identities and interests and promoted the cessation of grief and its ties to the past". "Grief work meant work against grief and an important attack on Victorian savouring of this emotional state."

## 2.6 Despair

> Be beginning; since, no, nothing can be done
> To keep at bay
> Age and age's evils – hoar hair,
> Ruck and wrinkle, drooping, dying, death's worst, winding sheets,
> Tombs and worms, and tumbling to decay
> So be beginning, be beginning to despair.
> (Gerard Manely Hopkins)

When one feels *despair* over one's aging one thinks about this process as something very bad that is happening to one, something one doesn't want to accept and yet can't do anything about. As a result, life seems impossible; at the same time, one's will is still engaged – one doesn't succumb to apathy but rather one is, so to speak, in a state of impotent revolt against reality.

Other instances of *despair* can be interpreted in similar terms. Even though the triggering event can be actually in the past, the situation can be construed as on-going ("something very bad is happening to me"), as in the case of *sorrow*, although *despair* – in contrast to *sorrow* – doesn't imply duration and can be short-lived like *grief*.

*Despair* presents, however, a greater threat to a person's capacity to live than either *sorrow* or *grief*. *Sorrow* is like long-term suffering that one can, in principle, live with. *Grief* is, prototypically, limited in time and in scope; it is intense and absorbing, but it is not completely incompatible with hope and with a desire to live. But *despair* seems to remove the ground from under a person's feet: not only does one feel unable to counteract the very bad things that are happening to one, but one simply doesn't know how one can live on. The incompatibility between one's volitional attitude ("I don't want this to be happening", "I want to do something because of this") and one's sense of total impotence ("I can't do anything") explains the great tension linked with *despair* (in contrast to *sorrow* and even to *grief*).

The etymology of *despair* suggests that this concept may have another aspect relating it to *hope* (cf. from Latin *sperare* "to hope", *desperare* "to lose hope"). In fact, *LDOTEL* (1984) defines *despair* as either "utter loss of hope" or a "cause of hopelessness or extreme exasperation". A loss of hope is also compatible with resignation, whereas *despair* is not, so the rough gloss provided by *LDOTEL* cannot be right; it does capture, however, that aspect of *despair* which is spelled out in the component "I can't think: some good things can happen to me" (compare the explication of *hope*, which includes the component "I think some good things can happen").

The component "I can't think: some good things can happen to me" links *despair* also with *depression*, whose two key cognitive components are "I can't do anything", and "nothing good can happen to me". But *despair* is more overwhelming and more directly life-threatening than *depression*, because of its all-embracing cognitive component "I don't know how I can live now".

> *Despair* (X felt despair)
> (a)  X felt something because X thought something
> (b)    sometimes a person thinks:
> (c)    "something very bad is happening to me
> (d)    I don't want it to be happening
> (e)    I want to do something because of this
> (f)    I can't do anything
> (g)    I can't think: some good things will happen to me
> (h)    I don't know how I can live now"
> (i)    when this person thinks this this person feels something
>        very bad
> (j)  X felt something like this
> (k)  because X thought something like this

## 2.7 Disappointment

> A fine morning, but I persuaded myself not to expect William,
> I believe because I was afraid of being disappointed. (Dorothy
> Wordsworth 1975[1802]: 181)

In its wide range of applications, spanning the very serious as well as trivial causes, *disappointment* is similar to *sadness*, and in fact it is sometimes presented in the literature as "a kind of sadness". For example, Johnson-Laird and Oatley 1989 have defined *disappointment* as "sadness caused by failure to achieve a goal". An analysis of this kind, however, is empirically inadequate, since it leads to false predictions. For example, it predicts that it should be odd to say "I am disappointed but I am not sad", as it would be odd to say:

> *It is a spaniel but it is not a dog.
> *It is a parrot but it is not a bird.

A closer examination of *disappointment* reveals, however, that it is not conceptualized as a kind of *sadness*, and (unlike *sadness, unhappiness, distress, grief,* or *despair*) it doesn't necessarily imply that "something bad happened". Rather, it implies that "something good didn't happen" – something that one had expected to happen.

A failure to achieve goals is not necessarily involved either: one can be *disappointed* if something desired and expected doesn't happen, even if one has never tried to do anything to bring that desired event about and has never seen it as a "goal". (For example, farmers may be disappointed if the promising-looking clouds fail to bring an expected and hoped for rain; one could hardly say, however, that the rain was the farmers' "goal".)

> *Disappointed (X was disappointed)*
> (a)  X felt something because X thought something
> (b)  sometimes a person thinks:
> (c)  "I thought that something good would happen
> (d)  I felt something good because of this
> (e)  I know now: this good thing will not happen"
> (f)  when this person thinks this this person feels something bad
> (g)  X felt something like this
> (h)  because X thought something like this

(As mentioned earlier this is in fact a mirror image of *relief*.)

## 2.8 Frustration

*Frustration* doesn't really belong in the present group either, but it is related to *disappointment* and it is useful to include it here for comparison.

As noted by R. Smith (1991: 80), "frustration is usually defined as the blocking of a goal", and this is clearly on the right track, although hardly sufficient. (In fact, we have seen that, for example, Harris 1989 defines a different concept – *anger* – in terms of "desirable goals blocked", contrasting it with "desirable goals lost" supposedly linked with *sadness*.)

A helpful introduction to *frustration* is provided by Ortony, Clore, and Collins (1988: 66), who have offered the following illustration:

> Consider, for example, the likely reaction of a person encountering a series of problems while attempting to prepare breakfast for his family. If the person forgets to start the coffee soon enough or burns the toast or overcooks the eggs or all of these, we would not be surprised to see behavioural evidence of frustration and arousal.

As this vignette suggests, what is characteristic of *frustration* is that one wants to do something (e.g. prepare breakfast), attempts to do it, and finds (usually through a series of mishaps) that, contrary to one's expectations, one can't do it. We could propose, then, the following explication:

> *Frustration* (X felt frustration)
> (a) X felt something because X thought something
> (b)    sometimes a person thinks:
> (c)    "I wanted to do something now
> (d)    I thought I could do it
> (e)    now I 'see' (have to think) that I can't do it"
> (f)    when this person thinks this this person feels something bad
> (g) X felt something like this
> (h) because X thought something like this

It is interesting to note that *frustration* is a highly culture-specific concept, very characteristic of modern Anglo culture, with its emphasis on goals, plans, and expected achievements. In other languages, the concept of "frustration" exists only as a relatively recent loan word from English (*Frustration* in German, *frustracja* in Polish, *frustracija* in Russian, *frustrasi* in Bahasa Indonesia, and so on); and as such, it has been spreading.

## 3 "Bad things can happen" and related concepts

Lazarus (1991: 235) opens his discussion of the "core relational themes" of the family of emotions identified by him as "fright-anxiety" as follows: "Fright, as I shall henceforth term fear, involves threats that are concrete and sudden." But if one makes such an arbitrary first move (deciding to call *fear* "fright"), one can't explore the differences, as well

as similarities, between concepts like *fright* and *fear* and one is under-
mining the empirical basis of one's own discussion. Unfortunately,
many psychologists often take a similarly cavalier attitude towards
conceptual distinctions drawn in natural language, while at other times
relying unwittingly on such distinctions as if they had some "scientific"
basis independent of the language. For example, in the very same
passage in which he decides to equate *fear* with *fright*, Lazarus leans
heavily on the lexical distinction that English draws between *fright* and
*anxiety* ("fright . . . is a more primitive reaction than anxiety"), quoting
at the same time (in an English translation) Freud's ideas on "anxiety",
oblivious of the fact that Freud was talking not about "anxiety" but
about the German "Angst".

In this section, I will analyse the concepts *fear, fright, dread, panic,*
*terror, horror, anxiety, apprehension, worry,* and *concern* (as well as *afraid,*
*alarmed,* and *nervous*), as they really function in English, recognizing
them for what they are: folk categories rooted in the English language
rather than some language-independent absolutes. The German concept of "Angst", much discussed by Freud and substantially different
from the English *anxiety*, will be analysed in detail in chapter 3. The
common theme of this section is that "bad things can (or will) happen".

### 3.1 Fear and afraid

> (i) Although the figure seemed to be beckoning them, they were
> afraid to approach her. (Durham 1995: 22)
> (ii) The authorities were immediately suspicious of the apparitions;
> they feared that the large crowds attracted to them would encourage
> political dissent, particularly a Croatian separatist movement that was
> active in the region. (Durham 1995: 24)

There are several differences between the concepts *fear* and *afraid*.
Firstly, *afraid* is inherently personal ("something bad can happen to
me") whereas *fear* is not ("some bad things can happen"). For example,
the sentence "grave fears are held for the safety of person X" implies
that "something bad can happen", not that something bad can happen
to the speaker. (Note the plural *fears*; hence the phrasing "some bad
things"). Of course *fear* can also be (and typically is) used in situations
when something bad can happen to the experiencer, but this is not
necessarily the case. On the other hand, if someone is *afraid*, this implies
that something bad can happen to this very person (or to someone that
they identify with, as in the sentence "I'm afraid for you"). For
example, if the children in sentence (i) above were *afraid* to approach
the apparition the apparent thought was that "something bad could
happen to us"; whereas in sentence (ii) the (Yugoslav) authorities

feared that "something bad can happen" (political dissent could spread).

Secondly, *fear* focusses on lack of knowledge as to what the future holds ("I don't know what will happen"). For example, the common phrase "missing, feared dead" emphasizes the lack of knowledge as to what is going to happen: it is possible that we will discover that the persons in question have died. *Afraid*, on the other hand, does not include such a component and it is more compatible with situations when the danger is immediate and tangible. For example, if I am *afraid* of a dog, I do not reflect about the future ("I don't know what will happen") but focus on the threat itself ("something bad can happen to me"). Partly for this reason the sentence "he is afraid of God" sounds odd, whereas "he fears God" does not (although the collocation linking *fear* with *God* is now archaic). The person who "fears" God is taking a longer as well as a broader view ("I don't know what will happen" plus "some bad things can happen") than someone who is "afraid of God": the latter seems to imply that God could punish me ("do something bad to me") right now. This focus on lack of knowledge (in *fear*) explains also why one can "fear the worst" but not *"be afraid of the worst" (one can be "afraid of the dog" but not *"afraid of the worst"): the phrase *fear the worst* implies that one doesn't know what will happen and that it could be "the worst". *Afraid* is also more specific than *fear*. When one is *afraid*, one thinks about something specific: "something bad can happen to me because of this" (e.g. because I have approached the apparition). *Fear*, on the other hand, can refer to some unspecified and unknown "bad things" (*fear of the unknown*).

Finally, *fear* is more likely to mobilize one to action, in particular, to make one run away from a potentially dangerous situation (although it could also have a paralysing effect), whereas being *afraid* is more likely to stop one from doing something:

> he was too afraid to speak
> he was afraid to cross the road
> *he feared to cross the road (to speak)

For this reason, I have posited for *fear* the component "I want to do something because of this if I can" (as well as the helpless "I don't know if I can do anything"). For *afraid*, however, I have only posited a helpless component, placing it directly after "I don't want this to happen", and enhancing it by the addition of the word "now". The sequence "I don't want this to happen", "I don't know if I can do anything now" implies a paralysing effect, which, as we have seen, is more characteristic of *afraid* than of *fear*. (For further discussion of *fear* see also the section on *hope*.)

*Fear* (X felt fear)
(a)  X felt something because X thought something
(b)     sometimes a person thinks:
(c)     "I don't know what will happen
(d)     some bad things can happen
(e)     I don't want these things to happen
(f)     I want to do something because of this if I can
(g)     I don't know if I can do anything"
(h)     when this person thinks this this person feels something
       bad
(i)  X felt something like this
(j)  because X thought something like this

*Afraid* (X was afraid)
(a)  X felt something because X thought something
(b)     sometimes a person thinks about something:
(c)     "something bad can happen to me because of this
(d)     I don't want this to happen
(e)     I don't know if I can do anything now"
(f)     when this person thinks this this person feels something
       bad
(g)  X felt something like this
(h)  because X thought something like this

## 3.2 Fright

> A telegram comes to you and you leave it on your lap. You are pale
> with fright. (Mary Boykin Chestnut 1975[1862]: 280)

*LDOTEL* (1984) defines the verb *frighten*, unilluminatingly, as "to make
afraid; scare", but its definition of the noun *fright* is more helpful: "(an
instance of) fear excited by sudden danger or shock; alarm". The
helpful element in this definition is the word "sudden".

     *Fright* is sudden because it is a response to something (e.g. a sudden
noise); and it implies that something has just happened ("something
has happened now") and that "I didn't know this would happen". It
also refers to what is perceived as an immediate and tangible danger
("something bad can happen to me now").

     The adjective (pseudo-participle) *frightened* differs from the noun
*fright* in so far as it doesn't necessarily imply the same immediacy of
either the stimulus or the perceived threat; nonetheless, collocations
such as "frightened out of her/his wits" do imply that there was some
"trigger". (One can't be *"afraid out of one's wits".) Sentences like "she

is frightened of the future" sound rather odd; and one can't be *"frightened to do something" as one can be "afraid to do something". All such differences point to the implication (in *frightened*) that "something happened" (probably, "now") and that "something will happen" (probably, "in a short time"). To illustrate: "the door suddenly opened and there, three or four paces within the chapel, he saw a beautiful young girl of seven or eight, dressed all in white . . . Noguer was dazzled by the sight and very frightened" (Durham 1995: 82). The sight was sudden and it immediately preceded the experience, and the perceived danger was immediate. In the case of the noun *fright* the temporal implications "something happened *now*", "something bad can happen to me *in a short time*" are even clearer.

> *Fright*
> (a)  X felt something because X thought something
> (b)      sometimes a person thinks:
> (c)      "something has happened now
> (d)      I didn't know that this would happen now
> (e)      I know now that something bad can happen to me in a
>            short time
> (f)      I don't want this to happen
> (g)      I want to do something because of this if I can
> (h)      I don't know if I can do anything"
> (i)      when this person thinks this this person feels something
>            bad
> (j)  X felt something like this
> (k)  because X thought something like this

### 3.3 *Terrified, petrified, horrified*

> One day . . . I was walking up the stairs with my baby in my arms and the three-year-old holding my hand, when again I was immobilized by pain. I was terrified of dropping the baby. (Spufford 1996: 35)

If one is *terrified*, what one is *terrified of* is seen not simply as "something bad" but as something "very bad". What one is *terrified of* is very real, for something very bad is already happening. And yet the target of terror is also partly in the future, because the present "bad event" is seen here as a source of a future threat, though not a distant one (" . . . can happen NOW"). This future threat is necessarily personal ("something very bad can happen TO ME NOW"). The experiencer's attitude is one of an intense non-acceptance ("I don't want this to happen"); at the same time, it is one of total helplessness ("I can't do anything").

*Terrified* (X was terrified)
(a) X felt something because X thought something
(b)    sometimes a person thinks:
(c)    "something very bad is happening
(d)    something very bad can happen to me now because of this
(e)    I don't want this to happen
(f)    I want to do something because of this if I can
(g)    I can't do anything now"
(h)    when this person thinks this this person feels something very bad
(i) X felt something like this
(j) because X thought something like this

*Petrified* appears to be a more specific version of *terrified*: it is a *terror* which leads to a kind of paralysis ("I can't move"). (Note, however, the further difference between "can happen" in *terrified* and "will happen" in *petrified*, which presents the latter as subjectively more inevitable).

*Petrified* (X was petrified)
(a) X felt something because X thought something
(b)    sometimes a person thinks:
(c)    "something very bad is happening
(d)    because of this something very bad will happen to me now
(e)    I don't want this to happen
(f)    I want to do something because of this if I can
(g)    I can't do anything now
(h)    I can't move"
(i)    when this person thinks this this person feels something very bad
(j) X felt something like this
(k) because X thought something like this

The main difference between *terror* and *horror* concerns the relationship between the experiencer and the victim: in the case of *terror*, the two are identical, whereas in the case of *horror* they can be, and usually are, different. One is *horrified* to see what has happened to someone else, just as one is *appalled* to see what has happened to someone else. A second difference between *horror* and *terror* (which is not unrelated to the first one) has to do with the present orientation of the former: since *horror* is, essentially, the feeling of a spectator, it concerns primarily what happened "now" rather than what will, or can, happen. (Strictly speaking, therefore, the term *horrified* should not be included in the present section at all; it is useful, however, to discuss it here for comparison with the intuitively closely related concept *terrified*.)

Unlike *appalled*, however, which is always an "on-looker's" reaction (see section 2.4.), *horror* can sometimes refer to some nightmare involving the experiencer himself or herself, as in the following story about an earthquake:

> At first he thought he was in a dream. Then he caught an image of having dived under his desk, and in a moment of stark horror he realized that this was very real. He screamed for help. All was silence . . . Then came the realization that he might slowly die in this terrible manner. More alone than he'd ever felt, his mind grew dark with terror. (Feinstein and Mayo 1993: 44)

It is particularly interesting to observe the experiencer's changing perspective from *horror* to *terror*. *Horror* is accompanied by the realization ("I know now") that "something very bad has just happened and in fact is still happening" (an earthquake). Then the perspective focusses on one's personal danger ("then came the realization that he might slowly die in this terrible manner"), that is, "something very bad can happen to me"; and there is no longer a sense of sudden discovery (one can be *terrified*, though not *horrified*, for a very long time).

In both cases, the experiencer is innerly opposing the terrible event ("I don't want this to be happening", "I don't want this to happen"), in both cases he/she would dearly want to do something to avoid it ("I want to do something because of this if I can"), and in both cases he/she feels powerless and helpless ("I can't do anything").

The present orientation attributed here to *horror* may seem to be inconsistent with the cases of a sudden discovery of some horrifying truths concerning the past. For example, in Helen Demidenko's novel *The Hand that Signed the Paper* (1994: 7) the heroine discovers some old photographs showing, among other war scenes, her father in an SS uniform chasing "a poor-looking man with a big star around his neck" and "wielding a rifle with deadly intent". Although the word *horrified* is not actually used, the reader may well understand that that's what the heroine feels, and one can well imagine the word *horrified* being used in such a scene ("she was horrified to see . . . ").

It is interesting to note, however, that in this case the photographs involved the experiencer personally (because of what they were telling her about her father), and that the experience could therefore be construed in terms of "something very bad has happened to me now" ("I've discovered some dreadful truths about my father") rather than necessarily in terms of "something very bad happened to some people there".

In fact, if the photographs were gruesome but involved only strangers it would be odd to say that the heroine was horrified to see them. One could say that they were horrific images but not that she was *horrified* to see them – unless they somehow involved her personally. Of course the experience of horror is not always personal, because one can indeed be only an on-looker, but it seems it can always be construed as involving the present: "something very bad happened now" (either to someone else – the victim, or to me the discoverer).

*Horrified* (X was horrified)
(a)  X felt something because X thought something
(b)    sometimes a person thinks:
(c)    "something very bad has happened now[1]
(d)    I didn't think that something like this could happen
(e)    I want to do something because of this if I can
(f)    I can't do anything"
(g)    when this person thinks this this person feels something very bad
(h)  X felt something like this
(i)  because X thought something like this

### 3.4 Dread

> . . . I learned to dread the monotonous, constant, routine repeat of them [pains] over and over and over again. (Spufford 1996: 51)

*Dread* refers to an event or events seen as not simply "bad", but "very bad". In this respect, it is similar to *terrified*, *petrified* and *horrified* rather than to *afraid* or *fear*. But *dread* refers to a future event, and not even necessarily an imminent one ("something very bad will happen to me"), whereas *horror* refers to the present and the immediate past ("something very bad has happened now"), and *terror* to the immediate future. Consequently, the reality of the dreaded event is purely subjective: one doesn't really know that it will happen; on the other hand, one thinks that one knows exactly what will happen to one if and when this hypothetical event happens. Consider also the following sentences (from a medical-journal paper):

> Throughout much of history the now treatable disease of leprosy was the most dreaded of medical afflictions. The reason for this dread was . . . that it inexorably caused ghastly and chronic disfigurement or deformity.

The word "inexorable" provides a helpful clue here: people *dreaded* leprosy because they knew what would happen (to those afflicted). If *dread* were to be replaced in this sentence with *fear* the emphasis would be on what one didn't know rather than on what one did. *Fear* implies: "I don't know what will happen", whereas *dread* implies "I know what will happen to me (if X happens)".

The great vividness of *dread* appears to stem from the combination of imagination and subjective certainty: the experiencer is not quite certain that the dreaded event will take place (e.g. that he/she will get leprosy), but "knows" exactly what its consequences will be. These consequences are experienced as very real, but since they are in the future, the imagination is not constrained by evidence.

The future orientation of *dread* links it with *fear*, and its personal character ("something very bad will happen TO ME") links it with *afraid*. But *fear* implies uncertainty ("I don't know what will happen"), and *afraid* is at least compatible with uncertainty ("something bad CAN happen to me"), whereas *dread* implies subjective certainty – if not as to the future event itself then at least as to its consequences. This is why the sentences (i) and (ii) below invite quite different inferences:

> (i)   She was afraid to go to the dentist.
> (ii)  She dreaded going to the dentist.

Sentence (i) implies that the action will probably not take place, whereas sentence (ii) implies that it probably will, and also that its consequences are quite clear in the person's mind. Similarly, the phrase "the fear of flying" can refer to people who never fly (because of their fear of flying), but if someone "dreads flying" this implies that they probably do (or will) fly, and that they know exactly what they can expect if and when they do fly.

> *Dread*
> (a) X felt something because X thought something
> (b)    sometimes a person thinks about something:
> (c)   "if this happens, something very bad will happen to me
> (d)    I know what
> (e)    I don't want this to happen
> (f)    I want to do something because of this if I can
> (g)    I can't do anything"
> (h)    when this person thinks this this person feels something
>          very bad
> (i)  X felt something like this
> (j)  because X thought something like this

## 3.5 Alarmed

> a local newspaper . . . made its way into our house, wrapped around the rhubarb. . . . I hid it where our son could not possibly find and read it. To my alarm, it disappeared from its hiding place (Spufford 1996: 39)

The person who is *alarmed* has just become aware of some event which works like a warning: if I don't do something now, something bad will happen. An alarm clock is not meant to alarm us in the emotional sense of the word, but it does provide a useful simile: the sleeping person wakes up becoming suddenly aware that "something has happened now", that they have to do something now (get up), and that if they don't do it something bad will happen. The emotional *alarm* has all the same essential elements: the suddenness, the mobilisation to action, the awareness of an impending danger, and of the need to act "now". In addition, however, it appears to have an element of uncertainty, linking it with confusion and even panic: the alarmed person does not have things under control and does not have a clear plan of action. This is reflected in the component "I don't know what I will do". This uncertainty, together with the sudden onset of the emotion, links the emotional *alarm* with *fright*.

*Alarmed (X was alarmed)*
(a)  X felt something because X thought something
(b)     sometimes a person thinks:
(c)     "something has happened now
(d)     because of this I know: something bad can happen in a short time
(e)     I don't want it to happen
(f)     because of this I have to do something
(g)     I don't know what I will do"
(h)     when this person thinks this this person feels something bad
(i)  X felt something like this
(j)  because X thought something like this

## 3.6 Panic

> As I ferreted in this [the nappy bucket], my hands sticky with dextrose, a cry of panic went up from the six-year-old, "Mummy, the gerbils have escaped into the garden, and the *owl* will get them!" (Spufford 1996: 58)

*Panic* is a feeling which might overcome a student at an exam. The topic is announced ("something has happened now"). The student realizes that she hadn't expected this kind of topic and knows nothing about it and so has to write about something that she knows nothing about; the situation, therefore, is assessed as "bad" ("something bad is happening"). The student has to mobilize herself to action – otherwise the exam will be a disaster ("if I don't do something, something very bad will happen to me"). Of course, the student doesn't want that disaster ("I don't want this to happen"). Consequently, something has to be done immediately ("because of this, I have to do something NOW"). Presumably, something CAN be done. But what? The panic-stricken student does not know what she can do ("I don't know what I can do"); she cannot collect her thoughts ("I can't think now").

As this analysis shows, *panic* is related in various ways to *alarm* (in particular, in the sudden realization that something is wrong and that something has to be done immediately), and to *terror* (in particular, in the vividness, the immediacy, and the intensity of the impending danger: "something very bad can happen to me now"). It is also related to concepts such as *distress* ("I don't know what I can do"). *Panic* mobilizes one into action, as does *fright*, and at the same time it prevents us from effective action, as does *terror* or the feeling of being *petrified*. The component "I can't think now" of *panic* is analogous to the "I can't move" of *petrified* and to the "I can't do anything" of *terrified*. At the same time, the active component "I have to do something (now)" makes *panic* very different from such paralysing emotions. In *panic*, the ineffectiveness is due not to any paralysis, but rather to confusion and to unfocussed agitation.

> *Panic* (X felt panic)
> (a)  X felt something because X thought something
> (b)     sometimes a person thinks:
> (c)     "something is happening now
> (d)     if I don't do something now something very bad will happen to me because of this
> (e)     I don't want this to happen
> (f)     because of this I have to do something now
> (g)     I don't know what I can do
> (h)     I can't think now"
> (i)     when this person thinks this this person feels something bad
> (j)  X felt something like this
> (k)  because X thought something like this

## 3.7 Anxiety

*Anxiety* can be, as psychologists say, "free-floating", in the sense that the bad events threatening me are unidentified ("I don't know what will happen"). These "bad events" appear also to be more subjective than grounded in some danger with an identifiable basis ("MAYBE something bad will happen to me" rather than "something bad CAN happen to me"). The resulting feeling is debilitating as it makes one feel helpless ("I can't do anything now"). It is related, in different ways, to *worry* and *dread*, as well as to *fear*. It is not, however, a passive attitude; rather, it has an active aspect ("I want to do something if I can"), which in combination with the helpless "I can't do anything now" element leads to something like impotent agitation.

> *Anxiety* (X felt anxiety)
> (a)  X felt something because X thought something
> (b)  sometimes a person thinks for some time:
> (c)  "I don't know what will happen
> (d)  maybe something bad will happen to me
> (e)  I don't want this to happen
> (f)  I want to do something because of this if I can
> (g)  I can't do anything now"
> (h)  when this person thinks this this person feels something bad
> (i)  X felt something like this
> (j)  because X thought something like this

For example, a student awaiting the results of examinations may well be in a frame of mind producing anxiety: "I don't know what will happen" (i.e. what my results will be), "maybe something bad will happen to me" (i.e. I will discover that my results are bad), "I don't want this to happen" (the student is not resigned but actively wishes for good results), "I want to do something because of this" (the student is agitated and eager to do something to influence the outcome), "I can't do anything now" (he/she realizes that at that stage nothing can be done).

Of all the concepts discussed so far *fear* seems to be the closest to *anxiety*; there are, however, two important differences between the two. First, *fear* can be impersonal ("something bad can happen"), whereas *anxiety* is always personal ("maybe something bad will happen to me"). For example, as mentioned earlier, the phrase "missing, feared dead" implies that "something bad can happen", not that "something bad can happen to me". And second, *fear* is not quite as helpless as *anxiety* (cf. "I don't know if I can do anything" vs. "I can't do anything now"). For example, *fear* can lead to an attempt to run away, but *anxiety*, which is often associated with waiting, has to be simply endured.

### *3.8 Nervous*

> He had enjoyed it, seeing Bonnie out in public, nervous, but nonetheless smiling, talking to people (Capote 1967: 5)

Like *anxiety*, being *nervous* implies that "I don't know what will happen", and that "maybe something bad will happen". Unlike *anxiety*, however, it doesn't imply that maybe something bad will happen "to me" personally.

Furthermore, unlike *anxiety* and unlike most other concepts in this field, *nervous* focusses specifically on "risks" accompanying future actions: I can only be *nervous* if I am going to do something, and if I think that something bad can happen while I am doing it. (For example, I am going to make a speech, and I could forget what I was going to say; or I am going to meet people in public, like Bonnie in the example, and I think I could make a faux pas in the process.) One way or another, something can "go wrong".

The attitude of a person who is *nervous* is not completely passive and helpless, as is that of a person experiencing *anxiety* ("I can't do anything now"), but a sense of not being fully in control is certainly there ("I don't know what I can do").

> *Nervous* (X was nervous)
> (a)  X felt something because X thought something
> (b)  sometimes a person thinks:
> (c)  "I have to do something
> (d)  I don't know what will happen when I am doing it
> (e)  maybe something bad will happen
> (f)  I don't want this to happen
> (g)  I want to do something because of this if I can
> (h)  I don't know what I can do"
> (i)  when this person thinks this this person feels something bad
> (j)  X felt something like this
> (k)  because X thought something like this

### *3.9 Worry*

> In that fortnight, inevitably, an ophthalmic appointment we had been waiting for for months came up for Bridget at the Hospital for Sick Children. We were deeply worried about her eyesight: it seemed

essential I should go to hear what the new specialist said. (Spufford 1996: 96)

If *alarmed* suggests a sudden onset of emotion, *worried* and *worry* suggest a long-term thinking process. One is *worried about* something (as one is *concerned about* something), and this "aboutness" of *worried* reflects its link with an on-going thinking process ("for some time").

*Worry* is rooted in uncertainty. Unlike *fear*, it refers primarily to the present ("something is happening *now*"), but it also has a future dimension: what is happening now may lead to something bad.

For example, in the quote adduced above the parents are worried about their child's eyesight because they have noticed some "worrying signs". The signs are in the present, but the danger is in the future ("something is happening to her eyesight; something bad can happen because of this"). Similarly, if a daughter is late in coming home the *worrying* mother may think: "something is happening to my daughter – something bad can happen to her". If one has a healthy and thriving baby one may still *fear* all sorts of bad things that might happen to him or her; but if one *worries* about one's baby then one must have noticed something in the present that could lead to something bad. One doesn't want anything bad to happen and one wants to do something because of this; but one doesn't know what one can do. Thus, the attitude is not passive and resigned but rather active and agitated; it is lacking, however, in a sense of direction ("I want to do something", "I don't know what I can do". These last two components indicate a kind of inner conflict and jointly account for the fruitless agitation implied by this concept.

> *Worried* (X was worried)
> (a)  X felt something because X thought something
> (b)  sometimes a person thinks for some time:
> (c)  "something is happening now
> (d)  something bad can happen because of this
> (e)  I don't want it to happen
> (f)  because of this I want to do something
> (g)  I don't know what I will do"
> (h)  when this person thinks this this person feels something bad
> (i)  X felt something like this
> (j)  because X thought something like this

## 3.10 Concern

The concepts *concerned* and *worried* are closely related, yet they differ in some important respects. To begin with, one is usually *concerned* about someone else, whereas *worry* is often linked with thoughts about one-self (cf. "she is worried about her own health" vs. slightly dubious "she is concerned about her own health"). In addition, *worried* is focussed entirely on bad things which may happen to people; by contrast, *con-cerned* implies a desire for good things, as well as a "dis-want" of bad ones. For this reason, having *concern* for someone is also related to *caring* for someone; *worry* is much further from *care* (although *cares* in the plural are closer to *worries* than *care* in the singular is to *worry* in the singular). Furthermore, *concern* does not imply the same agonizing uncertainty ("I don't know what I can do") as *worry* does. Finally, *concern* is not necessarily a "bad", undesirable feeling, whereas *worry* is (cf. "this person feels something" vs. "this person feels something bad").

> *Concern* (X was concerned)
> (a)  X felt something because X thought something
> (b)     sometimes a person thinks for some time about someone:
> (c)     "something bad can happen to this person
> (d)     I don't want this to happen
> (e)     I want good things to happen to this person
> (f)     because of this I want to do something if I can"
> (g)     when this person thinks this this person feels something
> (h)  X felt something like this
> (i)  because X thought something like this

### 3.11 Apprehension

*Apprehension* is a fairly mild emotion, as compared with *fear, afraid, fright,* or *scared* (not to mention *dread* or *terror*). The explication proposed below accounts for this in two ways: first, it refers to bad things that only CAN – rather than WILL – happen; and second, it emphasizes the experiencer's uncertainty as to whether these bad things will happen at all ("I don't know if it will happen").

> *Apprehension* (X felt apprehension)
> (a)  X felt something because X thought something
> (b)     sometimes a person thinks:
> (c)     "something bad can happen
> (d)     I don't want this to happen
> (e)     I don't know if it will happen"
> (f)     when this person thinks this this person feels something
>          bad, not very bad

(g)  X felt something like this
(h)  because X thought something like this

## 4 "I don't want things like this to happen" and related concepts

Evaluation and will typically go hand in hand: we want "good things" to happen, and we don't want "bad things" to happen. In the area of emotions, however, the relation between will and evaluation is not always as simple as that. Sometimes, "bad things" happen that we feel something about but that do not engage our will; and sometimes we don't want something to happen (or to be happening) not because we think it is "something bad" but simply because it is contrary to our will.

Often, what is involved is not simply "I don't want this to happen (or: to be happening)", but rather, more generally, "I don't want things like this to happen", that is, an attitude including both a kind of protest against something that has already happened and an opposition to any future repeats. In this section I will focus on concepts of precisely this kind, that is, on *anger, indignation, fury,* and *outrage,* including also, for comparison, *rage, shocked,* and *appalled.* (For an earlier discussion of *irritated, annoyed,* and *mad,* and some other related concepts, see Wierzbicka 1994a.)

### 4.1 Anger

*Anger* is one of the most frequently discussed emotion concepts, and the range of the interpretations varies widely. Some authors (e.g. Harris 1989) write about "goals blocked", others (e.g. Lazarus 1991: 122) link *anger* with "a demeaning offense against me and mine", or with an "affront" (e.g. Averill and More 1993), still others (e.g. Stein, Trabasso, and Liwag 1993: 287) claim that "almost any type of loss or aversive state can evoke anger when a belief about goal reinstatement is strongly held".

But consider, for example, the situation of a mother who becomes angry when she discovers that her unruly child has broken a precious vase. There is no question here of "goals blocked", of "affront", of a "demeaning offense", or of a "belief about goal reinstatement"; it is consistent, however, with the normal understanding of such a sentence to interpret it in terms of the following simple scenario (in the angry person's mind):

> this person did something bad
> I don't want this person to do things like this
> I want to do something because of this

We can now test this scenario against a wide range of situations where *anger* is attributed to people – including those where people's goals are indeed "blocked", or when a "slight" occurs, or where a desire for "retaliation" may be involved. If we do so, it emerges that the simple scenario proposed here applies to them too.

Over the years, I have experimented with a number of different scenarios for *anger* myself, including components like "I want to do something to this person because of this", "I (would) want to do something bad to this person because of this", and "I want this person to feel something bad" (see e.g. Wierzbicka 1992c and 1994a). Upon further testing, however, it transpired that the more general form of the *anger* scenario outlined above is more accurate and more consistent with the contemporary usage (at least for the basic meaning of *angry*, which I will call *angry*(1) to distinguish it from a more recent sense, *angry*(2), to be discussed later).

> X was angry(1) (with Y)
> (a) X felt something because X thought something
> (b)   sometimes a person thinks about someone:
> (c)   "this person did something bad
> (d)   I don't want this person to do things like this
> (e)   I want to do something because of this"
> (f)   when this person thinks this, this person feels something bad
> (g) X felt something like this
> (h) because X thought something like this

The explication outlined above refers to sentences where the word *angry* is used in the frame "angry with" ("person X was angry with person Y"). There is, however, another modern usage of the word *angry*, typically associated with the frame "angry at" (rather than "angry with"), as in the following example: "Dying people may feel angry [. . .] Some people feel angry at God for allowing them to get sick, at their doctors for not being able to find a cure, at the government for putting money into weapons instead of medical research, or at the world in general" (Callanan and Kelley 1993: 44).

In this more recent usage the implication is not that "someone did something bad" but rather that "something bad happened because someone did (or didn't do) something". For example, when some dying people are "angry at God" or "angry at their doctors" the implication is not that God, or the doctors, did something bad, but rather, that "something bad happened" (the illness), and that God, or the doctors, failed to do something to prevent it or cure it. Typically, this second usage implies less control than the first one ("I want to do something because of this IF I CAN"; with an invited inference that perhaps I can't do much at all).

> *X was angry$_{(2)}$ at Y*
> (a)  X felt something because X thought something
> (b)    sometimes a person thinks:
> (c)    "something bad happened
> (d)    because someone did (didn't do) something
> (e)    I don't want things like this to happen
> (f)    I want to do something because of this if I can"
> (g)    when this person thinks this, this person feels something bad
> (h)  X felt something like this
> (i)  because X thought something like this

## 4.2 Indignation

*Indignation* is similar to *anger* in so far as it, too, is based on the judgment that "someone did something bad" and is active rather than passive. In this case, however, the judgment is more likely to concern an unspecified person ("someone" rather than "this person") and the volitional impulse is less likely to be directed against a specific person and is also less likely to be acted upon.

For example, on reading a newspaper story about a group of highly paid public servants demanding a high pay rise and threatening to strike should their demand not be met, a person-in-the-street is perhaps more likely to be *indignant* than to be *angry*. The exclamations which one might hear in such a situation are "How could they!", or "What arrogance!" There is no question of doing anything in response, because usually one feels unable to either identify or affect the culprits; at the most, one can write an indignant letter to the newspaper. One thinks ("indignantly"): "I don't want things like this to happen", but there is no purposeful "I want to do something" air about it. Above all, one wants to express one's opinion about the "bad action" ("I want to say what I think about this").

Lazarus (1991: 227) states that "indignation and outrage clearly imply having been wronged", but as the above example indicates, this is not always the case. On the contrary, although one *can* be indignant when one feels wronged (e.g. when one is unjustly accused of cheating), typically *indignation* is linked with more general concerns. The proposed components "someone did something bad" and "I don't want things like this to happen" account for this. (There is no "someone-did-something-bad-to-me" component here.)

Finally, *indignation* appears to be somehow related to *surprise* (and, since this surprise is caused by something bad, it is also related to *dismay*, *shock*, and *outrage*). The thought underlying this emotion is not merely "someone did something bad" but also "how could they have done something like this". In the explication, this element of unexpectedness is portrayed by means of the component "I didn't think that someone could do something like this".

> *Indignation* (X felt indignation)
> (a)  X felt something because X thought something
> (b)  sometimes a person thinks:
> (c)  "I know now: someone did something bad
> (d)  I didn't think that someone could do something like this
> (e)  I don't want things like this to happen
> (f)  I want to say what I think about this"
> (g)  when this person thinks this, this person feels something bad
> (h)  X felt something like this
> (i)  because X thought something like this

### 4.3 Fury

At first sight, *fury* (that is, being *furious*) may seem to be just a variety of *anger* (a particularly strong or intense *anger*). In fact, however, the scenario linked with the word *furious* differs qualitatively from that linked with the word *angry*, and in some respects comes closer to the scenario of *outrage*. Above all, *furious* – like *outraged* – implies that something very bad has happened.

The fact that one can be *furious* "with someone" – as one can be *angry* "with someone" – suggests that the bad event is seen as due to somebody's action ("something very bad happened because someone did something"). But unlike in the case of *anger* (*anger$_{(1)}$*) the action itself doesn't have to be regarded as "bad". For example, if a husband mentions, accidentally, a fact which his wife has asked him to keep secret she can be *furious* with him (because of what she sees as the very bad consequences of his indiscretion), but she doesn't need to think that "he has done something bad". Nor does the infuriating action have to be seen as unexpected (the wife could even regard her husband's "infuriating" action as quite typical of him).

But although the action may be seen as neither "bad" nor unexpected the emotion occasioned by it is very strong ("this person feels something very bad", rather than simply "this person feels something bad", as in the case of *anger*). What is more, *furious* implies not only an impulse to do something (as does also *angry*) but an impulse to do something to the person responsible for what has happened. Thus, an *angry* person may simply slam the door and leave; but someone who is *furious* is more likely to "want to do something (bad) to" the person involved. On the other hand, this impulse of the *furious* person to "do something to the other person" is usually short-lived ("I want to do something to this person now"), whereas the impulse of the *angry* person to "do something" can last much longer ("I want to do something because of this").

Solomon (1997: 11) asks: "Does it matter whether we call [it] 'anger' or rather . . . 'fury' or 'outrage' or 'moral indignation'? (What are the differences here?)" And he replies: "'fury' suggests violence, 'outrage' indicates violation, and 'moral indignation' suggests righteousness". Unfortunately, Solomon doesn't tell us what exactly he means by "violence", "violation", and "righteousness". But his statement that *fury* suggests violence is compatible with the component "I want to do something (bad) to this person now".

If we consider that the person with whom the experiencer is *furious* is not regarded as having done something bad but only as having done something because of which something (very) bad happened, the violent impulse implied by *fury* may well seem irrational and unjustifiable. This is consistent with the somewhat pejorative connotations of the word *furious*: one can sometimes be "justifiably angry", but hardly "justifiably furious".

As we will see, the irrationality of *fury* is somewhat less pronounced than that of *rage*, which implies also a lack of control and an inability to think. Unlike *rage*, *fury* can be "cold" and "calculating". Nonetheless the phrase "justifiable fury" sounds as odd as "justifiable rage"; on the other hand, one can perhaps be "understandably furious", though not "understandably enraged". I think that the explications of *fury* sketched below and that of *rage* in the next section account for all this.

> *Fury* (X was furious with Y)
> (a)  X felt something because X thought something
> (b)  sometimes a person thinks about someone else:
> (c)  "something very bad happened
> (d)  because this person did something
> (e)  I don't want this person to do things like this
> (f)  I want to do something bad to this person now"
> (g)  when this person thinks this this person feels something
>      very bad
> (h)  X felt something like this (for a short time)
> (i)  because X thought something like this

*4.4 Rage*

> I sat down and wrote to my husband, words so much worse than
> anything I can put in this book [her diary], and as I wrote I was blinded
> by rage . . . Years, death, depopulation, bondage, fears (Mary Boykin
> Chestnut, 1975[1865]: 285)

The best clues to the concept of *rage* are provided by common collocations involving this concept, such as "blind rage", "impotent rage",
"tears of rage", "rage and frustration", "get into a rage", "fit of rage",
or "uncontrollable rage". Trying to follow these and other similar clues,
I propose the following tentative explication:


Rage
(a)  X felt something
(b)      sometimes a person thinks:
(c)      "something very bad is happening to me now
(d)      I don't want this to be happening
(e)      I have to do something now
(f)      I don't know what I will do
(g)      I want to do something bad
(h)      maybe something bad will happen because of this
(i)      I don't want to think about this (about what will
         happen)"
(j)      when this person thinks this this person feels something
         very bad
(k)  X felt something like this


*Rage* appears to be centred on things happening to the experiencer, or to
someone with whom she/he identifies, and on things happening in the
present rather than on something that has happened in the past (component (c)). What is happening to the experiencer doesn't have to be
due to any human action. In fact, one can "fly into a rage" over gadgets
which refuse to work, for example, a television set or a lawn-mower. In
accordance with popular beliefs, *rage* can be attributed to a bull who is
being teased with a red rag. The bull is not believed to become *furious*,
but rather, to get into a *rage*, and the bull's presumed attitude appears to
be consistent with the proposed scenario: "something is happening to
me now" (I'm being teased with a red rag); "I don't want this to be
happening; I want to do something now". This part of the scenario of
*rage* is similar to that of *distress*, but the scenario of *rage* doesn't stop
here. The experiencer becomes desperate and obstinate at the same
time; and the impulse to act becomes "blind" ("I don't know what I will

do"), destructive ("I want to do something bad now"), and oblivious of the consequences ("maybe something bad will happen because of this – I don't want to think about this").

The "blindness" and "out-of-controlness" of *rage* are reflected in the combination of components "I will do something now" and "I don't know what I will do"; and its irrationality is reflected in the lack of connection between the destructive impulse "I want to do something bad now" and the unattainable goal "I don't want this to be happening". The proposed scenario suggests that the destructive impulse is caused by the experiencer's inability to attain the goal and the compulsion to act immediately in any way whatsoever rather than by any perception that by "doing something bad" he/she may somehow attain it.

The proposed scenario of *fury* is not similarly "illogical". The impulse "to do something (bad) to the person in question now" is not necessarily illogical from the point of view of the experiencer's apparent goal: "I don't want this person to do things like this". The sequence of components proposed for *fury* is therefore more coherent, although the attitude portrayed in it may still seem irrational for reasons mentioned earlier (the lack of proportion between the "offence": "this person did something", and the desired retaliation: "I want to do something bad to this person now").

## 4.5 Outrage

> We are outraged by recent decisions of the Vice Chancellor, which are detrimental to the best interests of our students and a further erosion of our working conditions. (from Goddard 1998)

In some ways, *outrage* is similar to *indignation*. In both cases, the experiencer thinks that "someone did something very bad" and that (roughly speaking) one wouldn't have expected something like this to happen; she/he takes an unaccepting, protesting attitude along the lines of "I don't want things like this to happen". But an *indignant* person may wish to do no more than to say what he or she thinks about the "bad action". An *outraged* person, however, cannot be similarly disinclined to do anything, and the attitude implied by this word is more active and more goal-oriented: "I want to do something because of this" rather than merely "I want to say what I think about this".

In addition, *outrage* implies a thought that "something very bad happened", whereas *indignation* implies only that "someone did something very bad" (whether or not there are some very bad consequences).

This last difference may account, to some extent, for the moral overtones of *outrage*, which *indignation* as such doesn't have (although *righteous indignation* does). For example, a teenager can be *indignant* at the suggestion that he has cheated in a game, thus implying that the accuser "has done something very bad", without necessarily implying that something bad has happened because of this (unless the injustice of the accusation itself should count as something very bad that has happened).

Even if we decided, however, to include in the explication of *indignation*, as well as that of *outrage*, the component "something very bad happened", the fact remains that *outrage* has a greater moral weight than *indignation*. This may be due partly to the social rather than individual character of *outrage*: the perpetrators must be, or represent, a group, and so must the victims, or those who identify with the victims. For example, if someone mistreats my child I would be *angry*, even *furious*, rather than *outraged*. On the other hand, if I discover that some teachers mistreat children in the school my child attends then I could indeed be *outraged*.

This last example helps us also to sort out the semi-personal, semi-impersonal nature of *outrage*. Pace Lazarus (1991: 227; quoted in the section on *indignation*), I cannot be *outraged* if someone mistreats or insults me personally, or even me and my friends, although I can be *outraged* (as a parent) if I hear that the children in my local school are somehow mistreated. At the same time, I can't be *outraged* over the treatment of some children in Uganda or Sudan (although I can be *shocked* and *appalled* by it). To be *outraged*, then, I have to have a role in the situation, a role which makes it imperative for me to take an interest in the matter and to act. This suggests the following formula: "I have to do something because of this", as well as "I want to do something because of this" (with the implication that I'm going to do something on other people's behalf, rather than defend my own personal interests or rights).

*Indignation* is compatible with a sense of individual or personal wrong (as when one is accused of cheating), but it doesn't imply any particular role requiring me to act (on behalf of other people).

This leads us to the following explication:

> *Outrage*
> (a)  X felt something because X thought something
> (b)  sometimes a person thinks:
> (c)  "I know now: something very bad happened to some people
> (d)  because some other people did something very bad
> (e)  I didn't think these people could do something like this
> (f)  I don't want things like this to happen

(g)    I want to do something because of this
(h)    I have to do something because of this"
(i)    when this person thinks this this person feels something
        bad
(j)  X felt something like this
(k)  because X thought something like this


*4.6 Appalled*

> When allegations of physical and sexual violence emanate from a
> classroom, parents are *outraged*, the community *appalled*. (Example
> quoted in Goddard 1998)

As the quote above illustrates, the concept of "appalled" is fairly close
to that of "outraged". In both cases, the (prototypical) experiencer
thinks that "something very bad happened" and that one wouldn't
have thought something like this could happen. But the same sentence
also illustrates some differences in the attitude. The parents feel responsible for their children; they want to do something about the situation
and they think they have to do so; the community, on the other hand,
reacts more as onlookers: onlookers can be *horrified* or *appalled*, but they
cannot be *outraged*. This suggests that we should not posit for *appalled*
the component "I want to do something because of this".

Another difference between *outraged* and *appalled* can be illustrated
with the following sentence (also from Goddard 1998):

> They were appalled (*outraged) to see the suffering of the
> people in the wake of the floods.

In this sentence, *appalled* sounds natural, for it suggests that "something
very bad happened to someone"; but *outraged* sounds odd here –
mainly, it seems, because it implies human action rather than a natural
disaster. This shows that while *appalled* and *outraged* share the implication that "something very bad happened", *appalled* doesn't carry the
further implication that it happened "because someone did something
very bad".

Unlike *outraged*, *appalled* has also a reflective quality – as if one felt
compelled to take note of and to reflect on terrible things that happen to
people. The fact that *appalled* frequently co-occurs with the phrases "to
see" or "to hear" ("I was appalled to see/hear") highlights its "eviden-
tial" and compelling character. I have tried to account for this aspect of
*appalled* with the component "I have to think now: very bad things
happen to people". On the other hand, *appalled* doesn't seem to imply a

sudden discovery ("I know now"), characteristic of *outraged* (it is not perceived as a sudden experience, although the experiencer's attention is focussed on some compelling evidence).

This brings us to the following explication:

> *Appalled* (X was appalled)
> (a)  X felt something because X thought something
> (b)     sometimes a person thinks:
> (c)     "something very bad happened to someone
> (d)     I didn't think that something like this could happen
> (e)     I have to think now: very bad things happen to people"
> (f)     when this person thinks this this person feels something bad
> (g)  X felt something like this
> (h)  because X thought something like this

Since *appalled* doesn't seem to refer to any human actions it may seem more closely related to *sad* than to *angry*. Unlike *sad*, however, it does refer to people. For example, I can be *sad* to see magnificent roses destroyed by the hail, but I couldn't be *appalled* by it. This "human factor" links *appalled* with the family of words which includes *anger, indignation, fury*, and *outrage*. But the decision to include *appalled* in the group of "*anger* and related words" rather than "*sadness* and related words" must be seen as basically arbitrary. Since *appalled* can also be seen as related to *horrified*, and *horrified*, which is closely related to *terrified*, has been placed together with *terrified* in the group of "*fear* and related words", *appalled* could also be included in that latter group. The truth of the matter is that there are no discrete classes here, and that different classifications are possible. What is discrete is the structure of each concept, with its strictly definable set of components.

### 4.7 Shocked

In many situations, *appalled* may seem to be interchangeable with *shocked*; for example, one can be either *shocked* or *appalled* by scenes of human suffering. But of course there are also differences.

To begin with, *shocked* – like *outraged* – implies not only a totally unexpected event ("I didn't think that something like this could happen"), but also a sudden discovery: "I know now (that something very bad happened)". Furthermore, *shocked* clearly doesn't include any reflective component like "I have to think now: very bad things happen to people". On the contrary, it implies a sense that one is unable to think (being, as it were, shell-shocked). Finally, it should be noted that *to be shocked* doesn't mean the same as *to get a shock*: the latter expression does not imply that "something very bad happened".

> *Shocked* (X was shocked)
> (a) X felt something because X thought something
> (b)  sometimes a person thinks:
> (c)  "something has happened now
> (d)  I know now: something very bad happened
> (e)  I didn't think that something like this could happen
> (f)  I can't think now"
> (g)  when this person thinks this this person feels something bad
> (h)  X felt something like this
> (i)  because X thought something like this

## 5. Thinking about other people

Many emotion terms are linked with scenarios which involve thinking about "someone else", with an explicit or implicit contrast with "me". These include (among others) *envy* and *jealousy*, *pity* and *compassion*, *Schadenfreude, gratitude, admiration* and *contempt*. The feelings involved can be either "good" (as in the case of *gratitude* and *admiration*) or "bad" (as in the case of *envy* or *contempt*); and the evaluative components of the cognitive scenario are not always aligned in value with the feeling; e.g. in the case of *envy* "something good" happens to another person, and yet one feels "something bad", whereas in the case of *Schadenfreude* something bad happens to another person, and yet one feels "something good".

### 5.1 Envy and jealousy

*Envy* involves thinking about good things that happen to other people and wishing that things like this would happen to us. It also implies a kind of comparison between oneself and other people leading to a negative assessment ("this is bad") and to a "bad feeling".

According to Parrott (1991: 23), "envy occurs when another has what one lacks oneself, whereas jealousy is concerned with the loss of a relationship one has". It seems clear, however, that (as the word is normally used), *envy* doesn't have to be focussed on possessions as such: strictly speaking, it is not a question of what another person "has" and of what I "lack", but rather, of "good things that have happened to another person and have not happened to me".

Obviously, the observation that some good things have happened to someone else and have not happened to me does not exhaust the full scenario of *envy*: a crucial part of this concept involves the experiencer's "wishes" or "wants". To state what these wishes are, Parrott divides envy into two types: "nonmalicious envy" and "malicious envy", and he states that "the focus of nonmalicious envy is 'I wish I had what you have' . . . whereas the focus of malicious envy, on the other hand, is 'I wish you did not have what you have.'"

But when we examine the ways the word *envy* is actually used we do not find sufficient grounds for positing two separate meanings here. Rather, we can say that in all its uses *envy* implies that "I want things like this to happen to me". Furthermore, in all its uses *envy* implies a negative evaluation of the observed state of affairs: "something good happened to this person", "it didn't happen to me", "this is bad". Whether or not this scenario appears to be associated with "malice" depends on the context. The evaluative component "this is bad" does lend itself to different interpretations, for it can be taken as referring especially to the component "something good happened to this other person" or to the component "it didn't happen to me". But since it can always be understood as referring to the combination of these two components, there is no need to posit polysemy here. Instead, we can posit the following unitary meaning:

> *Envy* (X felt envy)
> (a)  X felt something because X thought something
> (b)    sometimes a person thinks about someone else:
> (c)    "something good happened to this other person
> (d)    it didn't happen to me
> (e)    this is bad
> (f)    I want good things like this to happen to me"
> (g)    when this person thinks this this person feels something bad
> (h)  X felt something like this
> (i)  because X thought something like this

Let us turn now to *jealousy*, which Parrott defines as "an emotion experienced when a person is threatened by the loss of an important relationship with another person (the 'partner') to a 'rival'" (p. 15). I believe that this statement is essentially on the right track, as is also the statement that "What is also true is that jealousy involves a triangle of relations" (p. 16).

Parrott's further elaborations, however, notably that "at the heart of jealousy is a *need to be needed*" (p. 17) or that *jealousy* involves "a loss of self-esteem" or "a loss of a relationship", appear to be unfounded and unnecessary. For example, a child jealous of her sibling does not have to feel that she has lost the relationship with the mother. What is really essential is that *jealousy* involves (prototypically) three parties rather than two and that it has to do with other people's good feelings. For example, a *jealous* husband is thinking about his wife but at the same time he is also thinking about some third party; and his thoughts must involve his wife's feelings: the husband wants his wife to "feel good feelings" for him and he suffers because it seems to him that his wife "feels good feelings" for someone other than himself.

Unlike *envy*, *jealousy* doesn't necessarily imply any unfavourable comparison between myself and somebody else (the idea is not that my wife, or my parent, loves (or likes) someone else and doesn't love (or like) me). Nor is it necessarily a question of my wife, or my mother, loving (or liking) somebody else more than me. Rather, the *jealousy* scenario can be summed up in three key components which are not strictly speaking comparative: (1) "I want this person to feel good feelings for me"; (2) "I think this person feels good feelings for someone other than me"; (3) "this is bad". Everything else is variable. The relationship between these three key components of *jealousy* is left unspecified and is compatible both with an interpretation in terms of an invidious comparison and with one in terms of an exclusive claim on somebody else's affections or favours.

> *Jealousy* (X felt jealousy)
> (a) X felt something because X thought something
> (b)    sometimes a person thinks about someone else:
> (c)    "I want this person to feel good feelings for me
> (d)    I think this person feels good feelings for someone other than me
> (e)    I don't want this
> (f)    I can't not think about this"
> (g)    when this person thinks this this person feels something bad
> (h)  X felt something like this
> (i)  because X thought something like this

Parrott (1991: 23) asks "why these two emotions [*jealousy* and *envy*] should be so readily conflated". Parrott himself answers this question by suggesting that, first, both emotions involve "a loss of self-esteem", and second, "jealousy and envy may frequently co-occur". Neither of these explanations makes any reference to the inherent semantics of the two words. On the other hand, the explications proposed here do exhibit some commonalities. First, *envy* implies that "something good happened to someone else", while *jealousy* implies that "someone feels good feelings for someone else". Second, *envy* implies that "I want good things like this to happen to me", while *jealousy* implies that "I want this person to feel good feelings for me". Third, *envy* implies a negative evaluation ("this is bad"), whereas *jealousy* (which tends to be, as Parrott says, "more intense", more violent, more active) implies a greater volitional involvement ("I don't want this") and an (often obsessive) preoccupation ("I can't not think about this"). Clearly, then, while there are important differences between the two concepts, there are also striking similarities.

It should be added that, as noted by Parrott and others, the adjective *jealous* is sometimes used in an extended sense, which brings it closer to *envy*, as, for example, in the sentence "he is jealous of his brother's success". The noun *jealousy*, however, does appear to be restricted to triadic interpersonal relations, as suggested in the proposed explication.

Finally, we should note that (as documented by P. Stearns 1994) a major change occurred in this century in Anglo, and especially Anglo-American, culture with respect to *jealousy*, which came to be profoundly disapproved of and regarded as a sign of immaturity, possessiveness, and so on. Cross-cultural analysis (see e.g. Sommers 1984) has suggested that "Americans were far more likely to profess great discomfort with jealousy than were people from most other cultures" (P. Stearns 1994: 234), and studies conducted in America suggested that "an increasing number [of Americans] either denied jealousy or admitted deep personal responsibility for the emotion" (ibid.).

*Envy*, which used to be regarded as one of the seven deadly sins (cf. e.g. M. Bloomfield 1967[1952]), appears to be now seen as a less grave offence; after all, it can be said to imply only a desire for equality, which is one of the key modern ideals. On the other hand, "possessiveness", which is associated with *jealousy*, is one of the cardinal sins of modern times.

## 5.2 Pity and self-pity

*Pity*, like *envy*, involves comparing our own lot with that of other people. In the case of *envy*, the comparison is unfavourable to us: "something good happened to this person, it didn't happen to me"; in the case of *pity*, it is the other way around: "something bad happened to this person, it didn't happen to me".

The two concepts, however, are not fully symmetrical, for the assessment is in both cases negative: in the case of *envy*, I think it is bad that those good things didn't happen to me, in the case of *pity*, it is bad that those bad things happened to this other person.

The focus of *pity*, then, is on the other person (the one to whom bad things have happened) rather than on oneself, and so the feeling is "bad" rather than "good". In fact, it might even be questioned whether any comparison is involved at all. I would note, however, that it would be odd to say of a prisoner in a concentration camp that he or she felt *pity* for another prisoner in exactly the same position. *Compassion*, yes, but probably not *pity*. On the other hand a guard, whose position is quite different, could indeed be said to feel *pity* for a prisoner.

The implicit comparison between the unfortunate person and myself explains also the whiff of superiority that *pity* has: it is not exactly a fellow-feeling. Presumably, this is why people are so often afraid of other people's *pity* (while they are not afraid of their *compassion*): "I fear pain, dependency, ugliness, and loss of control. Pity from others. Being tolerated. Doctors with tubes and shots and knives and drugs" (Feinstein and Mayo 1993: 19).

> *Pity* (X felt pity)
> (a) X felt something because X thought something
> (b)     sometimes a person thinks about someone else:
> (c)     "something bad happened to this other person
> (d)     this is bad
> (e)     something like this is not happening to me"
> (f)     when this person thinks this this person feels something
> (g) X felt something like this
> (h) because X thought something like this

*Self-pity* may seem to be simply a special case of *pity*, but in fact it is not quite that: since *pity* involves an implicit comparison between another person and myself, one cannot be the target of one's own *pity*. *Self-pity*, then, is not a special case of *pity*, but rather, something like *pity* but focussed on one's own misfortunes and involving an implicit comparison with other people (by no means a detached one). Being a sort of misapplication and distortion of *pity*, *self-pity* has always a pejorative and as it were ironic ring, whereas *pity* does not.

Ortony, Clore, and Collins (1988: 106) state that *self-pity* requires a certain degree of "detachment" and "self-distancing" and that when people experience *self-pity* they "view themselves as though they were someone else, they view their misfortune as undeserved, and they complain 'Why me? What have I done to deserve this?'" I believe the point about the "complaining" character of *self-pity* (which implies, inter alia, that one feels "something bad") is well taken; but the words "detachment" and "self-distancing" seem less apposite. In fact, the "complaining character" of *self-pity* distinguishes it from *pity* and suggests an inability to look at oneself in a detached way, from the outside. One can look at oneself in this way if one is, for example, "angry with oneself" or "displeased with oneself" (as one can be angry, or displeased, with someone else), but not when one is wallowing in *self-pity*. One cannot genuinely *pity* oneself, as one cannot *envy* oneself, be *jealous* of oneself, be *grateful* to oneself, or feel *compassion* for oneself.

> *Self-pity* (X felt self-pity)
> (a)  X felt something because X thought something
> (b)    sometimes a person thinks:
> (c)    "something bad happened to me
> (d)    this is bad
> (e)    something like this is not happening to other people"
> (f)    when this person thinks this this person feels something bad
> (g)  X felt something like this
> (h)  because X thought something like this

### 5.3 Compassion

> The Vietnamese holy man [Thich Nhat Hanh] talked about how the suffering we see around us provides an opportunity to develop the compassion that the Buddhists think of as the noblest emotion. Instead of responding to others' misfortune with fear or pity or guilt – all of which create distance – he teaches that we can turn such events into opportunities to practice opening our hearts, to know our oneness with all other beings. (Feinstein and Mayo 1993: 50)

*Compassion* is relatively close to *pity*, but it differs from it in some significant ways. What the two share is the idea that something bad happened to another person. In the case of *compassion*, however, there is no potentially invidious comparison with myself, which could be interpreted as patronizing. Strictly speaking, therefore, *compassion* does not belong to the category discussed in the present section; it is useful, however, to include it here for comparison with *pity*.

*Compassion* implies also that the target person is aware of their own misfortune and is suffering, whereas in the case of *pity*, the target person need not be aware of any misfortune (yet another reason why *pity* may invite a suspicion of a superior and patronizing attitude on the part of the experiencer). This means that in the case of *compassion* the component "something bad happened to this person" needs to be accompanied by a further component "this person feels something bad because of this", while the comparative component of *pity* ("something like this didn't happen to me") should not be included here.

Finally, *compassion* implies an impulse, or at least a desire, to do something for the suffering person if it is possible ("I want to do something good for this person if I can"), which in the case of *pity* is absent.

> *Compassion* (X felt compassion)
> (a) X felt something because X thought something
> (b)  sometimes a person thinks about someone else:
> (c)  "something bad happened to this person
> (d)  this person feels something bad now
> (e)  I want to do something good for this person if I can"
> (f)  when this person thinks this this person feels something
> (g) X felt something like this
> (h) because X thought something like this

### 5.4 Schadenfreude

The concept of *Schadenfreude* has recently been the subject of intense world-wide discussions on the Internet. It has not, however, been the subject of any rigorous semantic analysis, and the discussions, animated and stimulating though they were, tended to be carried out in a theoretical vacuum. Apparently, the meaning of *Schadenfreude* was regarded by most discussants as self-evident – so much so that no attempt to state it precisely seemed needed; and, consequently, no thought seemed to be given to the need for a methodological framework suitable for undertaking such a task.

One point which seems clear is that in the prototypical scenario the experiencer thinks about someone else: "something bad happened to this person"; and also that while he or she thinks this he or she "feels something good".

But this is not the whole story. A person who feels something good while thinking that something bad happened to someone else could be a sadist, rather than someone experiencing *Schadenfreude*. To use again the example of a guard and some prisoners in a concentration camp, the guard could be cruel and inhuman, and could feel something good thinking of the suffering occurring all around, but she/he could hardly feel *Schadenfreude*. On the other hand, a guard who disliked another guard could feel *Schadenfreude* at this other guard's misfortune – especially if it were not a serious misfortune but rather some miscalculation in an attempt to obtain an advantage.

Typically, then, *Schadenfreude* occurs among people who are in a comparable situation. It is directed at someone who in the past has enjoyed good luck – perhaps (in someone else's view) excessively or undeservedly so. And it is likely to occur in a climate of competition and envy. The experiencer seems to perceive the world (or her/his local world) in terms of a wheel of fortune, where good and bad things happen to people, and where the distribution of good and bad things among people may often seem unfair – an imbalance which can sometimes be satisfyingly corrected. The experiencer doesn't think, cruelly, "I want bad things to happen to this person", but rather something along the lines of "it serves her right" (because she seems so arrogant and so complacent). The situation is seen more in terms of a satisfying reversal of fortune than in terms of a real misfortune.

> *Schadenfreude* (X felt Schadenfreude)
> (a)  X felt something because X thought something
> (b)    sometimes a person thinks about someone else:
> (c)    "many good things happened to this person before now
> (d)    this person thought: 'this is good'
> (e)    something bad has happened to this person now
> (f)    now I think: this is good"
> (g)    when this person thinks this this person feels something good
> (h)  X felt something like this
> (i)  because X thought something like this

## 5.5 Gratitude

*Gratitude* is clearly based on the thought that someone else has done something good for me. This central component of the *gratitude* scenario is so salient that it is easy to think that it is the only one. In fact, however, there is more to *gratitude* than that. For example, a small child, aware of all the good things that her mother is doing for her, may well respond with love rather than with gratitude, and in fact the word *gratitude* doesn't seem entirely appropriate, or natural, for this particular relationship. Somehow or other *gratitude* implies a certain distance. To account for this impression of distance I would propose for this concept a second component: "this person didn't have to do it". A small child may well think that her mother does good things for her, but she would be less likely to think that her mother "doesn't have to do it".

But even adding this second component to the first and most obvious one may not be enough. Conceivably, one could still say: "I know she did many good things for me, and I know she didn't have to do it, but I can't say I feel grateful". What appears to be missing is something about the experiencer's will: I don't necessarily want to reciprocate, but at least I want to think good things about my benefactor ("I want to think good things about this person because of this"). When this third element is also present (together with some "good feelings") then one could hardly say that "I am not really grateful".

Often, *gratitude* is taken to imply that the beneficiary owes the benefactor a debt, or that some strings may be attached to the benefit; or that the beneficiary simply wants to "repay the favour". All such associations, however, are contextual and variable, whereas the "gratuitous" nature of the benefit and some "good thoughts" about the benefactor do indeed seem to be part of the invariant.

> *Gratitude* (X felt gratitude)
> (a) X felt something because X thought something
> (b)  sometimes a person thinks about someone else:
> (c)  "this person did something good for me
> (d)  this person didn't have to do it
> (e)  I want to think good things about this person because of this"
> (f)  when this person thinks this this person feels something good
> (g) X felt something like this
> (h)  because X thought something like this

Ortony, Clore, and Collins (1988: 147–8) have described *gratitude* as a "compound emotion that results from the conjunction of the eliciting conditions of admiration and joy". Since the eliciting conditions of *admiration* and *joy* are "praiseworthy action" and "desirable event" respectively, this characterization of *gratitude* makes it in their system an opposite of *anger*, whose eliciting conditions are "blameworthy action" and "undesirable event".

In my view such a characterization of *gratitude* is rather artificial. For one thing, *gratitude* does not necessarily imply either *admiration* or *joy*; for another, it is not a conceptual opposite of *anger*. The basic thought behind *gratitude* is "this person did something good for me", whereas the basic thought behind *anger* is "this person did something bad", not "this person did something bad for me" (or "to me"). The action that one is *grateful* for is not seen as "something desirable" but as "something good for me". In fact, I can be *grateful* for something that at the time I didn't want at all but that I now appreciate as "good for me". One can admire the elegant symmetry of the definitions constructed by Ortony, Clore, and Collins (1988) but here the system they have constructed departs somewhat from empirical reality.

## 5.6 Admiration and self-admiration

> Her courage and resourcefulness are amazing. It's good to be able to admire one's own daughter. (Spufford 1996: 111)

*Admiration*, like many other emotion terms (e.g. *contempt* or *envy*), can be used as a name of a "disposition" as well as an "emotion" sensu stricto. In the explication proposed here, however, I will focus on the emotion, as in the frame "X felt admiration for Y" (rather than "X admired Y").

There are two key elements in the cognitive scenario of *admiration*: a very positive evaluation of somebody else's abilities ("this person can do some very good things"), and a comparative perspective ("not many other people are like this"). Each of these elements requires some discussion.

The word "ability" can be misleading in this context, for we can feel *admiration* for someone's attitude (e.g. in the face of adversity) rather than for any tangible achievements or accomplishments. But the semantic component "this person can do some things very well" can be understood more broadly, and can include inner activities: the way one (psychologically) confronts a threat, "battles" with illness, "works through" suffering and personal catastrophes, and so on. What the phrasing of this component does not include is, for example, good looks, but I think this is correct: normally it would be odd to say "I felt admiration for her huge blue eyes / for her gorgeous red hair" (although one can say, of course, "I admired her gorgeous red hair", using the word *admire* in a different sense: "to look admiringly").

The component "not many other people are like this" is clearly necessary: the thoughts which underlie *admiration* place the target person above the ordinary level. What is less clear is whether or not *admiration* implies also some kind of comparison with oneself: if I feel *admiration* for someone do I need to place them (in some respect) above myself? Although the matter requires further investigation, I am inclined to think that some component along those lines is indeed necessary, and I have included it in the explication (not in the form "I am not like this" or "I want to be like this" but rather a more hypothetical "I would want to be like this if I could"). In support of this component I would point out that parents who think about their children: "this girl/boy can do some things very well, not many other people are like this" could well be described as "proud" rather than "full of admiration". If, however, a mother or father thinks, in addition, "I would want to be like this if I could" this does indeed sound admiring rather than simply proud.

> *Admiration* (X felt admiration)
> (a) X felt something because X thought something
> (b)    sometimes a person thinks about someone else:
> (c)    "this person can do some very good things
> (d)    not many other people are like this
> (e)    I would want to be like this if I could"
> (f)    when this person thinks this this person feels something good
> (g) X felt something like this
> (h) because X thought something like this

Finally, a few words need to be said about *self-admiration*, which is clearly inconsistent with the above scenario. As in the case of *self-pity*, however (which is not *pity* but pseudo-pity), *self-admiration* is not a special case of *admiration* but a distortion of the real thing; and both words (*self-pity* and *self-admiration*) carry more than a tinge of mockery and moral disapproval.

> *Self-admiration*
> (a) X felt something because X thought something
> (b)    sometimes a person thinks:
> (c)    "I can do some very good things
> (d)    not many other people are like this
> (e)    other people would want to be like this if they could"
> (f)    when this person thinks this this person feels something good
> (g) X felt something like this
> (h) because X thought something like this

## 5.7 Contempt

*Contempt* may seem to be a mirror image of *admiration*; in fact, however, the relationship between the two is more complex than that.

To begin with, *contempt* is not focussed on what someone else can or cannot do. For example, if the Nazis had contempt for the "inferior races" (like Jews and Slavs), the implied attitude was not "these people can't do good things" but rather something like "these people are not people like those for whom I can have some respect". Thus, *contempt* seems to divide people (from the experiencer's point of view) into two categories: "those about whom I can think some good things" and "those who are not like this and about whom I can't think good things". More precisely, this attitude can be represented as follows: "I can think good things about some people – this person is not someone like these people – I can't think good things about someone like this".

One difficult point to decide on concerns any comparison between the person one feels *contempt* for and oneself. In the case of *admiration* I have posited the component "I would want to be someone like this if I could". In the case of *contempt*, it would be difficult to propose a symmetrical negative component: "I wouldn't want to be someone like this if . . ." (if what?). But a straightforward superiority component ("I am not someone like this" or "this person is not someone like me") doesn't sound quite right either. It would appear, therefore, that *contempt* doesn't involve any direct and explicit comparison with oneself, and that the suggestion of my personal superiority over the target of *contempt* is there only by implication (presumably, if I have *contempt* for person Y I am not like this myself). The fact that there is no such word as *self-contempt* corresponding to the well-established *self-admiration* suggests that in the case of *contempt* an element of explicit comparison with oneself is perhaps missing.

> *Contempt* (X felt contempt for Y)
> (a)  X felt something because X thought something
> (b)    sometimes a person thinks about someone else:
> (c)    "I can think good things about some people
> (d)    this person is not someone like these people
> (e)    I can't think good things about someone like this"
> (f)    when this person thinks this this person feels something
>        bad
> (g)  X felt something like this
> (h)  because X thought something like this

## 6. Thinking about ourselves

In this section I will discuss a group of emotions that, for example, Taylor (1985) (who devoted to them a whole book) calls "emotions of self-assessment", and that many other authors have characterized as "self-conscious emotions" (see e.g. Price Tangney and Fischer 1995). In my terms, what this group shares is the experiencer's idea that "other people can think something (either good or bad) about me" (*shame, embarrassment, pride*) or that the experiencer is thinking about his/her own actions (*remorse, guilt*). In all cases the attention is, or appears to be, focussed on the experiencer.

## 6.1 Shame

As noted, for example, by Miller (1993: 179), "In the English-speaking world . . . we have moved from a culture of shame to a culture of embarrassment". The point is well taken, and it is an important one, but to explain what really happened "in the English-speaking world" we have to pay some attention to semantics. For while it is true that *embarrassment* has come to occupy centre-stage, at the expense of *shame* (cf. P. Stearns 1994), it is also true that the meaning of *shame* has changed, and that the modern English *shame*, which is being continually squeezed out by the modern English notion of *embarrassment*, is not the same *shame* which, for example, Hamlet was referring to when he said to his mother: "O shame! where is thy blush?"

In Shakespeare's language (and for a long time thereafter) *shame*, which was then associated with blushing, was regarded as a good thing – a necessary thing, and not a bad thing at all (cf. e.g. Swinburne: "Man is a beast when shame stands off from him", quoted in Stevenson 1949: 1809). It is not just the importance of *shame*, then, which has changed, but also its very meaning. (The older meaning has survived in the adjective *shameless*: to be *shameless* is a bad thing, precisely because in that older sense *shame* was something good and necessary.) But to understand how the meaning of *shame* changed we first have to examine its current meaning. In current usage, *shame* often refers to something bad that we have done, and it often goes hand in hand with *remorse*. But people can also be *ashamed* of something for which they are not in any way responsible, for example, they can be *ashamed* of their parents, or of their origin. Furthermore, we can be *ashamed* of our shortcomings, of our inability to spell correctly, of our clothes. To account for all these different possibilities, I have phrased the first cognitive component of *shame* (in its modern sense) as "people can know something bad about me" (rather than as "I did something bad").

If there is some "shameful" truth about us that we would like to hide from other people it is because we don't want them to *think* something bad about us (rather than merely *know* it), but this bad opinion which we want to avoid would have to be based on some facts, i.e. on knowledge. Since the anticipated "bad thoughts" are grounded in knowledge, they are seen as having an objective basis, and this implies that the experiencer shares the negative judgment attributed in advance to other people.

As argued, in particular, by Gabriele Taylor (with reference to Sartre 1948), in *shame* the experiencer not only imagines an audience who will know, and therefore think, something bad about him or her, but also identifies with it: "the agent looks at his own action through the observer's eyes and so it is suddenly revealed to him what it amounts to" (Taylor 1985: 68); it is necessary, then, that "a person feeling shame judges herself adversely" (ibid.).

A similar point is made by Miller (1993: 149), who draws a vignette of a person discovered stealing from the offering dish: "Here I think we can still distinguish between the sensation of being exposed in a furtive act from the sensation of knowing yourself as a person who does shameful things. The former is an intense humiliation, the latter shame."

A fellow linguist once confessed that he was ashamed of the fact that he – a lecturer in linguistics – could not pronounce certain sounds which are routinely taught in courses on phonetics. It was clear that while this linguist didn't want this "compromising" fact to become widely known, he felt he had to agree with the negative judgment that, he thought, its discovery would lead to (and that in fact he found this self-judgment particularly painful). To account for this aspect of *shame*, I have posited for it the sequence of components: "if people know this they are 'bound to' (i.e. can't not) think something bad about me", "when I think about it I can't not think the same".

> *Shame* (X was ashamed)
> (a)  X felt something because X thought something
> (b)  sometimes a person thinks:
> (c)  "people can know something bad about me
> (d)  I don't want people to know this
> (e)  if people know this they can't not think something bad about me
> (f)  when I think about it, I can't not think the same"
> (g)  when this person thinks this this person feels something bad
> (h)  X felt something like this
> (i)  because X thought something like this

*Shame* is widely regarded as a "moral emotion" and is often linked with the notion that "I have done something bad" (cf. e.g. Harré 1990: 199). But as the last example shows, this is not necessarily the case. The notion that "I have done something bad" is necessarily involved in *remorse*, but not in *shame*. What is indeed necessary is that there is (as we see it) something bad about us that other people can know. For example, not being able to pronounce certain sounds may not be widely regarded as a very bad thing; to be *ashamed* of it, however, I have to think of it as something truly bad – and, moreover, as "something bad that people can know *about me*". Bad things that happen to me cannot normally be regarded as "something bad *about me*", but bad things that I am ashamed of can. In that sense, one could understand why *shame* – in contrast to, for example, *embarrassment* – may seem to "engage the moral" (Harré 1990: 199).

The older meaning of *shame*, I would suggest, didn't include the knowledge component: "people can know something bad about me". The "blush of shame" did not indicate that people know something bad about the blusher but only that the blusher didn't want other people to know, and to think, anything bad about her.

Hamlet's mother may well have been afraid that people could know bad things about her, but such an apprehension wasn't invariably associated with *shame*. In fact, the older English *shame* was often "forward-looking" and it implied the thought "I don't want people to know bad things about me (and therefore I will not do certain things)" rather than a thought implying a *fait accompli*: "people can know bad things about me (because there is something bad to know)". To quote the eighteenth century writer Edmund Burke:

> Whilst shame keeps its watch, virtue is not wholly extinguished in the heart. (quoted in Stevenson 1949: 1809)

As this quote illustrates, the older meaning of *shame* reflected a social climate in which other people's view of the individual was expected to act as a powerful means of control: it was expected that people wouldn't do certain things because they wouldn't want other people to know, and to think, bad things about them; and it was assumed that the very thought of other people's potentially negative view of a person could make this person blush.

The modern meaning of *shame*, however, does not reflect a kind of society where "other people's" anticipated view of us can be expected to act as a powerful regulator of our behaviour. In the modern Anglo society – as reflected in the mirror of semantics – other expectations and other concerns have come to the fore, as reflected, in particular, in the rise of the concept of *embarrassment* in modern English (to be discussed in the next section).

The change in the meaning of the English *shame* should also be a warning to all those who are inclined to absolutize *shame* as a "universal human emotion". What "shame"? The Shakespearian *shame*? The modern English *shame*? Or any one of a number of other emotions (such as, for example, the German *Scham* or the Polish *wstyd*), whose names are routinely translated into English as *shame* but which in fact do not mean the same?

John Braithwaite, the author of the important legal work *Crime, Shame, and Reintegration* (1989) states that "the most important work on shame in Western history is Norbert Elias's two volumes on *The Civilizing Process*", and he notes that "Elias sees shame in the ascendant rather than declining during the last 700 years". Braithwaite argues that "while Elias identifies an interesting trend toward the democratizing of shame, he overstates it" (Braithwaite 1989: 25); and he refers to Thomas Scheff's (1990: 16) observation that "during the twentieth century we became ashamed to be ashamed in certain ways and the very word *shame* atrophied in our vocabulary". Braithwaite concludes that "Half a century after Elias wrote, the withering of many types of shame has significantly reversed the most fundamental unilateral trend in his theory" (p. 27).

What appears to be overlooked in this discussion is the fact that Elias didn't write about *shame* at all, but rather, about the German *Scham* (which in fact is closer in meaning to the Shakespearian than to the modern English *shame*). As noted by P. Stearns (1994) and Miller (1993), the English *shame* declined largely at the expense of *embarrassment*; but German doesn't have a word corresponding to the English *embarrassment* as it doesn't have a word corresponding to the modern English *shame*; and no comparable process has occurred in the German language (whatever other changes may have occurred instead).

## 6.2 Embarrassment

*Embarrassment* is one of the most important emotion concepts in the modern Anglo world. Its ascent – at the expense of *shame* and also *guilt* – has been extraordinary. As Miller (1993: 199) notes, "Undoubtedly, as a historical matter, the realm of embarrassment expanded and continues to expand at the expense of shame." Miller endorses Harré's (1990) view that this expansion is due to the fact that "the category of morals has shrunk relative to the category of manners and convention". P. Stearns (1994) makes a number of similar comments, remarking, in particular, on the weakening of the association between *embarrassment* and blushing: "Blushing, rather charming in a Victorian context when embarrassment had few heavy duties, recedes in notice in our own age, when embarrassment is more central and its invocation more uniform than random individual proclivity to blushing can express" (p. 354).

What, then, is *embarrassment*, and how does it differ from *shame*? Harré (1990: 199) defines it as an emotion "occasioned by the realisation that others have become aware that what one has been doing . . . has been a breach of conventions and the code of manners, a judgment in which I, as actor, concur", and he contrasts it with *shame* in terms of "moral infraction" vs. "breach of convention", remarking that "shame engages the moral, embarrassment the conventional".

This is helpful, but clearly not sufficient, if only because a person can be embarrassed without being an "actor", that is, without doing anything. In fact, typically *embarrassment* is used with reference to situations where something (undesirable) is *happening* to a person rather than to situations when a person is *doing* something. For example, one can be acutely embarrassed if one's trousers split in public or if one's stomach produces loud rumbling noises – clearly, situations when "something is happening to me" rather than "I am doing something".

Harré's reference to other people's awareness of the experiencer's predicament appears persuasive; in the NSM framework, this aspect of *embarrassment* could be accounted for by means of the component "other people know that this is happening to me".

Since the embarrassing event is, prototypically, in the present rather than past (one finds oneself in an embarrassing situation), other people's awareness of it must mean (or at least invites the inference) that these other people are physically present. In P. Stearns' (1994: 147) words, the increasingly powerful emotion of *embarrassment* "assumed an audience", and presupposed an "audience response"; it also assumed a "sensitivity to others' reactions" (p. 148). This expected audience response takes, above all, the form of "audience attention": not only do "other people know what is happening to me" (as suggested by Harré), but "they are (I assume) thinking about me because of this".

Harré's references to "a breach of conventions" or "a code of manners" are, however, too specific. For example, if someone is embarrassed at being praised in public (cf. Miller 1993: 152) no breach of convention or manners needs to be involved. Since other people's potential "bad thoughts" are not caused by anything the experiencer has done but only by something that is happening to her (him) they cannot involve any moral judgment and may indeed have to do with manners and conventions, but strictly speaking it is not "manners" and "conventions" as such which provide a key to *embarrassment*. In fact the fear of embarrassment seems to control the lives of many people who would happily break conventions and depart from traditional codes of manners (cf. P. Stearns 1994). Indeed, the growing reliance on *embarrassment* in modern (Anglo) life can be seen as going hand in hand with a growing emphasis on "informality" and relaxation of rigid social conventions. P. Stearns (1994: 215) refers in this connection to the work of the Dutch sociologists who have emphasized "the new informality" of social relations of the later twentieth century, where "at least superficial democracy reduces detailed rules of emotional conduct but where the need to manifest appropriate responses and avoid embarrassment continues to define important constraints".

Prototypically, *embarrassment* involves being *seen* by other people: the "audience" that P. Stearns (1994) refers to is normally an "embodied" one, with their eyes on the experiencer. To quote Taylor (1985: 69–70):

> A pipe may burst and demand immediate attention . . . Whatever my emotional reactions under the circumstances, embarrassment can be one of them only if I believe myself to be watched . . . This seems to suggest that, unlike shame, embarrassment requires an embodied audience, or at least requires that the agent should imagine that such an audience is present. The demand relevant to embarrassment seems to be created not so much by the burst pipe as by the eyes which are upon me.

Consider, however, the following passage from a novel:

> There was in Ashley a quiet respect for things that Jim also respected. None of this had to be stated. Ashley was too incoherent to have explained and Jim would have been embarrassed to hear it, but he understood. (Malouf 1983: 7)

In this example, there is no question of being *seen* by other people; and if the only other participant in the situation, Ashley, were blind, this wouldn't have made this situation any less embarrassing for Jim either. In the situation envisaged by Malouf, something happens to Jim (Ashley openly discusses feelings and values with him), and it happens in the presence of a witness (Ashley himself). The point is not so much that Ashley would think something bad about Jim, but rather, that Ashley's attention would be focussed on him in the context of this situation (a situation of which Jim is not in control). And at this stage of the scenario the experiencer appears to generalize: "I don't want people to think about me like this". The concern, then, is with "self-presentation" in some general sense (cf. Goffman 1967), but this has to be mediated via some specific witness or witnesses, who are there and who can know (observe) what is currently happening to me and "see" me (think about me) in this light.

Exactly the same applies to C. S. Lewis' (1989: 21) comments about the *embarrassment* he can read in the faces of his stepsons when he attempts to talk to them about his grief over the death of his wife and their mother: "there appears on their faces neither grief, nor love, nor fear, nor pity, but the most fatal of all non-conductors, embarrassment. They look as if I were committing an indecency. They are longing for me to stop." The boys are embarrassed because something is happening to them which places them in an undesirable role; it happens in the presence of a witness (the stepfather himself); and the undesirable image (as boys talking "indecently" about emotions) is projected at "people" in general (presumably, the boys cringe at the thought of being thought of by "people" as involved in such conversations).

The last two examples may seem to corroborate Harré's definition of *embarrassment* quoted earlier, with its reference to people's judgment concerning "a breach of conventions, . . . a judgment in which I, as actor, concur". But this is not always the case. For example, a girl who feels embarrassed at being looked at admiringly by a man does not need to see the situation in terms of anybody's judgment with which she, the experiencer, concurs. Here, as elsewhere, however, it does make sense to interpret the experiencer's feelings with reference to the following underlying thoughts: "something is happening to me now not because I want it", "someone knows about it", "this person is thinking about me", and "I don't want people to think about me like this".

This leads us to the following explication:

*Embarrassment* (X was embarrassed)
(a)  X felt something because X thought something
(b)   sometimes a person thinks:
(c)   "something is happening to me now not because I want it
(d)   someone knows about it
(e)   this person is thinking about me
(f)   I don't want people to think about me like this"
(g)   when this person thinks this, this person feels something bad
(h)  X felt something like this
(i)  because X thought something like this

The situational embeddedness of *embarrassment* (component (c)), its assumption of other people's attention (components (d) and (e)), and its concern with "self-presentation" (component (f)), make this concept a unique cultural artifact, symptomatic in many ways of the society which has created it.

In a nutshell, what appears to have happened in the big shift from *shame* to *embarrassment* in Anglo culture can be presented as follows. At the basis of the older meaning of *shame* there was a concern "I don't want other people to know bad things about me", a concern which could regulate (to some extent) a person's conduct, and which could combine social and moral considerations. Then *shame* became recast in terms of bad things which *can* (already) be known about a person (thus losing its potential for prevention of "bad things", that is, losing its role as a regulator of conduct). More or less at the same time a new culturally salient concern asserted itself: concern with one's image ("I don't want people to think about me like this"), devoid of any references to "good" or "bad" and focussed on the idea of self-control (one doesn't want to be seen as a person to whom things happen not because this person wants them to happen). This new concern was the theme of the new concept of *embarrassment*. (On the importance of "self-control" in modern Anglo emotionology cf. P. Stearns 1994.) Then, gradually, the expansion of *embarrassment* at the expense of *shame* got under way, with the concerns about what Goffman (1958) called "self-presentation in interpersonal interaction" ("what is happening to me in other people's presence" and "how are other people thinking about me") coming increasingly to the fore, over and above the concern about "bad things" that other people can know about me.

The child psychologist Michael Lewis (1995) concludes his study of "embarrassed behaviour" (p. 201) in young children by stating that embarrassment, which is "the affective component of the cognitive process of self-awareness", "emerges developmentally at some time during the middle of the second year of life" (p. 215). This makes it sound as if the emergence of embarrassment were a developmental stage comparable to the emergence of the first teeth, or of the ability to walk. In fact, however, the concept of *embarrassment* is part and parcel of modern Anglo culture. It was unknown to Shakespeare (cf. Ricks 1974) and it is unknown in most other cultures of the world, which of course have their own culturally constructed "social emotions" (cf. e.g. Geertz 1976; Goddard 1996a; Harkins 1996; Myers 1986). It is difficult to see, therefore, how the "developmental emergence of embarrassment" could be meaningfully studied without a historical and cross-cultural framework.

## 6.3 Pride

We feel *proud* of our achievements, of good things that we have done, and also of good things that those close to us have done (if we emotionally identify with them). But one can also be *proud* of one's origins, or of one's beautiful singing voice; or even of one's beautiful long hair. Generally speaking, we are *proud* of something very good that people can know about us; we believe that people will have to think something good about us because of this, and we "can't help" thinking something good about ourselves.

Essentially, then, *pride* is a mirror image of *shame* (in the modern sense of the word): one may be *proud* of one's achievements as one may be *ashamed* of one's failures; one may be *proud* of one's hidden talents as one may be *ashamed* of one's hidden weaknesses; one may be *proud* of one's origins, one's family or the shape of one's nose, as one may be *ashamed* of one's origins, one's family, or the shape of one's nose.

According to Gabriele Taylor (1985: 24), the crucial feature of pride is "that it is reflexive", that is, that it includes a "reference to self": "at the time of its occurrence the person feeling pride believes that in a certain respect her own worth is confirmed or enhanced . . . there is at the moment of feeling it an awareness that she has reason to think well of herself". While agreeing in essence with these comments I would suggest an even "stronger" phrasing of the references to other people's, and our own, thoughts about ourselves: not only "there is reason" for people to think well of me, and for me to think well of myself, but I secretly believe that people will be "compelled" to think well of me: "if people know this they can't not think good things about me because of this", and I am similarly "compelled" to think something good about myself ("I can't not think the same").

> *Pride* (X felt pride)
> (a)  X felt something because X thought something
> (b)  sometimes a person thinks:
> (c)  "people can know something very good about me
> (d)  I want people to know this
> (e)  if people know this they can't not think good things about me
> (f)  I can't not think the same"
> (g)  when this person thinks this this person feels something good
> (h)  X felt something like this
> (i)  because X thought something like this

## 6.4 Remorse

"Remorse is memory awake" (Emily Dickinson), memory of something bad that I have done in the past.

*Remorse* is clearly based on the knowledge that one has done something bad ("I know: I did something bad"). This knowledge is not due to a sudden discovery or a sudden insight into one's past actions. I knew all along that I was doing something bad but at the time I didn't want to think about it. Now, however, "my memory is awake" and the thoughts about my bad action are coming back with a vengeance: this time the voice of my conscience speaks quite loud ("I can't not think about it now"). Linked with the notion of conscience, *remorse* is related to religious concepts such as *contrition* or *penance* (which to many people seem now rather old-fashioned). It is also related to *regret*; but *regret* can concern present and future events, as well as past ones, whereas *remorse* is restricted to the past:

> I regret very much that I won't be able to come to your party.
> *When I think that I won't come to your party I feel remorse.

Furthermore, *regret* can refer to events and states of affairs for which we are not responsible, whereas *remorse* applies only to our own (intentional) actions.

*Remorse* is like a judgment passed by our conscience, a judgment which keeps reverberating in our soul whether we want it or not. I did something bad, I knew it was bad, but I did it. It wasn't a mistake, it wasn't a faux pas, it wasn't an error of judgment. It was something for which I am fully responsible. Thinking about it is far from pleasant and I might wish to suppress these thoughts, but I can't; a secret voice in my inner self keeps repeating "this was bad", and I can't not hear it, I can't not think about it.

Does a person who feels *remorse* have to wish they could undo what they have done? According to Gabriele Taylor (1985: 105), this wish is indeed a necessary ingredient of *remorse*:

> we do expect some sort of action from her who feels remorse, though of course we may expect in vain. She wants to undo what she has done, and although it is evidently impossible to do just that, she would normally be expected to try and do something towards repairing the damage she takes herself to have brought about.

One can doubt, however, that such a wish for "undoing the past", let alone a wish for making reparations, is a necessary part of *remorse*. There are different kinds of remorse; some of them involve regrets, some lead to contrition and penitence, but some do not move beyond the gnawing thought "I know I did something bad", accompanied by very bad feelings. To quote Coleridge (*Remorse*, act 1, sc. 1, as quoted in Stevenson (1949:1697)):

> Remorse is as the heart in which it grows;
> If that be gentle, it drops balmy dews
> Of true repentance; but if proud and gloomy,
> It is the poison tree, that pierced to the inmost,
> Weeps only tears of poison.

In my own definition of *remorse*, therefore, I have refrained from references to the experiencer's desires and possible future actions, restricting the cognitive scenario to the awareness that sometime in the past I did something bad, to the past attempts to suppress this knowledge, and to the thoughts about this past action gnawing at me now:

*Remorse* (X felt remorse)

(a)  X felt something because X thought something
(b)    sometimes a person thinks:
(c)    "I know that some time ago I did something bad
(d)    I knew it when I was doing it
(e)    I didn't want to think about it then
(f)    I can't not think about it now"
(g)    when this person thinks this this person feels something
         bad
(h)  X felt something like this
(i)  because X thought something like this

Taylor (1985) frames much of her discussion of *remorse* with reference to Max Scheler's discussion of the German concept of *Reue*, which she apparently equates with *remorse*. But *Reue* doesn't really mean quite the same thing as *remorse*, and is in fact closer to *contrition* (although *contrition* can be an act of thought and will unaccompanied by feelings, whereas *Reue* does inherently engage feelings). As a result of this semantic misunderstanding, Taylor takes issue with Scheler's analysis of *Reue* (translated as *remorse*) and seems to be baffled by the great value which Scheler places on this emotion. Taylor argues (quite cogently) that *remorse* can be "as destructive and self-indulgent as guilt may be" (p. 102) and that "far from prompting repair work and bringing about a new and hopeful attitude towards the future, it may just torment the sufferer" (p. 102).

All this seems quite valid (and in fact not inconsistent with what Scheler said about *Reue*), but it seems hard to reconcile with what Taylor herself has said about the experiencer's desire "to undo what she has done" (p. 105).

While not all aspects of Taylor's analysis of *remorse* are convincing, however, her contrastive discussion of *remorse* and *guilt* is valuable and insightful, and I will draw on it in the next section.

## 6.5 Guilt

*Guilt* appears to be closely related to *remorse*, and often the two are used almost interchangeably. For example, if a man is unfaithful to his wife he may feel either *guilt* or *remorse*. On the other hand, if I cause, unintentionally, a car accident as a result of which someone dies or is severely injured, I can only feel *guilt*, not *remorse* – even if the accident was not due to my negligence, recklessness, drunken driving, or anything of the sort. It is enough that *I did something* and that something bad happened as a result. *Remorse* would not be used in this situation because *remorse* implies that "I did something bad", not that I simply "did something" (causing something bad to happen).

I agree with Taylor (1985: 91), then, that if "while driving my car I knock down and kill a child" it is enough to make me suffer from guilt, even if "I have not been negligent but have taken all possible care". On the other hand, I cannot quite agree with the following comment: "If I can feel guilty about my privileged position in society due to circumstances of birth then I see myself as an agent causally involved: it is *my* birth which has brought about the state of affairs which is my privileged position." Being born is not something one does, and therefore I cannot feel responsible for, and guilty about, my privileged position in society *due to birth*. To feel guilty about my privileged position in society I have to think of all the opportunities of doing something about it – that is, of giving up that privileged position or atoning for it. To feel guilty I do indeed need to see myself "as an agent causally involved"; this means, however, that I need to think about something I did (or failed to do), not about something that simply happened to me.

If one's old relative is very sick, and one feels one should stay with them but instead one goes to a party, and the relative dies, one may feel either *guilt* or *remorse*, depending on one's view of the situation. If it was, for example, one's father, and one thinks it was morally wrong to leave him, and if one was conscious of it at the time, then one will feel *remorse*. If it was a distant cousin and one didn't think that it was one's obligation to stay with them but that it was nonetheless a "bad thing" that they died alone, then one will feel *guilt*. Perhaps I didn't do anything bad (in going to that party), but I did something, and because of this, something bad happened (the old relative died alone); the memory of it is a burden to me, I can't not think about it. This is *guilt*.

Lazarus (1991: 122) suggests that the "core relational theme" of *guilt* is "having transgressed a moral imperative". In fact, such a characterization would be more apposite for *remorse* than for *guilt*. For example, the driver who killed a child (through no fault of his own) has not transgressed any moral imperative and so he would not feel *remorse* (he didn't do anything bad); he could, nonetheless, feel *guilt*.

Thus, *guilt*, too, implies that I feel somehow responsible for what has happened and that in my conscience I do not find myself innocent. I cannot forget what has happened; I cannot not think about it.

There is a peculiar tension in *guilt*, different from the inner change involved in *remorse*. *Remorse* implies a contrast between the past and the present ("I didn't want to think about it then – I can't not think about it now"). *Guilt* doesn't imply any such contrast; the feeling can be (almost) concurrent with the event. It does, however, imply a contrast between my conscious judgment (which may well exculpate me because it admits only that "something bad happened", not that "I did something bad"), and some other voice within me which nonetheless finds me "guilty" ("I can't not think that I did something bad"). This leads us to the following explication:

> *Guilt* (X felt guilt)
> (a) X felt something because X thought something
> (b)  sometimes a person thinks:
> (c)  "I did something
> (d)  something bad happened because of this
> (e)  because of this I can't not think that I did something bad"
> (f)  when this person thinks this this person feels something bad
> (g) X felt something like this
> (h) because X thought something like this

Taylor (1985) argues that *guilt*, in contrast to *remorse*, is "an emotion of self-assessment" (p. 100). *Remorse*, which "concentrates on the action rather than on the actor . . . seems the healthier emotion, for in turning the agent away from himself he [sic] is less threatened by the possibility of self-preoccupation and self-indulgence" (p. 101). On the other hand, in the case of a person feeling *guilt* the thoughts "are primarily on herself" (p. 104); "she believes that she has done something forbidden and that in doing what is forbidden she has disfigured and so harmed herself" (p. 103).

While I could not agree with all the details of this analysis (for example, why "forbidden" rather than simply "bad"?), I think that the basic idea is insightful. It is true that in the case of *remorse* one focusses on the action rather than on oneself as the actor, whereas in the case of *guilt* one focusses more on oneself. The explications proposed are consistent with this: the unequivocal component "I know that I did something bad" of *remorse* reflects this focus on the bad action, whereas the component "I can't not think that I did something bad" assigned to *guilt* reflects the focus on the inner tensions of the actor and the actor's thoughts about himself (herself).

## 7 Concluding remarks

While most of the widely used English emotion words (as well as some less widely used ones) have been discussed here, there are of course many others which have not. Perhaps the most glaring omission is that of *love*; an adequate treatment of this concept, however, would require a more lengthy study than can be accommodated here. For reasons of space, too, I have omitted *hate, humiliation, exasperation, enthusiasm, regret*, and many others, despite their historical and cultural interest. At the same time, however, I believe that a good deal of ground has been covered; that the "NSM" semantic method of analysis has been demonstrated and shown to be fruitful; and, finally, that the links between semantics, culture, and history have been illustrated and elucidated.

CHAPTER 3

# A case study of emotion in culture: German *Angst*

## 1 "Angst" as a peculiarly German concept

"Angst" is a peculiarly German concept. The fact that this word has been borrowed and is used in English for a different range of situations, highlights the *sui generis* meaning of the German *Angst*. Consider, for example, the following sentence from an English novel: "community was replaced by the fleeting, passing contacts of city life; people came into the university, and disappeared; psychiatric social workers were appointed, to lead them through the recesses of their angst" (Bradbury 1975: 64). As this example illustrates, *angst* in English suggests an existential condition which seems to have to do with a long-term state of deep-seated anxiety and alienation rather than with what is normally called *fear*. The German word closest to the English *fear* is not *Angst* but *Furcht*; and it is noteworthy that it was not *Furcht*, but *Angst*, with its very distinct semantics and its great salience in German culture, that was felt to be needed as a useful loan word.

As is often the case with loan words, however, the English word *angst* does not mean exactly the same as its German source, but reflects those aspects of the meaning of the German *Angst* which are particularly striking from an Anglo point of view: its indeterminacy and its "existential nature". In German, one can speak of "Existenzangst" (cf. e.g. Jaeger 1971: 26) or of the "existentielle Angst" (cf. e.g. Nuss 1993: 189) and "existentielle Ängste" (plural; see e.g. *Langenscheidt's Großwörterbuch* 1993: 308). In English, the loan word *angst* seems to have absorbed the meaning of these collocations, and seems to refer inherently to an "existential *Angst*" ("existentielle Angst") rather than to *Angst* as such. English *angst* reflects the links between the German *Angst* in general and existential insecurities and concerns – links extensively explored by German philosophers, and in particular, by Martin Heidegger.

In David Lodge's novel *Therapy* (1996: 43) the following dialogue takes place:

> "Cheers, darling. How's the knee?"
> I told her it had given me one bad twinge today, in the train.

123

"And how's the Angst?"

"What's that?"

"Oh, come, sweetheart! Don't pretend you don't know what Angst is. German for anxiety. Or is it anguish?"

"Don't ask me," I said. "You know I'm hopeless at languages."

Later on, the hero is reminded of this dialogue and of the question "How's the Angst?" and he looks the word up (pp. 63–9).

I was slightly surprised to find it in my English dictionary: 1. *An acute but unspecific sense of anxiety or remorse.* 2. *(In Existentialist philosophy) the dread caused by man's awareness that his future is not determined, but must be freely chosen.* I didn't fully understand the second definition – philosophy is one of the bigger blank spots in my education. But I felt a little shiver of recognition at the word "dread". It sounds more like what I suffer than "anxiety". Anxiety sounds trivial, somehow. You can feel anxious about catching a train, or missing the post. I suppose that's why we've borrowed the German word. *Angst* has a sombre resonance to it, and you make a kind of grimace of pain as you pronounce it.

Let us begin our exploration of the German *Angst* by comparing the use of *Angst* and *Furcht*. In German speech, *Angst*, in contrast to *Furcht*, is a very common word. According to a frequency dictionary of spoken German (Ruoff, 1981), *Angst* occurs 52 times in a corpus of half a million running words, whereas the verb *(sich) fürchten* occurs only 4 times, and the noun *Furcht* does not occur at all.

The main semantic difference between *Angst* and *Furcht* has undoubtedly to do with the basic "indeterminacy" of *Angst*, reflected in the fact that one can say *Ich habe Angst*, "I have *Angst*", without having to specify the reasons for that *Angst*, whereas one cannot normally say *Ich fürchte mich* (roughly "I am afraid") without specifying what one is afraid of. In English the sentence *I am afraid*, without a complement, is not unacceptable, but it sounds elliptical, and it invites the question "What are you afraid of?" But the German sentence *Ich habe Angst* does not sound elliptical at all, rather like the English sentence *I am depressed*. Of course a person's depression has some reasons, but the sentence *I am depressed* is perfectly self-contained semantically, without any further expansion.

*Angst*, one can say, is a "state", like depression, and the compound word *Angstzustand*, "a state of Angst", is commonly listed in German dictionaries. *Fear*, on the other hand (or being *afraid*), is not a "state", it is either a feeling, or a disposition to a feeling, linked with a thought about someone or something.

According to Bernard Nuss (1993: 193) a state of "Angst" was widespread in Germany in the seventies: "It was an epoch when millions of

Germans would say simply "Ich habe Angst", without even trying to specify the nature and cause of this *Angst*."[1]

According to Nuss, various specific justifications for that widely prevailing "Angst" could be offered, but they were all different expressions of the same underlying "Angst" rather than different underlying reasons; and those justifications were shifting:

> After the euphoria of the fifties and the sixties, there was a time when the Germans feared (had *Angst* of) everything possible: nuclear power, the oil sheiks, the unemployment, the Japanese, rockets, environmental pollution, the police state, the future . . . Every time one danger was overcome, another one would emerge and become entrenched in their mind (Nuss 1993: 193).[2]

Duden's (1972) dictionary of German defines *Angst* not only as "mit Beklemmung, Bedrückung, Erregung einhergehender Gefühlszustand [angesichts einer Gefahr]", ("an oppressive emotional state linked with nervous agitation") [in the face of a danger], but also as an "undeutliches Gefühl des Bedrohtseins", "a vague feeling of threat". The modifier "undeutliches" ("vague") again suggests some indeterminacy not so much of the feeling itself as of the perceived threat; at the same time, the characterization of *Angst* as "an emotional state" suggests an emphasis on what is happening to the experiencer rather than on the experiencer's thoughts directed towards some particular target.

Indeed, according to a number of commentators, the German *Angst* is, essentially, a "nameless *Angst*", or *Angst* linked with the human condition as such rather than with any specific dangers. Nuss (1993: 188–9) writes about it as follows (with reference to two characteristic figures from German literature, Georg Büchner's Lenz and Woyzeck):

> Uncertainty generates *Angst*. The more Germans are confronted with uncertainties, the more reason they discover to be worried. In this way, the feeling of *Angst* spreads further and further and engenders in some people a permanent state of *Angst*. It is nourished by a thousand trifles which gradually swell to form a constant sense of threat, against which it is impossible to struggle.
>
> For a German, the endless silence, which chokes Lenz, and the horror experienced by Woyzeck, express, in a striking way, the nameless *Angst* that is felt by every human being and that one can never quite grasp. It is omni-present, because everything represents a danger, so that one is nowhere really safe. The German fears not so much physical danger (he is by nature brave), or the various vicissitudes of life . . . as the unknown. Not to know what will happen, not to know clearly what problem one has to deal with, not to know one's opponent, this evokes much more *Angst* in him than a real danger.[3]

The key elements suggested by Nuss' (1993) analysis of *Angst* have to do with the unknown (*das Unbekannte*) and with the ubiquity and inescapability of (undefined and obscure) danger. Using the metalanguage of universal semantic primitives, we could represent these elements in the form of the following prototypical thoughts:

> I don't know what will happen
> bad things can always happen to me

## 2 Heidegger's analysis of "Angst"

The diffuse, indeterminate expectations of "bad things" in general, linked with the German *Angst* have been given a particularly strong emphasis in the writings of the German existentialist philosopher Martin Heidegger, who complained that the concepts "Angst" and "Furcht" are usually not distinguished from one another and that "als Angst bezeichnet wird, was Furcht ist, und Furcht genannt wird, was den Charakter der Angst hat" ("Furcht is described as Angst, and *Angst* is called *Furcht*"; Heidegger 1953[1926]: 185). In Heidegger's own philosophy – strongly influenced by that of the Danish philosopher Søren Kierkegaard – the concept of "Angst" plays a particularly important role, as does also the distinction between "Angst" and "Furcht". (On this point, too, Heidegger followed Kierkegaard, for whom the concept of "Angst", embodied in the Danish word *angest*, played an essential role.)

> The only threatening which can be "fearsome" and which gets discovered in fear, always comes from entities within-the-world . . .
> *That in the face of which one has anxiety* [das Wovor der Angst] *is Being-in-the-world as such.* What is the difference phenomenally between that in the face of which anxiety [*Angst*] is anxious [*sich ängstet*] and that in the face of which fear is afraid? That in the face of which one has anxiety [*Angst*] is not an entity within-the-world. Thus it is essentially incapable of having an involvement. This threatening does not have the character of a definite detrimentality which reaches what is threatened, and which reaches it with definite regard to a special factical potentiality-for-Being. That in the face of which one is anxious [*Angst*] is completely indefinite. Not only does this indefiniteness leave factically undecided which entity within-the-world is threatening us, but it also tells us that entities within-the-world are not "relevant" at all. Nothing which is ready-to-hand or present-at-hand within the world functions as that in the face of which anxiety [*Angst*] is anxious. Here the totality of involvements of the ready-to-hand and the present-at-hand discovered within-the-world, is, as such, of no consequence; it collapses into itself; the world has the character of completely lacking significance. In anxiety [Angst] one does not encounter this thing or that thing which, as something threatening, must have an involvement (Heidegger 1962[1926]: 230–1).[4]

The key elements in Heidegger's theory of *Angst* are the "Unbestimmtheit" of the "Bedrohung" (that is, the "indeterminacy" of the "potential dangers"), and the independence of the state of "Angst" of anything that may actually happen: it is not the thought of any specific events (real or potential) which causes the state of "Angst", but the very nature of the human condition, the very fact of human existence "in the world".

If we wanted to translate Heidegger's ideas into the language of semantic primitives we could say, once again, that the underlying hidden thought on which "Angst" is based is this: "bad things can always happen to me". It is not the thought of some particular "bad things" which causes "Angst" but the deep-rooted sense that "bad things can always happen to me" (for they are inherent to "being-in-the-world"). What these things are is unknown and unknowable ("unbestimmt"). Heidegger's notion that the human existential condition consists in a "Un-zuhause-sein", a "not-being-at-home", can be loosely paraphrased by saying that the world is not a safe place and not a predictable, familiar place. This again can be reduced to the semantic components suggested earlier:

> I don't know what will happen
> bad things can always happen to me

Of course Heidegger's philosophical speculations were aimed at the "phenomenon of Angst" rather than at the German word *Angst* as such. It seems clear, however, that in his analysis Heidegger was guided, to some extent, by the meaning of the German word *Angst*, and by the German lexical distinction between *Angst* and *Furcht* (as Kierkegaard was guided by the meaning of the Danish word *angest*, and by the lexical distinction between *angest* and *frygt*).

It should be added that Heidegger is by no means the only German philosopher for whom "Angst" is an important concept. Furthermore, "Angst" plays an important role also in the writings of various German theologians, and theologians-cum-philosophers such as, for example, Paul Tillich. Since Tillich – a German refugee in America – wrote in English (polished, he says, by his American friends), he talked about "Angst" using the English word *anxiety*, but he was aware that his own use of *anxiety* was an extension modelled on the German (and Danish) *Angst*. For example, he wrote (1957: 34–5):

> Man is not only finite, as is every creature; he is also aware of his finitude. And this awareness is "anxiety." In the last decade the term "anxiety" has become associated with the German and Danish word *Angst*, which itself is derived from the Latin *angustiae*, "narrows." Through Søren Kierkegaard the word *Angst* has become a central

concept of existentialism. It expresses the awareness of being finite, of being a mixture of being and non-being, or of being threatened by non-being. All creatures are driven by anxiety; for finitude and anxiety are the same. But in man freedom is united with anxiety. One could call man's freedom "freedom in anxiety" or "anxious freedom" (in German, *sich ängstigende Freiheit*).

But to what extent do Heidegger's (and other German philosophers' and theologians') speculations about "Angst" reflect the meaning of the German word *Angst* as it is used in everyday speech?

### 3 "Angst" in the language of psychology

Before we turn to the use of the German word *Angst* in everyday language, we should note that this word plays an important role in the language of psychology, and that German psychologists speak routinely about *Angstneurose* and *Angstpsychose*, using the word *Angst* in a sense very close to that attributed to it by Heidegger. As noted, for example, by the Duden dictionary (1972: 188): "in der Fachsprache der Psychologie wird öfter zwischen 'Angst' als unbegründet, nicht objektbezogen, und 'Furcht' als objekt-bezogen differenziert" [in the specialist language of psychology, a distinction is often drawn between "Angst" as something that has no reason and no object, and "Furcht" as something which does have an object'.]

In psychology, the distinction between *Angst* and *Furcht* (and also *Schreck*, "fright") was first introduced, and given a great deal of attention, by Freud, who clearly believed, however, that it was grounded in ordinary language: "I think *Angst* relates to the state and disregards the object, while *Furcht* draws attention precisely to the object. It seems that *Schreck* ... lays emphasis ... on the effect produced by a danger which is not met by any preparedness for anxiety [Angst]. We might say, therefore, that a person protects himself from fright by anxiety [*Angst*]". (Freud 1963[1917]: 395).

According to Duden (1972), however, the distinction between "Angst" and "Furcht" drawn by psychologists is not drawn by the ordinary language: "in der Allgemeinsprache ist die Differenzierung nicht üblich" ("in ordinary language there is no such differentiation").

But does this mean that in ordinary German there is no semantic difference between *Angst* and *Furcht* at all? And if there *is* a difference, is this difference quite unrelated to the distinctions drawn in the writings of Heidegger and in the technical language of psychology? Both these propositions seem inherently unlikely.

It is true that the differences between *Angst* and *Furcht* as used in everyday language are not as sharp as Heidegger's discussion might suggest, and that sometimes the two words seem to be used inter-changeably. For example, Ratinger (1968: 246–7) not only calls loneli-ness ("die Einsamkeit") "a region of *Angst*" ("die Region der Angst"), but also says that "the fear (Furcht) of loneliness is the *Angst* of a being that can only live together with others" ("die Furcht der Einsamkeit ist die Angst eines Wesens, das nur im Mitsein leben kann").

What is even more confusing is that in theoretical discussions *Furcht* can also be used to refer to existential fears unrelated to any particular dangers. Ratinger's discussion of *Furcht* is a good example of this:

> When a child goes alone at night through a forest in the dark, he is afraid, even if one demonstrates to him quite convincingly that he has nothing to fear. Once he is alone in the dark and feels utter loneliness, fear arises, the typical human fear, which is not a fear of something, but fear as such. A fear of something specific is basically harmless, it can be banished once one removes the object in question. For example, if someone is afraid of an aggressive dog, one can quickly straighten things out by putting the dog on a leash. Here we encounter some-thing much deeper: a person in a state of ultimate loneliness is afraid not of something specific that could be shown to be groundless; rather, he experiences the fear of loneliness, a mysterious exposure of his own being, which cannot be overcome by rational means (Ratinger 1968: 246).[5]

It is interesting to note, however, that even in this discussion of "objectless *Furcht*" Ratinger uses repeatedly the phrase "die Furcht der Einsamkeit" ("the fear of loneliness, the fear linked with loneliness"), whereas the word *Angst* appears throughout this discussion without modifiers, as simply *Angst*, not "die Angst der Einsamkeit".

In fact, in Ratinger's discussion of an "objectless *Furcht*" a specific thought *is* clearly present: "I am all alone" (in the case of the child, "it is dark and I am all alone"). Thus, *Furcht* may have no particular object and yet be linked with a specific thought (e.g. "I am all alone"). A semantic difference between *Furcht* and *Angst* is still possible, for *Angst* may have not only no particular object but also be linked with no specific thought. The fact that *Angst* is more readily used without modifiers than *Furcht* suggests that while both *Furcht* and *Angst* can be thought of as objectless they are nonetheless not synonymous.

It is also noteworthy that the word *Angst* (but not *Furcht*) appears in countless titles of popular books belonging to the self-help genre. Some examples among recent publications are:

1. Eugen Bisser 1986, *Überwindung der Lebensangst. Wege zu einem be-freienden Gottesbild. Erlösung von existentiellen Grundängsten.* ("Over-coming the *angst* of life. Ways to a liberating image of God.") Don Bosco Verlag.

2. Klaus Lange 1996, *Bevor du sterben willst, lebe! Auf der Reise nach innen verwandelt sich die Welt. Von Todessehnsucht, Krankheit, Schuldgefühlen, Angst und Einsamkeit zu Weite, Leichtigkeit, Freiheit und Vertrauen.* ("Before you die, live! During a journey inwards the world changes. From deathwishes, illness, feelings of guilt, *Angst*, and loneliness, to a feeling of space, lightness, freedom and trust.") Kreuz Verlag.
3. Verena Kast 1995, *Angst: Facetten eines Weges aus Angst und Symbiose.* ("*Angst*: ways out of *Angst* and symbiosis.") Munich: Deutscher Taschenbuch Verlag.
4. Jürgen Schutz (ed.) 1995, *Angst: Urgefühl.* ("*Angst*": a primeval feeling."). Munich: Deutscher Taschenbuch Verlag.
5. Gerhard Stöcker 1996, *Angst, laß nach! Wieder Lust am Leben finden. Umfangreicher Ratgeber bei allen Angstzuständen.* ("*Angst*, let go! How to find again joy of life. A comprehensive guide for all states of *Angst*.") Augsburg: Pattloch Verlag.

It would be difficult to maintain that titles of such books, aimed at the general reader, are totally divorced from the understanding of *Angst* in ordinary language. The fact that in everyday language, too, people can talk of "existential" *Angst* or "metaphysical" *Angst* confirms the close links between the technical and the everyday sense of the word. One example from a contemporary novel:

> Eine kleine metaphysische Angstwelle lief durch ihn hindurch. (Schwanitz 1995: 332)
> "A small metaphysical wave of *Angst* ran through him."

In fact, careful examination of linguistic evidence shows that in everyday speech *Angst* and *Furcht* do not have the same range of use (although their ranges overlap), and that the differences between their respective ranges are indeed related to the distinction drawn by Heidegger and by the technical language of psychologists. Let us review here some of these differences.

## 4 *Angst* in everyday language

In this section I will summarize, in the form of eleven points, the linguistic evidence for the everyday concept of *Angst* as outlined in this section.

1. As mentioned earlier, the expression *Angst haben* "to have *Angst*", is often used without any complements, as in the following example from a novel (Noll 1993: 104):

> Außerdem hatte ich grauenhafte Angst. Ich konnte mich im Augenblick überhaupt nicht zusammennehmen. "In addition I had a terrible *Angst*. I simply couldn't pull myself together."

Both the adjective *grauenhaft* ("terrible") and the following sentence indicate that the speaker is focussing on her inner state, and not on any thought about some particular danger. On the other hand, the noun *Furcht* or the verb *sich fürchten* are normally not used in this way. One can say "Ich habe Furcht vor dem Tod" ("I'm afraid of death") but hardly "Ich habe Furcht" or "Ich fürchte mich". With the non-reflexive verb *fürchten* an object is grammatically obligatory; with the reflexive verb *sich fürchten* an object is not obligatory in the same sense, but if this verb is used without an object the grounds for the feeling are usually made clear by an adverbial phrase or clause, as in Ratinger's own example about the child in the forest, or as in the following sentence from *Langenscheidt' Großwörterbuch* (1993):

> Das Kind fürchtet sich im Dunkeln.
> "The child is afraid in the dark."

It is also noteworthy that sentences with *Angst* are more acceptable than those with *Furcht* (or *sich fürchten*) in situations where the cause of the feeling is explicitly presented as unknown:

> Ich hatte Angst, ich wußte nicht wovor und warum.
> "I had *Angst*, I didn't know why or of what."

> ?Ich fürchtete mich, ich wußte nicht wovor und warum.
> "I was afraid, I didn't know why or of what."

Furthermore, *Angst* is often described as a subconscious feeling of which the experiencer herself (himself) is not even aware, as in the following sentence:

> Wie der Tod nicht aufhört zu existieren wenn wir nicht an ihn denken, so auch nicht die Angst. (Fritz Riemann, a motto in Schutz 1995.)
> "Just as death does not cease to exist when we don't think about it, neither does *Angst*."

2. The noun *Angst* is often used in the plural, and German dictionaries list expressions such as *in tausend Ängsten schweben* and cite many sentences with the plural form *Ängste*, both old and recent. For example:

> die Wolga hier hat nicht so viel der tropfen[6] als ängste mir an meine seele klopfen. (Fleming: 486, in Grimm and Grimm 1854: 358)
> "The river Wolga doesn't have as many drops of water as these *ängste* which come knocking at [the door of] my soul."

> Ihre Ängste vor einer verstrahlten . . . Umwelt sind eklatant (Wiener 1; in Duden 1993).
> "Their fears (Ängste) of a radioactively contaminated environment are striking."

The fact that *Angst* is frequently used in the plural and that people speak about "a thousand *Ängste*" supports the view that *Angst* focusses on a more general state of "Bedrohtsein" (existential threat) rather than on any specific danger. By contrast, *Furcht* is normally not used in the plural at all.

3. The dative construction "mir ist angst" or "mir ist angst und bange" suggests that the concept of "Angst" focusses on the subjective state of the experiencer rather than on the someone or something linked with that state (cf. e.g. "mir ist kalt" "I'm cold", "mir ist übel" "I feel sick").

4. The compound nouns *Angstzustand/Angstzustände* ("a state of *Angst*") and *Angstgefühl/Angstgefühle* ("a feeling/feelings of *Angst*") suggest that *Angst* is a state which can be considered independently of its external target.

5. The common adjective *angstvoll* (roughly, "nervous/anxious") and the adverb *ängstlich* ("nervously"), which describe a psychological state without reference to its cause or to the accompanying thought, point in the same direction. For example:

> Und so anmutig und jung, aufgeregt und angstvoll stieg ich am Samstag die ausgetretenen vier Steinstufen hinauf und schellte einfach an seiner Tür. (Noll, 1993: 53)
> "And so graceful and young, excited and nervous [*angstvoll*] I climbed on Saturday the worn out four stone steps in front of his door and simply rang the bell."

6. It is also interesting to compare the two symmetrical adjectives *furchtlos* ("fearless") and *angstfrei* ("angst-free"): the first implies that one does not betray "Furcht" (roughly, fear) in external situations in which other people could be expected to do so, whereas the second implies that one is, roughly speaking, free of anxieties, and does not refer to any external situations at all. It hardly needs to be added that *\*angstlos* and *\*furchtfrei* do not exist at all.

7. The imagery of *Angst*, often presenting it as "sitting inside" a person's body (e.g. *jemandem sitzt die Angst im Nacken*; see e.g. Duden 1972: 188) is consistent with the view of *Angst* as an enduring internal state, not necessarily linked with any conscious thoughts about particular targets.

8. The verb derived from *Angst, sich ängstigen*, refers clearly to a persistent state of inner turmoil (anxiety), rather than to a feeling linked with a particular thought. In this respect *sich ängstigen* can be compared to the English expression *to be anxious* rather than to the verb *to fear* or the expression *to be afraid of*. The clear difference in meaning between the verbs *sich ängstigen* and *sich fürchten* helps to see better the less obvious difference between the nouns *Angst* and *Furcht*: *sich ängstigen* implies that one can find no peace (because of an inner turmoil), whereas *sich fürchten* has no such implications and refers simply to a feeling caused

by a thought. The *WDG* (1964–77) dictionary of German cites, for example, the following sentence: "ein böser Traum hat mich beängstigt" ("a bad dream has brought *Angst* over me"). This sentence does not mean that the speaker is thinking about a dream and fears something because of this, but rather, that the dream itself has brought with it a certain mood and has set off a troubled inner state.

9. The word *Angsttraum* cited by many German dictionaries points in the same direction: it describes a certain type of dream, identifiable in terms of, roughly speaking, its mood, and not its content. Duden's (1972: 139) dictionary defines an *Angsttraum* as a "mit Ängsten verbundener Traum", "a dream linked with *Ängste* (plural)". The dictionary mentions the word *Alptraum* "nightmare" in this connection, but an *Alptraum* has a describable content (so much so that a real-life situation can be called, figuratively, an "Alptraum"), whereas an *Angsttraum* is quite vague (hence the plural *Ängste* in Duden's definition): it is an "atmospheric" kind of dream rather than a dream with a clear structure of events or thoughts.

10. The word *Angst* is more acceptable than *Furcht* in contexts where it is not clear at all what kinds of danger are being considered. For example, in the situation of anxiety (and related feelings) before an exam a sentence with the phrase *Angst haben* is much more acceptable than one with the verb *sich fürchten* (the noun *Furcht* is not acceptable in this context at all):

(a)  Er hatte Angst vor der Prüfung.
"He had *Angst* of the exam."
(b)  ?Er fürchtete sich vor der Prüfung.
"He was afraid of the exam."

If, however, the word *Prüfung* "exam" is replaced with the word *Hund* "dog" both *Angst haben* and *sich fürchten* are perfectly acceptable:

(c)  Er hatte Angst vor dem Hund.
(d)  Er fürchtete sich vor dem Hund.

Presumably, the reason is that in the case of a dog the nature of the danger is quite clear (one doesn't want to be bitten), whereas in the case of an exam, one doesn't know what will happen, and the situation is stressful even if one is not expecting to fail.

11. In situations in which the phrase *I'm afraid* can be used in English with reference to a known fact, in German only *ich fürchte* can be used, not *ich habe Angst*:

I'm afraid that's true.
Ich fürchte, das stimmt.
*Ich habe Angst, das stimmt.

## 5 Defining *Angst*

What, then, is the meaning of the word *Angst*? Is the definition suggested by Heidegger's speculations, or by the psychologists' use of the
term, acceptable for the everyday use of the word, or does it need to be
somehow modified, and, if so, how?

My own conclusion is that while the meaning of *Angst* in everyday
language is not identical with that of the *Angst* of psychologists and
philosophers, the core components are the same, and that basically the
distinction between *Angst* and *Furcht* drawn by Heidegger applies to
everyday language too. In support of this conclusion, I will first propose
two explications and then discuss the differences between them as well
as some apparent counterexamples. To facilitate the comparison, I have
put the distinguishing part of the two explications in capital letters.

*Angst* (e.g. *X hatte Angst vor dem Hund/vor der Prüfung*)
(a)  X felt something
(b)    sometimes a person thinks FOR SOME TIME:
(b')  "I DON'T KNOW WHAT WILL HAPPEN
(c)    MANY BAD THINGS can happen to me
(d)    I don't want these things to happen
(e)    I want to do something because of this if I can
(f)    I don't know what I can do"
(g)    because of this this person feels something bad FOR SOME
          TIME
(h)  X felt something like this

*Furcht* (e.g. *X fürchtete sich vor dem Hund/*vor der Prüfung*)
(a)  X felt something
(a')  BECAUSE X THOUGHT SOMETHING ABOUT SOMETHING
(b)    sometimes a person thinks ABOUT SOMETHING:
(c)    "SOMETHING BAD can happen to me BECAUSE OF THIS
(d)    I don't want this to happen
(e)    I want to do something because of this if I can
(f)    I don't know what I can do"
(g)    WHEN this person thinks this this person feels some-
          thing bad
(h)  X felt something like this
(h')  BECAUSE X THOUGHT SOMETHING LIKE THIS

If we now compare the explications of *Angst* and *Furcht*, we will note the following differences.

First, *Angst* is defined only via a prototypical scenario, and no thoughts are attributed to the experiencer: when one has *Angst* one feels LIKE a person does who thinks certain thoughts, and one doesn't necessarily think these thoughts oneself. This explains why one can feel *Angst* without knowing why one feels *Angst*. But one cannot feel *Furcht* without knowing what is the object of that *Furcht*, and so the explication of *Furcht* does attribute certain thoughts to the experiencer.

Second, the phrase MANY BAD THINGS in the explication of *Angst* differs from its counterpart SOMETHING in the explication of *Furcht*. This, too, accounts for the greater indeterminacy of *Angst* and for a more generalized sense of threat (*Bedrohtsein*); it also accounts for the use of the plural *Ängste*. It will be noticed that the phrasing "many bad things can happen", used in the explication of *Angst* proposed here, differs from the phrasing "something bad can always happen" used in the earlier discussion. This change has been introduced to cover the fact that while in its everyday sense, *Angst* is somewhat indeterminate ("*undeutlich*"), it is not quite as indeterminate as the philosopher's, or the psychologist's, "*Angst*". The word "always" implies an inescapable existential condition, the word "many" does not imply quite that, although it does go beyond the specificity of the singular ("something bad can happen to me").

Third, the subcomponent FOR SOME TIME in the explication of *Angst* accounts for its durative aspect, that is, for its "state-like" or "process-like" character.

Fourth, the explication of *Angst* includes the component I DON'T KNOW WHAT WILL HAPPEN, which accounts for the far greater uncertainty of *Angst* and for the inappropriateness of the word *Angst* in contexts where little or no uncertainty is involved.

Fifth, the distinction between BECAUSE OF in the explication of *Angst* and WHEN in the explication of *Furcht* accounts for the fact that in the case of *Angst*, a feeling can endure much longer than any underlying thoughts, whereas *Furcht* suggests a feeling coextensive in time with the thought. For example, it would be odd if the word *Angst* were replaced by *Furcht* in the following example (from Duden 1993):

> blieb Lea ein Gefühl der Bedrohung, das . . . Angst [?Furcht] auslöste.
> (Ossowski, Liebe ist kein Argument (Duden 1993: 357))
> "Lea was left with a sense of some threat, which triggered Angst."

Thus, *Angst* differs in meaning from *Furcht*, and everyday *Angst* is not as different from the *Angst* of psychologists as Duden's (1993) dictionary implies. It is true that *Angst* in the everyday sense of the word can, like *Furcht*, be "objektbezogen", e.g.

(i) Sie fürchtete, daß sie ihren Job verlieren würde.
"She feared that she would lose her job."

(ii) Sie hatte Angst, daß sie ihren Job verlieren würde.
"She had *Angst* that she would lose her job."

Is the use of *Angst* in sentences of this kind consistent with the analysis proposed here? Or should we rather admit that in this kind of context *Angst* (*haben*) and *fürchten* mean exactly the same?

Despite appearances, I do not think that the sentences mean exactly the same. Sentence (i) focusses on the thought: "I can lose my job", whereas sentence (ii) focusses on the subject's emotional state:

(i) "She thought: "I can lose my job"
when she thought this, she often felt something bad because of this

(ii) "She felt something bad (for some time)
she felt it because she thought: "I can lose my job"

Sentence (i) refers primarily to a thought, although it presents this thought as accompanied by a feeling. By contrast, sentence (ii) refers to a feeling, although this particular sentence presents this feeling as triggered by a thought. This focus on the emotional state is particularly clear in sentences in which the state is described in detail in various ways, as in the following two sentences:

> Gleichzeitig aber klapperten mir alle Knochen vor Angst, wenn ich an die Konsequenzen einer erfolgreichen Auferstehung dachte. (Noll 1993: 202)
> "At the same time all my bones rattled with fear [*Angst*], when I thought about the consequences of a successful resuscitation."

> Ich war halbtot vor Angst, daß auch mein Koffer inspiziert würde. (Noll 1993: 207)
> "I was half-dead with fear [*Angst*] that my suitcase too could be inspected."

It is true, then, that in everyday speech *Angst* can be presented as linked with a particular thought, that is as something that is "objekt-bezogen"; but when it *is* linked with a particular thought, *Angst* can still be thought of as a particular emotional state – a kind of state that is linked with uncertainty and with a sense of vulnerability.

In some contexts, when the feeling is linked with a specific thought, the difference between *Angst* and *Furcht* doesn't seem to matter much and native speakers may not be immediately aware of it. But there are many other contexts where the difference clearly does matter, and the linguistic facts discussed in this chapter provide sufficient evidence for different conceptual structures.

The fact that *Angst* is a basic German word (whereas *Furcht* is not) shows that the conceptualization encoded in *Angst* is particularly salient in German culture. This is consistent with the special place given to "Angst" in German philosophy and psychology and also with the special importance attached to this concept both by German writers (recall book titles such as *Angst: Urgefühl*, "Angst: a primeval feeling") and by outsiders commenting on German culture in a comparative perspective.

### 6 The German *Angst* in a comparative perspective

If one looks at the concept of "Angst" and its salience in German culture from a cross-linguistic and cross-cultural point of view one can't help being baffled by it. Most, if not all, languages appear to have a "basic" emotion term linked with the thought "something bad can/will happen to me" (cf. chapter 7). For example, English has the noun *fear* (and the adjective phrase *to be afraid*); French, the noun *peur* (and the verbal expression *avoir peur*); Italian, the noun *paura* (and the verbal expression *avere paura*); Spanish, the noun *miedo* (and the verbal expression *tener miedo*); Russian, the noun *strax* (and the verb *bojat'sja*); and so on.

In German, the noun closest in meaning to those listed above is *Furcht*, and the verb, *sich fürchten*. One might have expected, therefore, that these words would play a comparable role in German to that played by their closest semantic equivalents in the other languages mentioned. In fact, of course, this is not the case.

German–English dictionaries usually link the German word *Angst* with the English word *anxiety* or with a multi-word gloss starting with the word *anxiety*. On the other hand, *Furcht* is usually glossed with the word *fear*, or with a sequence of alternative glosses headed by *fear*. Conversely, the English word *anxiety* is normally glossed by English–German dictionaries with the word *Angst*, or with a series of glosses starting with *Angst*, while *fear* is glossed with the word *Furcht*, or with a series of glosses starting with *Furcht*. Similarly, dictionaries usually pair *Angst* not with *peur, paura, miedo*, or *strax*, but rather with *angoisse, ansia*, or *trevoga*, that is, with words closer in meaning to the English *anxiety* than to the English *fear*.

In a sense, then, one might say that the semantic distinction between *Furcht* and *Angst* drawn by the German lexicon is analogous to the distinctions drawn between *fear* and *anxiety* by English, between *peur* and *angoisse* by French, or between *strax* and *trevoga* by Russian. As we will discuss later, the meanings of the words in question are not identical, but the distinctions can nonetheless be said to be broadly analogous; and it is interesting to note that these distinctions have often been treated in the literature as identical, and also that considerable importance has been attached to them – by philosophers, psychologists, historians, and others.

For example, the eminent French historian Jean Delumeau (1978: 15) draws what he calls a fundamental distinction ("la distinction fondamentale") between "peur" and "angoisse" (in the English version, "fear" and "anxiety"), which he links with a distinction between specific fears ("les peurs particulières") and a climate of fear ("un climat de peur"). In Delumeau's view, the fact that the accumulation of various collective fears in Europe from the time of the Great Plague to the religious wars created a climate of fear, provides an important clue to the understanding of the history of Western civilization.

> "Specific fears": that is, "named fears". Here, the distinction established by psychiatry at the level of the individual between fear and anxiety, confused by traditional psychology, may become applicable on a collective level. For it is a matter of two poles around which words and mental facts gravitate which are both related and yet different. Apprehension, fright, terror, dread belong more to fear [*la peur*]; uneasiness, worry, melancholy, more to anxiety [*l'angoisse*]. The former is related to something known, the latter to the unknown.
>
> Fear has a specific object which one can confront. Anxiety does not and it is experienced as a painful expectation of a danger all the more frightful for not being clearly identified: it is a feeling of global insecurity. Consequently, it is more difficult to bear than fear . . . Since it is impossible to preserve one's internal balance when confronted over a period with a floating anxiety which is infinite and unidentifiable, it is necessary for a person to transform it and to fragment it into specific fears. "The human spirit manufactures fear permanently" in order to avoid a morbid anxiety which would lead to the annihilation of the self. (*Delumeau 1978: 15–16*)[7]

But if the conceptual distinction between, roughly speaking, *angoisse* (anxiety) and *peur* (fear) is so important (in philosophy, in psychology, and in history), how is it possible that a concept closer to *angoisse* (namely, "Angst") has come to occupy such an important place in German language and culture, over and above the concept of "Furcht", given that the opposite appears to be the case in most other languages and cultures, in Europe and elsewhere? Once again, we must conclude that there is something special about the German "Angst", something, therefore, that requires a special explanation.

I believe that a key to such an explanation can be found in the observation that while the German situation is indeed special (as compared with, for example, French, Italian, Spanish, or Russian), it is apparently not unique in Europe: an analogous situation appears to obtain in Danish, and perhaps in the other Scandinavian languages as well. The common denominator appears to be provided by the predominant religious tradition: the countries in whose languages a concept closer to a cross between "anxiety" and "fear" appears to be more salient than a concept closer to simply "fear" or "fright" are all predominantly Lutheran. Since, however, I cannot engage here in a detailed discussion of the relevant lexical data from Scandinavian languages, I will simply submit that it may pay to explore the possibility of there being a link between "Angst" (the German *Angst*) and the language and thought of Martin Luther; and in what follows I will try to do so.

## 7 Luther's influence on the German language

Luther's contemporary, Erasmus Alberus, said that Luther was "the father of the German language" (*"linguae Germanicae parens"*), and to a large extent this opinion has been shared by later generations. It is generally accepted that the newly invented printing press played an essential role in the popularization of Luther's writings, which "achieved a dissemination beyond anything that had ever happened before" (Keller 1978: 355). Luther wrote and wrote, the presses printed and printed, and the nation read, studied, and often learnt by heart – thus absorbing both the message and the language.

> In 1520 his famous treatises *An den christlichen Adel deutscher Nation* and *Von der Freiheit eines Christenmenschen* started a flood of German theological writing. Tracts, treatises, sermons, missives, dialogues, and pamphlets of abuse, condemnation and exhortation, poured from the printing presses. And there was above all else: the German Bible. The history of the German language took a new turn: the printed German written language reached every corner of the German-speaking countries and influenced and shaped the political destiny of the entire nation. (Keller 1978: 356)

One of the first serious grammars of German, written by Johannes Clajus and published in Leipzig in 1578, was based on Luther's writings: *Grammatica Germanicae linguae ex bibliis Lutheri Germanicis et aliis eius libris collecta*, and the influence of Luther's writings on the standardization of the German literary language and the development of

German literature is indisputable. To quote one German scholar (Bach 1965: 259–60):

> A work of the linguistic power of Luther's Bible which circulated in many thousands of copies throughout Germany, including the Catholic regions, and which coming at a time of rapidly expanding literacy was not only read but often also learnt by heart. Such a work could offer a firmer basis for a common national language than the languages of the state administration or the printing offices. (Bach 1965: 259–60)[8]

According to Jacob Grimm, often proclaimed to be the founder of German linguistics, the later flowering of German literature was possible only thanks to Luther's work, and the tenor of Grimm's remarks is typical of that of other authoritative commentators as well:

> Because of its almost miraculous purity and because of its deep influence, Luther's German must be considered the core and the fundament of the new German language. Whatever can be said to have nursed this language, whatever rejuvenated it so that a new flowering of poetry could result – this we owe to nobody more than to Luther. (Grimm 1882[1822]: 11; quoted in Erikson 1958: 227)

What had the greatest impact was – it is widely accepted – Luther's translation of the Bible, on which were also based the Catholic translations of Hieronymus Emser, Johann Eck, and Johann Dietenberger. The assessment given by Chambers and Wilkie's (1970: 42) *Short History of the German Language* illustrates well the general opinion on this point:

> the richness of vocabulary, the felicity of idiom, and the vigour and directness of style which characterize all his works – Bible and hymns, catechism and sermons, expository and polemical tracts – mark a new beginning in the development of the German language. In particular, his masterly translation of the Bible, which in the four intervening centuries has been read and studied and learnt by heart more than any other German book, has had a profound and incalculable stylistic influence – to say nothing of its spiritual effect – on every generation of speakers and writers until our own day.

Luther's translation of the Bible is also widely believed to have determined, to a large extent, the lexicon of the standard language. Its impact was not only lexical but also semantic. Significantly, "Many of Luther's own personal word creations have become part of the standard vocabulary" (Keller 1978: 449). Keller notes also new meanings due to Luther's influence, commenting that "The semantic aspect of the lexicon tends to reflect the great cultural and spiritual movements of an age as well as internal structural changes on the plane of meaning" (p. 452).

What is particularly interesting from the point of view of the history of "Angst", is that the expression *angst und bange* is listed as one of those whose spread was influenced by Luther, alongside some other expressions referring to emotions, such as *Hoffnung und Zuversicht* ("hope and confidence") and *bekümmern und vexieren* ("afflict and disturb") (Keller 1978: 449). Luther's creativity and impact in the area of the language of emotions has also been noted by other writers. For example, Chambers and Wilkie (1970: 42) comment that "Among his many gifts he had a remarkable feeling for the manifold variety of language and for its emotional nuances".

Clearly Luther's possible influence on the semantic history of "Angst" should be considered against the background of this general assessment of the role of his writings in general.

## 8 Eschatological anxieties of Luther's times

It seems to be generally accepted that – like many of his contemporaries – Luther believed in, and lived in imminent expectation of, the end of the world and the "Last Judgment". Discussing "the great eschatological anxieties" of the epoch, which "had a profound impact on the collective mentality", the eminent "historian of fear", Jean Delumeau (1978: 211) quotes Hugo Wölflin's observation, made in connection with Dürer's works, that a sense of the end of the world was at that time present in everyone's mind, and he observes:

> The birth of the Protestant Reform cannot be understood if it is not placed in the atmosphere of impending Doomsday which existed at the time in Europe and especially in Germany . . . Luther was haunted by the idea.

Like many other writers, Delumeau notes that "Luther's enormous popularity strengthened the conviction, already widely held, that the end of the world was near" (p. 216), and he discusses the key role of the invention of print in this regard:

> Luther . . . believed in the imminence of the Last Judgement; and the printing presses spread his works so widely that he is certainly one of the key contributors to the general expansion of eschatological fears, at least in the countries which opted for protestantism. (p. 210)

Discussing the colossal popularity of Luther's Bible and the impact of Dürer's apocalyptic engravings which illustrated it, Delumeau (1978: 210) points in particular to the conjunction of the planets in 1524 and 1525, which created a collective panic and alarmed both Luther and

Dürer, and he observes that the Protestant Reform was both an outcome of the deep eschatological ferment of the times and an important factor in its growth and expansion.

Thus, while eschatological fears were common in Europe in the 16th century, and the beginning of the 17th century, they were especially strong in Protestant countries and, in particular, in Germany. Delumeau (1978: 228) notes, for example, that of the 89 eschatological works included in Georg Draudius' catalogue in Frankfurt in 1625, only one was written by a Catholic author, whereas 68 were Lutheran, and 20 were by Calvinist authors.

In another work, Delumeau (1990: 527) points out that "throughout the sixteenth century, Lutheran discourse was laced with eschatological forecasts", and that, for example, Osiander "wrote an entire book (published in 1544) to demonstrate that by any method of calculation, the end of the world can be fixed for no later than 1672". It is this belief in the approaching end of the world which caused "the Protestants' indignant rejection of Pope Gregory XIII's calendar reform, which to them proved that the Pope did not believe in the end of the world" (p. 527).

Delumeau (1978) notes also that what applied to the fear of Judgment Day applied also to the (closely related) fear of Satan. "In Luther, there lived both a fear of the devil and a certainty that the final cataclysm was already on the horizon" (1978: 237), and the printing presses spread these fears both in learned volumes and in innumerable popular publications. The very success of Luther's works ensured that "Dr Martin communicated his fear of the devil to hundreds upon hundreds of thousands of readers" (1978: 239). As a result (asks Delumeau rhetorically), "how could have Germany of the sixteenth and beginning of seventeenth centuries not trembled from those two interrelated terrors?" (1978: 237). And thus, "demonic literature" replaced in 16th century Germany the popular medieval genre of the lives of the saints (1978: 239). It has been calculated (he reports) that in one decade 1560–70 one hundred thousand copies of works on the demon world were released in Germany, and that in the last twelve years of the century the story of Faust alone went through no less than 24 editions.

Delumeau points out in this connection a comment made in 1561 by a contemporary witness, André Musculus, who observed that "In no country of the world does the devil exercise a more tyrannical power than in Germany" (1978: 240). In the light of such observations, it seems remarkably fitting that the legend of Faust, born in Germany, should have come to occupy such a central and symbolic place in German culture.

## 9 The meaning of *Angst* in Luther's writings

Before we can assess Luther's impact on the formation and/or spread of the modern German concept of "Angst" we need to know how exactly Luther used the word *Angst*.

The "Theological German Vocabulary" based on quotations from Luther's Bible (Mosse 1955) glosses *Angst* as "anxiety, fear, distress", and includes as "synonyms" *die Furcht* "fear", *die Herzensangst* "the *Angst* of the heart", and *die Seelenangst* "the *Angst* of the soul".

This gloss suggests that the meaning of *Angst* in Luther's writings was probably different from its present-day meaning. For example, *Harrap's German and English Dictionary* (1963) glosses *Angst* (in English) as "fear, fright, dread; mental anguish; anxiety; Psy: angst". The range of suggested senses is similar, but the focus seems to have shifted from something more like "anxiety" and "distress" to something more like "fear". This impression is confirmed by the fact that earlier German dictionaries tend to emphasize anxiety in the first instance: for example, *Flügel's Complete Dictionary of the German and English Language* (1845: 32) glosses *Angst* as "anguish; anxiety; agony; pangs (of death); fear, terror" (with "fear" at the end rather than at the beginning); and Grimm and Grimm's (1854: vol. 1, p. 358) dictionary entry on *Angst* reads: "*angst* ist nicht bloss mutlosigkeit, sondern quälende sorge, zweifelnder, beengender zustand überhaupt" ("*Angst* is not just a lack of courage but tormenting worry, and a general state of oppressive doubt").

Some modern German dictionaries posit two separate meanings for *Angst*, one focussed more on a vague state of anxiety, and another, closer to "fear" (as in the English word *fear* or in the German word *Furcht*). For example, *Langenscheidt's Großwörterbuch* (1993) offers the following two definitions of *Angst* (supported by a putative difference in grammar):

> 1. *Angst* (pl. *Ängste*): Zustand von jemandem, der bedroht wird oder sich in Gefahr befindet ("a state of someone who is threatened or finds himself in danger").
> 2. *Angst* (only Sg.): die ernsthafte Sorge, daß jemandem etwas Schlimmes passiert, daß man jemanden/etwas verliert ("a serious worry that something bad will happen to one, that one will lose someone or something").

While both these putative meanings refer, in their own way, to the thought: "something bad will happen to me", the first postulated meaning focusses on the experiencer's state, whereas the second focusses more on the thought itself and the feeling caused by it.

But in Luther's writings, *Angst* is not invariably linked with the thought "something bad will/can happen to me" and in his translation of the Bible *Angst* is not used to translate the Latin words *timor* (noun) and *temere* (verb) or the Greek words *phobos* (noun), *phobeomai* (verb) (roughly, "fear"). Instead, Luther uses for this purpose the noun *Furcht*, and the verb *sich fürchten* (and in some contexts, *erschrecken*). Some examples:

1. Fürchte dich nicht, Maria.(Lk. 1, 30, Luther NT, p. 131)
   Do not be afraid, Mary (NEB, p. 93)
   ne timeas, Maria! (NTL, p. 152)
   mē phobou, Mariam (GENT, p. 151)

2. Sie fürchteten sich aber (Lk. 8, 25, Luther NT, p. 155)
   In fear and astonishment they said to one another (NEB, p. 111)
   timentes (NTL, p.182)
   phobetentes (GENT, p.182)

3. Fürchte dich nicht, du Tochter Zion! (John. 12,15, Luther NT, p. 240)
   Fear no more, daughter of Zion (NEB, p. 175)
   Noli timere (NTL, p.291)
   mē phobou (GENT, p. 291)

4. Es kam über alle Seelen Furcht an (Act. Ap. 2, 43, Luther NT, p. 269)
   a sense of awe was everywhere (NEB, p. 200)
   Fiebat autem omni animae timor (NTL, p. 326)
   egineto de pasē psykhē phobos (GENT, p. 326)

Furthermore, Luther uses consistently the word *Furcht (die Furcht Gottes, die Furcht des Herrn, Gottesfurcht)* for the "fear of God" (Mosse 1955: 46).

Thus, the Latin word *timor* and the Greek *phobos* were normally translated in Luther's Bible by *Furcht*, not by *Angst*. *Angst* was normally used to translate other words: the Latin words *pressura, angustia* and *tribulatio*, and the Greek words *stenoxoria, tlipsis,* and *synokhē*, all of which had meanings corresponding, roughly, to those of English words such as *affliction* or *distress*. Some examples:

*Pressura*
1. In der Welt habt ihr Angst (Joh 16, 33, Luther NT, p. 251)
   In the world you will have trouble (NEB, p. 183)
   In mundo pressuram habetis (NTL, p. 304)
   Greek: *tlipsis* (GENT, p. 304)

2. Ein Weib, wenn sie gebiert, so hat sie Traurigkeit, denn ihre Stunde ist gekommen. Wenn sie aber das Kind geboren hat, denkt sie nicht mehr an die Angst um der Freude willen, daß ein Mensch zur Welt geboren ist. (Joh. 16, 21, Luther, NT p. 250)

A woman in labour is in pain because her time has come; but when the child is born she forgets the anguish in her joy that a man has been born into the world. (NEB, p. 182)

Mulier, cum parit, tristitiam habet, quia venit hora eius; cum autem pepererit puerum, iam non meminit pressurae propter gaudium quia natus est homo in mundum. (NTL, p. 302)

Greek: *tlipsis* (GENT, p. 303)

*Angustia*

3. Wer will uns scheiden von der Liebe Gottes? Trübsal oder Angst oder Verfolgung . . . ? (Rom. 8, 35, Luther NT, p. 354)

Then what can separate us from the love of Christ? Can affliction or hardship? (NEB, p. 267)

Quis nos separabit a caritate Christi? Tribulatio an angustia? (NTL p.424)

Greek: *tlipsis* (GENT, p. 424)

4. Den ich schrieb euch aus grosser Trübsal und Angst des Herzens mit viel Tränen. (II Kor. 2, 4, Luther NT, p. 402)

That letter I sent you came out of great distress and anxiety; how many tears I shed as I wrote it! (NEB, p. 305)

Nam ex multa tribulatione et angustia cordis scripsi vobis per multas lacrimas. (NTL, p. 475)

Greek: *synokhē* (GENT, p. 475)

5. Die Angst meines Herzens ist gross; führe mich aus meinen Nöten! (Psalm 25:17; Luther, Werke vol. 10/1, p. 176)

The troubles of my heart have enlarged,
Oh bring me out of my distresses. (NKJV, p. 549)

Tribulationes cordis mei multiplicatae sunt, de necessitatibus meis erue me. (Luther, Werke, vol. 10/2, p. 205)

*Tribulatio*

6. Wenn mir angst ist, so ruffe ich den HERRN an, und schrey zu meinem Gott, so erhöret er meine stim von seinem Tempel, und mein geschrey kompt fur in zu seinen Ohren.

(Psalm 18, 6: Luther, Werke, vol. 10/1, p. 149)
In my distress I called upon the LORD,
And cried out to my God;
He heard my voice from his temple,
And my cry came before him, even to his ears. (NKJV,
p. 545)
In tribulatione mea inuocaui Dominum, et ad Deum meum
clamaui. Et exaudiuit de templo sancto suo uocem meam, et
clamor meus in conspectu eius introiuit in aures eius. (Lu-
ther, Werke, vol. 10/2, p. 201)

Looking at the semantics of the word *Angst* in a broader historical
perspective, it would seem that Luther constitutes a turning point in a
shift from a meaning close to "distress" and essentially unrelated to
"fear" (or "Furcht") to a meaning much closer to "fear" (or "Furcht"),
though still different from it and bearing distinct traces of the earlier
meaning.

Schematically the history of *Angst* can be rendered in three stages:

1. Old High German: *Angst* means (according to the *Althochdeutsches
Wörterbuch* (1968)) "seelische Bedrängnis, Erschütterung", that is, "affliction, anguish" (*Gegensatz zum Begriff des "Friedens"*, an opposite of
the concept "peace"); "Sorge, quälende innere Unruhe" ("a worry, a
tormenting inner turmoil, anxiety"); "Leid, schmerzvolle Bedrückung"
("suffering, painful oppressive feeling").

2. Luther's language: *Angst* seems to mean, essentially, the same as in
Old and Middle High German (and is used for translating *pressura,
angustia,* or *tlipsis* "affliction", rather than *timor* or *phobos* "fear"), but is
often used in contexts suggesting anxiety about the future, and therefore shifts – in connotations if not in actual meaning – in the direction of
"fear" (or *Furcht*).

3. Present-day language: *Angst* has lost its original meaning of, roughly
speaking, "distress, inner turmoil, anguish", and has come closer to
"fear" (or *Furcht*), preserving, however, some components of the older
meaning.

Since *Angst* has come to mean something closer to "fear" (*timor/
phobos*) than to "affliction" (*pressura/tlipsis*), it is hardly surprising that
in contemporary (late twentieth century) German translations of the
Bible *Angst* has often been used as a translation equivalent of the Latin
*timor* and the Greek *phobos*, that is to say, in passages in which Luther
used *Furcht*. Two examples:

Ich fürchtete mich vor dir, denn du bist ein harter Mann. (Luke 19, 21, Luther NT, p. 189)
Ich hatte nämlich Angst vor dir, weil du ein strenger Mann bist. (NGÜ(L), p. 73)
I was afraid of you, because you are a hard man. (NEB, p. 135)

Und da ihn die Jünger sahen auf dem Meer gehen, erschraken sie und sprachen: Es ist ein Gespenst! und schrien vor Furcht. (Matt. 14, 26, Luther NT, p. 43)
Als sie ihn auf dem Wasser gehen sahen, wurden sie von Furcht gepackt.
"Es ist ein Gespenst!" riefen sie und schrien vor Angst. (NGÜ(M), p. 40).
When the disciples saw him walking on the lake they were so shaken that they cried out in terror: "It is a ghost!" (NEB, p. 27)

But given the central role that Luther's translation of the Bible played in German culture, it is hardly surprising that his use of the word *Angst* has also found its way into modern translations, and that in these translations, too, one often finds the word *Angst* in contexts where, for example, in English translations *anxiety*, *distress*, or *trouble* (rather than *fear*) are used (and in French translations, *l'angoisse* rather than *peur*). One example, from Psalm 25 (17):

Die Angst meines Herzens ist gross:
führe mich aus meinen Nöten! (Luther, Werke, vol. 10/1, p. 176)

Mein Herz wird immer mehr von Angst gequält; befreie mich von jedem Druck! (*Die Bibel*, p. 499)

The troubles of my heart have enlarged,
Oh bring me out of my distresses. (NKJV, p. 549)

Mes angoisses m'envahissent;
dégage-moi de mes tourments. (*La Bible*, 1988, p. 813)

We can say, then, that in modern German translations of the Bible the word *Angst* replaces two different words from Luther's Bible, which for Luther had very different meanings: *Angst* ("affliction/distress") and *Furcht* ("fear"). But the meaning of this new word *Angst* doesn't correspond exactly to either of those two words (as they were used by Luther). Rather, being a descendant of the two, it is a new concept, whose identity reflects its complex – and unique – past.

Most importantly, what can be said about *Angst* as used in modern German translations of the Bible, can also be said about its use in contemporary German language in general: being a historical descendant of *Angst* "affliction/distress", which has drifted in the direction of *Furcht* "fear", the modern German *Angst* is a new concept, whose identity reflects its past.

## 10 Martin Luther's inner life and its possible impact on the history of *Angst*

Erich Fromm's famous – and admittedly hostile – characterization of Luther saw the key to his personality as lying in "Angst" – and in the quest for something that could quench it. According to Fromm (1980a [1941]), "he [Luther] was a man driven to despair, anxiety and doubt [*Angst und Zweifel*] and at the same time by . . . an ardent wish for certainty" (1980a[1941]: 65). His whole attitude towards the world was "one of anxiety and hatred" (1980a[1941]: 66), and his "need to conquer the unbearable doubt" led him to a "compulsive quest for certainty" (1980a[1941]: 66). "He was tortured by doubts as only a compulsive character can be, and was constantly seeking for something which would give him inner security and relieve him from this torture of uncertainty . . . His whole being was pervaded by fear, doubt [*Angst und Zweifel*] and inner isolation, and on this personal basis he was to become the champion of social groups which were in a very similar position psychologically" (1980a[1941]: 56).

Other writers on the subject don't necessarily attribute to Luther "hatred towards the world", but they do seem to agree with Fromm as far as "anxiety" is concerned. Dalbiez (1974) not only attributes to him a "neurose d'angoisse très grave" (p. 332; "a serious anxiety neurosis") linked with "l'angoisse morbide de culpabilité" ("a morbid guilt anxiety") and "un sentiment morbide de culpabilité d'une extreme violence" (p. 12; "a morbid sense of guilt") but goes so far as to "sum up" Luther in the words "pour moi, Luther n'est qu'angoisse" (p. 24; "for me Luther is nothing but anxiety").

The most striking pieces of evidence adduced by Dalbiez include the description of Luther's acute anxiety attacks given by his fellow reformer Philip Melanchton, the other famous *"praeceptor Germaniae"*, ("teacher of Germany"), Luther's own vivid description of states of anxiety caused by a sense of sinfulness, and the record of his suicidal tendencies (related to the same sense of sinfulness) contained in Luther's *Tischreden* and other writings. Thus, Melanchton (1939: 158) reports:

> Often, when he was thinking attentively about the wrath of God, or about some startling examples of divine punishment, he would be

suddenly struck by such terror as to almost lose consciousness. I myself have seen him suddenly struck by such consternation whilst taking part in some doctrinal debate, that he had to go to an adjacent room to lie down, where he would pray and intermittently repeat: "God has locked all people in sin in order to show mercy to everyone". He first experienced this intense terror in the year when a friend of his was killed in an accident . . .

In the meantime, he pored over the sources of divine doctrines, the writings of the prophets and apostles, in order to better understand God's will and to nourish his fear and his faith with solid testimony. He was impelled to undertake this study by his sufferings and his fears.

Luther's own description of anxiety reads as follows:

I, too, have known a man who said he often suffered great affliction, very briefly but with such infernal intensity that neither tongue nor pen could describe it, nor any who had not experienced it believe it; had these sufferings been yet more intense or had they lasted half an hour or even one tenth of an hour, the man would have perished and his bones would have turned into ashes.

God would appear then to be terribly angry, and with him, the whole creation. And then there would be no escape, no consolation, neither inside nor outside, but only this universal accusation. And then the man would say, crying, this verse: "I've been rejected far from your eyes". And he wouldn't even dare to say: "God, don't punish me in your fury" (Ps. VI, 7). At this moment, mirabile dictu, the soul cannot believe that it can never be redeemed or that the punishment can never be completed. And yet this punishment is eternal and the soul cannot regard it as temporary, so it is left with the sole desire to be helped, and with a horrible moan, but it doesn't know where to ask for help. (Dalbiez 1974: 339)

The passage of the *Tischreden* relating to Luther's (alleged) suicidal tendencies reads:

Mr Leonhard, pastor of Guben, said that when he was a prisoner, the devil maliciously tormented him, laughing heartily when he took a knife in his hand, and saying to him: "Well, kill yourself!" And often he had to throw the knife away. Similarly, when he saw a piece of thread on the floor he would gather up enough of it to make a cord with which to hang himself. And he (the devil) had pushed(?) him to the point that he was no longer capable of reciting "The Lord's Prayer" or of reading the psalms, as he normally did. And then doctor Luther replied: "It has happened to me too, that when I had a knife in my hand such bad thoughts would come over me that I couldn't pray and the devil would chase me out of my room." (p. 355)

According to Dalbiez (1974), this testimony of the pastor Leonhard is supported by Luther's own references to suicidal tendencies (described in the third person) as a consequence to which thinking about one's sinfulness may easily lead (if one doesn't have a strong enough and constant enough faith in Christ's redemptive power). To illustrate:

> To look at the sin in your own heart is a sacrilege. For it is the devil, not God, who locates the sin there. You must look at Christ, and when you see your sins fixed there, you will be safe from your sins, death, from the hell . . . A great effort is necessary to grasp these things by faith and to believe them to the point of being able to say: "I have sinned and I have not sinned", so that one can win over one's conscience, this powerful master who has often pushed people into despair, leading them to a knife or a rope. (*Esaïam prophetam Scholia* ch. 53; quoted in Dalbiez 1974: 352)

The subject of Luther's personality is of course a controversial one, and I have no intention of trying to get involved in this controversy here. As far as the subject of "Angst" is concerned, however, certain points do seem to emerge quite clearly.

First, Luther's life was marked by intense spiritual suffering – by an inner affliction and distress – and this suffering is reflected in his writings. Second, from Luther's translation of the Bible we know that Luther's word for affliction and distress was "Angst" (his translation equivalent of the Latin words *pressura, angustia,* and *tribulatio* and the Greek words *stenoxoria, synokhē,* and *tlipsis*). Third, nobody doubts that Luther's suffering was linked with his faith in God, his passionate need to be certain of his salvation, and his overpowering sense of sinfulness (human in general and his own in particular). Fourth, since for Luther the prospect of his salvation was linked with God's judgment, and since he thought that this Last Judgment was imminent, his distress at the thought of his sinfulness was inextricably linked with an intense anxiety over his eternal destiny. Fifth, since for Luther salvation depended on faith, and only faith, the very doubts which tormented him seemed to stand between him and his salvation; and so his present anguish was inseparable for him from anxiety over the future (a possible future hell was inseparable from what he called the "hell" experienced here and now).

There are reasons to think, then, that for Luther, the two phenomena – distress (inner suffering in general) and anxiety about the future in particular – were inextricably connected. When he used the word *Angst* (or the phrase *angst und bange*), it meant in his speech what it meant in the language of the time, that is, something like "distress in general", but he often used it in contexts which implied, roughly speaking, not only distress but also anxiety (rather than any other kind of affliction). In his writings, as in his life and his teaching, therefore, the two concepts ("affliction" and "anxiety") came to be closely related.

To put it differently, there was no greater suffering for Luther than uncertainty about one's eternal fate – and since he talked and wrote incessantly about the subject it is likely that his general word for something like "affliction", namely *Angst,* became tinged with connotations of something like "anxiety". This, in turn, is likely to have set off a semantic shift, of a very familiar nature, a kind of semantic narrowing (cf. Stern 1965[1932]), from "affliction" in general to affliction caused by uncertainty about the future, that is to say, to a kind of cross between "affliction" and "anxiety".

In addition to eschatological anxieties (which, given Luther's conception of eschatology, were also existential anxieties), there is another vital ingredient in Luther's theology which is consistent with the concept of "Angst": the idea that a man quite literally *can't do anything* which could improve his eschatological prospects. For salvation depends exclusively on faith, not on anything that one might do. Our own efforts to live well, to do "good things", can get us nowhere. To quote one (Lutheran) commentator, Althaus (1966: 245–6):

> Justification, and therewith all of salvation, is given to men through faith alone, *sola fide.* For justification and salvation depend only on God's mercy; and this can be received only in an act of faith. Man's ethical activity and "works" have no place here. They can neither cause nor preserve salvation for us. It is only through faith that we are preserved to eternal life.

Thus, the existential uncertainty ("I don't know what will happen to me) [after I die]", the eschatological fears ("many very bad things can happen to me"), and the theology of "faith alone" ("I can't do anything [to cause these bad things not to happen]") form a conceptual whole which is remarkably congruent with the German concept of "Angst" as it subsequently evolved.

Given the wide dissemination of Luther's writings, their great popularity, and their unquestioned impact on the German language, Luther's use of the key word *Angst* was likely to have an impact on the use of this word in German in general, and is more than likely to have contributed to the semantic shift which has demonstrably taken place: "affliction" (1000–1600), "affliction/anxiety" (1600–1900), "anxiety/ fear" (1900–2000).

But of course labels such as "affliction", "affliction/anxiety", "anxiety", and "anxiety/fear" are only very rough approximations. A more precise statement of these meanings, as well as further arguments in their support, will be offered in the next section.

## 11 Luther's possible role in the shift from *Angst* "affliction" to *Angst* "anxiety/fear"

As we have seen, Luther didn't use *Angst* as a quasi-synonym of *Furcht* (as, for example, modern translations of the Bible often do), but rather in a more general sense of, roughly speaking, "distress". But the contexts in which he used the word *Angst* had to do, typically, with death, sin, and the danger of hell, and they exuded anxiety. One example is provided by Luther's translation of Psalm 116, where the expression *angst der Hellen* appears:

> Stricke des *todes* hatten mich umbfangen,
> Und *angst der Hellen* hatten mich troffen,
> Ich kam inn jamer und not. (Luther, Werke, vol. 10/1, p. 489)

> "The pains of death encompassed me,
> And the pangs of Sheol laid hold of me;
> I found trouble and sorrow." (NKJV, p. 602)

Luther used here the expression *Angst der Hellen* (with *Angst* as a plural), to translate a Hebrew phrase rendered in the Vulgate as *pericula inferni* ("dangers of hell"), and in the English New King James Version as "pangs of Sheol". An even more characteristic example is furnished by Luther's famous hymn "In the midst of life we are":

> Mitten wyr im leben sind
> mit dem *tod* umbfangen
> Wen suchen wir der hulffe thu
> das wyr gnad erlangen?
> Das bistu alleyne.

> Mitten hyn dem *tod* anficht
> uns der *Hellen* rachen,
> Wer will uns aus solcher not
> freh und ledig machen?
> Das thustu Herr alleyne.

> Mitten hyn der *Hellen angst*
> unser *sund* uns treyben,
> Wo soln wyr denn flihen hyn
> da wyr mugen bleyben?
> Zu dyr herr Christ alleyne. (Luther, Werke, vol. 35, p. 454)

> "In the midst of earthly life,
> Snares of *death* surround us;
> Who shall help us in the strife
> Lest the Foe confound us?
> Thou only, Lord, Thou only.

> In the midst of *death's* dark vale
> Powers of *hell* o'ertake us,
> Who will help when they assail,
> Who secure will make us?
> Thou only, Lord, Thou only.

> In the midst of *hell*-born woe

All our *sins* oppress us,
Where shall we for refuge go,
Where for grace to bless us?
To Thee, Lord Jesus, only."

In the standard modern German version, the phrase rendered here as "hell-born woe" is "der Hölle Angst" (Polack 1942: 420), which of course suggests (to modern readers) the fear of hell, whereas in Luther's original version, the phrase "der Hellen angst" suggested indeed something closer to torment and "woe".

It is hardly surprising that in discussing this hymn, Althaus (1966: 410) describes it as expressing "anxious questions and prayers" and as voicing "anxiety [faith] feels when it confronts God in death". Luther used in the hymn the word *Angst*, but even though the word as such meant for Luther "affliction" rather than "anxiety", given the context, an interpretation in terms of "anxiety" is perfectly natural. The collocation *der höllen angst*, "the *angst* of hell" (to which I will return later), is particularly symptomatic in this respect: for Luther, it meant the "torment of hell" rather than the "fear of hell", but the image of the "gaping jaws of hell" (awaiting the sinner) exudes anxiety. (The phrase "snares of death" used in the standard English version of the hymn is less vivid than the original phrase "der Hellen Rachen", and Althaus' (1966: 406) version, "hell's jaws gaping at us", better preserves the tone of the original.)

Another very characteristic example of the link between *Angst, death, God's judgement, devil*, and *hell* in Luther's writings is provided by the hymn described as "a piece of Luther's autobiography" (Oberman 1983: 330) and referring to his illness:

Dem Teufel ich gefangen lag
im Tod war ich verloren,
mein Sünd mich quälte Nacht und Tag,
darin ich war geboren.
Ich fiel auch immer tiefer drein,
es war kein Guts am Leben mein,
die Sünd hatt' mich besessen.

Mein guten Werk' die galten nicht,
es war mit ihn' verdorben;
der frei Will haßte Gotts Gericht,
er war zum Gut'n erstorben;
die Angst mich zu verzweifeln trieb,
daß nichts denn Sterben bei mir blieb,
zur Höllen mußt ich sinken.

"Fast bound in Satan's chains I lay,
Death brooded darkly o'er me,

Sin was my torment night and day,
In sin my mother bore me;
Yea, deep and deeper still I fell,
Life had become a living hell,
So firmly sin possessed me.

My own good works availed me naught,
No merit they attaining;
Free will against God's judgment fought,
Dead to all good remaining.
My fears increased till sheer despair
Left naught but death to be my share;
The pangs of hell I suffered."
(Translation from Lutheran Hymn Book 1961: 281)

Here, Luther is speaking of "Angst" in the sense of torment and anguish (once again, with reference to hell), but the English version of the hymn renders this "Angst" as "fear". This is not inconsistent with the general atmosphere of Luther's hymn but does not represent accurately its exact meaning.

One can understand, then, why Mosse's (1955) dictionary based on quotations from Luther's Bible should assign to Luther's *Angst* not one but three glosses: "anxiety, fear, distress". The word's invariant in Luther's speech appears to have been "distress" rather than either "anxiety" or "fear"; but since, typically, the word is used in contexts inspiring fear and exuding anxiety, its very meaning may seem to be somewhat indeterminate and to span a wider range of emotions than it actually encoded.

The difficulty in sorting out the semantic invariant of *Angst* from the implications induced by the context is reflected, in an interesting way, in a controversy between the editor of the Middle High German dictionary (1854) Georg Friedrich Benecke and the brothers Grimm, the editors of the monumental dictionary of modern German published some decades later. In essence, Benecke emphasized the difference in meaning between the Middle High German *angst* (roughly, "affliction") and its modern meaning (roughly, "anxiety/fear"), whereas the brothers Grimm were inclined to see some mixture of "affliction" and "fear" (or "anxiety") in both the earlier and the later meaning. Thus, Benecke wrote:

> The modern German *angst*, with which we usually link the concept of lack of courage, does not correspond at all to the old *angest*, or only incidentally. *angest* refers to a state, in which one feels that one is surrounded by trouble and danger, even when one tackles them with the greatest courage, or endures them calmly. The heroes in the

"Nibelungen" have plenty of *angest* [trouble/danger], but they have no *angst* [fear]. (Benecke 1854: vol. 1, p. 43)[9]

The brothers Grimm disagree:

> Benecke exaggerates the supposed difference in meaning between the Middle High German *angest* and the modern German *angst*. Why shouldn't today, too, some things arouse *angst* in a warrior without causing him to show the slightest cowardice? . . . *angst* is not simply a lack of courage but a tormenting worry, a general state of oppressive doubt. (Grimm and Grimm 1854: vol. 1, p. 358)[10]

But the account of the Grimm brothers fails to explain why Luther never used *Angst* to translate *timor* or *phobos* ("fear") and why he only used it to translate *pressura, angustia,* and *tribulatio,* or *tlipsis* and *synokhē* ("affliction/distress"). By contrast, Benecke's hypothesis does explain this fact – and at the same time it is not inconsistent with the Grimms' observation that nineteenth century *Angst* means not just "fear" but rather, roughly speaking, something between "fear" and "distress". (See also Dietz 1870.)

The evolution in the meaning of the compound word *Höllenangst* ("hell-*angst*") is particularly revealing in this respect. In modern (twentieth century) German this word is generally taken to refer to the "fear of hell" (i.e. fear that one might go to hell). In Luther's language, however, (as pointed out earlier) *Höllenangst* (or *der Höllen angst*) referred to the "torments of hell".

In fact, long before Luther and long after Luther, the torments of hell were described in German as the "angst of fire", as the following examples illustrate:

> der wirt schuldig zu der angst des feuers
> "he will deserve the *angst* of fire" 1382;
> (quoted in Reichmann 1989: 1190)

> Da liegt er [Satan] in dem Flammen-Meere,
> Ihn foltern ewig Angst und Pein.

> "there he (Satan) lies in a sea of flames,
>   tortured eternally by *Angst* and pain"
> (Goethe; quoted in the *Goethe Wörterbuch* 1966: 57)

The editors of the Goethe dictionary comment in this connection that "angst" was understood as a "symptomatic experience of hell" ("als symptomat. Erleben der Hölle"). Luther's references to the "angst of fire" or to the "angst of hell" should be seen in this perspective.

As noted, for example, in Reichmann's (1989) "Frühneuhochdeutsches Wörterbuch", in pre-modern German *angst* was associated, in particular, with Christ's suffering before his death ("Passio Christi,

Todesangst Christi", p. 1190), and with religious and didactic use of language ("religiöse und didaktische Texte", p. 1191). But for Luther, thoughts about death (including Christ's death) were inextricably linked with thoughts about God's judgment and the possibility of eternal damnation.

The characteristic link between "Angst", "Todesangst" (present also in Jesus' agony), and "Höllenangst", which came to be associated with Lutheran theology in general, is clearly articulated in Paul Tillich's discussion of this concept (rendered by him in English as "anxiety"):

> If man is left to his "having to die," the essential anxiety about non-being is transformed into the horror of death. Anxiety about non-being is present in everything finite. It is consciously or unconsciously effective in the whole process of living. Like the beating of the heart, it is always present, although one is not always aware of it . . . The dramatic description of the anxiety of Jesus in having to die confirms the universal character of the relation of finitude and anxiety.
>
> Under the conditions of estrangement, anxiety has a different character, brought on by the element of guilt. The loss of one's potential eternity is experienced as something for which one is responsible in spite of its universal tragic actuality. Sin is the sting of death, not its physical cause. It transforms the anxious awareness of one's having to die into the painful realization of a lost eternity. (Tillich 1957: 67–9)

But to appreciate the full force of Luther's references to *Höllenangst* we must take into account Luther's theology and, in particular, Luther's eschatology, and we must pay attention to the fact that for Luther hell was not just a matter of a person's possible eternal future, but also very much a matter of a person's spiritual distress in the present. To quote Asendorf's (sympathetic) account of Luther's eschatology:

> The Last Judgment will not happen at some distant point in time; rather, it is one's immediate present. One's conscience is hell. The Judgment, wrath, sin and death are all present at the same time . . . When we feel our conscience, then we feel hell and we think we are lost for all eternity. (1967: 57)

> [it was pointed out that] through a bad conscience hell, that is the eschaton itself, is thrust into this life, in such a way that impotent curses raised towards God are no more than an expression of utter separation from God and of utter despair. Here, the person experiences, in pain, what it means to be remote from God's visage; as Luther himself had fully experienced, before he chose the path of the Reform. The borders to the eschaton are open. One suffers God's eternal judgment here and now. (1967: 59–60)[11]

Thus, for Luther, "Angst" was very much linked with the idea of hell, but not just in the frightening images of a place of eternal damnation; rather, and above all, with "hell" as intense anguish suffered here on earth and linked with a subjective experience of God's wrath and rejection. It is hardly surprising that given this conception of "hell" and this conception of "Angst", the notions of "anguish" and "anxiety" became closely linked in Luther's writings, and – one must hypothesize – in Luther's spiritual and linguistic heritage in Germany. The fact that we can see traces of this heritage not only in Germany but in other Lutheran countries as well, lends additional support to this hypothesis. The importance of "angst" in Danish language and philosophy (recall Paul Tillich's remarks quoted earlier) is relevant here.

It is also interesting to note Luther's use of the words *Hölle* and *infernum* (Latin for hell) as labels for pain and anxiety, as in his 1527 letter to Melanchton, written when he [Luther] seemed to be mortally ill:

> For more than a week I have been thrown hither and thither in death and hell, I felt beaten throughout my whole body, all my limbs were trembling. Driven by floods and storms of despair and blasphemy against God, I all but lost Christ. But thanks to the prayers of the faithful, God started to show me mercy and to tear my soul from the bottom of hell. (Luther quoted in Oberman 1983: 335)[12]

Speaking of the "Angst" which Luther showed on this occasion (when he thought he was on his deathbed), a sympathetic commentator, Oberman (1983: 335), remarks:

> It was not the encounter with death which caused him so much *Angst* and fright. Physically, Luther improved quickly, as he reports. What he experienced on the outbreak of the sickness as an attack of the devil, was only to come into full swing as his health improved. Nor was he tormented by any doubts about the truth of the Gospels. What worried him [caused him *Angst*] was the question whether he himself could hold on to this truth. (Oberman 1983: 335)[13]

Since for Luther salvation (and heaven) depended on faith alone, the doubt which he experienced (not a doubt about God but a doubt about his own salvation) was for him, by his own testimony, a source of intense torment and anxiety – of "hell" – not in a modern metaphorical sense of the word, but in a literal sense: to feel that one was cut off from God was for Luther what he understood by "hell". Anguish and anxiety were for him one: "infernal anguish" and "fear of hell" were one and the same thing.

Thus, the semantic shift from *angst* "anguish" to *angst* "anxiety/ fear", which took place in the German language at some time between the sixteenth century and modern times mirrors a synchronic shift which we can observe in Luther's own language and thought: a shift from *angst* as a translation equivalent of the Latin words *pressura*, *angustia*, and *tribulatio* ("anguish/distress") to *angst* as a word associated with anxiety-inspiring thoughts about death, the devil, and hell.

## 12 The great social and economic anxieties of Luther's times

In the view of many historians, the times when Luther lived were marked by a wide-spread anxiety, linked with the dissolution of feudalism in Europe and the birth pains of capitalism. In the words of Erich Fromm (1980a [1941]: 67), "the old order was breaking down. The individual had lost the security of certainty and was threatened by new economic forces, by capitalists and monopolies; the comparative principle was being replaced by competition". This state of affairs led to wide-spread anxiety [*Angst*]:

> The breakdown of the medieval system of feudal society had one main significance for all classes of society: the individual was left alone and isolated. He was free. This freedom had a twofold result. Man was deprived of the security he had enjoyed, of the unquestionable feeling of belonging, and he was torn loose from the world which had satisfied his quest for security both economically and spiritually. He felt alone and anxious. (1980a[1941]: 85)
> (Er fühlte sich nun allein und war voller Angst. Fromm 1980b: 275)

Again and again, the word *Angst* reappears in Fromm's discussion of those times as a key word. Fromm asks: "What is the connection of Luther's doctrines with the psychological situation of all but the rich and powerful towards the end of the Middle Ages?" (1980a [1941]: 67). And he replies that the new religious doctrines carried a special appeal to the urban middle class, to the poor in the cities, and to the peasants, "because they gave expression to a new feeling of freedom and independence as well as to the feeling of powerlessness and anxiety [*Angst*][14] by which their members were pervaded" (1980a [1941]: 53). Luther's picture of man mirrored (Fromm remarks), these people's dilemma: "Man is free *from* all ties binding him to spiritual authorities, but this very freedom leaves him alone and anxious [*angsterfüllt*]" (Fromm 1980a [1941]: 68; 1980b: 264). I will adduce a few more quotes highlighting the psychological climate at the end of the Middle Ages which helps to explain the birth of the concept of "Angst":

> the new religious doctrines not only gave expression to what the average member of the middle class felt, but, by rationalizing and systematizing this attitude, they also increased and strengthened it. (1980a[1941]: 87)

> Protestantism was the answer to the human needs of the frightened, uprooted, and isolated individual who had to orient and to relate himself to a new world. (ibid. p. 87)

> It was also satisfying psychologically, since such action answered the needs and anxieties of this new kind of personality. (ibid p. 89)

This free, isolated individual is crushed by the experience of his individual insignificance. Luther's theology gives expression to this feeling of helplessness and doubt. (ibid p. 69)

[They] were an answer to psychic needs which in themselves were brought about by the collapse of the medieval system and by the beginnings of capitalism . . . freedom *from* the traditional bonds of medieval society, though giving the individual a new feeling of independence, at the same time made him feel alone and isolated, filled with doubt and anxiety [*Angst*] (ibid. p. 89)

Thus, "Angst" plays in Fromm's analysis a crucial role, representing as it were a meeting place of history and theology.

## 13 Uncertainty vs. certainty, *Angst* vs. *Sicherheit*

According to some commentators, the salient role of the concept "Angst" in German culture is linked with the cultural value of "certainty", of knowing exactly what one should expect and what one should do. As Bernard Nuss (1993: 188–9) put it in the passage quoted earlier, "[for Germans] uncertainty generates *Angst* . . . Not to know what will happen . . . arouses [in Germans] much more *Angst* than a real danger".

Nuss' remarks about the value of "certainty" in German culture tally with comments on the importance of certainty that one encounters in the writings of many German scholars. One characteristic example is provided by the following passage from a foreword to a popular book on theology, with the characteristic title "Vergewisserung" ("acquisition of certainty" or "becoming certain"):

"I am certain!" – Is this a sentence from our time? . . . It seems that nowadays certainty is more rarely found, and that searching for it requires a greater effort. But who would really forsake certainty? To be certain: of oneself, of one's goals, of another person – and above all: of one's own beliefs – this is necessary for life. It is impossible to live in uncertainty. Even the more or less trivial uncertainties of everyday life are difficult to bear. Often they make us ill, and in this way demonstrate how much people suffer from them. Uncertainty in the basic questions of life threatens life itself. (Rössler 1979: 6)[15]

As the above quote illustrates, the adjective *gewiß* can be matched with the English adjective *certain*, and the noun *Gewißheit*, with the noun *certainty*. The adjective *sicher*, in one of its meanings, can be regarded as an equivalent of *gewiß*, and the noun *Sicherheit*, as an equivalent of *Gewißheit*. (As *Langenscheidt's Großwörterbuch* (1993) puts it, *Gewißheit* means "das sichere Wissen in bezug auf etwas = *Sicherheit*", i.e. "a certain knowledge about something, that is, *Sicherheit*".)

The following sentence from a novel illustrates the use of the word *sicher* in the sense of *gewiß*.

> *Mag sein, daß Ivy mich liebte. (Sicher war ich bei Frauen nie.)* (Frisch 1969: 43)
> "Maybe Ivy loved me. (With women, I was never certain.)"

In addition, however, both the adjective *sicher* and the noun *Sicherheit* are widely used in German in a sense which, roughly speaking, combines the ideas of "certainty", "safety", and "security". *Langenscheidt's Großwörterbuch* (1993) defines this second sense of *sicher* as follows: "vor Gefahren oder Risiken geschützt < ein Versteck, ein Weg, ein Arbeitsplatz, ein Einkommen" ("protected from dangers or risks < a hiding place, a road, a job, an income"). If something is "sicher" in this second sense, one can be certain that one can rely on it and that nothing bad will happen to one because of that. This meaning of *sicher* is so salient and so important in German culture, that the adjective *sicher* in this sense has become semi-grammaticalized and is used widely in compounds such as *diebessicher* "thief-proof" or *fälschungssicher* "secure against forging" (of a document, for example, a passport). Langenscheidt's dictionary describes this use of *-sicher* as "very productive".

To appreciate the differences between the meaning of the German words *sicher* (adjective) and *Sicherheit* (noun) and any English words with which they may be compared, consider the following two German sentences:

> (i) Erwähnen möchte ich noch, daß ist nicht weiß, ob ich vor Verzweiflungsanfällen sicher bin. (Hahnemann, 1995: 61)
> "I would also like to mention that I don't know whether I am certain/ secure from attacks of doubt." (not acceptable in English)

> (ii) Wer in seinem Schicksal einen Sinn sieht, der kann versuchen, ein Lebensprinzip zu finden, durch das er Sicherheit für sich selbst, für die anderen und für die gesamte Welt, in der er lebt, gewinnt. (Harder 1995: 69)
> "He who sees a meaning in his life [fate] can try to find a life-principle, through which he can win *Sicherheit* [certainty/security] for himself, for others, and for the whole world in which he lives."

What these sentences clearly show is that *Sicherheit* (in the sense in which it is used here) means neither "certainty" nor "security" but, as it were, a combination of the two: a kind of security which is found in certainty.

To be *sicher* in that characteristically German sense does not mean to be immune from dangers but rather to be, so to speak, free from *Angst*; it implies not only that one is safe, but also that one can be *certain* of being safe. To put it differently, *Sicherheit* is an opposite of both danger and doubt: it suggests a deeply satisfying sense of being free from danger and doubt at the same time.

The semantic relations between the concepts under discussion ("doubt", "certainty", "safety", "security", *Sicherheit*₁ and *Sicherheit*₂) can be clarified by means of explications formulated in the Natural Semantic Metalanguage. Thus, the meaning of the English word *doubt* (and the German word *Zweifel*) can be portrayed as follows:

> *doubt* (e.g. I doubt it that X happened)
> I can't think: "I know that X happened"
> I think: "maybe it didn't happen"

The meaning of the English word *certainty*, and of the German word *Gewißheit* (and also one meaning of *Sicherheit*) can be represented as, essentially, an opposite of doubt:

> *certainty/Gewißheit/Sicherheit*₁ (e.g. I am certain that X happened)
> I can think: "I know that X happened"
> I don't have to think: "maybe it didn't happen"

The concepts of "danger" (in German, *Gefahr*) and "safety" (no exact equivalent in German) can also be represented as opposites:

> *safety* (e.g. person X is safe)
> I know something about person X
> because of this I can think:
> > "nothing bad will happen to person X
> > this is good for X"
>
> *danger* (e.g. person X is in danger)
> I know something about person X
> because of this I cannot think:
> > "nothing bad will happen to person X"
> I have to think:
> > "something bad can happen to person X
> > this is bad for X"

The English word *security* implies, so to speak, more than *safety*, because it promises that not only "nothing bad WILL happen (to someone or something)" but that "nothing bad CAN happen (to someone) because of [something]". But the German word *Sicherheit* (in the relevant sense, *Sicherheit*₂) promises even more than *security*: not only CAN

nothing bad happen to one if one has that "Sicherheit", but one can be
CERTAIN that nothing bad can happen to one:

> *security* (e.g. security screen, security lock)
> people can know something about X
> because of this, people can think:
> > "if person Y has object X nothing bad can happen to this
> > person
> > because of this, if Y has X, it is good for Y"

> *Sicherheit₂*
> person Y knows something
> because of this, person Y doesn't have to think:
> > "I don't know what will happen
> > maybe something bad will happen to me"
> person Y can think:
> > "I know that nothing bad can happen to me"
> this is good for person Y

The concept of "Sicherheit₂", combining, as it were, the ideas of
"certainty", "safety", and "security", is widely regarded as a key
German value (cf. e.g. Syberberg 1995: 122), and as a positive counterpart of "Angst". The key role that the word *Sicherheit* plays in German
advertising (including permanent signs displayed over shops and busi-
nesses) provides some evidence for this perception, as do various
linguistic facts, such as the wealth of derivates and compounds involving this concept, including, for example, the verbs *sichern, sicherstellen*,
and *sichergehen*. For example (taken from *Langenscheidt's Großwörterbuch*
1993), the sentence:

> Wir müssen sicherstellen, daß nicht noch mehr Vogelarten
> aussterben.
> "We must ensure that no more bird species die out."

means that we must do something so as to be certain that some bad
thing will not happen. Similarly, the phrase:

> die Tür durch ein doppeltes Schloß gegen Einbruch sichern
> "to secure the door against a break-in by a double lock"

means that if one does this to a door one can be certain because of this
that nothing bad will happen to that door (no one will be able to break
in). And the sentence:

> Sie wollte sichergehen und fragte deshalb noch einen Arzt.
> "She wanted to run no risks so she asked another doctor for a
> second opinion."

means that the person in question wanted to do something thanks to which she could be certain that something bad would not happen to her.

The notion of "Sicherheit" is also linked with the specifically German ideal of "Geborgenheit" (from *geborgen* "sheltered"), that is, of being in a place where one can feel safe and protected (that is, so to speak, a feeling of being in a place where one doesn't have to feel *Angst*). This in turn is related to the specifically German concept of "Heimat" – that is, roughly, "homeland, or home region, seen as a place where one was a child and where one could feel safe and protected". (For detailed discussion, see Wierzbicka 1995e and 1997a.)

German–English dictionaries often translate the word *Geborgenheit* as "safety" or "security", but in fact the concept of "Geborgenheit" is quite unique and there is no word for it in English. Roughly speaking, it stands for a feeling of existential security (rather like *Angst* stands for a feeling of existential insecurity); and it could never be used with reference to such practical matters as, for example, "safety pins" or "security belts". On the other hand, it is perfectly suited to talk about a more or less mythologized native country, that is, *Heimat*.

As is often pointed out in the abundant literature on "Heimat", the very word *Heimat* suggests something like a lost paradise, the only place where one could feel "Geborgenheit" and be free of "Angst". If *Angst* represents, as Heidegger put it, a state of *un-zuhause-sein* ("not being at home"), *Heimat* represents a metaphorical (and metaphysical) "Zuhause", that is, "home". To quote Nuss (1993: 178):

> Through such images there arises for the Germans a state of "Geborgenheit", in which, as in the bosom of one's family, one is no longer exposed to the vicissitudes and dangers of life. The worst thing that can happen to a German is to lose his *Heimat*. Then it seems to him that he has been robbed of his very soul.[16]

Thus the concept of "Angst" is not only language- and culture-specific, but occupies moreover an important place in a whole network of language- and culture-specific concepts. It is closely related to other independently identifiable cultural attitudes and cultural values; along with *Sicherheit*, these values include *Ordnung*.

## 14 Certainty and *Ordnung*

In addition to the basic dictionary equivalents of the English words *certain* and *certainty* (*gewiß* and *Gewißheit, sicher*₁ and *Sicherheit*₁), German has also four "special", highly colloquial words implying certainty: *bestimmt, genau, klar,* and *Bescheid*. The very frequent use of these words in everyday conversation appears to confirm the great salience of the value of "certainty" in German culture. I will discuss these words briefly one by one.

*Bescheid* is a common colloquial word, which, however, has no equivalents in other European languages. According to Duden's (1981) dictionary, the noun *Bescheid* comes from the verb *bescheiden* as used in "Amtssprache" (the language of bureaucracy), whose meaning is given as "jemandem behördlicherseits eine Entscheidung über etwas mitteilen" ("to inform someone of a decision taken by the authorities"). In its colloquial use, however, *Bescheid* refers simply to a desirable state of knowing "with certainty" how one should proceed in a given situation. *Langenscheidt's Großwöterbuch* (1993) defines this concept as "eine erwartete Information über etwas" ("expected information about something") and illustrates it with the following examples:

> Sag mir bitte Bescheid, ob du zu meiner Party kommen kannst!
> "Tell me please *Bescheid* if you can come to my party."

The bureaucratic meaning of *Bescheid* provides a clue to its everyday meaning. The official sense of the word implies that to know what I have to do, I have to know something "with certainty", and that I can only know it if some official body tells me what this body has decided. The everyday sense of *Bescheid* has a reduced but clearly related meaning:

> I want to know something "with certainty"
> when I know it, I will know what I have to do
> I can know it if someone else says something to me about it

The adverb *bestimmt* (homophonous with the past participle of the verb *bestimmen*) is described by Langenscheidt (*Langenscheidt's Großwörterbuch* 1993) as a synonym of *gewiß* "certain/certainly" and is given two definitions: (1) "used to indicate that one holds something for very probable"; and (2) "without doubt, with absolute certainty". The illustrative sentences are:

> Du wirst bestimmt Erfolg haben bei deiner Arbeit!
> "you will certainly achieve success in your work!"

> Weißt du das bestimmt?
> "You know this for sure?"

The dictionary notes also the common everyday collocation *ganz bestimmt* "quite certainly" ("for sure"). A nice example of this phrase used in combination with the word *geborgen*, "emotionally and existentially sheltered", that is with reference to the ideal of *Geborgenheit* is provided by the following aphorism by the Lutheran pastor and resistance hero Dietrich Bonhoeffer (quoted in Claessen 1995: 38):

> Von guten Mächten wunderbar geborgen
> erwarten wir getrost, was kommen mag.
> Gott ist mit uns am Abend und am Morgen
> und ganz bestimmt an jedem neuen Tag.
>
> Wonderfully sheltered (*geborgen*) by Good Forces
> comforted we await whatever might befall us.
> God is with us by morning and by evening.
> And quite certainly (*ganz bestimmt*) through each new day.

*Genau* is, in its primary sense, an equivalent of the English word *precise*. But it is also frequently used in another sense, as in the sentence (from *Langenscheidt's Großwörterbuch* 1993):

> Wißt ihr schon Genaues über den Unfall?
> "Do you know anything definite about the accident yet?"

*Langenscheidt's Großwörterbuch* (1993) distinguishes also several other senses, including the one illustrated by the following phrase: "sich etwas genau merken", which it glosses as "bewußt and konzentriert" ("consciously and with full concentration"). The dictionary also notes the common conversational exclamation *genau!*, used "to confirm, answer a question in a positive way" or "to confirm a supposition". What these different uses of *genau* have in common (apart from the sense "precisely") is something like the combination of "good" and "certainly". An "emphatic confirmation" conveys something like "good, certainly", and "focussed, conscious, concentrated observation" allows one to come to have "good and certain" knowledge. In both cases the idea of "certainty" seems clearly involved.

The word *klar* means, above all, "clear", but it has also developed uses which relate it to certainty. *Langenscheidt's Großwörterbuch* (1993) recognizes these links explicitly when it glosses the colloquial expression *(Na)klar!* as "selbstverständlich, sicher" ("of course, certainly"), and also when it glosses the expression *über etwas klar/im klaren sein* ("to be clear about something") as "etwas genau wissen und deshalb sicher darüber urteilen können" ("to know something exactly and therefore be able to judge about it with certainty"). In fact, even the common conversational phrase *Alles klar!* (lit. "all clear") suggests not only that "now I know" or "now I understand [what you mean or what you know]" but also, and even especially, that "now I have no doubts", that is "now I am certain I know all I need to know".

Thus, German has a number of language-specific conversational routines which seem to reflect a special interest in "certainty", and a special importance attached to it.

It has often been said that German culture is characterized by a "Vorschrifts- und Ordnungsethos" (Hentig 1996: 59), that is, an ethos based on regulations and the notion of "order", and it is tempting to think with Nuss (1993) and others that the apparent German predilection for regulations and strict order is related to the value of "certainty". The numerous regulations and prohibitions characteristic (according to most observers) of German life can be seen as a secure framework reducing the uncertainty of life and, hopefully, the accompanying *Angst*. As Nuss (1993: 195) put it, "It is clear in daily life what an incessant struggle the Germans unconsciously lead to eliminate their tacit fears [*Ängste*, pl.]. Both materially and psychologically, they have a need to live in a secure/certain framework."[17]

These ideas are certainly consistent with the ubiquitous *Verboten* ("Prohibited") signs (cf. Wierzbicka 1998a), which may indeed have something to do with the cultural value of *Sicherheit* ("certainty/security"), as well as the central value of *Ordnung* ("order"). To quote Nuss (1993: 123) once more:

> For Germans, it is indispensable to have *Ordnung* (order) and to live in a world governed by *Ordnung*. In fact, only *Ordnung* is able to secure them an inner peace. For the head to be able to function in an orderly fashion and for the soul to be able to feel free, the body has to live in an ordered framework. The German cannot bear it when he cannot "find himself" – among his objects and in his thoughts, in his profession as in his emotional life. He likes clear relationships. He wants to know where he stands and how he should proceed. He is a creature of habit and he would like to see everything precisely regulated. The unknown oppresses, even frightens him. He has a need to investigate and to mark out the terrain where he moves. Only when this has happened, does he feel safe/secure/certain.[18]

## 15 Conclusion

Fear is supposed to be a fundamental human emotion – an emotion determined by human biology, not by culture (see, e.g. Kemper 1987; Plutchik 1994). But in the German intellectual tradition, and also in the prevailing German "naive" psychology, it is not fear (or, in German, *Furcht*) which is widely regarded as a "primeval" feeling (an *Urgefühl*), but something that the Germans call "Angst", and for which English and most other European languages don't have any equivalent.

In this chapter, I have tried to show that the concept of "Angst" to be found in German psychology, philosophy, and theology is rooted in everyday language, and that it is actually quite close to the concept of "Angst" with which ordinary speakers of German operate on a daily basis. I have also tried to trace the origin of the peculiarly German concept of "Angst", in the spiritual, cultural, and linguistic legacy of Martin Luther.

Having explored Luther's own use of the word *Angst*, and the kinds of context in which this word appeared in Luther's religious writings, I have proposed that there may be a link between Luther's theology and the emergence of the new concept of "Angst" – a concept different from that encoded in the sixteenth century word *Angst* but which may have been suggested by the contexts in which this word tended to appear in Luther's voluminous and hugely influential writings.

On a more general level, I have tried to show that the concept of "Angst" is a cultural creation, and that the boundaries between "different emotions" such as "Angst", "anxiety", or "fear" are in the eye of the beholder – the collective beholder – defined above all by a given language. This doesn't mean that these boundaries between "different emotions" are not real: they are real, but they are imposed by different cognitive scenarios with which the words in question are associated, and the cognitive scenarios themselves are shaped not just by universal human biology but by culture, which in turn is shaped by history, religion, and way of life.

Above all, I have tried to show that by studying the semantic system of a language in a rigorous way and in a coherent methodological framework, we can both reveal and document the cultural underpinnings of emotions – even the most elusive and unfathomable ones such as *Angst*.

# CHAPTER 4

# Reading human faces

## 1 The human face: a "mirror" or a "tool"?

The current debate on facial expressions is sometimes cast in terms of a choice between two opposing views: human faces as "read-outs" of inner emotions (e.g. Ekman 1972, 1989, 1994a and b; Izard 1971, 1977, 1994, 1997) vs. human faces as "social signals" (e.g. Fridlund 1994, 1997). By using the term "reading", I am not in fact opting for the "Emotional Expression Approach" as against the "Social Communicative Approach" (Chovil 1997). I believe that both these conflicting positions embody part of the truth, but only part.

Ekman's position can be illustrated with the following quote:

> The same facial expressions are associated with the same emotions, regardless of culture or language . . . There are some facial expressions of emotion which are universally characteristic of the human species . . . While facial expressions of emotion will often be culture specific because of differences in elicitors, display rules and consequences, there is also a pan-cultural set of facial expressions of emotion . . . The evidence now proves the existence of universal facial expressions . . . Regardless of the language, of whether the culture is Western or Eastern, industrialized or preliterate, these facial expressions are labelled with the same emotion terms: happiness, sadness, anger, fear, disgust and surprise. (Ekman 1980: 137–8)

And more recently (Ekman 1992a: 175): "The strongest evidence for distinguishing one emotion from another comes from research on facial expressions. There is robust, consistent evidence of a universal facial expression for anger, fear, enjoyment, sadness, and disgust".

In the past there was also a strong emphasis in this approach on the "discreteness" of the so-called "basic emotions" (cf. e.g. Ekman and Friesen 1971: 124: "The results provide evidence in support of the hypothesis that the association between particular facial muscular patterns and discrete emotions is universal"), and this is how this approach has been generally understood. (Cf. e.g. Oatley and Jenkins 1996: 67: "Investigators have found expressions specific to discrete emotions. Emotions may be considered discrete in the sense that they are produced and recognized panculturally.") In his recent work Ekman (e.g. 1992b, 1994b) continues to insist that his "basic emotions" (that is, those supposedly linked with "pancultural facial expressions") are anchored in distinct neural patterns (Izard's (1991: 17) phrase is "innate neural programs"):

> There is evidence . . . for distinctive patterns of autonomic nervous system (ANS) activity for anger, fear and disgust, and it appears that there may also be a distinctive pattern for sadness . . . It is necessary to posit emotion-specific central nervous system (CNS) activity in my account of basic emotions . . . There must be *unique* [original emphasis] physiological patterns for each emotion, and these CNS patterns should be specific to these emotions and not found in other mental activity. (Ekman 1994b: 17–18)

By continuing to talk about "each emotion" Ekman continues, in effect, to present the so-called "basic emotions" as discrete phenomena. He also continues to imply that these "discrete phenomena" can be identified by means of English lexical categories such as "anger" or "sadness". From this perspective, English lexical categories such as "sadness" or "anger" appear to cut nature at its joints and correspond to distinct neural programs, whereas the lexical categories of languages like Ifaluk or Pintupi (cf. Lutz 1988, Myers 1986; see also Wierzbicka 1992a and c) can only correspond to "blends".

Arguing against the doctrine of "basic emotions", Van Brakel (1994: 188) wrote: "Why should 20th century English name these universal emotions correctly? It can only be because Ekman believes that English is at the pinnacle of the evolution of naming of the structure of the experiential world". The logic of Ekman's approach seems to imply, indeed, not only that the English lexical categories name the structure of the experiential world "correctly" but also the functioning of the central nervous system!

Ekman's claims have been challenged by different scholars, from different points of view (cf. in particular, Fridlund 1994; Ortony and Turner 1990; Camras 1992; Russell 1994; Van Brakel 1994). In my own work (cf. Wierzbicka 1986a, 1990d, 1992a and c, 1993b, 1995b) I have questioned above all Ekman's use of English words like *anger, fear,* or *sadness* to describe what he claims to be universal facial expressions, "regardless of language". The speakers of other languages in fact think about human experience in terms of other, non-matching, conceptual categories (e.g. *rabbia* rather than *anger* in Italian, *grust'* and *pečal'* rather than *sadness* in Russian, and *Angst* rather than *fear* in German (see chapters 1 and 3)); they do not "read" any human faces as "angry, "sad", or "fearful", but rather interpret them in terms of their own language-specific categories.

I have also argued that the use of global labels like *angry, sad,* or *happy* (or *enjoyment*) does not do justice to the ways speakers of English "read" human faces either. As Ekman himself acknowledged in his more recent work (cf. e.g. Ekman 1994a), different facial configurations can be described by speakers of English as "angry", whereas the same face can often be interpreted by different people (and even by the same person at different times) differently (e.g. as "frustrated", "gloomy", "determined", "aggressive", and so on).

Admittedly, in his more recent work Ekman does acknowledge that emotion labels do not match across cultures. In particular, in his unfortunately somewhat tendentiously titled "Reply to Russell's mistaken critique" (Ekman 1994a: 270) he states that "There is no reason to expect that every culture will label the emotions in exactly the same way", adding that he and his associates "never claimed that facial expressions evolved to represent specific verbal labels". Nevertheless in this paper, too, he does revert to earlier formulations, for example, when he says the following (p. 276):

> Russell complained that we and others preselected our expressions [i.e. emotion labels] . . . We had theoretical and empirical reasons to expect that certain expressions would be universal, and of course, we selected just these stimuli . . . By showing only expressions selected according to an a priori criterion to people from different cultures, we determined whether *those* expressions were interpreted the same way over cultures.

But the point is that, as empirical cross-linguistic studies show, there are simply *no* emotional expressions (i.e. labels) interpreted the same way across cultures.[1]

The fundamental problem remains: how can the "basic emotions" be identified across languages and cultures if the labels are variable and unreliable? Ekman's polemical strategy on this point is a familiar one (cf. Wierzbicka 1995f): like Lazarus (1995) and others, he declares that he is not interested in *words* but in *emotions* and *facial expressions,* and he makes light of the objections of those (like Russell) whom he sees as interested in mere words.

> From my theoretical perspective, emotions are not reducible to labels. An emotion label is a shorthand that stands for a number of processes and responses that occur during an emotion . . . Russell is interested in emotion words, not in emotions per se and certainly not in facial expressions. I have not been primarily interested in emotion words but in facial expression and more generally in emotion. (Ekman 1994a: 282)

But if a label like "fear" or "anger" is just a shorthand abbreviation for something else, surely it is legitimate to ask: What is it shorthand for? How are we to know what Ekman and his colleagues are talking about when they say, for example, that "A number of separate, discrete, emotional states such as fear, anger, and enjoyment, can be identified which differ not only in [facial] expression but probably in other important aspects"? (1992a:170) By refusing to take an interest in words, Ekman and his colleagues end up relying on English words; as a consequence, despite all their disclaimers, they absolutize the English folk-taxonomy of emotions.

Having introduced in his more recent work the notion of "family of emotions", Ekman talks about "each emotion family" as having "a theme and variations", and, for example, of the "anger family" he says that while "there are more than 60 anger expressions" nonetheless "in all members of the anger family the brows are lowered and drawn together, the upper eyelid is raised and the muscle in the lip is tightened" (1992a: 172). It is not explained, however, exactly what is meant by "the anger family". Although it is now acknowledged that a term like *anger* is not reliable as a tool for identifying human emotions, it has not been replaced by anything else. But if we are not to take the term *anger* as crystal-clear, how are we to know what is meant by "the anger family"? We are told that the combination of "lowered and drawn together brows, raised upper eyelids and tightened muscle in the lip" is a pancultural expression of *something*, but we are not given any clues (other than the avowedly unreliable English word *anger*) as to what this something might be.

None of this of course is intended to call into question the great value of Ekman and his colleagues' pioneering research which has reawakened scholarly interest in emotions and in their universal facial correlates; but as Mandler (1997) and others have suggested, the time has come for a change of paradigm. To opt for a change of paradigm, however, does not mean that one has to give up the stimulating metaphor of "reading human faces". I would argue that faces can indeed be "read", and that some facial configurations (and behaviours) can indeed be "read" in the same way by different people within one culture or across all cultures, as Ekman and his associates have argued for decades. The questions which I will try to address in this chapter are these: What exactly can be "read" from human faces? What meanings can be associated with what facial behaviours? and, above all, in what metalanguage can these meanings be formulated (if they are not to be formulated in terms of English labels like *happy*, *angry*, or *sad*)?

It is also extremely important to clarify what exactly we mean by the metaphor of "reading human faces". Do we mean "reading" a person's inner states which are involuntarily "mirrored" in the person's face or do we mean some "messages" which may or may not correspond to what is actually going on "behind the face" (in the person's "heart" and "mind")?

Ekman appears to imply that he is talking about a person's "authentic" emotions rather than about any "social signals". Although he does talk about different "display rules" (cf. e.g. Ekman 1984, 1989), he seems to mean by that that people may be suppressing the expression of their authentic emotions, or that they may be putting on false expressions for social reasons (e.g. false smiles).

On the other hand, Fridlund (1997) emphatically rejects the distinction between "authentic" and "false" expressions, arguing that all facial expressions are, essentially, social. According to Fridlund, "facial expressions are not readouts of an 'emotional state'" (1997: 127); rather, they are "messages" (p. 104). Even when we are alone or "talking to ourselves . . . we often act as if others are present", and our faces are "communicative" even then (p. 119). Consequently, he argues, "we must finally dispatch the notion that the face mirrors the passions of the soul" (p. 124).

I believe Fridlund's points are well taken, and a valuable corrective to the decades of dominance of the "Emotional Expression" paradigm. In particular, I strongly agree that "facial displays are not 'expressions' of discrete emotional states" (Fridlund 1997: 104). It is to be hoped that the doctrine of "discrete emotional states" (and the concomitant doctrine of "blends") will soon be put to rest. The fact that the main proponent of the older paradigm, Paul Ekman, has now himself started to talk about "families of emotions" and "families of facial expressions" (cf. Ekman 1992a, 1994a and b), rather than "discrete emotions", as he did in the past, is very encouraging from this point of view (although it is difficult to see how this new view coheres with the doctrine of distinct neural patterns, associated with "distinct emotions").[2]

But if faces embody "messages", why should we abandon the term "readouts"? The metaphor of "reading" seems particularly appropriate to "messages" which can be "read" – not like scientific instruments in a lab, but as human sentences can be "read" (i.e. understood) by fellow human beings.

## 2 From the "psychology of facial expression" to the "semantics of facial expression"

The analogy between "facial behaviour" and language stressed by Fridlund is both valid and important. But if we accept that facial expressions are, in some respects, analogous to linguistic utterances, then we are moving from the domain of "the psychology of facial expression" to that of "the semantics of facial expression"; and then we have to take the basic assumptions and the methodological experience of the discipline of semantics into account.

In comparing "facial displays" to linguistic units and in stressing (quite correctly) the role of context in the interpretation of linguistic utterances, Fridlund (1994) appears to ignore the notion of "semantic invariants", that is to say, of those aspects of meaning which do *not* depend on context. For example, he writes:

> For the behavioural ecologist, the same smile would likely be labelled an "about to appease" display, and it would deliver the same message as the words, "I give in" or "Whatever you say" . . . By analogy with language, I may use the word *pen* to denote a writing implement in one context and a holding area in another, and there is no requirement that the writing *pen* be pronounced any differently than the cattle *pen*: the context determines the word's signification. Similarly, I may smile both when I am giving a gift and when I am exacting revenge. The context determines whether the smiles signify "I like you" or "Gotcha!", and the faces needn't be different. (p. 107)

But the analogy between a word like *pen* and a smile is spurious. The English word *pen* is simply polysemous: it has two distinct meanings, which have to be stated in a dictionary as such, and not one meaning with context-dependent elaborations. The context may help other people to understand which of the two meanings the speaker has in mind, but the polysemy of the word *pen* is a fact about the English language (as a semantic code), not a creation of the context (the words for "pen" in other languages do not share the same pattern of poly-semy). Crucially, the two meanings of the English word *pen* do not have a common denominator (a shared invariant), present in all its uses.

The status of a smile, as a semiotic category, is quite different: a smile is not polysemous (it doesn't have a fixed number of distinct meanings), and it does have one semantic invariant identifiable independently of context. As I have argued in earlier publications (cf. Wierzbicka 1993b, 1995b and d), the core meaning of a smile (that is, roughly speaking, of the configuration of facial muscles in which the corners of the mouth are raised, and of the movement which produces this configuration), can be stated as follows: "I feel something good now". Various possible interpretations of smiles such as those mentioned by Fridlund ("I give in", "Whatever you say . . .", "I like you", "Gotcha!", and so on) do indeed depend on the context; but they are compatible with the one meaning proposed here as the invariant core meaning of a smile ("I feel something good now"), and can be regarded as context-dependent elaborations of this invariant rather than as context-independent dis-tinct invariants, as in the case of *pen*. For example, the "appeasing smile" can be interpreted as signalling the message "I don't want you to

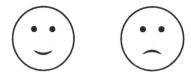

Figure 1

think that I feel something bad now, I feel something good now, I don't want to do anything bad". The "I like you" smile can be interpreted as signalling the message "I think good things about you, when I think about you I feel something good, I feel something good now", whereas a "revengeful" ("Gotcha!") smile can be interpreted along the following lines: "I want to do something bad to you (because you did something bad to me), I can do it now, because of this I feel something good now".

Since I am talking here about the semantics of smiles, not the psychology of smiles, no claims are being made about the smiling person's actual feelings, or actual thoughts, but only about the meaning of the observable "displays" (whether these "displays" are sincere or not does not affect their *meaning*). We can't "read" a person's actual feelings from their facial expression, but we can "read" the message associated with some forms of "display". In particular, from the raised corners of the mouth we can "read" the message "I feel something good now", whereas from the lowered corners of the mouth we can read the message "I feel something bad now". In Anglo culture (but also, for example, in Japanese culture; cf. Thayne and Suzuki 1996) this is sometimes symbolized by means of the schematic drawings in Figure 1 (cf. also Cüceloglu 1970) which are meant to signal either "good feelings" or "bad feelings".

It is true, then, that a smile sends a message, and that this message has a meaning. I would argue, however (pace Fridlund), that this meaning is identifiable, and that it has a context-independent invariant. The fact that in studies such as Kraut and Johnston (1979) "Smiles were observed more frequently when individuals were in social contact with others than when they were not facing or interacting with others" and that "people smiled more often *to* other people than as a result of some pleasurable experience" (Chovil 1997: 324) is perfectly compatible with the proposed semantic invariant of a smile. Often, it makes a great deal of sense for people to send to others the message "I feel something good now" (e.g. "when I see you"), whereas a pleasurable solitary experience doesn't have to be reflective and there is no reason to expect that it would often be accompanied by a message "I feel something good now" addressed either to oneself or to an imaginary addressee.

At the same time, I would argue (against Ekman, Izard, and others) that the meaning of a smile cannot be identified by means of one particular English word, such as *happy*, because, first of all, some smiles would often be interpreted as "amused", "cheerful", "serene", "joyful", "playful" etc. rather than necessarily "happy", and second, because other languages have other interpretive categories and so it would be ethnocentric to interpret all human messages (verbal or non-verbal) in terms of English lexical categories such as "happy". (In fact, Ekman himself alternates in his interpretation of smiling between different words, such as *happy* and *enjoyment*, as if these words meant exactly the same.)

Similarly, a facial configuration with the corners of the mouth lowered has an identifiable constant (context-independent) meaning, but this meaning, too, cannot be validly interpreted by means of some global and language-specific label such as *sad* or *unhappy*. It can be, however, validly interpreted by means of a language-independent semantic formula phrased in lexical universals such as "I feel something bad now".

For scholars like Ekman or Izard, who argue for the universality of human facial expressions, it should be congenial to be able to state those hypothetical meanings in universal terms (i.e. in terms which have exact semantic equivalents in each of the world's languages), rather than portraying them through the prism of the researcher's own language and culture.

### 3 "Social" does not mean "voluntary"

One crucial feature that facial "messages" have in common with verbal utterances is that they, too, express meanings which can be identified in the same metalanguage of universal semantic primes in which all verbal meanings can be identified. This means, in effect, that all facial messages can also be expressed verbally; for example, the message "I feel something good now" can be expressed either verbally or facially.[3]

On the other hand, the reverse is not true: there are many messages which can be expressed verbally but cannot be expressed facially, for example, "She feels something good now" or "I felt something good yesterday". As these examples illustrate, facial messages are necessarily "first person, singular, present-tense" ones (like performative verbs; cf. Austin 1962). In this restriction to the speaker's (actor's) current state facial expressions are similar to exclamations and interjections. An utterance like *Damn it!* or *Shit!*, too, can only express a first-person, singular, present-tense, meaning (very roughly, "I feel something bad now, I want to do something because of this"; cf. Wierzbicka 1991). As in the case of facial expressions, the meaning of an exclamation doesn't have to correspond to the speaker's actual current feelings: it can be sincere or "put on", but the meaning itself has an inherent first-person orientation. (Even if someone exclaims "Ouch!" to empathize with somebody else's pain, the expressed meaning includes the component "I feel something bad now", not "you feel something bad now".)

The analogy with exclamations and interjections can, I think, help us to clarify the issue of voluntariness of facial expressions. In Ekman's model, facial expressions appear to be essentially involuntary (and biologically based), unless they are "put on" for social reasons and therefore "false". Thus, summing up the results of his celebrated study comparing the "facial displays" of Americans and Japanese, Ekman (1984: 321) wrote: "In private, when no display rules to mask expressions were operative, we saw the biologically based, evolved, universal facial expressions of emotion".

Fridlund attacks this position and emphasizes the voluntary character of facial expressions; I think, however, that he goes too far in this direction, unnecessarily linking "meaning" with "voluntariness". In his model, people are said to "issue" certain faces (rather like one can "issue" orders, or official statements). For example, he writes: "In order to flourish, one must issue faces that primarily serve social motives, not any quasi-reflexive emotion" (1997: 105).

But one doesn't "issue" exclamations like "Shit!" or "Damn it!", although one may utter them more or less deliberately. The question is not whether such utterances are "voluntary" or "involuntary", but what they *mean*; and the important point is that they encode meanings which are social ("public") and which can be identified by semantic analysis, quite regardless of any particular speaker's state of mind or degree of premeditation. Similarly, one doesn't "issue" smiles or raised eyebrows, although one may produce them more or less deliberately. Again, the question is not whether such facial expressions are voluntary but what they *mean*.[4]

I also think that Fridlund may be exaggerating the "evolutionary advantage" of keeping one's feelings to oneself or displaying them only in a controlled and self-serving intentional way. Consider, for example, the following passage:

> Signals do not evolve to provide information detrimental to the dis-
> player. Displayers must not signal automatically but only when it is
> beneficial to do so (i.e., when such signalling serves its aims within an
> interaction). Automatic readouts or spillovers of drive or emotion
> states (for example, "facial expressions of emotion") would thus be
> extinguished early in phylogeny in the service of deception, economy,
> and privacy. (p. 109)

But, first, "privacy" is an Anglo cultural ideal, not a universal human value. Furthermore (as we will see in chapters 5 and 6), some cultures, for example Russian culture, value "spontaneous emotional expression" much more highly than does Anglo culture or than Fridlund would allow. It also seems that Fridlund takes a rather narrow view of what is "beneficial to the displayers". To begin with, it can be beneficial to the group if its members know what the other people in the group are feeling and what their needs are. Furthermore, although some "automatic readouts" (i.e. involuntarily betrayed emotions) may not be beneficial within a particular interaction, spontaneous displays of emotion may be seen (within a particular culture) as valuable and "advantageous" on a different level, e.g., by helping create closer bonds between people. We need to be careful not to absolutize the "evolutionary advantage" of values like "privacy" and "self-control", which are, after all, highly culture-specific.

What matters in the present context is that some "facial expressions" are indeed "social signals" which have an identifiable meaning. Whether a particular smile is voluntary, involuntary, or semi-voluntary, or "false", sincere, or semi-sincere, is irrelevant from the point of view of this smile's social meaning: no matter what a smiling person actually feels, or thinks, or wants, a smile as such never means "I feel something bad now"; it always means "I feel something good now".

### 4 What kind of "messages" can a face transmit?

If we leave aside the psychological issue of voluntariness, and focus, instead, on the semantic issue of what certain identifiable facial expressions mean, we are bound to recognize that the set of messages which can be expressed by our faces constitutes only a tiny fraction of the messages which can be expressed verbally. Some proponents of the "Social Communicative Approach" tend to exaggerate the semantic potential of human faces, and, in particular, fail to acknowledge their first-person present-tense limitations. For example, Chovil (1997: 322–3) states that "within a communicative approach, facial displays are hypothesized to be symbolic representations of a *wide variety* of meaning" (emphasis added); and also, that "they (...) enable individuals to communicate effectively and efficiently with others *on a variety of topics*" (emphasis added).

In my view, this is an exaggeration. There is only one topic on which "facial displays" enable us to communicate "effectively and efficiently", and this topic is "myself"; and not even "myself in general" but "my inner self now"; more precisely still, "some aspects of my inner self now" (cf. Wittgenstein 1967: 84). Above all, my face communicates what I *feel*, and also, in a very limited way, what I think, what I know, and what I want.

Speaking specifically of "faces in dialogue", Bavelas and Chovil (1997: 337) maintain that "facial displays . . . signify rather than reveal". I think the disjunction is not necessary: they certainly "signify", but no doubt they "reveal", too. What needs to be emphasized at this stage, when a change of paradigm appears to be finally under way (cf. Mandler 1997), is that they *also* signify; and that their signification can be studied in rigorous and methodologically coherent ways.

Chovil (1997) claims that faces can "depict" past occurrences, and that they can carry messages about the external situation such as "Danger" in addition to "first-person" messages such as "Fear" (i.e. "I feel fear" or "I am afraid"). But the fact that actors or story-tellers can "depict" in their faces emotions which they don't currently feel does not demonstrate that an actor's smile can *mean* "She felt something good at that time" rather than "I feel something good now". The words uttered by an actor also "depict" somebody else's thoughts, feelings, and actions, but this doesn't mean that the meaning of the words used by an actor is different from the meaning of the same words used in ordinary life. What is different is the pragmatic context, and the background assumptions, but not the meaning of the words.[5]

### 5 Messages are not "dimensions"

If we want to regard facial expressions as "messages", however, our hermeneutics should be intuitively plausible and should aim at representing the actor's, rather than the "observer's" (i.e. the scientist's), point of view (cf. Shore 1996). In particular, it is important to note that a "dimensional" model, such as those often used by psychologists in the past, and more recently resurrected (as he put it himself) by Russell (1997), cannot reveal the *semantics* of a facial "message" (whatever else it may or may not achieve), because the "dimensions" of this kind reflect the scientist's, not the actor's point of view.

Consider, for example, the face discussed by Russell (1997: figure 13.3) and reproduced here as figure 2. Russell notes that according to Ekman and Friesen (1975) and Matsumoto and Ekman (1988) this face shows an expression of fear, and he suggests an alternative interpretation in terms of three dimensions: "intense displeasure, very high arousal, and visual attention" (Russell 1997: 310).

Whatever the merits of such an analysis might be, it must be noted that it uses highly technical language and proposes a technical set of "meanings", not an ordinary person's language and an ordinary person's set of meanings. It shows how a psychologist might analyse a

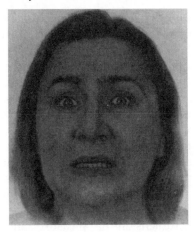

Figure 2

facial expression, not how a non-specialist could describe her own state of mind. (To say this is not to criticize the "dimensional" approach but merely to point to the obvious: it is a specialist "observer's model", not a non-specialist "actor's model".)

From this point of view, the traditional label "fear" (interpreted as meaning: "I feel fear now") is preferable to the proposed set of dimensions: if the person portrayed is a speaker of English, she could conceivably think, and say, "I feel fear" (or "I feel afraid"), but certainly not "[my] displeasure is intense, [I am] very highly aroused, [I am paying] visual attention".

Nonetheless, I would agree with Russell that the actual message sent by the face in question is less specific, and of course less culture-dependent, than "I feel fear" or "I feel afraid". Trying to articulate this message in an "actor's model", we could experiment with semantic formulae such as "I feel something bad now", "I think that something bad is happening", "I think that something bad can happen", "I want to know more about it", etc.; that is, formulae which an ordinary person could, in principle, say and understand, and which could be exactly translated into any other human language (for they rely exclusively on universal human concepts).

Russell (1997: 304) states that "In the psychology of emotion, a traditional debate has pitted categories of emotion against dimensions", and he argues, in my view quite convincingly, against the "standard account", that is, against interpreting faces in terms of categories like "happy", "angry", or "afraid (fear)". In fact, Russell's own studies (especially Russell 1991, 1994, and 1995) have played a major role in bringing about the "change of paradigm" hailed by Mandler

(1997). What these studies have done is to demonstrate that the "standard" account of emotions and facial expressions is questionable.

But the "dimensional" account is not the only possible alternative to the "standard" account. Looking at photographs such as the one in Russell's Figure 13.3 (1997: 310) (reproduced here as figure 2), which the "standard" approach interprets as "an expression of fear", and which Russell himself has analysed in terms of the three dimensions of "intense displeasure", "very high arousal", and "visual attention", I would propose a third type of analysis, portraying the *actor's* meaning, not the *observer's* (i.e. the scientist's) meaning, and doing so in terms of universal semantic primes, along the following lines: "I feel something bad now", "I think that something bad is happening", and "I want to know more about it".

Russell's proposed dimensions of "pleasure" and "displeasure" are of course akin to components like "I feel something good now" and "I feel something bad now", posited here. But the other dimensions proposed by him (such as "agitated vs. sleepy") do not translate equally easily into intuitively intelligible sentences formulated in universal human concepts; and the claim that "judgments about . . . pleasure and arousal are made quickly and automatically by all human beings, whatever their language or culture" (p. 298) appears to me unfounded. Moreover, since other languages don't have words corresponding exactly to the English *arousal* or *pleasure*, imputing to all other people, "whatever their culture or language", a "quick and automatic" judgment based on these notions seems to me to suffer from the same flaw as imputing to people all over the world English categories such as "happy", "angry", or "sad".

Regardless of what the basis for the proposed "dimensions" might be, they cannot be rooted directly in the judgments of non-specialists, "whatever their language and culture". Furthermore, "dimensions" of this kind cannot even be *tested* with untrained informants, because they do not relate to ordinary people's experience or understanding. By contrast, formulae such as "I feel something bad now" or "I want to know more (about it)" are "experience-near" (cf. Geertz 1984[1976]) and intuitively intelligible, and can be tested against actors' and experiencers' own intuitions.

## 6 "The face alone" or "the face in context"?

Opposition to the "standard account" of human faces would be more effective if it were not so frequently accompanied by claims that no firm generalizations about the meaning of facial actions can be made at all. After all, the appeal of the "standard account" was based largely on the strong generalizations this account offered. If these generalizations are now being refuted or questioned without any alternative generalizations being proposed, this can hardly look like a cause for rejoicing. And yet some opponents of the "standard account" seem to be doing just that: claiming that no generalizations can be made and presenting this conclusion as a very positive development.

For example, Chovil (1997: 330) writes (echoing Fridlund's remarks on the vital importance of "context" in the interpretation of facial signals): "Research discussed here, as well as other work on nonverbal communicative acts, has revealed that the meaning or function of the display may not be apparent when the display is viewed out of context. The same action(s) may serve several different functions." Chovil also links the "emerging view that emphasizes the social and communicative function of facial displays" with "the assumption that facial displays are expressive *to* another person rather than expressive *of* an underlying state", and she opposes the view of facial displays as "a route into psychological processes" to one which analyses them "in terms of the messages they convey to others in communicative situations" (p. 321).

What she appears to overlook is that we can also speak of the *meaning of* a certain type of facial display, regardless of what it happens to *convey to* various addressees in various communicative situations. In doing so, she appears to be jumping from the "psychology of emotions" directly to the "pragmatics of communication", and ignoring semantics – the study of the context-independent *meaning* of "social signals" (the meaning *of* something, not the information conveyed by it, in context, *to* a particular person). When Russell (1997: 313) argues that "the meaning attributed to a given facial stimulus even when seen alone still depends on context", it sounds as if he, too, believed that no firm and context-independent generalizations about the meaning of any facial movements or actions can be made.

Russell (1997: 313) questions Izard's (1997) argument "that we need to study judgements of the face alone in order to examine 'the independent signal value of the facial signals'" and comments: "The notion that the face alone has but one specific meaning (a specific basic emotion on the standard account) presupposes that the meaning attributed to the face is invariant across a reasonable range of observational contexts..." (p. 314). In my view, however, Izard's point is well taken, although I would suggest one correction: to establish the independent semantic value of "facial signals" we need to study "the face alone", not "*judgements* of the face alone".

Russell (1997) has demonstrated quite convincingly that "the face alone" cannot be interpreted in terms of an invariant global (i.e.

"gestalt") meaning such as "fear", "anger", or "surprise". He has not demonstrated, however, that no "independent signal value" can be attributed, regardless of context, to specific components of facial behaviour, such as a smile or a frown. Nonverbal signs, like words, require careful semantic analysis and cannot be established by "judgments" of untrained observers. To precisely identify the meaning of a word like *envy*, or *Schadenfreude*, or *remorse*, the semanticist must carefully examine a given word's range of use, sift through dozens of examples, and also dozens of sentences in which the word could *not* be appropriately used, and come up with an interpretive hypothesis (formulated in terms of more elementary concepts) which would best approximate the observed range of use. If the meaning of a word were to be established on the basis of casual comments by untrained observers, we would have to conclude that words have no stable meanings any more than smiles or frowns do. The biologist Nigel Wace (1981), who went around asking people what the word *weed* meant, collected no less than 2000 different "definitions", but this doesn't mean that the word *weed* has no stable and identifiable meaning (cf. Wierzbicka 1985a: 89–90).

Similarly, to establish the meaning of a smile or a frown we need to use proper techniques of semantic analysis, rather than merely to question casual observers; and we have to look for what remains constant across a variety of contexts.

## 7 Analysing facial behaviour into meaningful components

Semantic analysis presupposes structural analysis: to establish the meaning of a sign (e.g., a word) we have to delimit this sign from the complex within which it occurs. Similarly, to establish the meaning of a facial configuration we have to analyse it into simple (or simpler) signs which can be shown to carry their own meaning.

In "facial analysis" such a structural analysis is often done by establishing a list of what Russell (1997: 301) calls, following Snodgrass (1992), "single action units" or "elemental facial movements". Russell (1997: 301) reports some of Snodgrass' results in the form of a table which lists, among others, the following "units": "Inner brow raised", "Outer brow raised", "Brow furrowed", "Upper eyelid raised", "Cheek raised", and "Lower eyelid raised".

But the experience of modern linguistics suggests that a structural analysis of signs has to go hand in hand with semantic analysis: we cannot establish what the "minimal units" are if we don't ask from the outset what the "minimal *meaningful* units" are. In the case of the human face, it is doubtful that movements such as "cheek raised" or "lower eyelid raised" do have any identifiable invariant meaning at all;

or whether "inner brow raised" and "outer brow raised" can be shown to have two distinct meanings (identifiable by ordinary people in ordinary interpersonal communication).

On the other hand, if structural analysis of the face is carried out jointly with semantic analysis, the following eight movements at least emerge as meaningful minimal units of facial behaviour:

1. "Brow furrowed" (i.e. eyebrows drawn together)
2. Eyebrows raised
3. Eyes wide open
4. Corners of the mouth raised
5. Corners of the mouth lowered
6. Mouth open (while not speaking)
7. Lips pressed together
8. Nose wrinkled

The matter requires of course further investigation, in a variety of cultural settings. To be fully productive and reliable, however, such an investigation requires a rigorous semantic methodology. As mentioned earlier, it will not do to record casual ad hoc judgments of untrained "informants". What we can do instead is to formulate careful hypotheses phrased in English exponents of universal human concepts (such as, e.g. "I feel something bad now" or "I don't know what I can say now"), and to translate them into the matching configurations of elementary concepts in several different and culturally distant languages (e.g. in Russian "ja *čuvstvuju teper' čto-to ploxoe*", "*ja ne znaju, čto ja mogu teper' skazat'*"), and to test them with trained native consultants, familiar with the basic principles of semantic analysis and semantic methodology. In this chapter I can do no more than formulate, and briefly comment on, a handful of interpretive hypotheses, as a starting point for further cross-linguistic and cross-cultural testing.

Since the facial meanings pursued in this chapter are presumed to be universal rather than culture-specific (a presumption open of course to testing and in need of verification), it is reasonable to expect that their basis will turn out to be either iconic or indexical (in Peirce's sense; cf. Peirce 1932) rather than symbolic and conventional. For example, if we attribute to wide opened eyes the semantic component "I want to know more (about it)" it is clear how such a meaning could be gleaned, universally, from the gesture itself (with its implied message "I want to see more"), without the help of any local conventions. Similarly, if we attribute to an open yet silent mouth the semantic component "I don't know what I can say", it is clear how this meaning could be "figured out" (whether consciously or unconsciously), without the help of any local conventions.

What I mean by "iconic" and "indexical" is that the basis for decoding lies either in similarity ("like") or in co-occurrence ("when"). For example, the wrinkling of the nose (usually linked in the literature with "disgust") can convey that I feel "something bad" *like* a person does *when* she has to smell something bad that she doesn't want to smell. The gesture (which feels uncomfortable if we try to perform it) looks like a rather futile attempt to remove one's nose (or at least the bottom part of one's nose) from close contact with something malodorous, and so it can be seen as implying a message along the following lines:[6]

> I think this is bad
> I don't want to know anything about this
> I can't not know anything about it now
> I feel something bad now

There is an inferential leap here from "smell" to "know" (and in the case of wide open eyes from "see" to "know"), but this leap makes sense in the light of ordinary experience of people as "embodied beings"; and the same applies to other similar leaps "from body to mind" in the interpretation of facial behaviour. This is why facial gestures can function as social signals, that is, as messages which can be uniformly interpreted by other people, regardless of languages and cultures. (As Messinger, Fogel, and Dickson (1997: 213) put it, "facial expressions are simultaneously experiential and social".)

To say that gestures of this kind have an iconic and indexical basis is not to deny that they may be innate, as suggested by the fact that they can be observed in blind children, too (cf. Eibl-Eibesfelt 1972). A visible iconic basis may reinforce an invisible innate disposition; and besides, an iconic basis is, above all, experiential (a blind person has "muscular", if not visual, knowledge of frowns, smiles, and other facial gestures).

Of course there are also various culture-specific facial gestures, based on convention; and the interpretation of these – like the interpretation of verbal utterances – does depend on knowledge of the relevant conventions (cf. e.g. Hasada 1996). In this chapter, however, I will focus on a set of hypotheses concerning a number of facial gestures which appear to be iconic and/or indexical and therefore universally interpretable.

Before proceeding to present these hypotheses, however, let me make one general point. A "componential" analysis of the semantics of the face has been likened, not without justification, to the analysis of linguistic meanings into semantic primitives. In particular, Izard (1992: 563) has written:

Ortony and Turner (1990) also argued that some components of emotion expressions may be basic even though the emotions themselves are not. This is similar to the idea, discredited by many, that some components of words (semantic primitives) are simpler and more basic than the words themselves. Regardless of the merit of this controversial notion in semantics, its generalization to the bio-psychological phenomena of emotions is questionable.

Although Izard doesn't say who is responsible for advancing the theory of semantic primitives and using it as a basis for research into language, culture, cognition, and emotion, I think he can only mean the present writer. He does not, however, explain why he regards this idea as "discredited" or who exactly the "many" are who have "discredited" it. While he dismisses both the theory of semantic primitives and the "componential" approach to facial expressions, in fact, Izard's own theory of "differential emotions" suffers from the same problems that beset Ekman's theory of "discrete universal emotions" and their supposedly universal facial reflections. In this chapter I will try to show how the two related ideas – that of universal semantic primitives and that of identifiable facial "components" with identifiable meanings – can bear fruit in the interpretation of human facial expressions and how this approach can provide a viable alternative to the older paradigm.[7]

## 8 Summing up the assumptions

These are, then, my basic assumptions, on which the analysis proposed in this chapter is based:

1. We need to distinguish the "semantics of human faces" from the "psychology of human faces".
2. Semantic analysis (whether of verbal utterances or of facial expressions) must distinguish between the context-independent invariant and its contextual interpretations.
3. Certain facial configurations do have identifiable, context-independent meanings.
4. The meanings of facial configurations can be identified in the form of messages formulated in simple universal human concepts (e.g. "I feel something good now").
5. The meanings of facial configurations have an inherent first-person and present-tense orientation, and to be correctly identified must be represented in this mode (e.g. "I feel something good now" or "I want to know more").
6. The meanings of some facial expressions are universally intelligible and can be interpreted without reference to any local conventions.

7. To be fruitful, the semantic analysis of facial expressions needs a methodology. This can be derived from the methodological experience of linguistic semantics, and its basic theoretical tools, such as the notion of "polysemy", the notion of "semantic invariant", or the notion of "semantic component".

8. A semantic analysis of the human face has to be linked with a structural analysis, and requires the identification of minimal meaningful units of facial behaviour. This means, in effect, that to be fruitful, the semantic analysis of the face has to adopt a "componential" approach to the task, as suggested by Ortony and Turner (1990), Scherer (1984 and 1992), Smith and Scott (1997), and in fact, to a large extent, Darwin (1955[1872]).

9. The basis for the interpretation of facial gestures is, above all, experiential. One has no experience of, for example, raising one's cheeks (it is not something that one can do at will, and be conscious of doing), and so there is no meaningful facial gesture of "raising one's cheek" (even if our cheeks *are* actually raised when we raise the corners of the mouth). On the other hand, the raising of the corners of one's mouth is something that one can feel oneself do (as well as see in other people's faces), and so this gesture can indeed be regarded as meaningful (it is both experiential and social).[8]

10. The "semantics of the human face" can rely on the same "natural semantic metalanguage" which has been tested, over three decades, in linguistic semantics, and which has been applied to large-scale studies of semantic domains such as emotions, speech acts, and social interaction. Using this metalanguage, we can formulate the meanings of "facial expressions" from the actor's point of view, which we need to do if we really believe that "faces" send "messages". It is ordinary people, not scientists, who communicate by means of faces. Scientists can of course build their own models ("observers' models"), to communicate with one another; but if we want to understand messages that ordinary people send to one another (e.g. by means of a smile, a "frown", or raised eyebrows), we must put ourselves in ordinary people's shoes and posit messages which make sense to ordinary people. The use of the Natural Semantic Metalanguage allows us to do just that.

## 9 In what terms should facial behaviour be described?

Before we try to assign meanings to specific elements of facial behaviour we have to decide in what terms we are going to describe such behaviour. For example, are we going to talk about the function of the "corrugator supercilii" or about the meaning of a "frown"? And are we going to talk about "wide opened eyes" or about a face in which "the upper lid is raised, exposing the sclera (white) above the iris" (Ekman and Friesen 1975: 52)? Generally speaking, are we going to use scientific (anatomical and physiological) categories or more or less "naive" categories, reflecting the perspective of the "person in the street"?

If what we are really after is the meaning of certain facial expressions then the answer seems to be clear: we have to focus on those aspects of facial behaviour which are noticeable and apparently meaningful to "ordinary people". Words such as *frown* or *smile* and expressions such as *raised eyebrows* and *pursed lips* provide linguistic evidence for the psychological reality of certain perceptions: they demonstrate that people do notice "raised eyebrows" or "pursed lips" and attribute meaning to them. By contrast, there is no comparable linguistic evidence demonstrating that people are aware of the "raising of upper eyelids" or of "the skin below the brow [being] stretched" (Ekman and Friesen 1975: 45).

On the other hand, "naive" categories such as "a frown", "a smile", or "a pout" cannot be taken for granted either, because they are language-specific and their meaning may be partly due to "local" linguistic and cultural conventions. For example, while in ordinary English people speak of "opening one's eyes wide" (e.g. in surprise or fear) rather than of the "whites of the eyes showing (above the iris)", in Japanese, the reverse is the case (Hasada 1996); and in Russian one can speak not only of "opening one's eyes wide" (as in English), but also of making "big eyes", "round eyes", or even "square eyes" (Iordanskaja and Paperno 1996: 53; see also chapter 5) – options which are not available in English.

If people all over the world can communicate to some extent by means of facial behaviour, the meaning of the relevant facial signs must be both noticeable (perhaps even salient) to "ordinary people" (i.e. non-scientists) and "decodable" on some sort of universal basis. It may be premature to make any assertions as to the nature of this universal basis but the existing literature on facial expression does allow us to venture some hypotheses. In doing so I will try, as usual, to stay as close as possible to the level of linguistic and conceptual universals. I will not try to avoid "naive" and near-universal words like *eyes*, *eyebrows*, or *mouth* (cf. Goddard forthcoming a), although I will avoid references to "inner brow", "outer brow" or "lower eyelids", for which most languages, including English, do not seem to have distinct words or common descriptive phrases.

Trying to speak in "naive" but not overly language-specific terms, I will propose analyses of the following eight facial gestures which emerge from the literature as possible universals (no doubt not an exhaustive list):

1.   One can deliberately move one's eyebrows so that they will be (relatively) close together. This movement suggests, iconically, that "I want to do something" (as I want to move my eyebrows). It also appears to suggest, as does any deliberate movement in the part of the face above the eyes, that "I'm thinking now".

How do people know (other than "innately") that the gesture of drawing one's eyebrows together can convey the message "I'm thinking now"? Arguably, the basis of this knowledge (innate or not) is also experiential and in any case it can be experientially tested: just try to think hard for a moment about anything whatsoever, and the chances are that you will find yourself "frowning". (Of course in many cultures thinking can also be associated with other parts of the body in addition to the head in general and the forehead in particular: the heart, liver, kidneys, and so on; but this is not incompatible with an experientially testable association between thinking and moving some parts of one's face above the eyes.)[9]

In fact, the existence of an experiential basis is also the reason why I believe the drawing of the eyebrows is meaningful whereas their lowering is not: although we can feel ourselves raising our eyebrows we can't feel ourselves lowering them; on the other hand, we *can* feel ourselves drawing our eyebrows together. Thus, it is the drawing of the eyebrows together, not their lowering, which has an experiential basis and can be meaningful to the "actor" (even in the case of a blind person).

The gesture in question could, then, be described in a "naive", non-scientific way as follows: a person is doing something with her eyebrows as one would if one wanted to draw one's eyebrows close together. (For a fuller discussion see below, section 10.)

2.   One can move one's eyebrows upwards. Like other movements in the area of the face above the eyes, this, too, can be interpreted as suggesting that I'm thinking about something. In addition, it can be said that when I move my eyebrows upwards I am moving them as if I wanted to see more. To quote Stephen Peck (1987: 98), author of the *Atlas of Facial Expression*: "Not only does brow raising facilitate lid raising, but it also further increases the field of vision . . . Raised brows can be a part of many different attitudes, but the reason is almost always the same: to increase the visual field".

The claim that the *reason* for raised brows is "almost always the same: to increase the visual field" is somewhat fanciful, but it is not an exaggeration to *describe* the gesture in question with reference to such a goal: when I raise my eyebrows I move them *like* a person does when she moves her eyebrows upwards because she wants to see more above her. It is easy to guess at least part of the implied message: "I want to know more". (For a fuller discussion see section 11.)

3. One can "open one's eyes wide", or make them "big", or "round", or, in more general terms, do something with one's eyes like a person would who would want her eyes to be big (for a short time) so that she can see more. I am not trying to state and justify the core meaning of such a gesture here (I will do this in section 12), merely to "describe" the gesture itself. But here, too, it is easy to guess the implied message: "I want to know more".

4. One can do something with one's mouth in such a way that the corners of one's mouth move upwards (a "smile").

There is of course more to a prototypical "smile" than just the raising of the corners of the mouth: for the scientist, there is also the contraction of the muscle "orbicularis oculi which raises the cheek and gathers the skin inwards form around the eye socket" (Ekman 1989: 155); and for the naive observer, one might add, there is also the "showing of the teeth". All these facial events, however, are subsidiary to the core event (the raising of the corners of the mouth). Experientially, neither the wrinkles around the eyes (the famous "Duchenne smile"), nor the "raising of the cheek" have any semiotic value of their own, and "ordinary people" don't have to be aware of them as a necessary, or even typical, aspect of smiling (one can't produce these effects at will and one can't feel oneself doing these things); and a baby's toothless "smile" is still thought of, by "ordinary people" (as well as by scientists) as a "smile".

Assuming, then, that what we mean by "smiling" is, essentially, the voluntary raising of the corners of one's mouth, let us briefly consider this gesture's core meaning: if the core meaning of a "smile" is indeed, as I have often argued, "I feel something good now" (cf. Wierzbicka 1993b, 1995b and d), then how – on what basis – can people identify this meaning? I propose, roughly speaking, the following iconic and experiential basis for this apparently universal interpretation: the mouth of a "smiling" person looks like the mouth of a laughing person; and laughter is pleasurable to the laughing person; that is, in my terms, when a person is laughing she feels "something good" (cf. Plessner 1970[1961]); accordingly, a "smiling" mouth can be experientially linked with feeling "something good".

Normally, of course, a laughing person has a reason to laugh, and this reason may lie in a pleasant feeling of amusement, delight, or whatever. But my point is that, in addition, laughing itself "feels good", and so a "laughing-looking mouth" indexes "feeling something good";

and since a "smiling mouth" looks like a "laughing mouth" (minus the sound), a smiling mouth, too, can convey the message "I feel something good now". To quote Darwin (1955[1872]: 209):

> Between a gentle laugh and a broad smile there is hardly any difference, excepting that in smiling no reiterated sound is uttered . . . the habit of uttering loud reiterated sounds from a sense of pleasure, first led to the retraction of the corners of the mouth and of the upper lip, and to the contraction of the orbicular muscles; and that now, through association and long-continued habit, the same muscles are brought into slight play whenever any cause excites in us a feeling which, if stronger, would have led to laughter; and the result is a smile.

The fact that in many languages the same (or closely related) words are used for both "laughing" and "smiling" (lexically distinguished in English as two different activities) supports this: e.g. in Polish *śmiech* vs. *uśmiech*, in French *rire* vs. *sourire* (literally, "under-laugh"), in German *lachen* vs. *lächeln* (with a "diminutive" suffix for "smiling"); and in Vietnamese *cu'ò'i*, for both "laughing" and "smiling" (Nick Enfield, personal communication).

5. I can also "do something with my mouth" by deliberately moving the corners of my mouth downward. It seems likely that the core meaning of such a facial gesture would be universally understood as the opposite of that of a "smile", that is as, in essence, "I feel something bad now". The semiotic basis for this interpretation could lie simply in the diametrical contrast between two positions:

$$\cup \rightarrow \text{I feel something good now}$$
$$\cap \rightarrow \text{I feel something bad now}$$

The grimace moving the corners of the mouth down feels, I suggest, uncomfortable (that is, in simple terms, the person making it "feels something bad" – a suggestion open to experiential verification), and this could be an additional basis for the message which would be attributed to such a face (possibly, universally): "I feel something bad now".

6. Another thing that one can do with one's mouth (not necessarily deliberately) is to "open it" and to keep it like this for some time. Usually a gesture of this kind is linked with surprise or astonishment. Darwin (1955[1872]: 279) quoted in support of such an interpretation Shakespeare's line (from "King John"): "I saw a smith stand with open mouth swallowing a tailor's news". As mentioned earlier, the iconic basis for such a gesture's meaning is clear: if I do this, I'm doing something with my mouth like a person does who wants to say something and then, against expectations, I don't say anything. To avoid the English-specific term "open" in favour of universal concepts such as

"do" and "move", we could describe this gesture in just such quasi-functional terms, that is, we could say that the person whose expressive behaviour we are describing is moving her mouth like a person does who wants to say something and yet doesn't say anything. As suggested earlier, the implied message of such a gesture is likely to be: "I don't know what I can say".

7.   One other widely recognizable gesture which one can make with one's mouth or, more precisely, with one's lips is to press one's lips tightly together. Ekman and Friesen (1975: 83) speak in this connection of "the closed, lip-pressed-against-lip mouth", which they call "the anger mouth" (alongside the "open, square anger mouth") and which they claim is linked with two quite different kinds of anger: "It occurs when the person is engaging in some form of physical violence, bodily attacking another person. And it occurs when the person is attempting to control a verbal, shouting anger, and presses the lips together in an attempt to keep from shouting or saying something hostile" (p. 87).

In fact, the implied message of such a gesture is not necessarily that of "anger" (see section 14 below). The gesture has a clear iconic basis: by deliberately pressing my lips tightly together I convey the impression, on the one hand, that "I want to do something" (as I'm doing something with my lips), and, on the other hand, that "I don't want to say anything". Again, to avoid both scientific language and "naive" but language-specific expressions such as *pursed lips*, we can say that the person making such a gesture is doing something with her mouth like a person would who would want to prevent her mouth from being able to move.

In sections 11–15, I will discuss some of these facial gestures in more detail, focussing on their meaning and the semiotic basis for their interpretation. First, however, some general comments are in order about using the same framework for analysing verbal and non-verbal communication.

## 10 Humans and primates: a unified framework for verbal, non-verbal, and preverbal communication

While this chapter focusses on the semantics of human faces, the framework applied here is also applicable to the analysis of other aspects of non-verbal as well as verbal communication. For example, the message "I want to know more", which can be assigned to raised eyebrows, is closely related to the message "I want to know something", which can be assigned to rising intonation; and the message "I don't know what I can say" assigned to an open (but silent) mouth is closely related to the message "I don't know what I can say, I don't want to say anything about this to you now", which can be assigned to the gesture of shrugging one's shoulders.

As Goodenough (1994: 263) observes, "A theory or interpretation that accounts for more of the phenomena under consideration is preferable to one that accounts for fewer of them. One that is consistent with interpretations that account for other kinds of phenomena is preferable to one that is not." On this criterion alone, a theory which provides a unified framework for both verbal and non-verbal communication, and for facial as well as non-facial (bodily) non-verbal communication, should be preferable to theories which present different communication systems as completely unrelated.

For example, when Ekman and Friesen (1975) assign to raised eyebrows two entirely different interpretations: "surprise" and "question" (calling the latter an "emblem") they are clearly missing something that the two have in common. An invariant component such as "I want to know more (about it)" identifies the missing link.

The abyss which separates so-called "formal semantics" dealing with verbal language (cf. e.g. Chierchia and McConnell-Ginet 1990; Cann 1993) from the study of non-verbal communication (and which also ignores emotions, interjections, exclamations, and so on) is particularly striking. As the anthropologist David Parkin notes (1996: 115):

> much theoretical linguistics depends, for its data, on the fiction of the socially decontextualised speech event: it focuses on strings of grammatically acceptable sentences that are supposed to have truth-values, but completely omits any reference to the vital paralinguistic properties of gesture, mood and sentiment . . . The anthropological corollary would be the absurd claim that there exists a linguistically decontextualized culture, one that operates without language and that can be studied as such. I find such an idea preposterous, as I do the idea of separating out verbal language from non-verbal communication. Indeed, the category of the verbal, set up by such separation, is itself an analytic fiction.

The very fact that intonation is a necessary aspect of spoken language, distinguishing, for example, statements from questions, supports the validity of Parkin's comment; and the fact that one can, so to speak, ask questions with one's eyebrows, as well as with one's intonation or with interrogative particles such as *czy* in Polish or *li* in Russian, further highlights the underlying unity of verbal and non-verbal communication.

This is not to deny, needless to say, the central role of (verbal) language in human life, but rather to recognize its links with other types of communication, including that of non-human primates, and the desirability of a framework within which such links can be explored and accounted for. To quote Mandler (1997: ix):

> Nearly 100 years ago, Wilhelm Wundt in the first volume of his monumental *Völkerpsychologie* noted that "language presumably developed out of the simpler forms of expressive movements". Among the expressive skills that surely contributed to the early communicative behaviors of preverbal *H. sapiens* were facial, gestural, vocal, and "body language" expressions. Even today, other primates communicate not too badly by the use of these devices. Should early humans have been expressively mute by comparison? And if not, is it unlikely that some of these devices survived into the present, just as so many other aspects of our bodily equipment did?

The framework developed in this book is applicable to the communication of primates as much as it is to human communication, both verbal and non-verbal. For example, the literature on primate communication can be said to suggest the following meanings conveyed by more or less ritualized visual displays as well as vocal signals:

1. I want to do something bad to you now
   (so-called "threats" and "aggressive displays", in which "a tendency to attack is greatly preponderant", Moynihan 1976: 247)

2. I think: something bad can happen now
   I want everyone to know this
   (so-called "warning signals", cf. e.g. Simonds 1974: 141–2)

3. I think: something very bad will happen to me now
   I can't do anything
   (so-called "squealing", "fear-signals", cf. e.g. Simonds 1974: 146)

4. I know: something very bad is happening now
   I have to do something because of this now
   (so-called "alarm patterns in which a tendency to escape is greatly preponderant", Moynihan 1976: 247)

5. I say: I am here
   I want everyone to know this
   (cf. Tomasello and Call 1997: 257: "it is safe to say that the function of chimpanzee pant-hoots is currently unknown, although they almost certainly serve to announce to groupmates the caller's location.")

Assigning NSM meanings of this kind to visual and auditory signals of primates may seem anthropomorphic, but in fact it is no more so than the traditional language of primatology, including expressions such as "warning displays" or "alarm calls". To quote one primatologist, Pamela Asquith (1984: 170), the author of a paper entitled "The inevitability and utility of anthropomorphism in description of primate behaviour": "Terms such as 'threaten', 'submission', 'dominance', 'beg', 'chase', 'play' are so much part of the literature that they do not jolt or surprise the reader. However, the fact that other terms, such as 'refrain', *do* surprise the reader is a reminder that the metaphorical process is constantly in the background and constantly implying the human reference of the terms."

As Roy Harris (1984: 174) notes in his comment on Asquith's paper, "we have no plausible alternative but to use an anthropomorphic conceptual framework in our analyses of animal communication". (Harris (ibid.) also rightly points out that in fact there is no reason "to construe the application of communication vocabulary to animal signalling as being metaphorical" – a point which Asquith concedes (pp. 175–6).)

NSM formulae such as "I want to do something bad to you now" do jolt or surprise the reader more than "threat" or "warn" because they are less familiar and more explicit, but in fact they are no more anthropomorphic than the conventional primatological labels.

By applying the same system of semantic primitives to both human and animal communication we are not obliterating the profound, and indeed fundamental differences between the two but are rather making comparisons between them possible, just as by applying the same interpretive framework to verbal and non-verbal human communication we are making it possible for the two to be compared at all. We are also allowing for a relation of continuity and evolutionary development from animal to human, and from non-verbal to verbal communication.

Mandler blames the stagnation in research into non-verbal communication partly on Chomskian linguistics, with its innate "Language Acquisition Device", which supposedly sprang up in the human species ex nihilo (ibid.):

> The virtual abandonment in the literature . . . of a discussion of gesture language is an embarrassment for both the psychology of language and the psychology of emotion. The former, in its "miracle" Chomskian and neo-Chomskian mode, yields no place for any extensive communication skills in humans prior to the emergence of spoken language; the latter has, until recently, ignored the communicative functions of expressive movements (consisting of facial, bodily, and vocal expression and gestures).

But although Chomskian linguistics, with its disregard for meaning and communication, has deterred both psychology and anthropology from looking to linguistics for insights or methodological inspiration (cf. Steiner 1992, Keesing 1994, Tuite 1998, Goddard forthcoming b), there is more to modern linguistics than Chomskianism; and in fact the foundations for a "new psychology of language" (cf. Tomasello 1998) have already been laid.

Within the framework of this "new psychology of language" we can now ask questions which were entirely beyond the pale of the older paradigms; and this includes questions about the semantics of non-verbal communication.

## 11 The meaning of eyebrows drawn together

The English word *frown* is not a reliable way to identify a facial gesture with a universal or near-universal significance. The English expression *to frown upon* implies that someone (the "frowner") thinks that someone else is doing something bad, and even the word *frown* by itself may imply more than any particular facial gesture would do. (Some dictionaries of English, e.g. The *Longman Dictionary of the English Language* (*LDOTEL* 1984), attribute to the word *frown* two meanings, one more general and one restricted to "displeasure".) In what follows, I will avoid this word as far as possible and I will speak instead of the gesture of drawing one's eyebrows together, regardless of what feelings or thoughts appear to be conveyed by it in any given case and regardless of anything else that may or may not happen in the person's face – for example, of whether the eyebrows are lowered or raised at the same time. (Although, as mentioned earlier, we can feel ourselves raising our eyebrows, we can't feel ourselves lowering them; on the other hand, we *can* feel ourselves drawing them together. It is the drawing together of the eyebrows, then, not their lowering, which has an experiential basis.)

The over-all meaning of each facial configuration depends of course on all its components, and, arguably, on the interaction between the components as well, but in each case it should be at least compatible with the meaning that we wish to attribute to a particular facial gesture (e.g. the "frown") as such.

For example, Ekman and Friesen (1975) link the gesture of drawing one's eyebrows together not only with what they call "the anger brow" ("the eyebrows are drawn down and together", p. 82), but also with what they call "the fear brow", and (optionally) with what they call "the sadness brow". In "the fear brow", they say, "the eyebrows are raised and drawn together" (p. 50), whereas in "the sadness brow", "the inner corners of the eyes are raised and may be drawn together" (p. 117). If we wish to isolate the likely meaning of the gesture of drawing one's eyebrows together as such, we have to try to come up with something that would fit Ekman and Friesen's "fear brow" and "knitted-brow–sadness-brow" as well as their "anger brow", and all the other facial contexts in which the gesture of drawing one's eyebrows together may occur.

Many researchers have speculated about the meaning of a "frown" using the English word *frown* but without explaining clearly what exactly they meant by it. I presume that in most cases they, too, meant the gesture of drawing one's eyebrows together, but it is often not clear whether they didn't have something else in mind as well (in particular, the lowering of the eyebrows). Be this as it may, the answers they have come up with appear to suggest that some basic intuitions about the gesture of drawing one's eyebrows together are shared. Since, however, the way these intuitions are expressed differs from writer to writer, it is never quite clear whether, or to what extent, these differences represent genuine disagreement, since the interpretive hypotheses are usually not formulated in a way which would facilitate comparison.

Darwin considered what he called "frowning" an expression "of something difficult or displeasing encountered in a train of thought or in action" (1955[1872]: 222). He seems to have been the first scholar who linked the "frown" with the notion of "obstacle": "A man may be absorbed in the deepest thought, and his brow will remain smooth until he encounters some *obstacle* [emphasis added] in his train of reasoning, or is interrupted by some disturbance, and then a frown passes over his brow". The "obstacle" in the course of an action is illustrated as follows: "a man in doing even so trifling a thing as pulling on a boot frowns if he finds it too tight" (p. 221).

Darwin (p. 220) also quoted, with apparent approval, the idea of an earlier author, Charles Bell, that the muscle chiefly responsible for the effect of "frowning", that is, the so-called corrugator supercilii, "knits the eyebrows with an energetic effort, which unaccountably, but irresistibly, conveys the idea of mind".

A century later, Scherer (1992) "translated Darwin's observations into a proposal that the eyebrow frown is associated with the perception of some type of discrepancy between one's needs or goals and one's actual circumstances" (Smith and Scott 1997: 239). Others apparently understood Darwin differently: "In contrast, Smith (1989) interpreted Darwin's statements as implying that the frown was associated with anticipating the need to expend effort to cope with one's situation" (Smith and Scott, ibid.)

In the last decade or so, however, "frowning" has become increasingly strongly linked with the notion of "obstacle", apparently at the expense of the notion of "effort"; and "obstacle" has been increasingly interpreted in terms of "goal obstacles", "goal blockage", or "goal discrepancies".

Thus, Smith and Scott (1997: 241) report that "follow-up analyses suggested the eyebrow frown is more closely related to perceived goal obstacles than to anticipated effort, thereby supporting Scherer's (1984) interpretation of meaning of this component over Smith's (1989) . . . A series of regression analyses indicated that the relation between goal obstacles and eyebrow frown was more direct than that between anticipated effort and the eyebrow frown". Smith and Scott (1997: 242) also report that this result, favouring "obstacle" rather than "effort" as a key to the interpretation of a "frown", was also replicated in a later study by Pope and Smith (1994). "In this study, no evidence was obtained for a relation between anticipated effort and the eyebrow frown, but brow region activity was found to be positively correlated with perceived goal obstacles and goal discrepancies and negatively correlated with subjective pleasantness".

But while the notion of "obstacle" appears to be currently favoured over the notion of "effort", the key interpretive notions keep shifting and forming new alliances: what is the difference between "goal obstacles" and "goal discrepancies"? or between "goal discrepancies" and "need-goal discrepancies" (Smith and Scott 1997: 242)? Or between all of those and Scherer's (1992: 162) "lack of goal conductiveness" or Ortony and Turner's (1990: 321–2) "goal blockage"?

As I have suggested in an earlier discussion of the semantics of drawn-together eyebrows (Wierzbicka 1993b), to clarify the confusion surrounding this problem we have to abandon complex and shifting terms and phrases like "goal discrepancies", "goal obstacles", or "goal blockages", and replace them with intuitively comprehensible combinations of self-explanatory conceptual primes such as WANT and DO. To begin with, what the frequently recurring terms "goal" and "obstacle" suggest is that the actor is seen as someone who "wants to do something". Speaking from an actor's, rather than an observer's, point of view we could formulate on this basis the following semantic component of a "frown" (as I, too, called this gesture in my earlier work):

(a) I want to do something now

The wide-spread use of terms like "obstacle" and "blockage" in the discussions of "frowns" suggests, in addition, some negative component along the lines of

(b) I think I can't do it

(I am not positing component (b) as valid, but showing how it could be phrased.) If we were to agree with Ortony and Turner (1990) that the "obstacles" or "blockages" suggested by a "frown" have to be "unexpected" we would need to propose some further component along the lines of

(c) I didn't think this would happen

(Again, I am not positing component (c) as valid, but showing how it could be phrased.)

Semantic components such as (a), (b), and (c) above may or may not be correct as a representation of the perceived meaning of a "frown", but they have the advantage of being sufficiently clear and explicit to be able to be tested in a variety of contexts; and such testing across a variety of contexts is absolutely necessary if the invariant meaning of a "frown" is to be discovered and clearly identified. Components such as (a), (b), and (c) can also be tested cross-linguistically, for unlike "goal discrepancies" or "goal blockages" they are readily translatable into any language whatsoever.

From this point of view, the wide-spread practice of discussing "frowns" in connection with "anger" is unfortunate, for first, it makes cross-cultural testing impossible, and second, it brings to mind an "angry frown" rather than a whole range of possible "frowns" and possible experiential contexts in which those "frowns" may occur. In fact, I would suggest that the concentration on "goals", "obstacles", and "blockages" in the discussions of "frowns" may be skewed towards "angry frowns" or "frustrated frowns" instead of being focussed on invariant ("dissociable") semantic components of drawn-together eyebrows as such. Consider, for example, the following discussion of "frowns", "goals", and "blockages" in Ortony and Turner (1990: 321–2):

> Consider first the furrowed brow that plays such a large role in the prototypical expression of anger. This component of the anger expression seems to reflect not anger per se, but a mental state in which the person is conscious of being unable to attain a goal, due to some unexpected blockage. This interpretation is compatible with the evidence that a frown often accompanies states such as frustration, puzzlement, concentrated attention to a problem, a difficulty encountered in a task, and so on . . . The reason a frown is part of the prototypical anger expression might therefore be that one of the common components of the eliciting conditions of this emotion is the frustration of an attempt to attain a goal: One is frustrated by (and angry at) the car that refuses to start or a person who stands in the way of what one wants. Recently, C. A. Smith (1989) reported empirical evidence for the connection between the perception of an obstacle (goal blockage) and the frown. (pp. 321–2)

In my earlier discussion of "frowns" (Wierzbicka 1993b) I took as my primary point of reference Ortony and Turner's formulation: "a mental

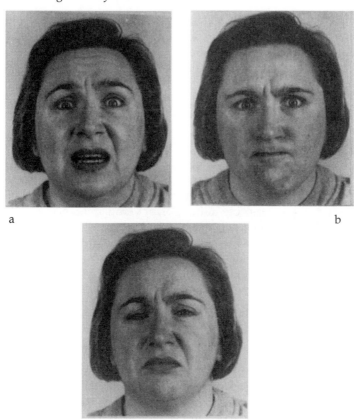

a

b

Figure 3                                        c

state in which the person is conscious of being unable to attain a goal, due to some unexpected blockage"; and I suggested a formulation in the form of the three components: (a) I want to do something (now); (b) I think I can't do it; and (c) I didn't think this would happen (as given above). To simplify further discussion, let us now discount, straight away, component (c), in recognition of the fact that the "target" or occasion of a "frown" does not have to be "unexpected". As noted by Darwin, stutterers frequently "frown" in speaking, and yet the "obstacles" they encounter are anything but unexpected.

But is it true that the other two hypothetical components, (a) and (b), are compatible with all cases of drawn-together eyebrows? Consider, for example, the three photographs in figure 3 (from Russell 1997), in which the gesture of drawing one's eyebrows together occurs in different environments: A. in combination with raised eyebrows, wide-open eyes, and semi-open mouth; B. in combination with lowered eyebrows and compressed lips; and C. in combination with semi-closed eyes and down-turned corners of the mouth. I would argue that of these three faces at least one, face B, doesn't convey the impression that "I want to do something and I think I can't do it": on the contrary, face B appears to suggest that "I want to do something and am determined to do it".

When looking for an invariant meaning which can be attributed to *all* instances of drawing one's eyes together (regardless of context), the starting point should probably be the iconic basis of a "frown" discussed earlier, with its apparent double message: "I'm thinking now (about something)" and "I want to do something now". These two components seem consistent with the expressions A, B, and C, as well as all other pictorial representations of, or verbal references to, "knitted eyebrows". As Charles Bell (quoted earlier) put it, the "knitted eyebrows irresistibly convey the idea of mind", or in my terms, the idea of "thinking" ("I'm thinking now"). Furthermore, the apparent "effort" displayed in the deliberate action of drawing one's eyebrows close together "irresistibly" conveys the idea that "I want to do something now", even if, as in the case of face A, I don't know what I can do, if anything, or, as in the case of face C, I am highly ambivalent about doing anything (e.g. I want to throw out that rotten piece of meat but I feel disgusted at the thought of actually touching it).

But while the two components of "thinking" and "wanting to do something" appear to be entirely plausible as the invariant core of drawn-together eyebrows, something seems to be still missing: the intuitions behind the recurring terms like "discrepancy", "obstacle", or "blockage" remain unaccounted for. To account for these intuitions I propose the following hypothesis: in the meaning of drawn-together eyebrows the component "I want to do something now" co-occurs with the "discrepant" component "I know I am not doing it now", arguably also rooted in the apparent logic of the facial behaviour itself.

For we can think about it like this: when I am trying to draw my eyebrows together, my face conveys the impression that, on the one hand, I want to do something (draw my eyebrows so that they are together) and, on the other hand, I'm conscious of not quite doing it (at least not yet): "I know I'm not doing it now" (my eyebrows are not fully "together", after all).

This is, then, I suggest, the "facial logic" which enables observers to attribute to "knitted eyebrows" the two "discrepant" semantic components "I want to do something now" and "I know I'm not doing it now".

Once again, we must resist the temptation of positing the component "I think I can't do it" (what I want to do), because this would be incompatible with the "frown" of a person determined to do something (as in the face B). We must also resist the temptation of adding to the formula the word *yet* ("I know I'm not doing it yet"), for this wouldn't be consistent with faces like A, where there is no expectation that the "discrepancy" will be resolved. It would appear, however, that in every case (including the faces A, B, and C above) the "frown" is compatible not only with the thought "I want to do something" but also with the thought "I know I'm not doing it now". If I am frightened or worried then maybe I can't do what I want to do (hence the idea of "obstacle" and "goal blockage"); but if I am angry and determined to act I may still be aware that I'm not doing (yet) what I want to do. (In fact, it would seem strange to keep the "frown" on once I am beating someone up). Similarly, if I am "frowning" while trying to thread a needle, or to pull on a tight boot (Darwin's examples), my attitude doesn't have to be one of "I can't do it", but it may well be one of "I know I'm not doing it now".

In the final resort, then, Scherer's notion of "discrepancy" appears to be more apposite to the interpretation of *all* "frowns" than the idea of an "obstacle" or a "goal blockage". For this idea to be truly explanatory, however, it has to be made clear in what this "discrepancy" consists; and I am suggesting that this can be articulated in the form of the two semantic components "I want to do something now" and "I know I am not doing it now".[10]

Ekman (1989: 157) has suggested that "Brow lowering acts as a sunshade, decreasing the light coming in from the superior visual field" and that it also "helps to protect the eyeball from blows, and also may enhance focal illumination by diminishing background light". I would suggest a different perspective on the gesture. First, I see the drawing of the eyebrows together, and not their lowering, as the most salient (and experientially real) aspect of the gesture and as a key to its semantic interpretation; and second, I propose a semantic invariant which seeks to explain the whole range of this gesture's use, including "concentration" and "worry" as well as "anger". "Concentration" and "worry" do not involve protecting one's eyeballs from either sunlight or from blows; but they, too, can be explained in terms of the three components proposed here: "I'm thinking now", "I want to do something", and "I know I'm not doing it now".

## 12 The meaning of "raised eyebrows"

In their discussions of the meaning of "raised eyebrows" scholars usually follow one of two main tracks: they either link this gesture with "surprise" or they talk, instead, of something that they call "attentional activity". To start with the latter approach, Smith and Scott (1997: 239) wrote recently about the raising of the eyebrows as follows:

> there is a general consensus that raising the eyebrows and raising the upper eyelids are both associated with something related to attentional activity. However, individual investigators differ in the specific meanings they associate with these actions. Darwin [1985(1872)] associates both activities with attentional activity, whereas Scherer (1984) associates them with the perception of novelty in the environment. Smith (1989), in contrast, associates raising the upper eyelid with attentional activity and raising the eyebrows with uncertainty about some aspect(s) of one's circumstances. Finally, Frijda (1969) associates raising the upper eyelid with attentional activity but does not address the significance of the raised eyelids.

The problem with this approach is that it is not quite clear what precisely is meant by "attentional activity", and since this expression does not belong to ordinary language we can't use our ordinary linguistic intuition to interpret what exactly the writers really have in mind. Of course, they mean something to do with "attention", that much is clear, but unfortunately no more than that. (Cf. Darwin (1955[1872]: 278: "Attention is shown by the eyebrows being slightly raised.")

From the point of view of intelligibility, the other, alternative approach to the interpretation of "raised eyebrows" is more promising. For example, when Peck (1987: 101) states that "raised eyebrows have always been and will continue to be synonymous with surprise itself" we may agree or disagree with him, but at least we know what he means, because he is using an ordinary English word ("surprise") in its ordinary, everyday meaning.

But clearly, statements such as Peck's, while intelligible, cannot be regarded as fully satisfactory either, given that, as he in fact noted himself, "raised brows can be a part of many different attitudes" (ibid.). For example, Peck points out, the eyebrows can be raised "in an effort to recall" or "as an act of empathy". (And of course many other languages don't have a word for "surprise"; cf. e.g. Goddard 1997b.)

Ekman and Friesen (1975), too, linked the gesture of raising one's eyebrows with "surprise", so much so that they invented the term "the surprise brow", linking it, above all, with raised eyebrows. The section entitled "the surprise brow" in their book starts as follows:

> The eyebrows appear curved and high . . . The skin below the brow has been stretched by the lifting of the brow, and is more visible than usual . . . The lifting of the eyebrows produces long horizontal wrinkles across the forehead . . . Not everyone shows these wrinkles. Most young children do not show them, even when the eyebrows are raised, and some adults do not either. (pp. 37, 39)

Since the horizontal wrinkles may or may not accompany the raising of the eyebrows they are clearly not an inherent part of the meaningful gesture in question: the meaning is conveyed by the raising of the eyebrows as such. Whether or not the eyebrows appear "curved" is probably not essential either; and neither is the fact (of which most ordinary people would not even be aware) that "the skin below the brow has been stretched by the lifting". What matters is the action of moving one's eyebrows upward (like a person does who moves her eyebrows to see more). The resulting wrinkles, the stretched skin, and the shape of the eyebrows, are all inessential.

What, then, is the meaning of this gesture, if we reject the exaggerated and inaccurate claim that it is "synonymous with surprise itself"?

Ekman and Friesen (1975), who, as we have seen, also link this gesture with "surprise", have nonetheless noted that when this gesture is not accompanied by other facial features like "wide-open eyes and dropped jaw" it may convey something other than surprise:

> When the brow is held in place for a few seconds or more, this is an *emblem* which means doubt or questioning . . . often this emblem will express mock doubt, the listener's incredulity or amazement about what she has just heard . . . If the surprise brow is joined by a disgust mouth, then the meaning of the emblem changes slightly to sceptical disbelief. (p. 39)

Trying to isolate the semantic invariant behind disparate notions such as "surprise", "doubt", "incredulity", "disbelief", and "interest" (the latter not mentioned in the quote above but often also linked with the raising of the eyebrows, cf. e.g. Izard 1991), we should, I suggest, let ourselves be guided once again by the "logic" of the facial behaviour itself. The act of moving one's eyebrows at all conveys, I believe, the idea that "I'm thinking now" and so I would assign this component to the gesture of "raising the eyebrows" as much as to the gesture of drawing one's eyebrows together. In addition, the "raising of the eyebrows" suggests, iconically, a desire "to see more". It is not that the gesture of "raising one's eyebrows" is *motivated* by a person's desire to see more, but rather, that the person raising her eyebrows is moving them "like a person does who wants to see more".

Ekman (1989: 157) remarks that "All those who have written about the origin of brow raising have noted that this action increases the visual input, by increasing the superior visual field". To avoid misunderstanding, let me stress that in contrast to those earlier studies I am not talking about the *origin* of brow raising but about its *meaning*; and the meaning posited for the gesture is not "I want to see more", but rather, "I want to know more (about this)". At the same time, however, I am suggesting that an action increasing a person's visual field can serve as a semiotic basis for the message "I want to know more (about this)".

Technically, the link between the raising of the eyes and an increased field of vision involves also the raising of the upper lids: the movement of the eyebrows pulls also the eyelids upwards, thus widening the exposed part of the eye and increasing the field of vision (cf. Peck 1987: 96). "Ordinary people", of course, need not be aware of the role of the eyelids, but the description of the gesture in terms of "moving one's eyebrows upward like a person does who moves her eyebrows to see more" is well within the scope of "naive" folk-psychology.

As mentioned earlier, the apparent facial message suggested by the raising of the eyebrows, that is "I want to see more (above me)", translates naturally into a more abstract message "I want to know more" (especially given the concurrent message "I'm thinking now"), and thus provides a natural iconic basis for the interpretation "I want to know more (about this)".

The message "I want to know more (about it)" could explain the links between raised eyebrows and questions, doubt, incredulity, disbelief, puzzlement, interest, surprise, amazement, and so on. Depending on other aspects of the facial behaviour, and depending on the situation, the raising of the eyebrows can be interpreted in any one of these different ways, but the underlying message "I'm thinking now, I want to know more (about this)" is clearly compatible with them all. It is also clearly compatible with Peck's observation quoted earlier that eyebrows can be raised "in an effort to recall" or "as an act of empathy". When I'm trying to recall something I'm clearly thinking about something and I want to know more (than I do now); and when I'm empathizing with someone it is very likely that I'm thinking about their situation, and their emotions, and trying to know (understand) more about it.

The proposed component "I want to know more (about this)" is also highly consistent with the finding that in research done with babies, eyebrow raising "was typically related to infants raising their heads and/or eyes to gaze at an object presented above their line of sight" (Messinger, Fogel, and Dickson et al. 1997: 206).[11]

Is this the whole meaning of the gesture, then? Or are there any other components? I suspect that there may be one more component, which would explain the tendency of the raised eyebrows to be linked with "novelty" (cf. Scherer 1984), "unexpectedness", and the occurrence of some external stimulus. It is not an accident, I think, that, as pointed out by Ekman and Friesen (1975), the raising of the eyebrows often occurs as a response to something someone else has just said (whereas "frowning" can also easily occur in solitude, when one is simply concentrating on a task, without any triggering external events; cf. Cacioppo, Berntson, and Klein 1992).

The third hypothetical semantic component for the raised eyebrows is this: "I know something now". In a sense, such a component is already implied by that proposed earlier ("I want to know more"). The two components: "I know something now – I want to know more" form a logical sequence. But the reference to "now" invites the inference that the knowledge which I have is very recent, that is, that something has just happened, and that this is why "I want to know more (about this)". At the same time, the proposed formula ("I know something now") is sufficiently vague as not to exclude less typical situations, such as Peck's "effort to recall": when I'm trying to recall something I must have some bit of knowledge in my mind which serves as a foothold in my effort to "know more" (by dragging something out from the "back of my mind", that is, by thinking). This is, then, the full meaning proposed for the "raising of the eyebrows":

> I know something now
> I want to know more (about this)
> I'm thinking now

This formula is not inconsistent with interpretations relying on the technical expression "attentional activity"; it is, however, much clearer and less "scientific" and therefore more verifiable. It is also phrased from the "actor's", rather than an "observer's", point of view. For whatever the gesture of raising one's eyebrows may mean, presumably nobody would argue that it means "I am now engaged in an attentional activity". It *can* be argued, however, that it conveys first-person meanings like those given in the formula above.

Importantly, simple sentences of this kind, which are phrased in universal concepts, can be easily translated into any other language and can be tested with native speakers. For example, Nick Enfield (personal communication) has provided the following word-for-word Lao translation (while commenting that it would be impossible to render "attentional activity" in Lao):

| kuu | huu | 'an-daj-'an-nïng | diaw-nii | | |
|-----|-----|-----|-----|-----|-----|
| I | KNOW | SOMETHING | NOW | | |

| kuu | jaak | huu | ('an-daj-'an-nïng) | 'iik | (kiaw-kap 'an-nii) |
|-----|-----|-----|-----|-----|-----|
| I | WANT | KNOW | (SOMETHING) | MORE | (ABOUT THING-THIS) |

| kuu | kamlang | khït | diaw-nii |
|-----|-----|-----|-----|
| I | PROGRESSIVE:MARKER | THINK | NOW |

The use of untranslatable technical English expressions such as "attentional activity" to represent universal human meanings can be seen as an instance of what Goddard (forthcoming a) calls "terminological ethnocentrism". By contrast, the use of such simple, intuitively intelligible, readily translatable, and actor-oriented formulae phrased in universal human concepts allows us to avoid this form of ethnocentrism, as well as facilitating comparisons between the meanings of different gestures. In this particular case the use of such formulae allows us also to differentiate and compare the meanings of two related but non-synonymous gestures, often subsumed in the literature under one technical label "attentional activity", that is, of the gesture of raising one's eyebrows and the gesture of opening one's eyes wide, to which I will now turn.

### 13 The meaning of the "wide open eyes" (with immobile eyebrows)

This gesture has two variants which are physically and semantically quite different: one can open one's eyes wide while at the same time raising one's eyebrows and one can open one's eyes wide without raising one's eyebrows.

If I open my eyes wide and raise my eyebrows at the same time, the two events will, I think, be normally interpreted as forming a unitary event. In fact, it seems virtually impossible to raise one's eyebrows without opening one's eyes wide at the same time: the two go naturally together. If the wide open eyes mean anything in this case it can only be "I want to know more", that is to say, they merely reinforce one of the semantic components of the eyebrow gesture.

Opening the eyes wide while at the same time keeping one's eyebrows immobile, conveys a quite different message.

To begin with, to open one's eyes wide without at the same time raising one's eyebrows is unlikely to be deliberate, rather it is something that might *happen to* one. As noted by Darwin (1955[1872]: 281), it is actually quite difficult to open one's eyes wide without at the same time raising one's eyebrows, and the "unnatural" combination of wide open eyes with immobile eyebrows conveys a message of its own. The expected position of the eyebrows would be to have them raised, and their unexpected (under the circumstances) immobility appears to add to the message another component: "I can't do anything now", that is to say, "I can't even move my eyebrows" (so powerless am I at the moment).

The wide open eyes again suggest that, first, "I know something now" and second, "I want to know more (about this)"; at the same time, however, the strangely immobile (as if paralysed) eyebrows send the message "I can't do anything now". Given this combination of components it is hardly surprising that the facial behaviour in question is likely to be interpreted in terms of "extreme fear" (or even "horror"), as

Figure 4

in Ekman's (1975) photograph, reproduced in figure 4.

As mentioned in the section on the "raising of the eyebrows", Ekman and Friesen (1975: 50) have described what they called "the fear brow" as "raised" rather than "immobile" ("the eyebrows appear raised and straightened"). As for what they call "the fear eye", they described it in the following terms: "The upper eyelid is raised, exposing sclera [i.e. the whites], and the lower eyelid is tensed and drawn up" (p. 63). Thus, apart from various minor differences described in somewhat technical terms, Ekman and Friesen (1975) attributed the raising of the eyebrows and the wide open eyes to both "surprise" and "fear" (as did Darwin 1955[1872]: 289). At the same time, however, they noted that a face expressing, as they put it, "a frozen, horrified fear" failed to show any raising of the eyebrows. They commented on this face as follows: "Interestingly, the intensity of the expression of fear is not reduced by the lack of involvement of the brow (it is a neutral brow). Instead, the absence of brow involvement causes the expression to appear immobilized or frozen" (p. 60). These comments support, I think, the interpretation proposed here: the references to a "frozen", "immobilized" expression are fully consistent with the semantic component "I can't do anything now".

Consider from this point of view Bruno Epple's painting of a child's funeral, reproduced on the cover of this book. People could argue whether the faces shown in the centre of this picture (with the whites of the eyes showing above the irises) express "horror", "disbelief", "incomprehension", "bewilderment", or something else. All these interpretations, however, would be consistent with the three components posited here: "I know something now" (presumably, "this little child is dead"), "I want to know more about this" (presumably, "I want to understand how things like this can happen"), and "I can't do anything now" (presumably, "I can't do anything about it now").

The reference to the whites of the eyes showing above the irises in the last paragraph requires a comment. I do not think that it is essential to the gesture of opening one's eyes wide that the whites of the eyes should be showing above the irises, and if they do show observers may not even be aware of this. In a still picture or photograph, however, it is impossible to distinguish eyes which are naturally big from eyes which seem big because they are wide open at the time, and so the whites above the irises can serve as a way of signalling to the viewer that the eyes are wide open.

Just as raising the eyebrows tends to be accompanied by the appearance of horizontal wrinkles in the forehead, so the gesture of "opening one's eyes wide *without* raising one's eyebrows" tends to be accompanied by the showing of the whites above the irises. But just as the semiotic value of the raised eyebrows doesn't seem to depend on the presence of the wrinkles, so the semiotic value of the wide open eyes unaccompanied by the raising of the eyebrows does not seem to depend on the visibility of the whites above the irises.

### 14 The meaning of a down-turned mouth

In a section entitled "On the depression of the corners of the mouth" Darwin (1955[1872]: 191) wrote: "this action is affected by the depressores anguli oris . . . The expression of low spirits, grief or dejection, due to the contraction of this muscle, has been noticed by everyone who has written on the subject." Darwin commented that in children the expression in question is linked with crying: "Sometimes, when they are struggling against a crying fit, the outline of the mouth is curved in so exaggerated a manner as to be like a horseshoe; and the expression of misery then becomes a ludicrous caricature" (p. 192).

These comments are illustrated in Darwin's book with the two photographs reproduced in figure 5. I have suggested that a mouth with its corners turned downward suggests unambiguously that "I feel something bad now". A semantic description of this kind, however, is clearly insufficient, because there are "bad feelings" (such as, for example, "rage") which cannot be expressed in this way, and because there are other facial gestures (such as, for example, a wrinkled nose) which also

a

b

Figure 5

convey some "bad feeling" but which nonetheless are not synonymous with a down-turned mouth.

Ekman and Friesen (1975) link turning down the corners of the mouth predominantly with "sadness", but they make this interpretation contingent on the appearance of other parts of the face. In the section entitled "the sadness mouth" they refer to two photographs (their figures 53A and 53B) as follows:

> In Figure 53A and 53B Patricia shows two sadness mouths. The mouth that is most often confused with it, a disgust-contempt mouth, is shown in 53C . . . In Figure 53A Patricia shows the corners of the lips down, in Figure 53B she shows the loose-lip characteristic of the mouth when it is trembling . . . When sadness is shown only in the mouth (no involvement of the eyelids or forehead), the facial expression is ambiguous . . . The expression in 53A might be a pout, but this is not certain. The message in 53B is completely ambiguous; it might be mild distress, defiance, or anything.

According to this account, if the corners of the mouth are down, this may – but doesn't have to – suggest "sadness". It is also interesting to note that in the series of faces included in Ekman (1975) the only one with clearly down-turned corners of the mouth is labelled by the author as expressing "disgust". (Note also the down-turned mouth in the "disgusted" photograph C in section 10.) Darwin (1955[1872]: 257), too, saw the downward movement of the corners of the mouth as typical of "disgust", linking it with the "movements around the mouth identical with those preparatory to the act of vomiting". But if a down-turned mouth can be linked with emotions as different as "sadness" and "disgust" – but not, for example, "rage" – what *is* the constant and invariant meaning of this gesture, beyond the obvious "I feel something bad now"?

A semantic component which would allow interpretations in terms of something like "sadness" as well as "disgust", and yet exclude an interpretation in terms of something like "anger" or "rage", can be formulated as "I know I can't do anything". Speaking loosely, one could call this a "passive" or "withdrawn" attitude: a person with down-turned corners of the mouth does not look like someone who is about to fight, to act, or even to speak.

In fact, it would be difficult to speak with the corners of one's mouth turned down, because it is virtually impossible to open one's mouth in this position. Up-turned corners of the mouth ("smiling") do not prevent a person from opening her mouth and speaking, and in fact a full, prototypical "smile" involves a partially open mouth, with the teeth showing. By contrast, it is difficult to imagine a face with the corners of the mouth turned down and with the teeth showing. Thus, a mouth which looks like an "upside-down" smile has to be a closed mouth, and so a mouth which can't speak (although, as noted by Darwin, it could still cry).

Of course a person with tightly closed lips (to be discussed in the next section) cannot speak either, but the message of the tightly closed lips is "I don't want to say anything" rather than "I can't say anything", and this is linked with the voluntary (almost deliberate) character of the gesture in question. By contrast, the gesture of turning down the corners of one's lips doesn't have to be voluntary, so there is nothing in this gesture to suggest that "I want to do something" or that I *deliberately* "don't want to say anything" (inferred from "I can't say anything"). Rather, the message seems to be "I know that I can't do anything". I would propose, then, the following semantic interpretation for the gesture of turning down the corners of one's mouth:

> I feel something bad now
> I know I can't do anything

This, of course, is just the invariant skeleton: the details of the interpretation are to be filled in by the context (facial, verbal, and situational). But this invariant skeleton is compatible both with emotions like "sadness" and with emotions like "disgust", whilst not being compatible with "action-oriented" emotions and attitudes such as "anger", "rage", or "determination". It is also highly consistent with the idea of helpless crying.

## 15 The meaning of tightly pressed lips

As noted earlier, Ekman and Friesen (1975: 83) saw the gesture of tightly pressing one's lips together as a manifestation of "anger", and they linked it with "physical violence" and with attempts to "control a verbal, shouting anger".

Other writers on the subject have pointed out, however, that the facial gesture in question is not restricted to anger, and supported Darwin's idea that it is linked with "determination" or "resolve". Thus, Ortony and Turner (1990: 322) wrote:

> Another common, and related, component of anger is a determination or resolve, usually to take some unpleasant action, typically not aggression against the instigator, but perhaps action to remove the source of the goal blockage. As Darwin (1955[1872]) suggested, determination appears to be expressed in the face by the compression of the lips (Frijda, 1986, offered the related and interesting suggestion that this response may reflect an attempt at self-control). Again, this com-

ponent of facial expression is dissociable; it is not essential to anger, nor limited to it, and seems to appear only when the appropriate mental state occurs. (p. 322)

Evidently, Ortony and Turner believe that Darwin's and Frijda's analyses have a common core, and, although they don't say expressly what this common core is, they appear to support both the idea of "determination" and the idea of "self-control".

Following a similar line of thought, but seeking to portray the actor's perspective and to do so in simple and universal concepts, in my earlier work on this topic (Wierzbicka 1993b) I proposed for "compressed lips" the following message:

(a) I want to do something now
(b) I know: if I do it I can feel something bad
(c) I don't want not to do it because of this

As I commented at the time, this formula is consistent with Ortony and Turner's analysis. The references to an intended action (component (a)) and to an anticipated "bad feeling" (component (b)) are consistent with Ortony and Turner's reference to an "unpleasant action"; the combination of components (a), (b), and (c) suggests something like "determination"; and the combination of (b) and (c) is consistent with the idea of "an attempt at self-control".

Looking at this formula several years on, I would want, above all, to seek a possible semiotic basis for the proposed semantic components, and, if necessary, to modify these components so that the final formula rests on an explicitly formulated, non-arbitrary basis.

To start with component (a) ("I want to do something now"), I believe it can be justified with reference to the deliberate action of the lips. When I press my lips tightly together I'm doing something with my mouth because I want to, and this deliberate action provides a clear iconic basis for the component "I want to do something now". In this respect (but only in this respect), the deliberate action of pressing one's lips together is "synonymous" with the deliberate action of drawing one's eyebrows together, to which I have also attributed the semantic component "I want to do something now".

Except for minor details, component (c) also appears to be justifiable in terms of the logic of "facial behaviour". The tight pressing of the lips together clearly suggests that "I don't want to say anything", and also that I don't want to say anything *despite* the fact that there may seem to be strong reasons for opening my mouth and saying something.

What is perhaps the most difficult thing to establish is the exact nature of the intermediate component (b), and the semiotic basis for this component, but we could try the following path: the deliberate action of the mouth results in an uncomfortable pressure on the lips (that is, "I feel something bad because of this", i.e. because of what I want to do with my mouth); it could be expected, therefore, that I might relent and say something. In fact, it is clear what exactly I could be expected to say: "I will not do it, after all (because I don't want to feel something bad")); but the maintenance of the tightly shut mouth denies these expectations, as if sending the message "I'm not going to say this" (i.e. "I'm not going to say that I'm not going to do it, after all"). Hence the conveyed message (component (c)): "I don't want not to do it because of this".

It seems to me that this explanation is viable, and so I am inclined to stand by the interpretation proposed in my 1993b article, including component (b): "I know: if I do it I can feel something bad". This is compatible with Darwin's, Frijda's, and Ortony and Turner's idea of "determination". Needless to say, the message of the "compressed lips" is not about the action of the mouth or the sensation in the lips as such, but the "bodily knowledge" associated with the gesture provides a comprehensible experiential basis for the proposed semantic interpretation.

## 16 Conclusion: the what, the how, and the why in the reading of human faces

Ekman (1975), assuming that the universality of human facial expressions of "the primary emotions" (i.e. "happiness", "fear", "surprise", "anger", "disgust/contempt", and "sadness") had been established, puzzled about the reasons for this universality: "Of course, we still do not know *why* these expressions are universal, or *why* these particular facial movements are associated with particular emotions. Why don't we press our lips tightly together and frown when we're happy?" (p. 39).

Ekman's view was that "all human beings share the same neural programming, which links facial muscles with particular emotions", and he looked to neurophysiology for the ultimate explanation. I believe, however, that we can at least put forward some meaningful hypotheses on this subject if we look at human faces from the point of view of human understanding rather than neural programming, that is to say, if we adopt a semiotic and experiential rather than a neurophysiological perspective.

Human faces send messages, and these messages must be decodable. Some messages can be decoded on the basis of local conventions, but those (if any) which are universally interpretable may have a "natural", i.e. iconic or indexical, basis (even if they are also genetically "hard-

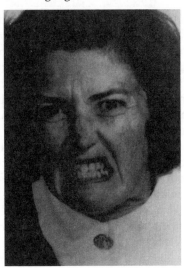

Figure 6

wired"). From an experiential and semiotic point of view it does make sense that facial gestures which are deliberate and which require an effort, such as a "frown" or tightly pressed lips, can convey a decodable message "I want to do something", but not a "happy" message such as "I don't want anything right now, I feel good as it is". Likewise, it does make sense that facial movements which feel uncomfortable to the actor, such as contortions or grimaces of the mouth, wrinkling of the nose, or hard pressed lips, can convey a decodable message "I feel something bad now" but not "I feel something good now".

It also makes sense that a gesture like a "frown", which (as discussed in section 11) suggests, iconically, that "I want to do something now" and that "I know I'm not doing it now" (cf. the notion of "discrepancy") is compatible with interpretations in terms of "frustration", "worry", "anger", or "concentration", but not in terms of "happiness"; or that a facial gesture which suggests, iconically, that "I want to see more" lends itself to an interpretation in terms of "I want to know more" but not, for example, in terms of "I feel something good now".

As a final example, consider the appearance of the mouth in the "bared teeth, square mouth" photograph (figure 6), which according to Ekman (1975: 38) shows "anger". Is it really surprising that whatever else people might associate with this mouth (e.g. "murderous rage", "vicious aggression", "insanity", etc.) they would certainly not associate it with "happiness"? First, our own "muscular knowledge" tells us that if we wanted to imitate such an expression it would feel uncomfortable, so part of the decodable message could be "I feel something bad now", but certainly not "I feel something good now". Second, the bared upper teeth and the squarish shape of the mouth seem to suggest that the person in the photograph "wants to bite"; and the apparent message "I want to bite someone now" readily translates into a more general message "I want to do something bad to someone now".

I have not included this gesture, striking as it is, in the foregoing survey of meaningful and probably universal facial gestures because many observers seem to feel that it is rare and perhaps even lies beyond the realm of what is "normal" in human beings (in contrast to dogs). But the semiotic basis of this gesture is quite clear and it has been noted already by Darwin (1955[1872]: 240):

> This retraction of the lips and uncovering of the teeth during paroxysms of rage, as if to bite the offender, is so remarkable, considering how seldom the teeth are used by men in fighting that I inquired from Dr. J. Crichton Browne whether the habit was common in the insane whose passions are unbridled. He informs me that he has repeatedly observed it both with the insane and idiotic.

Thus, by looking for a decodable meaning of individual facial gestures rather than for "distinctive patterns of autonomic nervous system (ANS) activity" linking (for reasons that aren't clear) global "emotions" (e.g. "happiness" or "anger") with global "facial expressions", we can not only isolate and describe but also, to some extent, explain some universal aspects of human facial behaviour.

Provine (1997: 173) closes his study of "yawns, laughs, smiles, tickles, and talking" with, as he puts it, "a caveat and a recommendation":

> Language, a precision tool of the intellect, may not serve us as well in the realm of emotion, empathy, and intuition. It is useful to approach human behaviour in an objective manner, as if we were studying another species, ethnologists stalking not the rain forest but city sidewalks and shopping malls, with a fresh eye and naive curiosity that permits us to see the familiar in new ways.

My own recommendation would be just the opposite: if we really want to look at human faces with a fresh eye and see the familiar in new ways, we should *abandon* the old practice of approaching human behaviour "in an objective manner, as if we were studying another species", and approach it in the spirit of participant observation, trying to understand both our fellow human beings and ourselves on the basis of our shared human experience and our shared language, that is, the simple and "naive" language of universal human concepts such as FEEL, THINK, KNOW, AND WANT.

# CHAPTER 5

# Russian emotional expression

## 1 Introduction

### 1.1 Linguistic evidence for cultural psychology

In a famous passage, Edward Sapir affirmed that "the worlds in which different societies live are distinct worlds, not merely the same world with different labels attached" (1949[1929]: 162). Three quarters of a century later, in the light of evidence that has accumulated in the interim, Sapir's insight can be extended: as members of different societies, we live not just in different worlds, but also among different people; and, moreover, we ourselves are different people.

As the growing field of "cultural psychology" demonstrates more and more clearly, we are different people because as members of different cultural groups we not only speak differently but also think differently, feel differently, and relate differently to other people (see e.g. Bond 1997; Kitayama and Markus 1994; Lutz 1988; Shweder and LeVine 1984; Stigler, Shweder, and Herdt 1990; White and Kirkpatrick 1985; Wikan 1990). But it is not only our "psyches" (and their external manifestations) which are culturally constituted; our bodies, and the behaviour in which they are involved, are different too: we laugh differently, we move our hands differently, we manage our faces differently, and so on (Cf. e.g. Hasada 1996; Russell and Yik 1996). In fact, as pointed out by Jenkins (1994: 319) (with reference to Csordas 1990, 1993), for many scholars the traditional view of culture as "located from the neck up" and the "traditional dualist idea that the closer we come to the body, the farther away we must be from culture" has now given place to "conceptualization of the body as a generative source of culture" (Jenkins 1994: 319).

Admittedly, differences in the cultural perceptions and uses of the body may be difficult to measure, to quantify, or to verify experimentally. But, as Shweder (1990: 20) has pointed out, the time of unquestioning acceptance of principles like "Do not think about anything that cannot be controlled and measured in a lab" has passed and we no longer need to be intimidated by them.

As I have argued for many years (see e.g. Wierzbicka 1992a, 1994b,

1997a), the best evidence for the differences, as well as similarities, between people as bearers and products of cultures, and cultures as "intentional worlds" inhabited and evolved by people, comes from languages. Cultural key words, like *duša* (roughly, "soul/heart/mind") or *drug* (roughly, "friend/soul-brother") in Russian, or *amae* (roughly, "sweet dependence") and *omoiyari* (roughly, "empathy-cum-kindness") in Japanese provide excellent evidence for insightful and at the same time methodologically informed cultural psychology.[1] And what applies to other conceptual domains applies also to the culturally extremely important domain of the human body.

But lexical semantics is only one area of evidence. Collocations, conversational routines, forms of address, semantically revealing grammatical constructions (e.g. in the area of emotions) – all provide rich data for cultural psychology, data which are amenable to systematic analysis within the interpretive framework of cross-linguistic and cross-cultural semantics. In this chapter, I will examine the data from one source: *The Russian–English Collocational Dictionary of the Human Body* (1996) (henceforth *RECDHB*); and focus on one theme: "the body and emotional expression".

## 1.2 RECDHB – a collocational dictionary of the human body

*RECDBH* is a most unusual publication. It is a relatively small thematic dictionary (one volume, 418 pages) devoted to a single domain, but one of fundamental importance and particular interest: the human body. Furthermore, while the number of entries is small (seventy odd), all the words treated in this dictionary are portrayed fully, with meticulous attention to detail, and in a systematic fashion (in accordance with the principles of "lexical portraits" and "systematic lexicography" developed by the Moscow linguistic school).

As the authors state at the outset, their "aim is to present *all* the information [emphasis added] necessary for the correct use of the corresponding Russian words and expressions". Given usual lexicographical practice, this aim is extraordinarily ambitious; and it is admirably met. The fact that the entries are organized according to the same schema and the same principles makes the information easily accessible and readily generates generalizations.

The format of the dictionary represents a simplified and "user-friendly" version of the one in the Mel'čuk and Zholkovsky *Explanatory Combinatorial Dictionary of Modern Russian* (1984). In contrast to that model, however, and to the whole line of "explanatory combinatorial" dictionaries based on it (see for example Mel'čuk et al. 1984, 1988, 1992), *RECDHB* is bilingual, and contains English translations of the Russian words and collocations. In this respect, *RECDHB* follows in the foot-steps of Apresjan and Rozenman's (1979) remarkable Anglo-Russian dictionary of synonyms (*Anglo-Russkij Sinonimičeskij Slovar'*).

The choice of thematic domain (the human body), the decision to use English to explain the meaning of the Russian words and expressions, the use of the methodology developed and tested in the whole series of "explanatory combinatorial dictionaries", and (last but not least) the adoption of a user-friendly format have jointly led to an extraordinarily interesting and illuminating publication – a real goldmine of facts and insights of many different kinds, and a model to emulate in future lexicography. In this chapter, however, I will confine myself to one aspect of this highly original lexicographic work: the insights it offers into Russian cultural norms concerning emotional expression, and into the differences between Russian and Anglo norms in this area.

## 1.3 The centrality of emotions in Russian culture

In my (1992a) study of the Russian language in its relation to culture I identified as one of the fundamental semantic themes of the Russian language "emotionality", that is, "the tremendous stress on emotions and on their free expression, the high emotional temperature of Russian discourse, the wealth of linguistic devices for signalling emotions and shades of emotions" (p. 395). This conclusion, based on detailed seman-tic analysis, was consistent with the key generalizations of earlier students of Russian culture. For example, the Harvard study of the "Russian national character" (Bauer, Inkeles, and Kluckhohn 1956: 141) characterized Russians as "expressive and emotionally alive", marked by "general expressiveness", "easily expressed feelings", and "giving in to impulse". In a similar vein, Gorer (1949: 160) wrote:

> Great Russians, with the exception of the Soviet elite, do take much pleasure in expressing aloud the emotions which are momentarily possessing them. There is a considerable Russian vocabulary for the expressing of the emotions, "pouring out one's soul" being one of the most common. For many Russians this is the most valued aspect of living. Indeed, feeling and expressing the emotions you feel is the sign that you are alive; if you don't feel, you are to all intents and purposes dead.

While in recent decades studies like those quoted above have often been regarded as impressionistic or based on uncertain methodology, rigorous linguistic analysis leads to similar conclusions. For example, Friedrich (1997: 86) notes "an enormous number of simple and complex affixes" with various "affective" meanings in Russian and he notes that "this affective suffixal system is more richly evolved in Russian than in any other Slavic language or, apparently, any language in the world". Friedrich calls the "highly dynamic" Russian system of expressive suffixation "imagination-boggling"; and he refers in this context to my own (Wierzbicka 1992a) analysis of the Russian expressive suffixes which, he says, "smashes the reductionist-structuralist components of traditional grammar, in order to construct propositional, pragmatic definitions of over a dozen major affective suffixes, many of them with many subtypes". (See also Zaliznjak and Levontina 1996.)

The *RECDHB* brings new evidence pointing in the same direction.

## 2 Emotion and the body

### 2.1 Laughter (smex and xoxot)

As RECDHB notes, Russian has not one but two nouns corresponding to the English word *laughter* (*smex* and *xoxot*), and not one but two verbs corresponding to the English verb *laugh*: *smejat'sja* and *xoxotat'*. Of course English, too, has other words for what might be regarded as kinds of laughter: *chuckle*, *giggle*, and *cackle*, but the relation of these words to the most basic words *laugh* and *laughter* is quite different from that between the Russian words *xoxot* and *xoxotat'* on the one hand and *smex* and *smejat'sja* on the other. In fact, all three English words *giggle*, *chuckle*, and *cackle* imply something less than hearty laughter. Of these three, the involuntary, uncontrolled *giggle* has its lexical counterpart in the Russian verb *xixikat'* (no corresponding noun), and the voluntary and controlled *chuckle* and *cackle* have no counterparts in Russian at all.

In contrast to *giggle*, *chuckle*, and *cackle*, *xoxot*, glossed in *RECDHB* as "laughter, loud laughter", is definitely laughter, full-blown laughter. *xoxotat'* is to laugh with abandon, without inhibitions, to one's heart's content.

The suggestion that the Russian *xoxot* is something quite different from "sub-laughing" behaviour designated by the English words *giggle*, *chuckle*, and *cackle* is supported by the collocations cited in *RECDHB*, such as the following:

> *umirat' ot xoxota* lit. "to be dying from *xoxot*"
> *to be dying from chuckling/cackling
> *pomirat' ot xoxota*
> (as above)
> *čut' ne umeret' ot xoxota* – lit. "to nearly die from *xoxot*"

Clearly, one cannot say in English that somebody was dying or nearly died "chuckling, cackling, or giggling". (It is also interesting to note that the English nouns *giggle, chuckle,* and *cackle* all refer to actions of relatively brief duration, whereas the Russian word *xoxot* stands for a prolonged activity.)

The other verbal expressions involving *xoxot,* listed in the *RECDHB,* are equally eloquent:

> *katat'sja ot xoxota* "to be rolling around with *xoxot*"
> *s nog valit'sja ot xoxota* "to be falling over from *xoxot*"
> *xvatat'sja za boka ot xoxota* "to (repeatedly) slap (lit. grab) one's sides from *xoxot*"
> *trjastis' ot xoxota* "to be shaking from *xoxot*"
> *život kolyšetsja ot xoxota* "someone's belly is rocking from *xoxot*"
> *na glazax slezy vystupili ot xoxota* "tears sprang to someone's eyes from *xoxot*"

Adjectives with which *xoxot* commonly combines are also different from those likely to co-occur with *giggle, chuckle,* or *cackle*:

> *gromkij xoxot* ?loud giggle/chuckle/cackle
> *veselyj xoxot* ?merry (cheerful) giggle/chuckle; ?cheerful cackle
> *zdorovyj xoxot* ?robust/healthy giggle/chuckle/cackle
> *družnyj xoxot* ?general (lit. harmonious, in concord) giggle/ chuckle/cackle
> *raskatistyj xoxot* *peals of giggle/chuckle/cackle (also: *raskaty xoxota*)

What these adjectives typically co-occurring with *xoxot* suggest is that in Russian culture the loud and unrestrained behaviour in question is not viewed (by the speaker and, presumably, by the speech community at large) with any disapproval, that, on the contrary, it is seen as "healthy". The *nomina personae xoxotun* (male) and *xoxotunja* (female) are particularly revealing in this respect, since they both imply a positive attitude to the person. This positive attitude is probably linked with the fact that *xoxot* must express genuinely "good feelings". Thus, while *smex,* like *laugh,* can sometimes be described as *gor'kij* ("bitter") or *sarkastičeskij* ("sarcastic"), *xoxot* cannot (*gor'kij xoxot, *sarkastičeskij xoxot*).

Since the words *xoxot* and *xoxotat'* are very common and highly colloquial in Russian, their special focus on loud and unrestrained laughter suggests a greater salience of this kind of behaviour in Russian culture: the message of the lexicon seems to be that, from the point of view of mainstream Russian culture, people are expected sometimes –

perhaps even often – to laugh loudly and without restraint, out of sheer merriment, and to do so without attempting to control the bodily expression of their good feelings (such as shaking, falling over, rocking, and so on); and also that behaviour of this kind is not only seen as normal and socially acceptable, but is in fact approved of. The absence of a word like *xoxot* (let alone *xoxotun, xoxotunja*) in the English lexicon, as well as the presence in it of the words *chuckle* and *cackle*, suggests that Anglo norms and expectations with respect to laughing are different from Russian ones.

This is further confirmed by the negative connotations of the English verb *guffaw*, which Russian–English dictionaries offer sometimes as an equivalent of *xoxot*. In contrast to *xoxot* and *xoxotat'*, however, *guffaw* is not a common word; and its very semantics reflect a condemnation of unrestrained loud laughter (whilst its low frequency suggests that such behaviour is not seen as very common).

An examination of the collocations of the Russian words *smex* and *smejat'sja* and their English counterparts *laughter* and *laugh*, to which we will turn next, points in the same direction.

Like *xoxot*, *smex*, too, has a number of collocations presenting it as intense and uncontrolled, with highly visible bodily manifestations. These include:

> *razrazit'sja smexom* "to burst out laughing", lit. "to break out with laughter (like a thunderstorm)"
> *nadorvat' sebe životiki* "to split one's sides (lit. belly, plural diminutive) with laughing"
> *čut' ne lopnut' ot smexa* "lit. nearly break (fly apart, suddenly and violently) from laughter"
> *pokatit'sja so smexu* lit. "to start rolling (as if sliding) with laughter"
> *čut' ne umeret' so smexu* "nearly die laughing"
> *zakatit'sja smexom* lit. "to start spinning with laughter"
> *prysnut' ot smexa* "to burst laughing, lit. to spurt out laughing"

While some of these expressions can be linked with English equivalents, the Russian expressions are both more numerous and more dramatic. The difference is particularly striking in the description of prolonged, on-going laughter, that is laughter that a person freely indulges in for some time, without trying to control it or stop it. In English there are a few expressions like "nearly died laughing", but not like "was dying with (or from) laughter". In Russian, however, there are many expressions involving imperfective verbs and referring to extreme forms of laughter, e.g.:

*zalivat'sja smexom* lit. "to be flooding oneself with laughter"
*nadryvat'sja ot smexa* lit. "to be tearing/splitting from (with) laughter"
*umirat' so smexu* "to be dying from (with) laughter"
*pomirat' so smexu* "to be dying from (with) laughter"
*davit'sja so smexu* "to be choking from (with) laughter"

Many such expressions involve visible involuntary movements of the laughing person's body:

> *zakatyvat'sja smexom* "to be rolling (as if spinning about) with laughter"
> *katat'sja ot smexa* "to be rolling (as if sliding along) with laughter"
> *trjastis' ot smexa* "to be shaking from laughter"
> *sotrjasat'sja: telo sotrjasaetsja ot smexa* "to shake: the body is shaking from laughter"
> *kolyxat'sja: život kolyšetsja ot smexa* "to sway: the belly is swaying from laughter"
> *trjastis': život trjasetsja ot smexa* "to shake: the belly is shaking from laughter"
> *korčit'sja ot smexa* lit. "to be contorted from laughter"

It is also interesting to note that the English expression *to roar with laughter*, which also depicts loud and unrestrained laughter, has somewhat coarse and animal-like connotations; by contrast, the Russian expression *zalivat'sja smexom* has positive and rather poetic connotations, as the same verb is often used about the "unrestrained" enchanting singing of nightingales.

Thus, not only the use of *xoxot* but also that of *smex* suggests that unrestrained, uncontrolled laughter is more salient, and viewed more positively, in Russian culture than it is in mainstream Anglo culture. *Xoxot* is a lexical reflection of this cultural salience of unrestrained laughter, whereas both *xoxot* and *smex* reflect it in their phraseological behaviour.

### 2.2 Tears

The Russian word *slezy* "tears" is used much more widely than its English counterpart with reference to external expression of emotions, and has a much wider range of collocations. To translate these collocations into English, one often has to change the meaning of the original expression, and the direction of this change is always predictable: it invariably consists in "toning down" the original meaning. One characteristic literary example is provided by a quote in *RECDHB* (p. 340) from Pushkin's *Eugene Onegin* and its English translation by Charles Johnston:

> Knjaginja pered nim, odna,
> Sidit, ne ubrana, bledna,
> Pis'mo kakoe-to čitaet
> I tixo slezy l'et rekoj
> Operšis' na ruku ščekoj.

> "The princess, sitting peaked and wan
> Alone, with no adornment on,
> She holds a letter up, and leaning
> Cheek upon hand, she softly cries
> In a still stream that never dries."

In the English translation, the princess cries "in a still stream", but in the Russian original, she "pours tears in a river", and this diminution of the flood of tears from a "river" to a "stream" is highly characteristic. For example, Russian expressions referring to crying include the following:

> *slezy lit'* "to pour tears"
> *prolivat' slezy* "to pour out (spill) tears"
> *zalivat'sja slezami* lit. "to flood oneself with tears"
> *oblivat'sja slezami* "to pour tears all over oneself"

The only English expression which could be compared with these is *to dissolve in tears*, but first, even this one has a slightly ironic or distancing tone, and second, it cannot be applied to an on-going activity: one can only "dissolve in tears" once, whereas in Russian, all the expressions listed above have imperfective versions, and thus allow the speaker to describe the activity of "flooding oneself with tears" as on-going, without any time limits.

The expression *ves' (vsja) v slezax* lit. "all in tears" has to be toned down in English to just *in tears*. For example:

> *Ona prišla vsja v slezax.* "She arrived in tears (lit. all in tears)".
> *Prišel domoj, a mat' vsja v slezax.* "When I came home, I found my mother in tears (lit. all in tears)."

Russian has a large set of expressions for describing the process of tears pouring out from a person's eyes. These include the following:

> *teč'/poteč,* "run/flow"
> *u N slezy tekut ruč'em (or: v tri ruč'ja) (iz glaz)* lit. "to him tears are

running/flowing in a stream (or: in three streams)
from the eyes"

*lit'sja/polit'sja* "pour"
u N slezy l'jutsja ruč'em (or: v tri ruč'ja, or: rekoj) (iz glaz).
lit. "to him tears are pouring in a stream (or: in three streams,
or: like a river) from the eyes."

*katit'sja/pokatit'sja* "to roll"
u N slezy katjatsja (gradom) (iz glaz)
lit. "to N tears are rolling (like hail) (from the eyes)'

*bryznut'* "spurt/splash/spatter"
u N slezy bryznuli (iz glaz)
to N tears gushed (from the eyes)
"tears spurted from N's eyes"

*xlynut'* "gush"
u N slezy xlynuli (iz glaz)
to N tears gushed (from the tears)
"tears gushed from N's eyes"

*struit'sja* "to stream"
u N po ščekam strujatsja slezy
"to N tears stream down cheeks"
"tears stream down N's cheeks"

Furthermore, in Russian, the face, the eyes, and indeed the person as
a whole can be described as visibly changed for having cried. In an
English translation, the meaning of such descriptions has to be altered,
for there are no idiomatic ways of rendering it. For example, the
expression *zaplakannye glaza* is rendered in *RECDHB* as "tear-reddened
eyes", but it really means more than that: "eyes visibly changed, showing that the person has cried" (not just "reddened"). Similarly, the
expression *zaplakannoe lico* is glossed in *RECDHB* as "tear-stained face",
but it really means more than that: not just "stained", but visibly
changed from having cried. The word *stained* suggests some isolated
superficial traces on an otherwise intact surface, whereas a *zaplakannoe
lico* is likely to be red, swollen, and generally markedly altered. Likewise, the expressions *lico v slezax* and *lico zalito slezami*, glossed in
*RECDHB* as "face stained with tears", literally mean something like
"face in tears" and "face flooded with tears", that is, again, much more
than merely "stained".

The Russian expression *do slez*, glossed in *RECDHB* as "V until one
cries", is commonly used to describe a wide range of emotions, includ-

ing those designated by the following verbs and verbal phrases: *smejat'sja* "to laugh", *xoxotat'* "to laugh loudly", *pokrasnet'* "to blush", *smuščat'sja* "to become embarrassed", *obidno* "to feel insulted", *zavidno* "to feel envy", and *dosadno* "to feel annoyed". Needless to say, the phrase "until one cries" is not similarly used in English. What this appears to suggest is that tears are regarded in Russian culture, in contrast to Anglo culture, as a normal and common symptom of a wide range of emotions, including, for example, embarrassment, envy, annoyance, compassion, and so on. In English, one could sometimes encounter "tears of happiness", "tears of rage", or "tears of grief", but the range is clearly more limited.

A similar conclusion is suggested by the following Russian collocations and their (rough) English glosses:

> *slezy vostorga* "ecstatic tears"
> *slezy obidy* "tears of humiliation"
> *slezy raskajanija* "tears of repentance"
> *slezy dosady* "tears of disappointment"
> *slezy sočuvstvija* "tears of sympathy"

Not surprisingly, many collocations involving tears involve also the eyes, or the face as a whole, as we will see in the next two sections.

### 2.3 Face (lico)

The collocations of the Russian word *lico* in *RECDHB* suggest different cultural attitudes to facial expressiveness than those suggested by the common collocations of the English word *face*.

To begin with, in Russian, faces are often described as "lighting up", "lit up", or shining (with joy, with delight, with delighted enthusiasm, and so on), whereas in English there is only one such expression: *someone's face lit up*, which can only refer to a momentary event. For example:

> *u N lico sijaet ot radosti (radosti'ju)* "N's face is shining with joy"
> *ves' sijat'/prosijat'/zasijat' ot radosti* (or: *vostorga*) "to shine all over with joy/delight"
> *u N lico osvetilos' (radost'ju)* "N's face lit up (with joy)"
> *lico u N prosvetelo* lit. "light started to shine in N's face"
> *prosvetlennoe lico* "a face suffused with a clear light" (implies: exalted, uplighted, joyful)

Conversely, a face can also be described in Russian in terms of absence of light:

> *u N lico omračilos'* / *u N lico pomračnelo* "N's face darkened, N's face became gloomy"
> *u N ten' probežala po licu* "a shadow ran across over N's face"
> *u N lico pogaslo* "the light went out of N's face"
> *temnet'/potemnet' licom* "to become darker in the face"

A smile, too, can be described in Russian in terms of light (less common, though not impossible, in English):

> *ulybka osveščaet lico* "a smile lights up someone's face"

But the following collocations, combining the ideas of smiling and swimming, or smiling and crawling, do not have counterparts in English:

> *lico u N rasplylos' v širokoj* (or: *radostnoj*) *ulybke.*
> lit. "N's face swam in all directions in a broad (or: joyful) smile."
> *u N lico raspolzlos' v ulybke'*
> lit. "N's face crawled in all directions in a smile."

The latter two expressions, which are described in *RECDHB* as referring to a "joyous smile", imply a kind of "overflowing" of emotions, linked with a lack of control over one's features and a lack of a perceived need to exercise such a control.

Crying, too, is commonly described in Russian as affecting the face more than it usually is in English. For example, while the expression *lico zalito slezami* does have its counterpart in *a face flooded with tears*, the common expression *zaplakannoe lico* (lit. "a face visibly changed from crying") obviously implies a greater change in a person's face than the closest English expression *tear-stained face* would suggest (as discussed in the section on tears).

One is also struck by *RECDHB*'s long list of expressions describing faces without an emotional expression (often, with some negative implications). For example:

> *nevyrazitel'noe lico* unexpressive face
> *nepodvižnoe lico* immobile face
> *derevjannoe lico* wooden face
> *kamennoe lico* stone face
> *zastyvšee lico* set/frozen face (lit. hardened, like a liquid turned solid from lost heat)
> *u N lico zastylo* N's face hardened/froze

What these expressions (and their opposites) suggest is that a "normal" face is expected to be expressive (*vyrazitel'noe*), mobile (*podvižnoe*), lively (*živoe*), and that if a face is not expressive, this in itself is a bad sign (a sign of tragic experiences, a sign of heartlessness, and so on).

It is particularly interesting to ponder the implications of the expressions *zastyvšee lico* and *lico zastylo* on the one hand and *(someone's) face froze* on the other. The Russian expressions evoke an image of a hot fluid which congeals, and imply an expectation that, normally, a person's face should be warm and fluid. By contrast, the English expression implies an expectation that normally human faces should be, so to speak, at room temperature; it is not good when it "freezes", but there is no expectation that it should normally be either "hot" or "liquid".[2]

The common, colloquial Russian phrase *vyraženie lica* "facial expression", combined with an adjective of emotion, points in the same direction: in English, the phrase *facial expression* is rather technical, and common Russian phrases such as *radostnoe vyraženie lica* or *veseloe vyraženie lica* "joyful (merry) expression of the face" are difficult to render in English accurately. One does speak in English, of course, about a person's "expression" (referring to facial expression) but this doesn't refer necessarily to emotional expression. Adjectives and participles describing emotion appear also to co-occur less readily with the English word *face* than they do with the Russian word *lico*. For example (a question mark in brackets is more tentative than one without brackets):

> *radostnoe lico* (?)joyful face
> *veseloe lico* (?)merry face
> *ispugannoe lico* ?frightened face
> *udivlennoe lico* ?surprised face
> *zloe lico* (?)angry/mad face
> *nedovol'noe lico* ?displeased face

Some such expressions – for example, *sad face* – do sound natural in English, too, but the range appears to be more limited. Again, the conclusion suggests itself that Russian cultural norms allow and indeed encourage a greater facial expressiveness (in the service of emotions) than do Anglo norms.

### 2.4 Eyes and eyebrows

In Russian, the word *glaza* "eyes" enters into a wide network of collocations describing the expression of emotions – far wider, it seems, than the English collocations including the word *eyes*. To begin with, like the face (*lico*), eyes can also be described in Russian in terms of light. *RECDHB* cites the following examples:

> *glaza sijajut (ot radosti)* "someone's eyes are shining (with joy)"
> *glaza svetjatsja (ot radosti)* "someone's eyes are lit (with joy)"
> *v glazax vspyxnula radost'* "in someone's eyes joy flared up"

In contrast to the face (*lico*), eyes can also be described in terms of fire and burning:

> *ogon' v glazax; ognennye glaza* "fire in someone's eyes; fiery eyes"
> *glaza gorjat; glaza zagorjajutsja* lit. "someone's eyes are beginning to burn"

As *RECDHB* notes, both the above expressions "are used only to describe an emotional state, such as anger, joy, etc." In this respect, these expressions differ from the expression *glaza blestjat* "the eyes are shining", which may, but doesn't have to, refer to an emotion.

Several expressions referring to eyes imply anger. These include:

> *glaza sverkajut (ot gneva)* "someone's eyes flash/crackle/blaze (with anger)"
> *molnii sverkajut v glazax* lit. "lightning (repeatedly) flashes in someone's eyes"
> *glaza metajut gromy i molnii* lit. "someone's eyes are throwing thunders and lightnings"
> *glaza temnejut (ot gneva)* "someone's eyes darken (with anger)"
> *glaza nalivajutsja krov'ju* "someone's eyes become suffused with blood"
> *suž_ivat'/suzit' glaza* "to narrow one's eyes"

Above all, the word *glaza* is included in a number of collocations indicating surprise, amazement, and shock. These include:

> *udivlennye glaza* "surprised eyes"
> *izumlennye glaza* "astonished eyes"
> *sdelat' kruglye* (or: *bol'šie*) *glaza* "to make round (or: big) eyes"
> *sdelat' kvadratnye glaza* "to make square eyes"
> *taraščit'/vytaraščit' glaza* lit. to "goggle out" one's eyes"
> *vypučivat' glaza* lit. "to blow out one's eyes" (the verb *pučit'* is used with reference to a stomach bloated from gases, and *vy-* means "out")

*vykatit' glaza* lit. "to roll out/wheel out one's eyes"
*vylupit' glaza* lit. "to let one's eyes break out of their shells"
*vypučennye glaza* lit. "goggle eyes"
*glaza okrugljajutsja* "someone's eyes get round"
*glaza na lob lezut* "someone's eyes crawl onto their forehead"
*glaza vylezajut iz orbit* "someone's eyes pop out of their orbits"

In addition to these and many other collocations involving a person's eyes, *RECDHB* lists also numerous expressions involving eyebrows. These include:

> *naxmurivat'/naxmurit' brovi* "to knit one's eyebrows, to frown" (from *xmurit'sja* "to be overcast, cloudy")
> *(surovo) nasupit' brovi* "to (sternly) knit one's eyebrows"
> *naxmurennye brovi; nasuplennye brovi* "knitted eyebrows"; lit. "clouded eyebrows"

All these expressions are described as indicating "dissatisfaction, anger, or a bad mood" (p. 18).

An overlapping range of emotions (dissatisfaction, anger or concentration) is linked with the following collocations:

> *sdvigat'/sdvinut' brovi* lit. "to draw together one's eyebrows tightly, to scowl"
> *sdvinutye brovi* "knitted eyebrows, scowling eyebrows"

Several Russian expressions correspond to the English expression *to raise one's eyebrows*, implying surprise:

> *podnjat'/podnimat' brov'* "to raise one's eyebrows"
> *vskidyvat'/vskinut' brov'* (sg.) (or: *brovi*, pl.) lit. "to throw up one's eyebrows"
> *brovi podnjalis'* lit. "someone's eyes were raised"
> *brovi popolzli vverx* lit. "someone's eyebrows crawled upwards"

In contrast to the above, the following expressions can indicate not only surprise ("faint surprise"), but also "lack of understanding, or mistrust" (p. 19):

> *izgibat'/izognut' brov'* (or: *brovi*) "to raise one's eyebrow(s) slightly"
> *povodit'/povesti brov'ju* (or: *brov'jami*) "to move one's eyebrow(s)"

Again, we must conclude that both eyes and eyebrows appear to be treated as more expressive in Russian than they are in English.

## 2.5 The expressiveness of hands and legs

In Russian, not only the face is expected to be emotionally expressive but also the hands, and even feet or legs. To begin with the latter, English has one common set phrase referring to feet as a tool of emotional expression, namely, *to stamp one's foot* (although one could of course invent various descriptive expressions ad hoc). Russian, however, has several such common set phrases. To wit:

> *v gneve stuknut' nogoj* "to stamp one's foot (once) in anger"
> *neterpelivo stuknut' nogoj* "to stamp one's foot (once) from impatience"
> *topat' nogami (v jarosti)* "to stamp one's feet (repeatedly) (in rage)"
> *kolotit' (po polu) nogami* "to thump (on the floor) with one's feet" (usually about a child throwing a tantrum)

*RECDHB* cites also the following three expressions, all glossed as "to shift from one foot to another":

> *pereminat'sja s nogi na nogu*
> *perestupat' s nogi na nogu*
> *toptat'sja na meste*

All these expressions are said to describe behaviour seen as indicating "confusion, perplexity, indecisiveness, or embarrassment" (p. 227). *RECDHB* also cites expressions describing emotional gestures which involve a person's legs:

> *žat'sja/prižat'sja k nogam* "to press oneself against someone's legs"
> *buxat'sja/buxnuts'ja v nogi* "to fall to one's knees in front of someone" (lit. "to throw oneself into someone's legs")

The first of these expressions is said to refer "to the action of a child or a pet seeking affection or protection", and the second, "to a gesture of supplication" (p. 227).

Turning now to hands, we discover a remarkably wide range of Russian collocations describing "manual expression of emotions":

*potirat' ruki (ot udovol'stvija)* "to rub one's hands (from satisfaction)"

*lomat' ruki (v otčajanii)* "to wring (lit. break) one's hands (in despair)"

*zalamyvat' ruki (v otčajanii)* (as above)

*prižymat'/prižat' ruki k grudi* "to press one's hands to one's chest" (as a gesture of supplication or as a sign of sincerity)

*obxvatit' golovu rukami* lit. "to clasp one's head with one's hands (and to hold it like that)" ("a gesture of deep despair", p. 318)

*xvatat'sja/sxvatit'sja za golovu* "to clutch one's head" "a gesture of deep despair or a sign of a sudden realization of one's blunder", p. 318)

*sidet' (tjaželo) podperev golovu rukoj* "to sit with one's head propped on one's hand" (to describe someone who is "feeling depressed and deep in thought, usually painful and oppressive thought", p. 318)

*razvodit'/razvesti rukami* "to spread one's arms" ("a gesture of bewilderment or helplessness", p. 318)

*ronjat'/uronit' ruki* "to let one's arms fall to one's sides" (a gesture of sorrow and helplessness, p. 319; often used with the adverb *bessil'no* "helplessly")

*skladyvat'/složit' ruki na kolenjax* "to fold one's arms, resting one's hands in one's lap" (a phrase used to describe "a calm gesture"; often used with the adverb *smirenno* "meekly", p. 319)

*vspleskivat'/vsplesnut' rukami* "to fling one's hands upward, allow them to drop, then clasp them together at chest level" ("a gesture of surprise", p. 319)

*ne znat' kuda devat' ruki* "not to know what to do with one's hands" (a phrase used to describe "shyness or embarrassment", p. 319)

*stisnut' (komu-to) ruku* "to squeeze someone's arm/hand" (a phrase describing a presumed symptom "of fear or excitement", p. 319)

The English reader will no doubt recognize among the gestures described by the Russian phrases cited above some which can also be seen as expressing emotions in Anglo culture. In most cases, however, there do not seem to be any corresponding English phrases. Probably some of the gestures themselves are specifically Russian. This applies, in particular, to those designated by the Russian expressions *razvodit'(razvesti) rukami, vsplesnut' rukami* and *maxnut' rukoj*, which were singled out for special attention by Vladimir Nabokov and to which we will return later.

### 2.6 Head (golova)

Judging by the behaviour of the Russian word *golova* "head", the Russian head is also expected to be more expressive than the Anglo head. Movements of the head (*golova*) which are seen as expressive of emotional states include the following:

> *opuskat'/opustit' golovu*$_{ACC}$ "to hang (lit. lower) one's head" ("an expression which usually indicates sadness, shame, or embarrassment")

The following four expressions, which all describe involuntary gestures, imply sadness:

> *uronit' golovu*$_{ACC}$ na grud' "to let one's head drop to one's chest"
> *povesit' golovu*$_{ACC}$ "to hang one's head"
> *ponurit' golovu*$_{ACC}$
> "to hang one's head"
> *poniknut' golovoj*$_{INSTR}$ "to drop one's head" lit. "to droop with one's head"

If the verb *ronjat'(uronit')* "drop" is accompanied by a locative phrase (describing the resulting location of the head) the phrase as a whole implies (according to *RECDHB*) not sadness but grief:

> *ronjat'/uronit' golovu na stol* (or: *na ruki*)
> "to let one's head fall onto the table '(or: onto one's hands/ arms")
> (lit. to drop one's head)

*RECDHB* also lists three other related expressions:

> *sidet' (tjaželo) podperev golovu rukoj* "to sit with one's head (heavily) supported by one's hand" (an expression indicating "mental anguish or deep thought")
> *vtjagivat'/vtjanut' golovu v pleči* lit. "to draw one's head into one's shoulders"
> *vbirat'/vobrat' golovu v pleči* lit. "to take in one's head into one's shoulders" (both the above expressions "indicate fear, embarrassment, shame, resignation, or that one feels chilly")

*RECDHB* lists also a number of expressions describing voluntary gestures expressive of despair and of self-destructive impulses:[3]

> *bit'sja golovoj*$_{INSTR}$ *o stenu* "to beat one's head against a wall"; lit. "to knock oneself with one's head against a wall" (an expression indicating despair)
> *bit' sebja kulakom po golove* "to beat oneself on the head with one's fist" (an expression which indicates "a strong anger at oneself")
> *xvatat'sja/sxvatit'sja za golovu* "to clutch at one's head"; lit. "to grab oneself by the head" (an expression indicating "strong emotion, such as surprise, horror, or shock; it is also used figuratively, in the sense of: to suddenly see one's error")

From an Anglo point of view these expressions sound quite dramatic, and suggest cultural norms favouring more "exhibitionist" emotional behaviour.

### 2.7 Heart (serdce)

Since the heart is an internal and invisible part of the body, it is only usually seen as a seat of emotional experience rather than as an organ of emotional expression (although *RECDHB* does list three such expressions: *prižimat' k serdcu* "to clasp someone to one's heart", *prižimat' ruku/ruki k serdcu.* "to clasp one's hand(s) to one's heart", and *xvatat'sja za serdce* lit. "to clutch at one's heart"). Nonetheless, the Russian collocations involving the heart are also illustrative of the same characteristic attitude to emotions: giving them full sway without any attempt to control them.

The collocations of the word *serdce* "heart" listed in *RECDHB* point in this same direction of strong feelings being given full sway and allowed to be experienced to the full (more so than do English expressions involving the word *heart*). For example, the English expression *N's heart skips a beat* is given in *RECDHB* in addition to the semantically close Russian expression *u N ekaet serdce*, several other Russian counterparts, some of them distinctly more dramatic and hyperbolic.[4]

> *u N serdce zamiraet* "N's heart is (seems to be) dying"
> *u N serdce sžalos'* "N's heart squeezed"
> *u N serdce upalo* "N's heart fell" (cf. "N's heart sank")
> *u N serdce oborvalos'* "N's heart snapped (and fell)"
> *u N serdce ušlo v pjatki* "N's heart escaped into N's heels"

The English expression *N's heart is pounding* has three counterparts in Russian, at least one of them clearly more hyperbolic:

> *u N serdce kolotitsja* "N's heart is pounding (connotations of battering, smashing, thrashing)"
> *u N serdce b'etsja* lit. "N's heart is pounding (connotations of loud, desperate and violent movements)"
> *u N serdce gotovo vyskočit' iz grudi* "N's heart is ready to jump out of N's breast"

As *RECDHB* notes, these expressions "describe symptoms of fear, excitement, or joy", and they can be followed by the phrases *ot straxa* "from fear", *ot volnenija* "from excitement", and *ot radosti* "from joy".

Finally, *RECDHB* lists several Russian expressions describing anxiety, despair, and sorrow, again more numerous and more dramatic than the two English expressions listed in this section, namely, *N's heart aches* and *N's heart bleeds* (the latter being often an ironic reference to compassion, not necessarily genuine):

> *u N serdce noet* "N's heart aches/moans"
> *u N serdce ščemit* "N's heart aches/nags"
> *u N serdce rvetsja (or: razryvaetsja) na časti (or: na kusočki, or: po polam)* "N's heart is tearing into parts (or: into small pieces, or: into halves)"
> *u N serdce oblivaetsja krov'ju* "N's heart is pouring over itself with blood"

## 3 Conclusion

It is often said and indeed taken for granted that emotional expression differs significantly from culture to culture. The "inscrutable" Japanese face, the "exuberant gesticulation" of Greeks or Italians, the Russian "bear hugs" and "hearty kisses", the Anglo "peck on the cheek". Stereotypes of this kind reflect accumulated intercultural experience, and it would be foolish to simply dismiss them as not based on any scientific methodology. But it would of course be equally foolish to simply accept such stereotypes without any attempt to study the purported cultural differences on the basis of some more objective evidence and with reference to some rigorous analytical framework.

The task is complex and fraught with difficulties, but as RECDHB demonstrates, sophisticated collocational dictionaries can provide invaluable evidence in this area.

Consider, for example, Vladimir Nabokov's (1957: 41) comments on some characteristic "Russian gestures" as displayed by his hero Timofey Pnin, "a veritable encyclopedia of Russian shrugs and shakes" (for the benefit of the American scholar Laurence Clements):

> Laurence even made a film of what Timofey considered to be the essentials of Russian "carpalistics," with Pnin in a polo shirt, a Gioconda smile on his lips, demonstrating the movements underlying such Russian verbs – used in reference to hands – as *mahnut'*, *vsplesnut'*, *razvesti*: the one-hand downward loose shake of weary relinquishment; the two-hand dramatic splash of amazed distress; and the "disjunctive" motion – hands travelling apart to signify helpless passivity.

The fact that Russian has indeed set phrases such as *maxnut' rukoj*, *vsplesnut' rukami*, and *razvesti rukami* (used with reference to a display of emotion), and that there are no equivalent phrases in English and many other languages, does indeed provide supporting evidence for Pnin's (and Nabokov's) perception that these are characteristically Russian modes of emotional expression. But these are only three examples. *RECDHB* provides dozens, if not hundreds, of similarly revealing collocations, all presented in orderly fashion, thus paving a road to generalizations.

It is beyond the scope of this chapter to try to spell out and justify all the generalizations concerning emotional expression that *RECDHB* can be seen as a basis for. By way of example, however, let me point out that the Russian collocational material presented by *RECDHB* suggests a cultural model of a person which is different from the model reflected in the English language.

In his *Acts of Meaning*, Jerome Bruner (1990: 35) stated that "all cultures have as one of their most powerful constitutive instruments a folk psychology" and that "we learn our culture's folk psychology early, learn it as we learn to use the very language we acquire and to conduct the interpersonal transactions required in communal life." (Cf. also Shore 1996.)

I believe linguistic data of the kind discussed in this chapter provide evidence for different folk models of a person; at the same time, they also suggest some of the ways in which such culture-specific models may be learnt (through language and through linguistic interpretation of nonverbal behaviour). The Russian model of person suggested by the material discussed in this chapter includes the following two assumptions (A and B), stated in the Natural Semantic Metalanguage:

*Russian model of a person*

A  (a)  OFTEN when a person feels something
   (b)  this person IS DOING something with some parts of the

body because of this
(c) this person can do it FOR SOME TIME
(d) other people can see this
(e) because of this, other people can know WHAT this person feels

B. (a) OFTEN when a person feels something
(b') something is happening to this person because of this
(b) because something IS HAPPENING to some parts of this person's body
(c) it can be happening for some time
(d) other people can see this
(e) because of this, other people can know WHAT this person feels

As the material presented in *RECDHB* suggests, the assumptions A and B proposed as part of the Russian model of a person are not necessarily parts of the cultural model of a person reflected in the English language. This is not to say that the Anglo model includes no similar assumptions, but rather that the exact form of the corresponding assumptions embodied in that model may be somewhat different (A' and B'):

*Anglo model of a person*

A' (a) SOMETIMES when a person feels something
(b) this person DOES something with some parts of the body because of this
(c) ——————————————
(d) other people can see this
(e) because of this, other people can know THAT this person feels something

B' (a) SOMETIMES when a person feels something
(b') ——————————————
(b) something HAPPENS to some parts of this person's body because of this
(c) ——————————————
(d) other people can see this
(e) because of this, other people can know THAT this person feels something

While no detailed justification and discussion of these formulae will be undertaken here (see, however, Wierzbicka 1992a, 1994b, 1996c), the reader will note the distinction between "often" and "sometimes" in component (a), the presence vs. absence of component (c), and the difference in the phrasing of component (e) ("other people can know what this person feels" vs. "other people can know that this person feels something").

One point which does require some explanation in the present context concerns the presence of component (b') in the Russian formula, and the absence of a corresponding component in the Anglo formula. What component (b') is meant to capture is the fact that in Russian bodily processes are typically presented as involving the whole person, whereas in English they are presented as involving some parts of a person's body, without any reference to the person as such. For example, when one wants to say in Russian that someone's face was "shining with joy" one normally has to include a locative phrase referring to the person as a whole (lit. "at her"). The phenomenon of treating a part of a person's body as an aspect of that person (rather than as an independent "object") is of course well known and has been much discussed in the literature (cf. e.g. Bally 1926; Chappell and McGregor 1996; Mel'čuk 1995; Wierzbicka 1979, 1988a), but it is interesting to note that Russian language takes this attitude to the human body further than many other European languages, whereas English language allows it only to a very limited extent. These differences need to be reflected in the semantic formulae portraying the two models of a person: the one associated with the Russian, and the one associated with English.

It can also be argued that Russian culture (in contrast to Anglo culture) includes a general "script" related to the expression of emotions which can be phrased as follows:

> it is good if other people know what a person feels

In support of such a general "script" we could cite not only collocations such as *zdorovyj xoxot* ("healthy loud laughter"), but also phrases such as *duša naraspašku* "soul wide open (like a shirt thrown wide open)", which has positive connotations: the implication is that it is good, indeed wonderful, if a person's "soul" (heart), which is the seat of emotions, is flung open in a spontaneous, generous, expansive, impetuous gesture, expressing full trust in other people and an innocent readiness for communion with them.

The implications of English words and expressions such as *emotional, effusive, demonstrative, excitable* (negative connotations) are quite different.

This is not to say, of course, that Russian culture doesn't value emotional self-control under any circumstances, or that Anglo culture doesn't value emotional expressivity at all. After all, one could also point, for example, to the positive connotations of the Russian word *xladnokrov'e* (lit. "cold blood"), and to the negative connotations of the English expression *stiff upper lip*.

But the range of situations in which emotional expression appears to be valued in the two cultures is quite different. *Xladnokrov'e* – like the French *sang-froid* – suggests self-control in the face of danger, that is, when something bad can happen to us. (It is quite different, therefore, from the English expression *in cold blood*, which implies that one wants to do something bad to someone else and that one feels no qualms about that.) The positive concept of *xladnokrov'e* is not inconsistent with the cultural script "it is good if other people know what a person feels", for it implies an (admirable) absence of bad feelings in the face of danger rather than an (admirable) ability to hide one's feelings.

The English expression *stiff upper lip* does refer to a tendency to hide one's feelings, and does it disapprovingly, but it does not suggest that "it is good if other people know what a person feels" or that "it is bad if other people don't know what a person feels". It implies only that "it is bad if someone *always* thinks: I don't want other people to know what I feel" (and if one acts accordingly).

It is also interesting to note that while the English word *open* (used with reference to a person) has positive connotations, its implications are quite different from those of Russian expressions like *duša naraspašku* "wide open soul". In fact, *open* does not necessarily refer to our personal feelings at all: one can be "open" in saying what one thinks rather than in saying – or showing – what one feels; by contrast, the Russian *duša* is above all an organ of feelings, and the expression *duša naraspašku* refers necessarily to emotions – emotions which are seen as generously and unreservedly shared.

Needless to say, I am not proposing here anything as simple as: "English = control, Russian = expressivity". Rather, I would argue that simplistic labels like "control", "self-control", "expressivity", "display", and so on are inadequate for cross-cultural comparisons, and would propose instead a flexible framework of complex culture-specific "cultural scripts" – complex, but constructed out of very simple building blocks, and culture-specific, but based on universal semantic elements.[5]

As pointed out by a reader of an earlier version of this chapter, it can be said that in Anglo culture "it's good to be cool, bad to be cold; it's good to be warm, bad to be hot and bothered". It is interesting to note, however, that in Russian it is good to be "hot" (*gorjačij*), and it is *not* good to be just "warm" (*teplyj*); for example, in English, one can thank someone "warmly" but not "hotly", whereas in Russian the opposite is the case. In Russian one can also defend someone "hotly" (*gorjačo zaščiščat'*), with positive connotations, whereas in English one can at best defend someone "warmly". Furthermore, English expressions like *hot and bothered* or *hot under the collar* (with negative connotations) have simply no counterparts in Russian: in Russian when the word *gorjačij* "hot" is used in reference to feelings it always has positive connotations.

In proposing, in such a formulaic format, a "Russian model of person" and an "Anglo model of person" I do not mean to deny either the heterogeneity or the changeability of cultures. To quote Shore (1996: 47):

> Cultural models are born, transferred through use, and eventually die out. Their continued existence is contingent, negotiated through endless social exchanges. Such shared models are a community's conventional resources for meaning making. To gain motivational force in a society, these models must be reinscribed [in] each generation in the minds of its members. In this way, conventional models become a personal cognitive resource for individuals.

The fact that cultural models are subject to change and variation does not mean that they have no stability or demonstrable reality. Linguistic data of the kind discussed in this chapter provide indispensable evidence for testing the validity of such models. They must, however, be collected and interpreted in a systematic and methodologically informed way. In particular, if we had sophisticated collocational dictionaries of the human body such as *RECDHB* for other languages – for example, for Italian, Greek, Malay, Chinese, Japanese, and of course English – we could learn a great deal about cross-cultural differences in the norms of emotional expression. We could document many differences which in the past have usually been suggested on a purely subjective basis; we could describe such differences in much more specific and illuminating ways; and we could reach for both richer and firmer generalizations.

Finally, data of the kind discussed in this chapter support the view that there is no need and no justification for opposing "the anthropology of the body" to the "anthropology of the mind", or the "cognitivist" to "practice-based" theories of culture and language (cf. e.g. Bourdieu 1977, Hanks 1996). The body is largely in the mind (cf. Johnson 1987), and cultural practices are largely governed by "cultural scripts" which are both public artifacts (cf. Geertz 1973) and cognitive representations (cf. e.g. D'Andrade 1987); and which can be seen as an important aspect of what Shore (1996) calls "culture in the mind".

# CHAPTER 6

# Comparing emotional norms across languages and cultures: Polish vs. Anglo-American

## 1 Emotion and culture

Although human emotional endowment is no doubt largely innate and universal, people's emotional lives are shaped, to a considerable extent, by their culture. Every culture offers not only a linguistically embodied grid for the conceptualization of emotions, but also a set of "scripts" suggesting to people how to feel, how to express their feelings, how to think about their own and other people's feelings, and so on.

In fact, a culture's lexical grid and its repertoire of "cultural scripts", including "emotional scripts", are closely related. For example, the fact that the closest Malay counterpart of *angry* (*marah*) is incompatible with violence and aggression and can be seen as, in some ways, closer to English words like *resentful* and *upset* than to *angry*, is no doubt related to Malay cultural attitudes to aggression, violence, and emotional self-control (cf. Goddard 1997a). In addition to the basic lexical grid, however, a culture's "emotional scripts" manifest themselves in many other ways – in the lexicon, in grammar, and in discourse.

But to be able to see, and to interpret, the diverse links between emotion and culture (cf. Kitayama and Markus 1994), we need to reaffirm "culture" as a valid, and indeed indispensable construct.

Questioning this construct, one influential writer, Eric Wolf (1994), refers in this context to Franz Boas as someone who appreciated, ahead of his time, "the heterogeneity and the historically changing interconnectedness of cultures" and was therefore able to see cultures as "a problem and not a given". Wolf charges that, subsequently, anthropologists failed to fully appreciate the importance, and the full implications, of these points. Apparently forgetting that Boas himself was a major link in the historical tradition leading from Herder and Humboldt to Sapir and Whorf, Wolf contrasts the French "universalist" tradition with the German-style emphasis on *Volksgeist* and differences between cultures.

There can be no quarrel with the statement that cultures are not separate monads but, rather, heterogeneous, historically changing, interconnected, and "continually exchanging materials" (Wolf 1994: 5). But there is a difference between, on the one hand, rejecting "static culturologies", as does Regna Darnell (1994) in her commentary on Wolf's paper, and, on the other, embracing the view that cultures have no "content" at all, being no more than cross-currents of myriads of influences, as Immanuel Wallerstein (1994) seems to do in his commentary on the same paper.

No one is more acutely aware of the reality of cultures than a bilingual who lives his or her life in two languages and two cultures, and the testimony of bilingual and bicultural writers is loud and clear (Cf. Wierzbicka 1997a; chapter 1). For the same reason that bilingual witnesses are better placed than monolinguals to affirm the reality of different languages, bicultural witnesses are better placed than "monolingual monoculturals" to affirm the reality of different cultures, however heterogeneous and lacking in fixed contours these cultures may be. Wuthnow et al. (1984: 6–7) note that "for all the research that has been made possible by survey techniques and qualitative analysis, little has been learned about cultural patterns", and they ask "whether it is possible to construct cultural analysis as a basic tool capable of producing verifiable social scientific knowledge at all, or whether the study of culture necessarily remains a speculative venture" (p. 257).

This chapter, focussed on Polish "emotional scripts" (set against the background of Anglo-American "scripts"), seeks to demonstrate that patterns of culture can be studied in a verifiable and non-speculative way on the basis of linguistic semantics, rooted in empirically established linguistic and conceptual universals.

My claim is that when one analyses linguistic evidence concerning emotions and emotional expression in Polish culture, there emerge three basic "cultural scripts", or families of "scripts", which can be labelled, for the sake of convenience, the "scripts of sincerity", the "scripts of warmth", and the "scripts of spontaneity".

## 2 The scripts of "sincerity"

### 2.1 "Sincerity" and smiles

The "scripts of sincerity" concern the value of presenting one's feelings "truthfully", that is, of saying, and "showing", what one really feels, and not saying, or "showing", that one feels something that one does not in fact feel. Polish culture can be contrasted in this respect with Anglo-American culture, which values and encourages the display of "good feelings" that one may not necessarily feel, and the suppression of "bad feelings" whose display may be seen as serving no useful purpose and either damaging to our "image" or unpleasant for other people.

In particular, the two cultures have different norms and expectations concerning smiling. An American woman married to a Pole and living in Warsaw (Klos Sokol 1997: 117) writes that "Americans smile more in situations where Poles tend not to"; Poles don't *"initiate* an exchange of smiles in a quick or anonymous interaction"; in Poland "you may see faces that might look *really* grumpy", and she comments further:

> In everyday life, the approach to fleeting interactions in Poland is often take-me-seriously. Rather than the cursory smile, surface courtesy means a slight nod of the head. And some Poles may not feel like masking their everyday preoccupations. From this perspective, the smile would be fake. In American culture, you don't advertise your daily headaches; it's bad form; so you turn up the corners of the mouth – or at least try – according to the Smile Code.

The tacit assumption behind what Klos Sokol calls the American "Smile Code" can be represented in the form of the following cultural script:

1. *Anglo-American*
   [people think:]
   when I say something to other people
   it is good if these people think that I feel something good

Of course not all Americans live by this script, but they are all familiar with it. The component "people think:" opening the scripts reflects the fact that even people who personally don't identify with the content of that script are nonetheless familiar with it: they, too, belong to the community which shares familiarity with this script (and with other, related, cultural scripts).[1] In Polish culture, however, there is no similar (generally recognizable) tacit assumption. It is not surprising, therefore, that, as Klos Sokol notes, Poles who have lived in the United States are often struck by the American "Smile Code". For example:

> A Pole who has lived in the States for six years recently returned to Poland for a visit. During a round of introductions to some people in a cafe, she immediately spotted the American by his smile. "There's a lack of smiling here . . ." says the Pole. Another Pole says, "Americans, in general, smile all the time. Here, people in the streets look worried."

The evidence adduced above is of course purely anecdotal and subjective. There is also, however, objective – linguistic – evidence which points in the same direction. This evidence includes, in particular, the strongly negative connotations of Polish words like *fałszywy* "false" and *sztuczny* "artificial", used for condemnation of "put-on" smiles and other forms of non-spontaneous displays of "good feelings". The collocation *fałszywy uśmiech*, "a false smile", is particularly common, but there are others as well. Some examples (from *SJP* 1958–69):

> Gdy Lipecka starała się manifestować czułość i troskliwość dla męża, wypadało to tak sztucznie i *fałszywie*, że nie mogło ujść niczyjej uwagi. (Perzyński)
> "When Lipecka tried to show tenderness and care for her husband, the effect was so artificial and false that everybody was bound to notice it."

> W *fałszywie* uśmiechniętym dorobkiewiczu dojrzał . . . bezdeń podłości. (Gomulicki)
> "In the falsely smiling nouveau-riche he saw bottomless baseness."

> Był zawsze słodki i zawsze *fałszywy*! A wam się wszystkim podobał, że taki zakochany. (Nałkowska)
> "He was always sugary and always false! And you all liked him because you thought that he was so much in love."

> Na Klarze jej pocałunki sprawiały przykre wrażenie czegoś *fałszywego*, ale poddała się im uprzejmie. (Orzeszkowa)
> "To Clare her kisses seemed painfully false, but she submitted to them to be polite."

Particularly noteworthy is the use of the word *fałszywy* "false" to describe a person as a whole ("a false person"), which is glossed by the SJP as "hypocritical, insincere, cunning, traitor-like" and which is illustrated with the following examples:

> W ich usłużności i gotowości nie tkwiło nic *fałszywego*.
> "There was nothing false in their eagerness to help and to be of service."

> *Fałszywy*, zdradny i przewrotny dworak ten był znienawidzony powszechnie.
> "That false, cunning, and treacherous courtier was hated by everyone."

The semantic shift from "insincere, fake", to "cunning" and "traitor-like" is telling.

Collocations like *fałszywy uśmiech* "a false smile", *fałszywe pocałunki* "false kisses" or *coś fałszywego* "something false" imply that someone is displaying "good feelings towards another person" that in fact are not felt, and that "of course" it is very bad to do so. This can be represented in the form of the following cultural script:

> 2. *Polish*
> [people think:]
> it is bad
> when a person wants other people to think
>     that this person "feels something good towards these people"[2]
> if this person doesn't feel this

This script can be seen as a special instance of a more general script:[3]

> 3. *Polish*
> [people think:]
> it is bad
> when a person wants other people to think
>     that this person feels something
> if this person doesn't feel this

Laura Klos Sokol (1997: 177) remarks:

> Poles expect people to be direct with emotions, views, and reactions. A Pole who lives in the States and works with Americans says, "I'm the kind of person whose face reflects my feelings. When someone is feeling down but poses as happy, I don't like it. Sometimes it gets on my nerves."

The assumption that a person's face should reflect his or her feelings is far more than an individual preference: it is a cultural premiss, supported by linguistic evidence in the form, for example, of pejorative expressions like *fałszywy uśmiech* "a false smile" and *sztuczny uśmiech* "an artificial smile", to which we will now turn.

To begin with, I will note that although the word *sztuczny* ("artificial") doesn't sound quite as pejorative in Polish as the word *fałszywy*, the two go often together, as in the example quoted earlier:

> Gdy Lipecka starała sié manifestować czułość i troskliwość dla męża, wypadało to tak *sztucznie* i *fałszywie*, że nie mogło ujść niczyjej uwagi. "When Lipecka tried to show tenderness and care for her husband, the effect was so artificial and false that everybody was bound to notice it."

A few more examples:

> Takiś smutny . . . – Gdzie tam – zaśmiałem się *sztucznie*. (Kło-sowski)
> "You look so sad . . . who me? – I laughed phonily."

> Sam wiedział, że to, co mówi, brzmi jakoś *sztucznie* i *nieszczerze*. (Krzywicki)
> "He knew himself that what he was saying sounded artificial and insincere."

> Stłumił głęboką urazę *sztucznym* uśmiechem. (Moraczewski)
> "He suppressed his deep resentment beneath a false smile."

> Mówił *sztucznym*, aksamitnym głosem gruchając słodko przy każdym 'r'. (Braun)
> "He spoke in a velvety, phoney voice, fruitily rolling each 'r'."

All these examples illustrate the cultural assumption that "it is bad when a person wants other people to think that this person feels something if this person doesn't feel this". A quote from the writer Niemcewicz, adduced by *SJP*, sums it up as follows:

> Uczucia, które *sztucznie* udajemy, serca nasze oziębiają.
> "Feelings that we artificially display, make our hearts cold."

Both sociological analysis and linguistic evidence concur with the cross-cultural experience in the assessment that Anglo-American attitudes to "displays of good feelings" in general, and to deliberate, controlled "put-on" smiles in particular, are different.

The extraordinary importance of controlled smiles in American culture is epitomized in the training in smiling to which American flight attendants are widely subjected. A vignette from Hochschild's (1983) account of her visit to the Delta Airlines Stewardess Training Center illustrates this well:

> The young trainee sitting next to me wrote on her notepad, "Important to smile. Don't forget smile." The admonition came from the speaker in the front of the room, a crewcut pilot in his early fifties, speaking in a Southern drawl: "Now girls, I want you to go out there and really *smile*. Your smile is your biggest asset. I want you to go out there and use it. Smile. *Really* smile. Really *lay it on*." (p. 4)

As Hochschild emphasized, the smiles that the air hostesses are expected to have on their faces must be "spontaneous and sincere":

As the Pacific Southwest Airlines jingle says, "Our smiles are not just painted on." Our flight attendants' smile, the company emphasizes, will be more human than the phony smiles you're resigned to seeing on people who are paid to smile. There is a smile-like strip of paint on the nose of each PSA plane. Indeed, the plane and the flight attendant advertise one another . . . Now that advertisements, training, notions of professionalism, and dollar bills have intervened between the smiler and the smiled upon, it takes an extra effort to imagine that spontaneous warmth can exist in uniform – because companies now advertise spontaneous warmth, too. (p. 5)

Because passengers "are quick to detect strained or forced smiles", what flight attendants are required to do is not just smile and smile well (i.e. adroitly, skilfully), but to manufacture within themselves feelings that match the smile. Thus, a stewardess is required to "really work on her smiles" and is expected to "manage her heart" in such a way as to trigger a smile that will both seem and be "spontaneous and sincere" (Hochschild 1983: 105). The company lays claim not simply to her physical movements – how she handles food trays – but to her emotional actions as well and to the way these show in the ease of the smile (p. 107). American society at large appears to value not just "painted smiles", but smiles reflecting genuine cheerfulness, genuine enthusiasm, a genuine state of feeling "happy"; but in the dominant hierarchy of values "cheerfulness" appears to be above "spontaneity" and perhaps even above "sincerity".

### 2.2 "Cheerful" speech routines

In English, there are many common speech routines which manifestly reflect a cultural premiss to the effect that it is good to "feel good" – and to be seen as someone who "feels good". In particular, the common "How are you? – I am fine" routine implies an expectation that "good feelings" will be expressed, and if need be, "artificially displayed". Of course this expectation may be violated, but it is undoubtedly there, as highlighted by the dictum "don't tell your friends about your indigestion, 'How are you' is a greeting, not a question" (Arthur Guiteman, quoted in Leech 1983: 198).

The importance of positive expressives such as *Hi!* or *Great!* in American culture, and of positive conversational routines, is well illustrated by the following beginning of a conversation, offered in an American bestseller as a model of successful human interaction (M. Smith 1975: 93):

Pete:  Hi, Jean.
Jean:  Hi, Pete, how are you?
Pete:  I'm fine, how are you?

Jean:  I feel like having a good time.
Pete:  Great. So do I.

In fact, Anglo-American culture appears to have gone further in the direction of "positive" scripts than the Anglo-British or Anglo-Australian varieties have, and has apparently developed some emotional scripts of its own, two of which could be called the "enthusiasm script" and the "cheerfulness script". To quote an American witness (Klos Sokol 1997: 176) again (cf. Wierzbicka 1994d: 184):

> Wow! Great! How nice! That's fantastic! I had a terrific time! It was wonderful! Have a nice day! Americans. So damned cheerful.

Speech routines of this kind suggest a cultural script which can be formulated along the following lines:

4. *Anglo-American*
[people think:]
it is good to say often something like this:
"I feel something very good"

It is interesting to note in this connection that, for example, Sommers' (1984) cultural study of attitudes toward emotions showed that Americans place an exceptional emphasis on "enthusiasm" and value it far more highly than do the other cultural groups with which they were compared (Greeks, West Indians, Chinese). In a similar vein, Renwick (1980) contrasted the "Australian art of deadpan understatement" with the American penchant for "exaggeration and overstatement" and observed that "Australians also add a dash of cynicism to their conversation, especially when they want to counterpoint an American colleague's overenthusiasm" (p. 28).

One linguistic reflection of this attitude is the ubiquitous presence of the word *great* in American discourse (cf. Wolfson 1983: 93), both as a modifier (especially of the verb *to look*) and as a "response particle":

> You look great!
> Your X (hair, garden, apartment, etc.) looks great!
> It's great! That's great! Great!

(Cf. also the dialogue between Pete and Jean quoted earlier.) The basic meaning of the "great" conversational routine may be represented as follows:

(a)  I think this is very good
(b)  when I think about it, I feel something very good
(c)  I want people to know this

Component (a) spells out the positive evaluation; component (b) accounts for the role of *great* as an expression of enthusiasm and accounts for the emotive character of this adjective (cf. *"Objectively speaking, that was a great meal"); and component (c) accounts for the tendency of *great* to be used as a response particle.

Polish doesn't have speech routines corresponding to "How are you? – I'm fine", "How is it going?", or to the ubiquitous American "Great!" This is consistent with the subjective evidence such as that reported by Klos Sokol (1997: 176):

> To some extent, Poles enjoy the up-beat American pom-pom skating cheer. Who would dare claim that cheerfulness is bad? However, sometimes, Poles balk at American-style frothy enthusiasm. Ask a Pole to imitate American behaviour and chances are the result will include a wide smile, an elongated "Wooooow!" and "Everything is fine!" with a thumbs-up.
>
> One Pole said, "My first impression was how happy Americans must be." But like many Poles she cracked the code: "Poles have different expectations. Something 'fantastic' for Americans would not be 'fantastic' in my way of thinking." Another Pole says, "When Americans say it was great, I know it was good. When they say it was good, I know it was okay. When they say it was okay, I know it was bad."

The central importance of positive feelings in American culture is also reflected in the key role that the adjective *happy* plays in American discourse, an adjective that is widely used as a yardstick for measuring people's psychological well-being as well as their social adjustment. The crucial role of this adjective in American life has often been commented on by newcomers. For example, Stanisław Barańczak (1990: 13), professor of Polish literature at Harvard University, writes:[4]

> Take the word "happy", perhaps one of the most frequently used words in Basic American. It's easy to open an English–Polish or English–Russian dictionary and find an equivalent adjective. In fact, however, it will not be equivalent. The Polish word for "happy" (and I believe this also holds for other Slavic languages) has much more restricted meaning; it is generally reserved for rare states of profound bliss, or total satisfaction with serious things such as love, family, the meaning of life, and so on. Accordingly, it is not used as often as "happy" is in American common parlance . . . Incidentally, it is also interesting that Slavic languages don't have an exact equivalent for the verb "to enjoy." I don't mean to say that Americans are a nation of superficial, backslapping enjoyers and happy-makers, as opposed to our suffering Slavic souls. What I'm trying to point out is only one example of the semantic incompatibilities which are so firmly ingrained in languages and cultures that they sometimes make mutual communication impossible.

The pressure on people to be "happy" can only be compared with the pressure to smile: by being "happy", one projects a positive image of oneself (as a successful person). The fact that some American psychologists have elevated the state of being "happy" to the status of a basic human emotion is revealing in this respect: from a cross-cultural perspective, the word *joy* (with equivalents such as *Freude, joie, gioia, radost'*, etc. in other European languages) might have seemed a much better candidate for such a status. But in American culture, the concept of *happy* is indeed much more central than the concept of *joy*. It is easy to understand how the centrality of this concept in American culture may have influenced the researchers' perspective on human emotions in general.

To be *happy* is to feel something good for personal reasons – an ideal quite consistent with the general orientation of "a culture dominated by expressive and utilitarian individualism" (Bellah et al. 1985: 115). The fact that *happy* is an adjective, whereas its closest counterparts in other European languages are verbs (e.g. *sich freuen* in German, *se rejouir* in French, or *cieszyć się* in Polish) is also significant, because these verbs indicate a temporary occurrence (as the archaic verb *rejoice* does in English), whereas the adjective *happy* is compatible with a long-term state (the expected norm). As Barańczak points out, people can be expected to be "happy" most of the time, but can not be expected to "rejoice" most of the time (cf. Kitayama and Markus 1992: 23–5; for a fuller discussion of the concept *happy*, see chapter 2).

The concept of *enjoyment* mentioned by Barańczak is also culturally significant, as it links good feelings with the idea of an activity: in contrast to *pleasure*, which can be entirely passive, one can only *enjoy* something that one is *doing* (e.g. talking, swimming, dancing, sitting in the sun, and so on). The fact that other European (or non-European) languages do not have a word corresponding to the English *enjoy* highlights the characteristically Anglo nexus of feeling and control, and of actively achieving a desired emotional state:

> X is enjoying Y =
> when X does Y, X feels something good
> because of this, X wants to do Y

Equally revealing is the key Anglo (and, especially, Anglo-American) concept of *fun*, which also links the idea of doing something with that of feeling something good (and adds to it a further component of the speaker's own good feelings at the idea of doing something for pleasure). The sociologist Martha Wolfenstein (1975: 401) talks even in this connection of "the emergence of fun morality" in modern American culture: ". . . fun, from having been suspect if not taboo, has tended to become obligatory. Instead of feeling guilty for having too much fun, one is inclined to feel ashamed if one does not have enough." Wolfenstein illustrates the emergence of the "fun morality" by doing a content analysis of child-rearing handbooks, with their striking emphasis on "fun" and "enjoyment". One example:

> The new parents are told that they are making a good start if they can enjoy their baby . . . The child should learn that mother and father are "two people who enjoy each other" . . . Introducing the baby to solid foods will be "fun" and "amusing" for the mother, and the baby will "enjoy the new experience more if you are having a good time." (p. 401)

The importance of good feelings (such as "cheerfulness", "friendliness", "enthusiasm", "enjoyment", and "fun") in American culture and the absence of similar norms in Polish culture are illustrated particularly well in Eva Hoffman's (1989) reminiscences of different farewell rituals as she experienced them in Poland and in America:

> But as the time of our departure approaches, Basia . . . makes me promise that I won't forget her. Of course I won't! She passes a journal with a pretty, embroidered cloth cover to my fellow classmates, in which they are to write appropriate words of good-bye. Most of them choose melancholy verses in which life is figured as a vale of tears or a river of suffering, or a journey of pain on which we are embarking. This tone of sadness is something we all enjoy. It makes us feel the gravity of life, and it is gratifying to have a truly tragic event – a parting forever – to give vent to such romantic feelings.
>   It's only two years later that I go on a month-long bus trip across Canada and the United States with a group of teenagers, who at parting inscribe sentences in each other's notebooks to be remembered by. "It was great fun knowing you!" they exclaim in the pages of my little notebook. "Don't ever lose your friendly personality!" "Keep cheerful, and nothing can harm you!" they enjoin, and as I compare my two sets of mementos, I know that, even though they're so close to each other in time, I've indeed come to another country. (p. 78)

These contrasting attitudes can be formulated as follows:

5. *Polish*
[everybody knows:]
sometimes people feel something bad
because they can't be in the same place as someone else
[people think: this is good]

6. *Anglo-American*
[people think:]
it is good to think often that good things can happen to people
it is good to feel something good because of this

The reason why the Polish script (5) has been introduced in the frame "everyone knows" rather than "people think" is that the cultural attitude in question is best thought of as a cultural model rather than a normative cultural script. From a Polish point of view, it is "common knowledge" that people often suffer because they are separated from beloved, or familiar, people and places – "common knowledge" reflected in the language-specific concept of *tęsknota* "nostalgia/homesickness/longing/heartache". (For detailed discussion, see Wierzbicka 1986a, 1988b.) The model which acknowledges this "common knowledge" is culturally endorsed, and the words *tęsknota* and *tęsknić* (verb) have rather positive connotations in Polish. At the same time, however, there is no normative script recommending to people that they should feel something like *tęsknota*, as there are normative scripts of "positive thinking" or "cheerfulness" in Anglo-American culture.[5]

Social commentators agree that, far from suppressing all expression of emotion, Anglo culture fosters certain kinds of (carefully monitored) emotional expression. In particular, American culture fosters and encourages "cheerfulness". To quote Eva Hoffman (1989) again:

> If all neurosis is a form of repression, then surely, the denial of suffering, and of helplessness, is also a form of neurosis. Surely, all our attempts to escape sorrow twist themselves into the specific, acrid pain of self-suppression. And if that is so, then a culture that insists on cheerfulness and staying in control is a culture that – in one of those ironies that prevails in the unruly realm of the inner life – propagates its own kind of pain. (p. 271)

Assessments of the psychological costs of obligatory cheerfulness may or may not be correct, but few commentators would disagree with the basic idea that something like "cheerfulness" is encouraged by American culture. More precisely, the norm in question can be represented as follows:

7. *Anglo-American*
[people think:]
it is good to think often that something good will happen
it is good to often feel something good because of this
it is good if other people can see this

What can one do to comply with the above norm? One can, of course, smile – and, as we have seen, American culture is one of those cultures that value and encourage the "social smile" (cf. Wanning 1991: 19; for the concept of social smile, see Ekman 1989).

### 3 The scripts of interpersonal "warmth"

Turning now to the "scripts of warmth", I will note, above all, the importance of the concept of "serdeczność" (from *serce* "heart") in

Polish culture. Roughly speaking, to be *serdeczny* (adjective) means to show "good feelings towards another person". Being *serdeczny* is a little bit like being "cordial", but the Polish word – which, unlike *cordial*, is a common, everyday word – implies more intensive and more genuine "warmth", flowing "straight from the heart".

Unlike *cordiality*, *serdeczność* must be perceived as spontaneous and almost unintentional (it just "flows" from the heart); and unlike *warmheartedness*, it is personal, directed to a particular person. For example, common collocations with *serdeczny* include *serdeczny przyjaciel* and *najserdeczniejszy* (superlative) *przyjaciel* – literally, "heart-friend" and "most-heart-friend". The word *przyjaciel* itself means not just "friend" but "a close friend" (cf. Wierzbicka 1997a), and the adjective *serdeczny* implies here something like a loving bond. By contrast, one cannot speak in English of a "cordial friend". Generally speaking, "cordiality" is reserved for people who are *not* very close to us; it refers more to a conscious attitude, manifested mainly in somewhat formal encounters, than to a propensity for outpouring genuine interpersonal feeling, as the Polish *serdeczność* does. Some examples (from *SJP*):

> Był oczywiście *serdeczny* – wyściskał i wycałował przyjaciela. (Broszkiewicz)
> "Naturally he was very warm, hugging and kissing his friend."

> Była u mnie Cesia, moja *najserdeczniejsza* przyjaciółka i najdawniejsza, bo jeszcze na pensji przysięgłyśmy sobie przyjaźń. (Reymont)
> "Cesia came to see me, my oldest and best friend, with whom I exchanged vows of eternal friendship while we were still at school."

The plural noun *serdeczności* refers to a specific (verbal or non-verbal) outpouring of good feelings towards another person. For example:

> Chłopczyna zaczął go głaskać ręką po twarzy. Na zakończenie tych *serdeczności* objął go za szyję i uścisnął. (Sewer)
> "The lad began to stroke his face, and finally flung his arms around his neck and embraced him warmly."

> Przesyła wszystkim mnóstwo serdecznosci. (Chopin)
> "He sends everyone masses of warm greetings."

"Serdeczność" does not consist in doing good things for someone else or in intentionally displaying good feelings towards another person.

Rather, it consists in letting genuine good feelings "flow" spontaneously towards another person.

Hoffman (1989) reminisces on this point as follows:

> My mother says I'm becoming "English". This hurts me, because I know she means I'm becoming cold. I'm no colder than I've ever been, but I'm learning to be less demonstrative . . . I learn restraint from Penny, who looks offended when I shake her by the arm in excitement, as if my gesture had been one of aggression instead of friendliness. I learn it from a girl who pulls away when I hook my arm through hers as we walk down the street – this movement of friendly intimacy is an embarrassment to her.

Hoffman's reference to "coldness", which her mother perceives as typical of "Anglo" behaviour (as compared with typical Polish behaviour), can be understood in two different ways: from Hoffman's mother's point of view, to be "cold" means, roughly speaking, to be lacking in "feeling" in general, and in particular, to be lacking in interpersonal "warmth". When Hoffman shakes her friend's arm in excitement, she is acting spontaneously, her action "flowing", so to speak, from her feeling, and "showing" other people what that feeling is. When Hoffman "hooks her arm through her friend's arm" she is again acting spontaneously, unreflectingly letting her "good feelings for her friend" express themselves in a bodily gesture. The gesture, "flowing" directly from the feeling, spontaneously displays that feeling, and since the feeling in question is affection (interpersonal "good feelings") for another person, the gesture is perceived as emanating "warmth".

All this is in accordance with the Polish "cultural model" (again, model rather than a normative script) which can be represented as follows:

8. *Polish*
[everybody knows:]
often when people feel something
they do something with parts of the body because of this
because of this other people can know what these people feel
[people think: this is good]

What is particularly "good" (from a Polish cultural point of view) is a spontaneous manifestation of "good feelings" towards another person (i.e. of interpersonal "warmth", "serdeczność"):

9. *Polish*
[everybody knows:]
often when people feel something good towards someone else

they do something with their body at the same time
they want to do it
when they do it parts of their body touch parts of the other
    person's body
because of this other people can know what these people feel
[people think: this is good]

From this perspective, the "spontaneity" in the display of "good feelings towards another person" is as important as having those "good feelings" in the first place: merely telling other people that we are fond of them would not count as "serdeczność", as "warmth". To quote Hoffman again:

> Perhaps my mother is right, after all; perhaps I'm becoming colder. After a while, emotion follows action, response getting warmer or cooler according to gesture. I'm more careful about what I say, how loud I laugh, whether I give vent to grief. The storminess of emotion prevailing in our family is in excess of the normal here, and the unwritten rules for the normal have their osmotic effect.

As Hoffman perceptively observes, the Anglo-American "unwritten rules for the normal" – that is, implicit "cultural scripts" which form the society's shared frame of reference – are different from the Polish ones, for the hierarchy of values governing interpersonal relations is different. Anglo "cultural scripts" encourage people to be "careful", to be "considerate", to be "thoughtful", to avoid "hurting other people's feelings". Generally speaking, they focus on the feelings of the "other person": one should be careful to avoid causing the "other person" to feel "something bad", and (as I will show shortly) one should try to make the "other person" feel "something good". By contrast, Polish "cultural scripts" focus not on the feelings of the addressee but on those of the speaker; what matters most is that the speaker has, and spontaneously displays, "warm" good feelings towards the addressee.

It is not an accident, therefore, that Polish doesn't have any words corresponding to the English words *considerate, thoughtful*, or even *kind*, or expressions like *to hurt someone's feelings*, all of which concentrate on the other person's feelings, not on our own (cf. Travis 1997). Nor is it an accident that English has no words corresponding to the Polish *serdeczny* (and its family of cognates), or to the important Polish emotion term *przykro*, which refers to a pain caused by what is perceived as "somebody's lack of warmth for another person" (cf. Wierzbicka, forthcoming a). The extensive Polish system of expressive derivation of personal names and other nouns used as terms of address, each with a different shade of "good feelings", also points to the Polish cultural emphasis on showing affection, tenderness, etc. (e.g. for *Maria, Marysia,*

*Marysieńka, Marysiulka, Marysiuchna, Marysiątko, Marysik, Marysieczka, Marysiunia,* etc.; cf. Wierzbicka 1992a), as does also the elaborate system of common endearments of various kinds, such as *ptaszku* "birdie", *żabko* "froggie", *kotku* "kitten", *koteczku* "little kitten", *słoneczko* "dear little sun", *złoto* "gold", *złotko* "dear-little-gold", etc. (cf. Wierzbicka 1994d).

From an Anglo point of view, then, Polish has both some astonishing lacunae (such as the absence of words corresponding to *kind, thoughtful, considerate,* and of expressions corresponding to *hurt someone's feelings*) and some areas of astonishing over-elaboration; and from a Polish point of view, English is similarly astonishing in both its apparent lacunae and its riches. The differences can be made sense of when they are shown to be systematic and reducible to general "cultural scripts" like the following:

> 10. *Anglo-American*
> [people think:]
> it is good
> if a person says something
> because this person doesn't want another person to feel some-
>     thing bad

> 11. *Polish*
> [people think:]
> it is good
> if a person says/does something
> because this person feels something good towards another
>     person

## 4 The scripts of "spontaneity"

### 4.1 "Compliments", "praise", and "criticisms'

Klos Sokol (1997: 97) suggests that in Polish, in contrast to English, compliments are often "treated with suspicion". For example:

> A Polish friend told me that my Polish has improved so I said thank you. "Oh, that wasn't a compliment", he corrected me, "It's just an observation". I told a Polish friend with a new spiffy haircut how great she looked with short hair. "You didn't think I looked good with long hair?" she asked.

Klos Sokol also comments that "You may also hear someone say '*To nie komplement. To prawda.*' ('That's not a compliment, it's the truth'), as if compliments are naturally on shaky ground" (p. 99); and she notes the expression *pusty komplement* "empty compliment" (to which can be added two near-synonyms: *czcze komplementy* and *zdawkowe komplementy*).

As I pointed out in my own earlier discussion of Polish attitudes to "compliments" (Wierzbicka 1994d), the very word *komplement* suggests, in Polish, something trivial and not-serious. A *komplement* may have its place in a playful, flirtatious exchange between the sexes, but in general by classifying an utterance as a "komplement" one indicates, in Polish, that it has little or no weight. The reason is not that what is seen as a "komplement" is suspected of being not true or not sincere, but rather that a Polish "komplement" wears on its sleeve the speaker's illocutionary intention of pleasing the addressee ("I say this because I want you to feel something good"). In English, such an intention can be treated as perfectly natural and acceptable, and a common routine of responding with "thank you" appears to recognize this intention as valid and beneficial to the addressee (one "thanks" the speaker for having made an effort to please us). From a Polish point of view, however, a professed intention of pleasing the addressee tends to rob the utterance of its interpersonal value: praise is valued if it is seen as spontaneous, flowing straight "from the heart" and caused by the speaker's own "good feelings" rather than by his or her desire to make the addressee feel good.

From an Anglo point of view, then, it is seen as "good" if someone expresses admiration or some similar good feelings for another person in order to make this other person feel good:

12. *Anglo-American*
[people think:]
it is good
if a person says something to someone else
because this person wants this other person to feel something
   good

From a Polish point of view, however, if a person expresses admiration or some similar feelings "merely" to make me feel good (rather than to "pour out" the feelings of their own heart) this has little value for me. Even when the admiration is genuine, if its expression is "calculated" to make me feel good, this detracts from the value of this admiration. On the other hand, a spontaneous exclamation of admiration is perceived as valuable. But to be credible, exclamations of admiration and similar feelings must be balanced (in a particular relationship) with exclamations of criticisms, with spontaneous negative "personal remarks". A remark like "Your hair looks nice" sounds more credible (from a Polish perspective) against the background of remembered spontaneous remarks like "This haircut doesn't suit you" or "This skirt doesn't look good on you."

Klos Sokol comments (from her perspective as an American teaching English to Polish students):

> All this Yankee mega-cheery stuff isn't crime; it's just confusing. When Poles hear again and again how wonderful! great! and fine! things are, they don't know what to believe or how to react. Or where they stand, complains a Pole. In the classroom, when giving students on-the-spot evaluations, I listed all the good points before getting to the meaty criticism. One student interrupted me, "Yes, yes, I know. Great. Great. Great. How did I really do?" (p. 176)

Clearly, the Anglo-American cultural script enacted by Klos Sokol encourages her to try to make the addressee feel "something good" and to avoid making the addressee feel "something bad". On the other hand, the Polish students expect her to adopt a different cultural script and to say what she really thinks and how she really feels about their work.

This is entirely consistent with the testimony of Eva Hoffman, who reports having had similar experiences *à rebours*:

> I learn also that certain kinds of truth are impolite. One shouldn't criticise the person one is with, at least not directly. You shouldn't say, "You are wrong about that" – though you may say, "On the other hand, there is that to consider." You shouldn't say, "This doesn't look good on you," though you may say, "I like you better in that other outfit." I learn to tone down my sharpness, to do more careful conversational minuet. (1989: 146)

Of these last two different patterns, insightfully noted by Hoffman, the Anglo one ("I like you better in that other outfit") is clearly based on the cultural premiss that it is good to try to avoid "hurting the other person's feelings", whereas the Polish one ("this doesn't look good on you") is based on the cultural premiss that it is good to say what one really thinks and what one really feels. But to follow the Anglo cultural premiss one has indeed, as Hoffman suggested, to be "more careful about what one says" (to dance a "more careful conversational minuet"), whereas to follow the Polish cultural premiss one has to speak "spontaneously", moving directly (to use Hoffman's expression) "from impulse to expression". This can be represented as follows:

13. *Polish*
[people think:]
it is good
when a person says: "I feel something now"

because this person feels something at that time

14. *Polish*
[people think:]
it is not good
when a person says "I feel something now"
because this person wants another person to feel (or think)
    something


### 4.2 *"Spontaneity" vs. "control" over emotions*

Polish culture encourages uninhibited expression of emotions in general (in addition to good emotions directed at the addressee). As Hoffman (1989) put it, the "storminess of emotions" in a Polish family (like her own) is in excess of what is normal in Anglo culture: and the word *storminess* refers here to both intensity and spontaneity of emotional expression.

In an earlier book (Wierzbicka 1991), I represented the uninhibited emotional expression characteristic of Polish culture in terms of the formula "I want to say what I feel." But this may require slight modification, because Polish culture encourages people to *show* emotions (verbally or non-verbally) rather than to *speak* about them. Polish culture does not have a tradition of elaborate verbalization of emotions or of highly developed analysis of one's own emotions (characteristic of mainstream modern American culture). Polish culture encourages spontaneity, not introspection. To quote Hoffman again:

> Between the two stories and two vocabularies, there's a vast alteration in the diagram of the psyche and the relationship to inner life. When I say to myself, "I'm anxious," I draw on different faculties than when I say, "I'm afraid." "I'm anxious because I have problems with separation," I tell myself very rationally when a boyfriend leaves for a long trip, and in that quick movement of self-analysis and explanation the trajectory of feeling is re-routed. I no longer follow it from impulse to expression; now that I understand what the problem is, I won't cry at the airport. By this ploy, I mute the force of the original fear; I gain some control . . . I've become a more self-controlled person over the years – more "English," as my mother told me years ago. I don't allow myself to be blown about this way and that helplessly; I've learned how to use the mechanisms of my will, how to look for symptom and root cause before sadness or happiness overwhelm me. I've gained some control, and control is something I need more than my mother did. I have more of a public life, in which it's important to appear strong. I live in an individualistic society, in which people blend less easily with each other, in which "That's your problem" is a phrase of daily combat and self-defense. (1989: 269–70).

This time, Hoffman interprets her mother's epithet "English" not in terms of interpersonal warmth but in terms of control over one's emotions, control that is based on self-analysis. Hoffman's comments based on personal experience echo those of social commentators who have often pointed out the paramount importance of constant scanning of one's feelings in American culture. Bellah et al. (1985) link this cultural preoccupation with the place of psychotherapy in American society and with the role of psychotherapy as a model of human relationships. They point out that "practitioners [of psychotherapy] stress the primary importance of 'knowing how you're feeling'" (p. 128). The culturally endorsed attitudes in question can be represented as follows:

15. *Anglo-American*
[people think:]
it is good if I know what I feel
it is good if I know why I feel like this
it is good if I think about this

This constant attention to one's feelings and the inclination to analyse and verbalize them is clearly reflected in American popular literature, where the authors often seem to be at pains to describe exactly how they or their heroes were feeling at any given time. For example, in Elizabeth Glaser's (1991) moving autobiography there are references to feelings on almost every page and often several times on one page:

I still felt . . . nonstop nervousness when we were in public. (p. 170)
[I] feel lucky that I get to call her a friend. (p. 171)
I felt devoid of almost any optimism. (p. 171)
I began to think that I would feel dead until I died. (p. 171)
I knew I would feel cold and black inside. (p. 171)
just how wretched I felt inside. (p. 172)
It was wonderful to feel momentarily alive. (p. 175)
I felt so devastated. (p. 175)
We felt like detectives (p. 176)
I felt bleak and overwhelmed. (p. 185)
I felt scared. (p. 183)
I feel so frightened and helpless. (p. 185)
Paul and I felt awful. (p. 184)
I could feel my head reverberate. (p. 189)

Self-analysis and self-control are particularly encouraged in the case of negative feelings. To quote Hoffman (1989) again:

In the project of gaining control, I've been aided by the vocabulary of self-analysis, and by the prevailing assumption that it's good to be in charge. "I've got to get some control," my friends say when something troubles them or goes wrong. It is shameful to admit that sometimes

things can go very wrong; it's shameful to confess that sometimes we
have no control. (p. 270)

The cultural attitude referred to in this passage can be represented as
follows:

16. *Anglo-American*
[people think:]
when I feel something bad, it is good to think about it
if I think about it, I don't have to feel like this any more

The ability to analyse one's feelings rationally is important in Anglo
culture because self-analysis enables people to gain some distance from
their emotions, and this distance is a prerequisite for emotional self-
control, in the double sense of controlling emotional expression ("I will
not cry at the airport") and of changing one's feelings (shaping them
and decreasing their intensity).

Culture plays a role at every level of this process: (a) One identifies
one's feelings in terms of concepts provided by a language-and-culture
system (e.g. *anxious* or *afraid*); (b) the element of thinking about one's
feelings and of looking for their causes reflects the general emphasis of
Anglo culture on rational analysis and on explanations; (c) the idea of
"controlling" one's feelings is part of the general Anglo emphasis on
control, on shaping events in accordance with one's will; and (d) the
suppression of involuntary expressive behaviour (such as crying) reflects the general distrust of the involuntary and the irrational.

Hoffman's personal testimony that in gaining "control" she was
aided by the vocabulary of self-analysis, tallies with the general cultural
norms reflected in American English and the American ethnography of
speaking. In particular, crucial conceptual categories such as *stress*,
*depression*, or *relaxation* (and the corresponding adjectives *stressed out*,
*depressed*, *relaxed*) bear witness to the enormous influence of psycho-
therapeutic language on everyday emotion talk. A comparison of the
English and the Polish lexicon in this regard is revealing because Polish
does not have common everyday words for any of these concepts. The
recent emergence in Polish of English loan words such as *stres* and *relaks*
highlights the absence of concepts of this kind in Polish folk psychology. The Polish word *przygnębiony* could be said to be not too different
from *depressed*, but it has no clinical connotations, and apart from the
fact that it seems to be used much more rarely than *depressed*, it is rarely
used to describe purely internal states:

I feel depressed.
? *Czuję się przygnębiony.*

*Przygnębiony* is closer in its use to English words and expressions such as *downcast, dejected,* or *in low spirits,* which are most naturally used about other people (or about oneself in the past), rather than about one's own current state, and which are not entirely natural in the "I feel" frame:

> He was downcast/dejected/in low spirits.
> ? I feel downcast/dejected/in low spirits.

The most common Polish emotion terms used about one's own current (negative) state appear to be *zdenerwowany, zły, wściekły, zmartwiony,* and *przykro (mi),* all of which imply a lack of control over one's emotional state.[6] *Zdenerwowany* is an extremely common word, with no equivalent or even near-equivalent in English, which implies a state of abnormal inner agitation and readiness to "explode" (a kind of opposite of calm). *Zły* (literally, "bad") implies a kind of crude anger that one has no wish to control. *Wściekły* comes close to *furious* or *mad,* but it is much more readily used in self-reports referring to the speaker's current state:

> *Wściekła jestem!*
> ? I am mad (furious)!

*Zmartwiony,* which could be glossed very roughly as "worried", does not have the active (though uncontrolled) character of *zdenerwowany, zły,* or *wściekły,* but it does imply a passive kind of out-of-controlness not unlike that implied by the English word *upset.* Finally, *przykro* (to which I have devoted a separate study, see Wierzbicka forthcoming a) can be loosely described as a painful feeling comparable to those linked in English with the words *hurt, upset,* and *sorry.*

It is particularly interesting to note that none of these five common words for negative emotions corresponds to any of the supposedly universal basic emotions. None of them corresponds exactly to the English word *angry* or *anger.* As mentioned earlier, the closest Polish equivalent of *anger,* namely *gniew,* is not nearly as common and intuitively basic as *anger* is in English. It implies a level of awareness, discernment, and control that makes it inapplicable to children, and it is undoubtedly less common and intuitively basic than *złość* (literally, "badness"), which implies neither discernment nor control and which is, nonetheless, not pejorative like the English word *tantrum.*

In Polish culture, then, the dominant attitude towards emotions is different from that of American culture. Instead of seeking to know "what I feel" and "why I feel like this", one wants *others* to know "what

I feel" (or rather "how I feel"). In this cultural universe, there is no need for me to know what I feel or to think about what I feel, or why I feel like this. Rather, there is a need to *express* my feelings and to express them *now*, without thinking about them and without trying to analyse, shape, or suppress them:

> Once, when my mother was very miserable, I told her, full of my newly acquired American wisdom, that she should try to control her feelings. "What do you mean?" she asked, as if this was an idea proffered by a member of a computer species. "How can I do that? They are my feelings."
>
> My mother cannot imagine tampering with her feelings, which are the most authentic part of her, which are her. She suffers her emotions as if they were forces of nature, winds and storms and volcanic eruptions. She is racked by the movements of passion – *passio*, whose meaning is suffering. (Hoffman 1989: 269)

The American folk philosophy stressing the need for "control" over one's emotions is reflected revealingly in the interviews on emotion conducted with fifteen American men and women by Lutz (1990). As Lutz observed,

> One theme that frequently arises in the interview is what can be called "the rhetoric of control" (R. Rosaldo 1978). When people are asked to talk about emotions, one of the most common set [*sic*] of metaphors used are those in which someone or something controls, handles, copes, deals, disciplines or manages either or both their emotions or the situation seen as creating the emotion. (p. 4)

To illustrate, one of Lutz's female respondents spoke as follows of a friend grieving over her son's death two years earlier: "You've got to pick up and go on. You've got to try and get those feelings under control" (p. 74).

Hoffman's and Lutz's emphasis on the prevailing ideology of "control" over emotions in contemporary American culture is consistent with the conclusions reached by many other commentators, including Carol and Peter Stearns, the authors of the *History of Anger in America* (see also Stearns and Stearns 1988b):

> Contemporary Americans seek to regulate not only behaviour but the feeling itself. Indeed, during the past two hundred years, Americans have shifted in their methods of controlling social behaviour towards greater reliance on direct manipulation of emotions and, particularly, of anger . . . For at least a century past Americans have been character-ized not by unusual readiness to express their tempers but by a complicated ambivalence that has focussed on the need for control. (Stearns and Stearns 1986: 2–3)

### 4.3 *"Spontaneity" in grammar and in non-verbal behaviour*

The Polish cultural emphasis on the involuntary character of feelings is reflected in Polish grammar, which has a productive pattern for talking about involuntary emotions. For example:

> (i)  *Jaś*               *był*    *smutny.*
>     Johnny-NOM    was    sad-ADJ
>     "JOHNNY WAS SAD."
> (ii)  *Jasiowi*          *było*         *smutno.*
>      Johnny-DAT    was-IMP    sadly-ADV

In the (i) pattern, the experiencer is in the nominative case, the copula agrees with the subject in gender (masculine), and the predicate word is an adjective; in the (ii) pattern, the experiencer is in the dative, the copula has an impersonal (neuter) form, and the predicate word is an adverb. Semantically, pattern (i) corresponds to the English gloss ("Johnny was sad"); pattern (ii), however, has no exact English equivalent (the closest being perhaps "sadness came over Johnny").

Pattern (ii), which plays a very important role in the Polish conceptualization of emotions, does not always have a pattern (i) counterpart at all, for it can be based on a predicate that in its adjectival form does not designate an emotion. For example:

> *Jasiowi*          *było* ˙    *tam*     *źle.*
> Johnny-DAT    was-IMP    there    badly-ADV
> "Johnny didn't feel well there."

Because this grammatical pattern focusses entirely on the experiencer's subjective feeling, it occurs most often and most naturally in the first person:

> *Było*          *mi*          *gorzko/nieprzyjemnie/przyjemnie.*
> was-IMP    me-DAT    bitterly/unpleasantly/pleasantly-ADV
> "I felt bitter/I had an unpleasant/pleasant feeling."

> *Było*          *mi*          *ciężko/lekko*          *na*    *sercu.*
> (it) was-IMP    me-DAT    heavily/lightly-ADV    on    heart-LOC
> "My heart was heavy/'light'."

In addition, Polish has a voluntary pattern for talking about emotions, but this voluntary pattern does not indicate that the feelings are controlled, but rather, that the experiencer is, as it were, giving in to a feeling. For example, verbs such as *smucić się* (from *smutny*, "sad"), or *złościć się* (from *zły*, "angry/cross/bad-tempered") imply a kind of voluntary (unchecked) wallowing in a feeling, and therefore can hardly be linked with emotional self-control. The fact that Polish is very rich in verbs of this kind (many of them without any corresponding adjectives) highlights the salience of this perspective on emotions in Polish culture. Some examples:

| | |
|---|---|
| *cieszyć się* | rejoice |
| *martwić się* | worry |
| *denerwować się* | (cf. *nerwy* "nerves") |
| *wstydzić się* | (cf. *wstyd* "shame") |
| *gniewać się* | (cf. *gniew* "anger") |
| *niepokoić się* | (cf. *niepokój* "anxiety") |
| *złościć się* | (cf. *zły* "bad" or "angry/mad"). |

Far from suggesting any control over one's emotions, verbs of this kind suggest that the experiencer is acting out an involuntary impulse, amplifying it, and giving it full vent. They imply nothing of that "re-routing of the trajectory of feeling" (from impulse to expression) that Hoffman (1989) linked with "the quick movement of self-analysis and explanation" encouraged by Anglo culture (p. 269). On the contrary, they imply both a voluntary attitude of giving in to the impulse and an immediate expression of the feeling.

There is a clear difference in this respect between the adverbial–dative pattern and the verbal pattern. For example, the sentence:

*Wstyd      mi*
shame-ADV me-DAT
"I feel ashamed."

means, roughly speaking, that I feel ashamed and that I cannot do anything about it, and refers to a passive inner state inaccessible to external observers; whereas the corresponding verbal construction:

*Wstydzę        się*
shame-VERB-1Sg    REFL
"I am ashamed"

implies not only an active inner attitude (as if one were intentionally amplifying the involuntary feeling) but also some sort of external expression. The passive versus active contrast is reflected in the differential use of the imperative construction:

(i) *Nie wstydź się!*
    Don't be ashamed! (lit. "Don't shame yourself!")

(ii) ? *Niech ci nie będzie wstyd!*
    Don't feel ashamed!

The difference with regard to external expression is reflected in the fact that an external observer is more likely to report someone else's emotion in the verbal pattern than in the adverbial–dative construction:

> (i) *Zauważyłem, ze Jaś zawstydził się.*
>     I noticed that Johnny got ashamed (verb).
> (ii) ? *Zauważyłem, że Jasiowi zrobiło się wstyd.*
>     ? I noticed that Johnny became (inwardly) ashamed (adverb).

Thus, both the involuntary pattern of talking about emotions and the voluntary one suggest a view of emotions different from that embodied in the Anglo folk philosophy with its stress on self-control. The fact that emotion verbs in English are not only rare but also (as noted earlier) tend to develop pejorative connotations provides further linguistic evidence for this folk philosophy. For example, verbs such as *sulk* or *fume* suggest the same combination of voluntariness and external expression as the Polish verbs of emotion discussed earlier, but they also reflect the culture's negative attitude to this kind of uncontrolled emotional reaction.

Again, linguistic evidence parallels in this respect "participant observations" on non-verbal behaviour, such as Hoffman's comment about her friend Penny, who "looks offended when I shake her by the arm in excitement, as if my gesture had been one of aggression instead of friendliness". From an Anglo point of view, behaviour such as Hoffman's is lacking in the necessary restraint and reserve: the emotion itself ("excitement") should have been restrained and harnessed; and whatever the emotion, it should not be allowed to express itself in uncontrolled physical behavior (shaking someone's arm).

From an Anglo cultural point of view, the idea of shaking another person is particularly unacceptable because this action combines uncontrolled emotional expression with violation of another person's bodily autonomy (as well as of their personal space). But even if this kind of assault on another person's territory and bodily integrity is absent, the unchecked flow of emotion translating itself into action is discouraged in the Anglo cultural world while treated as "normal" in Polish culture:

> 17. *Polish*
> [people think:]
> when I feel something
> I want other people to know what I feel

18. *Anglo-American*
[people think:]
when I do something I want to know:
"I do it because I want to do it
(not because I feel something)"

The Polish script (17) reflects a tendency to spontaneous emotional expression, whereas the Anglo script reflects the cultural emphasis on self-control. The Anglo script (18) can be seen as a special case of the more general script of "personal autonomy" (cf. Wierzbicka 1991, 1996b, 1998a):

19. *Anglo-American*
[people think:]
when I do something I want to know:
"I do it because I want to do it
not because of anything else"

One might be tempted to propose for Anglo culture an emotional script more directly opposite to the Polish one (especially as far as negative feelings are concerned), along the following lines:

19a. *Anglo-American*
[people think:]
when I feel something
I don't always want people to know what I feel

But the apparent Anglo tendency to suppress spontaneous expression of feelings appears to be in fact a by-product of a norm encouraging controlled behaviour. Control over expression of emotions is not the same thing as suppression of emotional expression. To quote one of Lutz's (1990) American informants: "Let me explain control. It's not that you sit there and you take it [some kind of abuse] and, you know, I think controlling them [emotions] is letting them out in the proper time, in the proper place" (p. 9). The norm underlying these comments can be represented as follows:

20. *Anglo-American*
[people think:]
it is good if other people know what I feel
    when I want them to know it
it is good to say what I feel
    when I want other people to know it

## 4.4 "Spontaneity" and the "living speech" of the face

The metaphor of "the face's living speech" was coined by Hoffman, who reports having experienced the different expectations with respect to "facial life" as another major dimension of difference between Polish and American culture.

> Because I'm not heard, I feel I'm not seen. My words often seem to baffle others . . . Anyway, the back and forth of conversation is different here. People often don't answer each other. But the matt look in their eyes as they listen to me cancels my face, flattens my features. The mobility of my face comes from the mobility of the words coming to the surface and the feelings that drive them. Its vividness is sparked by the locking of an answering gaze, by the quickness of understanding. But now I can't feel how my face lights up from inside; I don't receive from others the reflected movement of its expressions, its living speech. People look past me as I speak. What do I look like, here? Imperceptible, I think; impalpable, neutral, faceless. (p. 147)

Thus, the "spontaneity" of feelings valued (according to Hoffman) in Polish culture in contrast to the more "controlled" approach to feelings in Anglo-American culture concerns also the emotional accompaniment of speech: from a Polish cultural point of view, even when the speaker is not saying anything about his or her feelings, it is good if some feelings are non-verbally expressed, and it is good if the addressee responds to them and reinforces them with appropriate facial expressions of their own. What this means is not controlled management of one's facial expressions but rather permitting the free play of feelings in the speaker's face.

Linguistic evidence supports Hoffman's subjective evidence in a number of ways. To begin with, Polish doesn't have a verb corresponding to *stare* (elaborately glossed in English–Polish dictionaries along the lines of "to look at someone fixedly and impudently"; cf. e.g. Stanisławski 1969). The expression *patrzeć w oczy* "to look in the eyes" has positive connotations in Polish, and unlike the English expression "to look someone in the eye" carries no implications of defiance or readiness for confrontation.

It is interesting to note in this context Jerome Bruner's remarks on the potential dangers of looking other people in the eye:

> As we know, prolonged eye-to-eye contact is a feature of infant–caretaker interaction, one that appears just before infant–caretaker joint attention to objects. It is also known that prolonged eye-to-eye contact is virtually absent in our nearest kin, the chimpanzee. But with good reason. Below man, anything longer than momentary eye contact precipitates attack and threat behavior by the dominant animal – especially in Old World monkeys and baboons – which in turn is a reminder that we should be careful about prolonged eye-to-eye

contact with human strangers in strange places, like the subway: it will always be overinterpreted. If one is about to propose a general theory about the role of eye contact in human intersubjectivity, one had better be mindful of this troublesome bit of primate evolutionary history. (1990: 163–4)

Bruner is no doubt right. One wonders, though, whether his perspective on eye-contact is not influenced, partly, by cultural factors: that is, by culture-specific Anglo-American norms concerning eye-contact. As noted by Edward T. Hall, in Arabic culture, the norms concerning eye contact are rather different (cf. also Rieschild 1996):

Arabs who interact with Americans report experiencing a certain flatness traceable in part to a very different use of the eyes in private and in public as well as between friends and strangers. Even though it is rude for a guest to walk around the Arab home eyeing things, Arabs look at each other in ways which seem hostile or challenging to the American. One Arab informant said that he was in constant hot water with Americans because of the way he looked at them without the slightest intention of offending. In fact, he had on several occasions barely avoided fights with American men who apparently thought their masculinity was being challenged because of the way he was looking at them. As noted earlier, Arabs look each other in the eye when talking with an intensity that makes most Americans highly uncomfortable. (1990: 161)

Polish tacit norms concerning eye contact are by no means identical with the Arabic ones (as described by Hall 1990: 161), but they are also different from the main-stream Anglo-American ones. In particular, they require that the speaker looks at least intermittently in the eyes of the addressees. This requires, in turn, that the addressee will meet, again and again, the speaker's gaze; but the emphasis appears to be on the *speaker*'s eyes, and the addressee's gaze is perceived, as Hoffman puts it, as "an answering gaze".

In fact, there is an expression *nie patrzeć w oczy* "not to look in the eyes", which suggests evasion (typically, on the part of the speaker), and has negative implications. A sentence like:

Mówił nie patrząc jej w oczy.
"He was speaking without looking into her eyes."

suggests that speaking without looking frequently (if not continuously) into the other person's eyes is abnormal, unpleasant, and suspect.

English shows no evidence of linguistically embedded expectations of this kind. Certainly, occasional eye contact with the addressee is expected, but not looking continuously, or even frequently, into the addressee's eyes. Furthermore, in English it is apparently the addressee who is expected to be looking at the speaker's face (in a conversational exchange), and not even the addressee is expected to be looking for long stretches, but rather to show willingness to periodically "meet the speaker's eye". Expressions like *he averted his eyes* imply that the addressee is failing to fulfil this minimal expectation of "meeting the speaker's eyes", but do not imply an expectation of frequent and prolonged eye contact.

In Polish culture, the expectation seems to be that the expression of a person's face mirrors their current psychological state, and that to fully understand another person one has to engage not just in verbal dialogue, but also in a "facial dialogue" of the kind referred to by Hoffman. It is therefore important to look at the speaker not only to show that one is listening but also to be able to "read" and respond to the other person's face. In this connection, it is interesting to note descriptions like the following, commonly occurring in Polish literature (examples from *SJP*):

> Jego nieporównanie wyrazista i ruchliwa twarz mieniła się wszystkimi odcieniami uczuć.
> "His incomparably expressive and mobile face reflected all shades of feelings."

Not only people's faces but also their eyes are frequently described in Polish – positively – as extremely *ruchliwe* "mobile", *żywe* "lively" and *wyraziste* "expressive" (expressions which suggest, to use Hoffman's words, a "mobility driven by feelings"). In addition, eyes are described as "shining" (with inner life), as "lively" or "full of fire". For example:

> Oczy nadzwyczajnie ruchliwe rzucały spojrzenia pełne ognia.
> "The intensely expressive (lit. mobile) eyes cast fiery glances."

> Jego giętki, podatny ulotnym odcieniom głos, wyrazista mimika ruchliwej twarzy
> "His supple and subtly modulated voice, the expressive play of his mobile features"

The word *mimika* ("expressive facial behaviour") and the expression *wyrazista mimika* (where the adjective *wyrazista* means by itself "highly expressive") have no counterparts in English.

Furthermore, the word *wyraz* "expression" has a wide range of collocations referring to different emotions which can be read in a person's face. The *SJP* dictionary lists the following:

> Wyraz boleści, cierpienia, smutku, zakłopotania, żalu (na

twarzy, w twarzy). Wyraz twarzy. Oczy, spojrzenie, usta mają, przybierają jakiś wyraz, tracą wyraz.
"An expression of pain, suffering, sadness, embarrassment, regret (on the face, in the face). An expression of the face. The eyes, the gaze, the mouth have or assume an expression, or lose some expressions."

The range of common patterns referred to in this passage is illustrated with the following quote:

Z wyrazem dumy spoglądała dokoła.
"She was looking around with an expression of pride."

With this kind of cultural expectations, a successful interpersonal interaction requires participants to "watch" each other's faces like movies, and to look "into each other's eyes" while talking – if not continuously then at least frequently. The fact that Polish doesn't have a word like *stare* but does have expressions like *mówić nie patrząc w oczy* "to talk without [continuously] looking into the eyes" provides linguistic evidence for the validity of such perceptions, as does also the use of common expressions like *wyraz twarzy* "the expression of the face" (unlike the technical English *facial expression*), *wyraz oczu* "the expression of the eyes", and (pejorative) *bez wyrazu* "without expression."

All these facts support the model of communication in which it is good if people can "see" what a person feels, and in which what is valued is not a conscious "display" of feeling but a "free play" of feelings in a person's face.

What applies to a person's eyes, and face, applies also to a person's voice: from a Polish cultural point of view, it is good if the voice, too, spontaneously conveys emotional information, whereas from an Anglo point of view it is good if the voice is kept under control.

For example, the adjective *gorący* "hot" and the adverb *gorąco* "hotly" are used in Polish with positive connotations to describe an appealing presence of strong and good feelings in a person's voice or eyes – in marked contrast to the positive connotations of the word *cool* in English, and the negative connotations of expressions like *hot under the collar* or *hot and bothered*. What is particularly striking in this connection is the fact that Polish expressions like *mówić gorąco* "to speak hotly", *prosić gorąco* "to ask hotly", or *dziękować gorąco* "to thank hotly" (all with very positive connotations) have, in most cases, no equivalents in English (one can perhaps *speak passionately*, but not *ask passionately* or *thank passionately*).

The cultural attitudes in question can be represented in the form of the following cultural models:

21. *Polish*
[everyone knows:]
often when a person is saying something
other people can know what this person feels
because they can see this person's face
[people think: this is good]

22. *Polish*
[everyone knows:]
often when a person is saying something
other people can know what this person feels
because they can hear this person's voice
[people think: this is good]

## 5 Conclusion

Cultures – like languages – are heterogeneous and changeable, but are nonetheless both objectively and subjectively real. The best evidence for their objective reality is linguistic evidence – lexical, phraseological, grammatical – such as that discussed in this chapter.[7] The best evidence for their subjective reality comes from the testimony of bilingual and bicultural writers (for detailed discussion see Wierzbicka 1997b).[8] The theory of "cultural scripts" provides a framework within which cultural norms and expectations can be studied in a methodical and intersubjective way.

While aspiring to description which is intersubjectively and interculturally valid, I have not attempted in this chapter to present a fully "objective", neutral, and entirely even-handed treatment of the cultures discussed. Some readers might suspect some sort of pro-Polish bias. I should acknowledge, therefore, that my point of view is indeed subjective and influenced more by my native Polishness than by my thirty-year old immersion in Anglo culture. I do not claim that the treatment of the two cultures in the chapter is even-handed, because I didn't try to produce a full picture of all the differences, concentrating, rather, on those differences which over the years have struck me most; and these, inevitably, do reflect my personal history, experience, and, no doubt, prejudices. (Cf. Wierzbicka 1997b)

Nonetheless, the scripts themselves are phrased, I believe, in an unbiased way; and if the discussion of the topics were to be extended to cover other areas of difference, the overall picture might well strike the Anglo reader in a different way. In particular, I could develop the theme of the emphasis on "tact", "considerateness", and "kindness" in Anglo culture; and on the relative unimportance of such values to Polish culture.

It is all very well to be sincere, affectionate and spontaneous. But when one considers that the emphasis on such values may be associated with, and indeed lead to, telling people (on impulse) that their views are absolutely wrong, even crazy, that what they say is obvious nonsense, that they look awful, that their haircut doesn't suit them at all, that they "must" do X, Y, and Z, then some Anglo cultural scripts may appear – to an Anglo person – in a more positive light.

For example, as I have discussed in detail elsewhere (Wierzbicka 1994b), Polish particles like *przecież, skądże, skądże znowu, ależ skąd* and *no*, with which Polish conversation is frequently peppered, express messages of the kind "you are obviously wrong". Such attitudes are far less acceptable from an Anglo point of view. It is no accident that there are no comparable particles in English, as there are no particles in Polish comparable to the diplomatic English *well* (e.g. "well, yes"; "well, no"). Similarly, contrasts like that between saying "This doesn't look good on you" and "I like you better in that other outfit" (Hoffman's example) reflect profound differences in underlying cultural assumptions and are linked with different "fundamental schemas" (cf. Shore 1996: 53). Roughly:

> *Polish*
> > it is good to say what I think
>
> *Anglo*
> > it is not always good to say to another person what I think about this person
> > if I say it this person can feel something bad because of this

Scripts of this kind are always formulated from the insider's point of view. In Shore's (1996: 54–6) terms, they are "actors' models", not "observers' models"; and they are inherently sympathetic – and empathetic – to the insiders' point of view. They try to articulate the "native's" tacit knowledge rather than an outsider's objectivist and experience-distant representations of human experience and competence. At the same time, being formulated in universal human concepts, they can be intelligible to outsiders, too.

Thus, if this chapter reflects a predominantly Polish perspective it does so in the choice of the material discussed, not in the treatment of this material. For a more comprehensive, and therefore, more stereoscopic, presentation see my larger study of cultural scripts (cf. Wierzbicka forthcoming c).

# CHAPTER 7

# Emotional universals

## 1 "Emotional universals" – genuine and spurious

It is often assumed that to emphasize the differences in ways of speaking about "emotions" that we find in different languages and cultures is to embrace cultural relativism and reject the possibility of there being any "emotional universals". This isn't necessarily true. But false universals are a major obstacle in our search for true universals; and in searching for the latter we must, first of all, debunk the former. Since false universals mainly arise from the absolutization of distinctions drawn by one's native language, close attention to such ethnocentric traps is of prime importance. The idea (championed recently by the cognitive scientist Steven Pinker) that "mental life goes on independently of particular languages" and that in other cultures, too, concepts encoded in the English lexicon "will be thinkable even if they are nameless" (Pinker (1994: 82)) is naive and ethnocentric.

In applying this idea to the domain of "emotions" Pinker (1997) ignores the work of anthropologists like Michelle Rosaldo (1980), Catherine Lutz (1988), or Fred Myers (1986), and falls into the trap described more than a decade earlier by Lutz (1986: 47) as "the tendency to treat [English] emotion concepts as conceptual primitives and universals". As Lutz pointed out at the time, "in the cross-cultural context, Western ideas about the nature of emotion have set the terms for descriptions of the emotional lives of cultural 'other'". One can only hope that with time this realization will reach the darkest corners of contemporary "cognitive science" – where at the moment great syntheses are being forged on "how the mind works" blithely ignoring the data stemming from empirical cross-cultural investigations.

To repeat here what was said earlier, the phenomenon of ANGER is of course real, but it is no more real or more revealing of human nature than the phenomena of RABBIA (identified by the Italian word *rabbia*; cf. Wierzbicka 1995c) or SONG (identified by the Ifaluk word *song*; cf. Lutz 1988; Wierzbicka 1992a). Similarly, the phenomenon of EMOTION is of course real enough, but it is no more so than German GEFÜHLE or Russian čuvstva (cf. chapter 1).

Research into "colour universals" provides a useful analogy here.

Many languages don't have a word for "colour", and in many societies people talk habitually about visual experience without separating the "colour" of various things from other aspects of their appearance. Even in English there are words like *gold* or *silver* (referring not only to colour but also to a shining appearance), and in many other languages words of this kind appear to be the rule rather than an exception. A classic example is Hanunóo (cf. Conklin 1955), where, for example, the closest equivalent of *green*, *latuy*, is more properly glossed as "looking like plants when they have a lot of juice inside" (i.e. fresh, succulent-looking, probably – but not necessarily – green).

The search for "colour universals" initiated by Berlin and Kay's 1969 classic has ultimately proved misguided (see, e.g. Van Brakel 1993; Saunders and Van Brakel 1996; Dimmendaal 1995; Lucy 1997; Wierzbicka 1990c, 1996a (Chapter 10) and forthcoming b) precisely because it approached human ways of thinking and talking about "seeing" (a universal notion) in terms of a preconceived and non-universal notion of "colour"; and also in terms of preconceived and non-universal concepts such as "black", "white", "red", and "green".

While Berlin and Kay's error proved fruitful (for although their theory finally collapsed, a great deal was learnt in the process), this error should not be repeated in the case of "emotions". The concept of "emotion" is no more universal than the concept of "colour", and conceptual categories such as "anger", "sadness", or "surprise" are no more universal than the conceptual categories "white", "red", "green", or "blue". For example, as discussed earlier, the English concept of "anger" (as in *angry with*) is linked with a cognitive scenario which includes the following components: (a) this person did something bad; (b) I don't want this person to do things like this; (c) I want to do something to this person because of this. By contrast, the cognitive scenario linked with the Ifaluk concept "song" includes components (a) and (b) above, but not (c); on the other hand, it includes an additional component (d), which it shares with concepts embodied in the meaning of English words such as *reproach* and *admonition*: (d) I want this person to know this. By assigning to the words *angry (with)* and *song* such overlapping but non-identical cognitive scenarios we can explain why "song" may manifest itself in sulking, refusal to eat, or even attempted suicide, whereas "anger" (as in *angry with*) normally manifests itself in an action aimed at the offender, not at oneself. (See Lutz 1988; Wierzbicka 1992a.)

Just as the English concept of "blue" doesn't match the Russian concept "goluboj" ("sky blue"), the Polish concept "niebieski" or the Japanese concept "aoi" (cf. Wierzbicka 1996a, Chapter 10), so the English concept of "anger" doesn't match the Ifaluk concept "song" or the

Italian concept "rabbia". This doesn't mean that there are no "universals of seeing", or that there are no "universals of feeling", but it does mean that in our search for these universals we should carefully listen to how people in different cultures talk about what they see and how they feel (cf. White 1992; Fridlund 1994); and that we should avoid analytical categories based on culture-specific aspects of our own languages.

## 2 A proposed set of "emotional universals"

In this chapter (sections 2.1–2.12) I am going to survey ten or so "emotional universals" which emerge from linguistic and ethnographic studies of various languages and cultures. Some of these universals are firmly based, but most have only the status of working hypotheses.

The studies of the concept FEEL included in the volume *Semantic and Lexical Universals* (Goddard and Wierzbicka 1994), which was devoted in its entirety to an empirical search for conceptual universals, contain a particularly thorough analysis of the various methodological dilemmas involved. But a wealth of relevant data and observations can be found in a variety of modern "grammars" and other descriptive linguistic studies, particularly those focussed on "emotions". A great deal of information is also available in recent anthropological literature, and in particular, in the writings of such scholars as M. Rosaldo (1980), Lutz (1988), Howell (1981), Myers (1986), and White (1993). The hypothetical universal 4 (referring to human faces) is supported, above all, by the cross-cultural work of psychologists, especially Ekman and his colleagues.

On the basis of the evidence gleaned from both cross-linguistic and cross-cultural studies I would like to propose the following set of working hypotheses:

1. All languages have a word for FEEL.
2. In all languages, some feelings can be described as "good" and some as "bad" (while some may be viewed as neither "good" nor "bad").
3. All languages have words comparable, though not necessarily identical in meaning, with *cry* and *smile*; that is words referring to bodily expression of good and bad feelings.
4. In all cultures people appear to link some facial gestures with either good or bad feelings, and in particular, they link the raised corners of the mouth with good feelings (cf. Ginsburg 1997) whereas turned

down corners of the mouth or a wrinkled nose appear to be linked with bad feelings.

5. All languages have "emotive" interjections (i.e. interjections expressing cognitively based feelings).
6. All languages have some "emotion terms" (i.e. terms designating some cognitively based feelings).
7. All languages have words linking feelings with (i) the thought that "something bad can happen to me", (ii) the thought that "I want to do something", and (iii) the thought that "people can think something bad about me", that is words overlapping (though not identical) in meaning with the English words *afraid, angry,* and *ashamed*.
8. In all languages, people can describe cognitively based feelings via observable bodily "symptoms" (that is, via some bodily events regarded as characteristic of these feelings).
9. In all languages, cognitively based feelings can be described with reference to bodily sensations.
10. In all languages, cognitively based feelings can be described via figurative "bodily images".
11. In all languages, there are alternative grammatical constructions for describing (and interpreting) cognitively based feelings.

In what follows, I will discuss these putative universals one by one.

## 2.1 A word for FEEL

As discussed earlier (cf. chapter 1), all languages have a word for FEEL, undifferentiated between "bodily feelings" (sensations) and "cognitively based" feelings ("emotions"). This word doesn't have to be a verb – it can be an adjective, or a noun – but cross-linguistic surveys conducted to date suggest that all languages do have some word corresponding in meaning to the English *feel* – not in all its senses (and certainly not in the sense involving intentional touching), but in the basic "psychological" sense which can be illustrated with the following sentences:

> I feel like this now.
> I don't feel anything.
> I can't describe what I felt.
> How are you feeling?
> I felt as if I was going to die.

The claim that all languages do have a word for FEEL (in this sense) has often been denied, but a closer examination of the evidence suggests that such denials are misguided. In particular, the claims that a given language doesn't have a word for FEEL are often followed by a statement that in this language to say the equivalent of "I feel good" or "I feel bad" one has to say "my liver is good" and "my liver is bad", or "my insides are good" and "my insides are bad" (see e.g. Lutz 1988; Howell 1981; Levy 1973). What statements of this kind show is that the languages in question do have a word for FEEL (in the relevant sense) but that this word is not a verb (as in English), but a noun, and that it is a noun which, in a different sense, means "liver" or "insides".

For example, in Ifaluk there is the word *niferash*, which Lutz primarily glosses as "our insides". Her data suggest, however, that *niferash* means "feel" as well as "insides", and that it can refer to physical as well as psychological feelings, just like the English verb *feel*: "To say 'My insides are bad' (*Ye ngaw niferai*) may mean either that one is feeling physically bad or experiencing bad thoughts and emotions, or both. The exact meaning, as with the English phrase 'I feel bad,' is determined by context" (Lutz, 1985: 47).

Cross-linguistic investigations show that the pattern of polysemy which links "feel" with "liver", "insides", or "stomach" is very common (cf. Goddard 1994). Facts of this kind cannot possibly be interpreted in terms of "vagueness". A sentence like "I don't feel anything", for example, cannot be vague between a "no feeling" and a "no stomach" interpretation, even if the word which here means "feel" in other sentences means "stomach". So they are perfectly compatible with the claim that FEEL is a lexical and semantic universal.

Goddard (1996b) argues convincingly that sentences like "my *tjuni* (stomach/feel) is bad" are neither vague nor metaphorical. The very notion of "metaphor" implies that a distinction can be made between the metaphorical and the literal. As Ricoeur (1981) points out, without such a distinction everything becomes "metaphorical" and the notion of "metaphor" loses its usefulness. It makes sense to say that an English expression like "boiling with rage" is metaphorical, because the meaning of this expression can be explicated in a non-metaphorical way (see below, section 2.9); but it makes no sense to claim that a sentence like "my *tjuni* is bad" (for "I feel bad") is metaphorical, given that there is no other way of saying that "I feel bad".

A metaphorical expression (e.g. "boiling with rage") can be explicated in a non-metaphorical way in the same language. But since an expression like "my *tjuni* is bad" cannot be explicated within the same language (Yankunytjatjara) at all, from a Yankunytjatjara point of view it cannot be regarded as metaphorical, and to claim otherwise would be to exoticize the Yankunytjatjara people in the spirit of old-fashioned "orientalism" (cf. Keesing 1994). This is not to deny that the Yankunytjatjara people may associate "feeling" with the stomach, as in English people associate "love" with the heart, but to claim that the Yankunyt-jatjara notion of FEEL is indistinguishable for them from that of stomach as a body part would be as unfounded as to claim that for speakers of English the notion of "love" is indistinguishable from that of heart as a body part.

In addition to the confusion which has often plagued discussions of the relation between "feeling" and body parts another area of confusion must also be mentioned here: that concerning the relationship between "feeling" and "thinking". Claims have sometimes been made that this or that indigenous culture makes no distinction between "feeling" and "thinking". For example, Lutz (1985) suggested that Ifaluk does not distinguish lexically between *feel* and *think*, and that the most relevant word in this area, *nunuwan*, "refers to mental events ranging from what we consider thought to what we consider emotion . . . Thus, *nunuwan* may be translated . . . as 'thought/emotion'" (p. 47). Lutz argued that "it is not simply that thought evokes, or is accompanied by, an emotion; the two are inextricably linked. *Nunuwan* is included in the definitions of various words we would consider emotion words. For example, *yarofali* 'longing/missing' is the state of 'continually *nunuwan* about [for example] one's dead mother'" (p. 48).

In fact, however, Lutz's careful and scrupulously presented data are compatible with a different analysis: namely, that *nunuwan* means "think" rather than "think or feel", and that its frequent emotive connotations are due to context rather than to the word itself. For example, one of Lutz's (1985) informants says of a pregnant woman R. that she "has lots of *nunuwan* because the health aide is leaving on the next ship which is coming, and she [R.] *nunuwan* that there will be trouble with the delivery of the baby" (p. 47). This is compatible with the interpretation that *nunuwan* always means "think", and that "emotions" are implied only by the word's context.

The suggestion that *nunuwan* can be linked with the primitive THINK and *niferash* with FEEL is supported by informants' comments such as the following one, cited by Lutz (1985): "T. said that if we had bad *nunuwan*, we will have bad insides [i.e. *niferash*], and if we have good *nunuwan*, we will have good insides [*niferash*]" (p. 47).

To take another example, Howell (1981: 139) has written that while popular conceptions in the West contrast the head and the heart as the organs of thought and feelings, the Chewong people of Malaysia "make no such explicit distinction . . . The liver, *rus* . . . is the seat of both what we call 'thoughts' and 'feelings', and they do not make any conceptual distinction between the two. In fact, they have no word for 'think' or 'feel'. Whenever they express emotional and mental states verbally, this is done through the medium of liver. Thus, they may say, 'my liver is good' (I'm feeling fine)".

But if the Chewong really made no distinction between thoughts and feelings, then why should the sentence "my liver is good" mean "I'm feeling fine" rather than "I think well"? The very gloss offered by Howell suggests that while one of the meanings of *rus* is "liver", the other one is simply "feel", not some mixture of feeling and thinking.

As for "thinking", it is noticeable that in the Chewong myths edited by Howell (1982 and 1984), references to "thinking" (Howell's word) do occur from time to time too, as in the following sentences:

> The woman thought she was pregnant. (1982: 255)
> Bòngso was born and the pandanus woman thought that he was a real baby. (1982: 255)
> They were asleep, but he thought they were dead. (1982: 253)

It is possible that the Chewong word translated here by Howell as "think" is a loan from Malay, for in a more recent work Howell (forthcoming) writes: "They [the Chewong] do not distinguish between thinking and feeling. In fact, as far as I could make out, they do not have indigenous verbs for these processes". But even if the verb for "think" is in fact a loan from Malay, this would not disqualify it from being a valid exponent of the primitive and universal concept THINK, for, first, a loan from Malay may have been in use for hundreds of years, and second, it may well have replaced an earlier indigenous word. Nor is it necessary for a valid exponent of either FEEL or THINK to be a verb: a noun like *rus* (1. liver, 2. feel) may well do as an exponent of FEEL if, as Howell herself tells us, "my *rus* is good" means, unambiguously, "I feel good" (cf. Goddard 1996b).

Linguistic evidence suggests that no languages fail to distinguish between THINKING and FEELING, and that in fact both these categories are necessary ingredients of the universal "folk model" of a person (cf. D'Andrade 1987; Bruner 1990) – alongside KNOW and WANT.

Where cultures do differ is in the extent, as well as the character, of their "feel-talk". But this, while important and interesting, is a different matter altogether: the basic conceptual and linguistic resources for talking about matters relating to feelings are always there. On the other hand, whether the main focus of such talk is psychological, moral, or social, depends on the culture. For example the great importance of "feel-talk" in American culture (cf. Bellah et al. 1985; Stearns and Stearns 1988), is clearly in sharp contrast to the avoidance of "feel talk" in many other cultures, such as, for example, Japanese culture (see e.g. Lebra 1976; Mori 1997) or Chewong culture (Howell 1981).

### 2.2 "Feel good" and "feel bad"

It appears that in all languages feelings can sometimes be described as "good" or "bad". For example, in English, one can say "I feel good" and

"I feel bad" or "I feel awful" and "I feel wonderful"; and, as mentioned earlier, in Chewong one can say "my liver is good" meaning "I feel well" or "my liver is bad" meaning "I feel bad".

Similarly, in the Australian language Yankunytjatjara, people say (see Goddard 1994: 239):

> Ngayulu    tjuni    palya/kura
> I          "belly"  good/bad
> "I feel good/bad"

And in another Australian language, Kayardild (Evans 1994: 212) one uses the word *bardaka* "stomach" to refer to good and bad feelings:

> mirraa bardaka
> good   stomach/feeling
> "I feel good"

> birdiya bardaka
> bad     stomach/feeling
> "I feel bad"

In other languages, too, one can readily combine a word for FEEL with a word for GOOD or BAD (as in English). Hale (1994: 269) provides examples from Misumalpan languages of Nicaragua, such as the following:

> yamni ka-daka-yang
> good  feel
> "I feel good"

Hill (1994: 317) provides a similar example from the Austronesian language Longgu:

> Nu   vadangi  meta/ta'a
> I    feel     good/bad
> "I feel good/bad"

In Japanese, one can also use the expressions *ii kimochi* ("good feeling") or *warui kimochi* ("bad feeling"), with reference to unspecified (physical or mental) feelings. One example (from a Japanese novel, quoted in Hasada 1996:93; see also Onishi 1994):

> Watashi wa konya wa, ii kimochi deshita. Bunji-san to Eiji-san

to anata to, rippa na kodomo ga sannin narande suwatte iru
tokoro o mitara, namida ga deru hodo, ureshikatta.
"I feel very good tonight. When I saw you and Bunji and Eiji
sitting next to one another, I was so happy I almost wept."

(For further illustrations and discussion, see Goddard and Wierzbicka
1994.)

The hypothesis that feelings can be described, universally, as either
good or bad is of course in keeping with the view often expressed by
psychologists that emotions are usually "valenced" or that they usually
have a positive or negative "hedonic tone". For example, Plutchik
(1994: 109) points out that "a common practice is to group emotion
words into two broad categories called *positive affect* and *negative affect*";
and he states that an "important characteristic that is part of our
experience of emotions is their bipolar nature" (p. 65). Some scholars go
so far as to regard this "bipolar" character of "emotions" as one of their
defining qualities. For example, Ortony, Clore, and Collins (1988: 13)
define "emotions" as "valenced reactions to events, agents, or objects,
with their particular nature being determined by the way in which the
eliciting situation is construed".

Linguistic evidence suggests that feelings are not always interpreted
as good or bad, and some "emotion terms" (such as, for example,
*surprise* or *amazement* in English) do not imply any evaluation (although
the closest counterpart in, for example, Malay, does imply evaluation;
see Goddard 1997b). On the other hand, it does seem to be true that
feelings are often conceptualized as either "good" or bad", and that in
all languages people can talk of "good feelings" and "bad feelings" (of
"feeling good" and "feeling bad").

To account for "mixed feelings" of different kinds, we need to distinguish "feeling good", which sounds idiomatic in English, from "feeling
something good", which does not but which is nonetheless intelligible.
(An alternative solution would be to say, instead, "to feel bad/ have a
bad feeling".) As for *feeling bad*, it is a kind of idiom in English (unlike,
for example, *feeling awful*) and it implies something akin to "feeling
guilty" (for detailed discussion, see Wierzbicka 1998b). To account for
all "bad feelings" we need to use an awkward expression like "feel
something bad" or, alternatively, "to feel (or have) a bad feeling".

In the semantic explications proposed in chapter 2 and elsewhere in
this book I have used the expressions "to feel something good" and "to
feel something bad", which sound much less natural and idiomatic in
English than "to feel good" and "to feel bad". For analytical purposes,
however, the use of such artificial and awkward expressions is preferable because they do not imply a global "well-being", or its opposite, as

"feel good" or "feel bad" ("feel awful") tend to do. From the point of view of "naive" ethno-psychology, one can feel "something good" (e.g. relief) and "something bad" (e.g. shame) at the same time. (For example, if I have suspected someone of planning a hostile act towards me and then discover that they were in fact planning an act of generosity, I may feel relieved and ashamed at the same time.)

### 2.3 Links between feelings and the body – "smile" and "cry"

All languages appear to have some word or words comparable in meaning to *smile* or *laugh*, and some word or words comparable in meaning to *cry* or *weep*.

The distinctions between "smile" and "laugh" or between "cry" and "weep" are by no means universal. The words described here as "comparable" to *smile* and *laugh* or *cry* and *weep* do not have to correspond to these in meaning exactly, but some shared components *can* be identified. These components can be formulated as follows (cf. Wierzbicka 1995b and d; see also chapter 4):

> *cry/weep*
> I think: something bad is happening
> I feel something bad now
>
> *smile/laugh*
> I think: something good is happening
> I feel something good now

I have formulated the core meanings of smiling/laughing and crying/weeping in a first-person mode, on the assumption that such behaviours can be (and usually are) interpreted as if they were messages (cf. chapter 4). Other bodily behaviours, which are normally assumed to be involuntary and which are likely to be interpreted as "symptoms" rather than "messages", will be discussed in section 2.8.

### 2.4 "Facial universals"

In all cultures, people are prepared to interpret facial gestures such as raised eyebrows, a wrinkled nose, or eyebrows drawn together as indicating certain thoughts and feelings. The words or expressions that people would use for this purpose differ from language to language and they don't necessarily match in meaning, but the willingness to attribute some thoughts and feelings to such gestures appears to be universal. While to a degree speculative, this hypothesis seems to be strongly supported by Ekman's cross-cultural research, despite the doubts that have been raised about some aspects of his methodology and conclusions (cf. Russell 1994, 1995; Fridlund 1994).

To say the least, it seems indubitable that given a suitable experimental design people all over the world would be found to recognize the message of raised corners of the lips as "I feel something good now". I am not suggesting that people all over the world would be found to actually feel good whenever they raise the corners of the mouth (cf. Fridlund 1997), but rather that people all over the world would be found to recognize the *message* of this facial gesture as "I feel something good now".

I would also hypothesize that given a suitable experimental design, people would also be found, across cultures, to recognize the message of lowered corners of the mouth, or of a wrinkled nose, as conveying (in part) "I feel something bad now"; for these latter two hypotheses, however, there is much less circumstantial evidence at this stage than for the universal semantic interpretation of a smiling gesture. (For other hypotheses concerning facial universals see chapter 4.)

## 2.5. Emotive interjections

All languages have special words ("interjections") which are used to express "cognitively based feelings", that is, feelings linked with specific thoughts, such as, for example, *gee!*, *wow!*, or *yuk!* in English. The shared meaning of all such words can be represented as follows:

> I feel something now
> because I think something now

What exactly one feels is not described directly but can be gleaned from the content of the thought on which the feeling is based.

For example, Ochs (1988: 173) in her study of Samoan language and culture acquisition cites the following Samoan interjections, among others: *ola* "surprise", *uoia* "surprise/sympathy etc.", *visa* "negative surprise", *isa* "annoyance", *a'e* "disapproval", *tae* "anger". Ochs' glosses are of course no more than approximations, but they clearly indicate a combination of a feeling ("I feel something") and a thought. On the basis of Ochs' hints, we can hypothesize that these thoughts may have the following content:

> *ola* → I didn't think this would happen
> *visa* → this is bad
> I didn't think this would happen

*voia* → something bad happened to this person
        I didn't think this would happen
*isa* → something bad is happening
        I don't want this to be happening
        I don't want to say: it is very bad
*a'e* → this person did something bad
*tae* → this person did something bad
        I don't want this person to do things like this

As noted by Wilkins (1992), interjections are present even in American Sign Language. Wilkins discusses, in particular, a sign usually glossed as "pity; sympathy; mercy". Presumably, the cognitive component of this sign can be represented along the following lines:

I think: something bad happened to this person
[I want to do something good for this person because of this]

(For a detailed discussion of interjections from languages as different as Swahili and Ewe (Africa), Arrernte and Mayali (Australia), or Thai, see papers in Ameka 1992; for a detailed analysis of many Polish and Russian interjections see Wierzbicka 1991.) The existence of such words in all languages shows that although the universal concept FEEL is undifferentiated and makes no distinction between "bodily feelings" ("sensations") and "cognitively based feelings" ("emotions"), all cultures recognize that some feelings are based on thoughts. It also shows that in all cultures people sometimes want to *voice* some feelings of this kind (by interjections), as well as depicting them in their faces.

*2.6 "Emotion terms"*

All languages have some words for describing (rather than merely voicing) feelings based on certain thoughts, such as, for example, *anger* (*angry*), *shame* (*ashamed*), or *surprise* (*surprised*) in English. These words don't have to match in meaning across languages, but they all combine (in addition to various others) the following two components:

someone feels something
because this person thinks something

Furthermore, words of this kind attempt to describe the nature of the feelings in question – not directly, but, as discussed in chapter 1, via a cognitive prototype. This can be represented as follows:

Person X was angry/afraid/ashamed/worried etc. ⇒

person X felt something
because X thought something
    sometimes a person thinks: [Y]
    because of this this person feels something
person X felt something like this
because X thought something like this

It is this general model, rather than specific "emotion terms" widely relied on in psychological literature, which can be regarded as universal. For example, the child psychologist Paul Harris (1989: 103) writes: "Thus, children do not begin their emotional lives by learning a script from their culture. They are born with the capacity to experience basic emotions of sadness, anger and joy when desirable goals are lost or blocked or achieved. They also come to understand that other people may experience those emotions." Harris's three scenarios (1. "desirable goals lost"; 2. "desirable goals blocked"; 3. "desirable goals achieved") are clearly modelled on the English lexicon, although here, too, the "fit" is far from perfect (for example, when my goals are achieved, I'm likely to feel pleased rather than joyful; both joy and sadness can be disinterested and unrelated to personal "goals"; furthermore, the metaphor of "losing one's goals" is unclear and could be applied to apathy rather than sadness; anger can be caused by an insult rather than by an obstacle to one's goals, and so on). (For further discussion, see Wierzbicka 1992a and c; see also chapter 2).

But even if we assume that the three cognitive scenarios formulated in terms of goals fit English folk-psychology well enough, they certainly don't fit that expressed in other languages. There is no reason to assume that these particular cognitive scenarios specified by Harris are innate, universal, and independent of culture. What are more likely to be innate are, first, universal concepts like WANT, FEEL, I, HAPPEN, DO, NOT, GOOD, and BAD, and second, certain ways of combining such concepts into meaningful configurations, such as, for example, "someone thinks something", "this person wants to do something", or "this person feels something bad". As argued in detail in chapter 4, it is also likely that some configurations of universal concepts are innately associated with certain experientially accessible (i.e. felt) facial movements (e.g. "I feel something good now", "I feel something bad now", "I want to do something now"). But again, there are no identifiable facial movements which can be always linked with English words such as *sadness, anger,* or *joy.*

But while the cognitive scenarios encoded in the English words *anger, sadness,* and *joy* (or Harris' approximations of them) are not universal and cannot be plausibly regarded as innate, the basic conceptual pattern combining a cognitive component ("I think X") with a feeling component ("I feel something") does seem to be universal, for all languages provide lexically encoded examples of it.

*2.7 The three recurring themes: "fear-like" words, "anger-like" words, "shame-like" words*

Different languages "choose", so to speak, different cognitive scenarios as reference points for their emotional concepts, and no such scenarios are universal. At the same time, there are certain *components* of the cognitive scenarios which appear to be universal as reference points for emotion concepts. For mnemonic purposes, these components could be described as "fear-like", "anger-like", and "shame-like". I will discuss these three categories in three separate sections (A, B, and C) below.

A. All languages appear to have some words overlapping in meaning with English words such as *fear, afraid, scared, fright,* or *anxiety.* In fact, in many languages the family in question (which can be called, roughly and arbitrarily, the "fear" family) is much more differentiated than it is in English. For example, Bugenhagen (1990: 208) makes the following comments about "fear-like" words and expressions in the Austronesian language Mbula (spoken in New Guinea):

> Life in an animistic society is very fragile. Dangers abound. Sickness, sorcery, malevolent spirits, jealous neighbours are all potential threats. It is hardly surprising, then, that out of all the different emotions, fear appears to have the broadest range of encodings. Key parameters in delineating the various encodings are:
>
> 1. Does the fear have a particular object?
> 2. Does one fear for oneself or for someone else?
> 3. Does one fear physical harm to oneself?
> 4. Is the feared entity proximate?
> 5. Is the fear the result of one's having done something?
> 6. Is the fear a response to having "felt" some sensation?
> 7. Is the feared entity a spirit?
> 8. Is the fear a response to something having happened?

Given that all these "fear-like" words in both English and Mbula differ in meaning from one another, we cannot assume that all languages will have a word for "fear" in some constant sense. What we can hypothesize, however, is that all languages will have some word or words including the following two semantic components:

something bad can happen (to me)
I don't want this to happen

These two crucial components can be combined with various other ones, and a language may have numerous lexical distinctions in this area, but the evidence available suggests that every language will have at least one word relating, roughly speaking, to "danger" and to "wish to avoid danger" ("something bad can happen to me, I don't want this to happen"). Given the human existential condition, this clearly makes sense.

B. All languages appear to have a word which shares at least two semantic components with the English word *anger*. These two components are:

I don't want things like this (to happen)
I want to do something because of this

In many languages, these two components are combined with a "negative judgement" component: "someone did something bad", but this doesn't have to be the case. For example, the Ilongot word *liget* (see M. Rosaldo 1980; for detailed discussion, see Wierzbicka 1992a), which can refer to, for example, "fierce work in one's garden", clearly does not include such a component. But *liget*, too, refers to something undesirable: the idea that people may think that I am not as good as other people. In addition, *liget* (glossed by Rosaldo, amongst others, as "energy" and "passion") contains (like *anger*) an "active" component: "I want to do something".

In the case of *anger* (*angry with*) and many other similar words in other languages, this "active" component refers to a punitive or retaliatory action, which in general terms can be represented as "I want to do something to this person (because of this)". But not all languages have a word including such a component; and, for example, the Ilongot *liget* does not. While the "liget" of young men taking part in a head-hunting expedition may seem to be highly compatible with such a component, the *liget* of people working "fiercely" (that is, with *liget*) in their gardens is clearly not.

In the case of *liget*, the absence of the component "I want to do something to this person" may seem to be due to the absence of the component "this person did something bad"; but the assumption that someone did something bad (present in *anger* but absent from *liget*) does not always lead to the presence of such a punitive or retaliatory component. For example, the Ifaluk word *song* (Lutz 1987, 1988;

Wierzbicka 1992a) does imply a negative judgment ("this person did something bad") but does not imply a desire for punishment or retaliation ("I want to do something to this person because of this"). What all these words (*anger, liget, song,* and so on) do imply is a desire for action ("I want to do something because of this"), where the causal subcomponent "because of this" refers to something undesirable or unacceptable ("I don't want things like this to happen").

Why should all languages have an "emotion term" comparable in these two cognitive components with *anger*? Some may seek an answer to this question in theories of "aggression" as a (supposedly) common ingredient of "human nature". But words like *liget* or *song* cannot be legitimately described in terms of "aggression", for they lack the crucial component "X wants to do something bad to Y". One cannot say, therefore, that if "fear-like" words are universally associated with an impulse, or need, to run away, "anger-like" words are universally associated with an impulse, or need, to fight. Rather, we have to conclude that "anger-like" words (including those like *liget* and *song*) document a universal human impulse, and need, to "act" (to do something), in order to prevent the occurrence, or the repetition, of some undesirable events.

C. Turning now to "shame-like" emotions, we must note, first of all, that the area in question is particularly variable, and that the idea that all languages and cultures would have a word and concept identical in meaning to the modern English *shame* is profoundly mistaken (see e.g. Harkins 1996).

Nonetheless, it seems likely that all languages have a word (or words) referring to what might be called "social emotions" (cf. Goddard 1995). This means, above all, words referring in their meaning to "people" and to what people may think about us, and in particular, conveying a concern about "bad things" that people may think about us. The cognitive components in question can be represented as follows:

> people can think something bad about me
> I don't want this to happen

Judging by lexical evidence, a concern of this kind appears to be universal, and it is universally linked with feelings. The universal core meaning of the words in question can, therefore, be represented as follows:

> someone thinks:
>   "people can think something bad about me

I don't want this to happen"
because of this this person feels something

Why should all languages have a word linking feelings with other people's (real or imagined) disapproval? Presumably, because we are not Robinson Crusoes and have to live among and with other people. In contemporary Anglo culture, with its marked individualism, this concern for other people's possible disapproval may appear to have diminished. (See the discussion of *shame* in chapter 2, section 6.1.) At the same time, however, another "social" emotion, "embarrassment", has emerged and come to play a key role in Anglo culture (see chapter 2, section 6.2).

As discussed in chapter 2, we could say, then, that the Anglo concept of "shame" links social concerns with moral concerns, whereas the (modern) Anglo concept of "embarrassment" explicitly dissociates the two. In many other cultures, no such distinction is drawn. But the core components of "social emotions", postulated here as universal, are relevant to both "shame" and "embarrassment", as well as to those concepts lexicalized in many other languages which combine in one semantic entity ideas separated in English under *shame, embarrassment,* and *shyness*:

people can think something bad about me
I don't want this to happen

It is interesting that of the three potentially universal categories discussed here, two – "fear-like emotions" and "anger-like emotions" – correspond to two hypothetical "basic human emotions" which seem to "appear on every list" (Plutchik 1994: 57), whereas the third – "shame-like emotions" – does not. This may be due to the prevailing biological emphasis of the literature on "basic emotions". The complex which extends over "shame", "embarrassment", and "shyness" (sometimes even "respect") clearly has a social focus (although Darwin, for one, did not hesitate to posit a biological basis for some "social emotions", linking "shame" with the biological phenomenon of blushing. See also Izard 1991; Nathanson 1992; Tomkins 1987).

*2.8 "Fear-like" emotions vs. "shame-like" emotions: can the line always be drawn?*

In an earlier essay on the conceptualization of "emotions" (Wierzbicka 1986a) I noted, with reference to Hiatt's (1978) work on "Australian Aboriginal Concepts", that not all languages appear to distinguish lexically between "fear" and "shame". In particular, Hiatt (1978: 185) pointed out that in the Australian language Gidjingali (now called Burarra) the same word *-gurakadj-* appears to cover both "fear" and "shame", and he offered the following vignettes (some from "real life" and some from texts):

1. a meeting decides to put an end to two notorious killers. Two volunteers later make a surprise attack. When they report a successful outcome, a spokesman for their grateful countrymen replies: "Good. Now we can sleep in peace, defaecate, urinate, go back to the camp, get up, urinate, defaecate, and so on, for we were afraid (*ara-gurakadj-a*) of those two men". (text)
2. A baby cries as I approach a family group. His mother says: "He is afraid (*a-gurakadj-a*) of you."
3. A woman says she was afraid (*ng-gurakadj-ira*) of encountering a ghost. (text)
4. A man sees a naked woman approaching. He feels embarrassed (*a-gurakadj-a*). (Text)
5. Gidjingali men are circumspect with respect to their mothers-in-law and sisters (they must not utter their names, look at them, go near them etc. . .) When asked why, a man replies that he is ashamed (*ng-gurakadj-a*).
6. In 1960 police arrested two young men for a felony committed in Darwin. At the time of their arrest, they were participating as novices in a Kunapipi ceremony at Maningrida, and as such were under strict injunction to keep away from women and children. After police had conducted them through the general camp, men spoke of the widespread shame/fear(?) that had been caused (*ngubura-gurakadj-a*).
7. A man, on deciding that it is time to arrange his son's circumcision, speaks first to the lad's MMB (mother's mother's brother). He indicates that he does not wish to raise the matter with the boy's mother, as this would cause him (the boy's father) embarrassment (*ng-gurakadj-a*). (Text) (Hiatt 1978: 185)

Hiatt considers the possibility that in all situations the word in question implies both "fear" and "shame", but he rejects it as incompatible with some of the examples, and suggests instead a common core: "a strong impulse to retreat from the stimulus" (Hiatt 1978: 186).

It is not quite clear, however, whether in Hiatt's view the Burarra people do or do not distinguish two distinct "emotions", comparable to English *shame* and *fear*. Although he looks for a common core he nonetheless repeatedly talks of "two emotions", for example:

> I have argued that, although situations arise among the Gidjingali in which fear and shame may be felt simultaneously, other situations occur in which only one or the other is present. Nevertheless, the same term is used in all three cases. Why should this be so? Perhaps it is because both emotions manifest a strong impulse to retreat from the stimulus, viz. snakes, ghosts etc. in the case of fear; mothers-in-law, sisters etc. in the case of shame. (Hiatt 1978: 186)

On the basis of Hiatt's data (confirmed by personal information from other linguists who have worked on Burarra and related languages) I concluded (in Wierzbicka 1986a) that a distinction between "fear-like emotions" and "shame-like emotions" is probably not universal.

In the intervening decade, however, a comprehensive Burarra dictionary has been published (Glasgow 1994), which allows us to see the situation in a different light. The dictionary shows that there are two different words in the language (the adverb *gona* and the verb *gurkuja*) which can be said to be associated with "an impulse to withdraw". While each of these two words is glossed in terms of both "fear" and "shame", the primary gloss offered for *gona* is "ashamed", and the primary gloss offered for *gurkuja* is "show fear; be frightened; be afraid". Both these primary glosses and the illustrative examples suggest that *gona* is in fact more "shame-like", and *gurkuja* more "fear-like". Particularly illuminating is the following example, in which both the putative "fear/shame" words occur:

> wurra an-ngaypa jawina gala barra a-gurkuja burrwa wurra gama gorlk rrapa minypa gona a-ni apula ngaypa rrapa gun-ngaypa janguny.
> "But my disciple must not be afraid of people and like be ashamed [sic] of me and my story."

The word translated in this case as "afraid" is *gurkuja* and the one translated as "ashamed" is *gona*. Although "people" are mentioned in the first case, and not in the second, in fact the first word (*gurkuja*) seems to imply the "fear-like" thought "something bad can happen to me", whereas the second implies the "shame-like" thought "people can think something bad about me".

This is not the place to undertake a detailed discussion of *gona*, *gurkuja*, and other related words in Burarra. From the data now available, however, it emerges that while the language doesn't have words corresponding exactly to *fear* and *shame*, it does have two words which could be roughly described as "fear-like" and "shame-like" (i.e. as containing on the one hand the "fear-like" component "I don't want something bad to happen to me" and on the other hand the "shame-like" component "I don't want people to think bad things about me").

Available evidence suggests that the two Burarra concepts in question are indeed closer to one another than *fear* and *shame* are in English; nonetheless the Burarra data are not incompatible with the set of "emotional universals" proposed here. As Hiatt suggested, avoidance (the "strong impulse to retreat from the stimulus") is, no doubt, the key factor in the apparent closeness of the "fear-like" and "shame-like" emotion concepts in Australian languages. Nonetheless, the available evidence suggests that Burarra, like other Australian languages, does draw a distinction between "fear-like" feelings and "shame-like" feelings.

### 2.9 What about "good feelings"?

The three categories singled out here as possibly universal ( "fear-like", "anger-like", and "shame-like" feelings) may strike the reader as being all "negative": what about happier, "joy-like" or "love-like" feelings?

In fact, emotions labelled here as "anger-like" do not necessarily involve any "bad feelings" at all. In particular, the Ilongot concept of *liget* (as described by M. Rosaldo 1980) is not necessarily linked with "bad feelings". The semantic components proposed here as the universal common core of the category in question are "I don't want things like this to happen" and "I want to do something because of this". What is "negative" about this category is the volitive component "I don't want things like this to happen", but the "hedonic tone" of the emotion does not have to be negative ("bad").

Some languages appear to rely largely on the collocation "feel good" and may not have any other words comparable to *joy* and *happy*. This impression may, however, depend more on the limitations of our knowledge than the limitations of the "emotional lexicons" in these languages. For example, Hiatt's prediction concerning Australian languages (1978: 181) may have been overly negative:

> After inspecting a small number of lexicons, I predict that all Aboriginal languages possess words for the following emotional states: anger, fear, sorrow, jealousy, and shame. In the context of Aboriginal society, I would call them the dramatic emotions. Words referring to affection and contentment may also be widespread, though I suspect that in Australia the tranquil emotions have not obtained the same degree of verbal representation as their counterparts.

In the intervening two decades, however, a number of detailed dictionaries and descriptive studies of Australian languages have appeared which show that words for "positive feelings" comparable to *happy* or *joy* do exist in the languages in question (cf. Goddard 1990 and 1994;

Evans 1992; Henderson and Dobson 1994). Obviously, the matter requires further investigation.

As for the "love-like emotions", in many languages words referring to them appear to be linked with thoughts of "bad things" happening to people and so to be akin, in some ways, to "pity", "compassion", "sadness", and even "anguish" rather than to "happiness" or "joy". The Ifaluk concept of *fago*, glossed by Lutz (1988) as "love/sadness/ compassion", is a good case in point, as is also the Russian *žalost'*, which could be loosely glossed as "loving compassion", or even "sorrowful loving compassion" (cf. Wierzbicka 1992a; Zaliznjak 1992). It will also be useful to quote here at some length what Levine (1981: 110–11) says about the Nyinba language of Nepal:

> The Nyinba moral system includes no precept and provides no grounds for the evaluation of love in the generalized western sense. Nor is there any comprehensive term or concept to describe the idea of "love", whether divine, parental or sexual. Although the relations between close kin, particularly parents and children, are informed by a special moral bond, the nature of this bond is not seen as a suitable topic for discussion and is thus poorly articulated. Parents speak of having a feeling of "compassion" or "compassionate love" (Tib. *snying rje*) for their children, but this, ideally, should be disinterested concern, comparable to the feeling of compassion prescribed towards all sentient beings by Buddhist ethics . . . Less commonly, parents may describe their children, as well as other close kin and friends, as persons "they hold dear" (Tib. *nga'i gce ba*). This, like expressed sentiments of "compassion", is typically applied to dependent and weaker persons. However, it also seems to imply a state of exclusive emotional attachment.
>
> In the Nyinba moral system emotional attachments are identified with the desire for material goods and condemned as covetousness or greed (Tib. *'dod pa*), considered one of the cardinal vices. All such attachments are thought to produce mental suffering, simply because they give rise to frustration and inevitable sorrow. Furthermore, this is a state of mind said to increase the individual's concern with worldly existence and thus to interfere with his pursuit of salvation. Sexual relationships are presumed to be especially conducive to the development of interpersonal attachments and to be motivated by or to motivate carnal desire, known as *dödchag* (Tib. *'dod chags*; these are considered a type of *'dod pa*). There is no other term which can be used to describe the sexual "love" of husbands, wives or lovers; nor is there any positive valuation of this phenomenon.

If we believe Levine (and other similar reports) we will have to accept that "love" (in the English sense of the word) is not a universal human notion. On the other hand, it seems possible that all languages have some word or words implying a desire to do good things for someone else, presumably modelled, prototypically, on the relationship between mothers (X) and their small children (Y), which can be represented as follows: "person X wants to do good things for person Y". At this stage, however, we do not know whether this is indeed universal.

In the past (Wierzbicka 1992a: 146–7) I have argued against the common assumption that "love" is a universal human emotion, pointing out that the concept "love" is no more universal than, for example, the Ifaluk "fago". I still think that the point is valid. I would now add, however, that all languages may nonetheless recognize lexically a distinct type of feeling linked with the semantic component "person X wants to do good things for person Y". But the matter requires further investigation.

### 2.10 Emotions described via external bodily symptoms

It appears that in all languages one can talk about "emotions" by referring to externally observable bodily events and processes understood as symptoms of inner feelings. For example, in English one can say:

> She blushed.
> She grew pale.
> Her hands (lips) were trembling.
> Her eyes became round [with fear].
> When I saw this, my palms started to sweat.

intending such sentences to be understood as referring to feelings rather than just to bodily events. Presumably, the folk model behind such sentences can be interpreted as follows:

> sometimes when a person feels something because this person thinks something
> something happens to a part of this person's body at the same time
> when other people see this, they can know that this person feels something

Unlike in the case of "smiling" and "crying", I am not suggesting that all languages will have special words referring to such symptoms. For example, while English has the special word *blush*, presenting a visible bodily process as a symptom of a thought-related feeling, in many other languages (for example, in Russian) the closest equivalent of *blush* is simply something like "go red", with no special reference to feelings. What I think might be universal in this area is the very fact that visible bodily events and processes (such as becoming red in the face) may be treated as symptoms of thought-related feelings, that is, may be reported (in everyday discourse) with the intention of conveying information about a person's feelings (linked with this person's concurrent thoughts).

Descriptions of symptoms referring to thought-related feelings can't always be literally translated into other languages, as their interpretation can be culture-specific (cf. Iordanskaja 1986). For example, as pointed out by Hasada (1996: 87), in Japanese a reference to "lowering one's eyes" (*mejiri o sageru*: lit. "lowering the outer corners of one's eyes") would refer to feeling pleased or satisfied, as in the following sentence from a novel by Kobayashi:

> [Ero-jishi de aru] Subuyan kara denwa o uke, tachimachi *mejiri o sageru* kyaku bakari to wa kagiranu.
> "True, some customers had to only receive a call from Subuyan [a pimp] to begin *salivating*." (lit. "lowering the edges of their eyes").

Hasada comments on this example as follows:

> Here the customers feel "pleased" to get a call from Subuyan who introduced a girl to them. However, in English the description of this Japanese facial expression would not be translated word-for-word as "drawing down the edge of one's eyes". This is because the equivalent English facial expression does not convey the intended meaning of the expression in the original text. It is translated as "salivating", which only partially corresponds to the original meaning, since it implies the customer's positive response, but expresses it through a different part of the body: the mouth.

Similarly, in Chinese the perceived bodily symptoms of "emotions" are different from those recognized in English. For example, Chun (1997: 3) cites the following expressions: *la chang lian* lit. "pull long face"; *la xia lian* lit. "pull down face"; *bian lian* lit. "change face" and comments: "All the above expressions describe that one gets angry and that therefore his or her face is no longer the same, and usually it appears to be long". In addition, Chun (1997: 4) quotes the following expressions, also understood as referring to what she describes as an "angry face": *zhang hong le lian* lit. "flow red face" and *lian hong buozi cu* lit. "red face expanded neck". (For other examples and discussion, see also Iordanskaja 1986.)

## 2.11 "Emotions" described via sensations

It appears that in most, and perhaps all languages "emotions" (cognitively based feelings) can be described via bodily feelings – either general or localized. For example, it seems likely that in all languages people can say something like this:

> When I saw (heard) this, I felt hot (cold).
> When I saw (heard) this, my ears got hot.
> When I heard this, my ears started to burn.
> When I heard this, my throat went dry.

Sentences of this kind describe bodily sensations implying that these sensations are not due to physical causes but to "appraisals" (thoughts), however fleeting or hidden from the light of full consciousness. The folk model reflected in such ways of speaking can be represented as either A or B below:

> A
> [when I saw/heard X] I thought something (Y)
> because of this, I felt something
> like a person feels when this person thinks something like this
> BECAUSE OF THIS, I felt something in my body
> like a person feels when something(Z) happens to this person's body

> B
> [when I saw/heard X] I thought something (Y)
> because of this I felt something
> like a person feels when this person thinks something like this
> WHEN I FELT THIS, I felt something in my body
> like a person feels when something (Z) happens to this person's body

Whether or not the bodily sensation is actually *caused* by or merely concurrent with a cognitively based feeling is a point that may be debated (cf. James 1890), but what is at issue here is the folk model, reflected in ordinary ways of speaking. The question whether this folk model is best portrayed in terms of "because" or in terms of "when" may also be disputed. In any case, cross-linguistic evidence suggests that feelings based on thoughts can be seen, universally, as linked with bodily feelings, and are sometimes described as *resulting* in bodily sensations.

For example, Mikołajczuk (1998) quotes Polish expressions glossed literally as "to choke from rage" or "exasperation chokes someone". Taylor and Mbense (1998: 203–4) quote Zulu sentences which they gloss as "He was so angry he choked", "When he heard, he warmed up", and "I felt my blood getting hot". Palmer and Brown (1998) cite among many Tagalog expressions describing "emotions" one which they gloss as "tightening of breath (feel terribly hurt)". Iordanskaja (1986) cites examples from a number of languages including, besides Russian, Tajik Tatar and the Bantu language Kuria, emphasizing the language-specific character of the expressions in question. For example, in Russian one says *dux zaxvatyvaet ot vostorga*, lit. "it cuts one's breath from ecstasy", whereas in Tajik the same (or similar) sensation is linked with fright (*nafasaš gašt* lit. "his breathing stopped [from fright]"). In Russian, one's eyes can, roughly speaking, "flash from anger" (*glaza sverkajut ot gneva*), whereas in Kuria one's eyes can "shake" from anger (*amaiso garagankana*). Finally, Reh's (1998) analysis of "the language of emotions" in the Nilotic language Dholuo includes examples with glosses such as "her heart beat wildly with fear".

Expressions of this kind are sometimes described as "metaphorical" (e.g. Taylor and Mbense 1998) or "figurative" (e.g. Palmer and Brown 1998). In fact, however, there isn't necessarily anything metaphorical or figurative about them and they should be distinguished from truly figurative expressions such as "stomach burns" (Dholuo), "shattered heart" (Tagalog), or "he is burning with roaring flames" and "my heart turned into blood" (Zulu), to which we will turn next.

## 2.12 "Emotions" described via internal "bodily images"

It appears that in all languages people can talk about cognitively based feelings in terms of figurative "body images", referring to imaginary events and processes taking place inside the body, such as the following ones in English:

> When I heard/saw this, my heart sank.
> It [the news, etc.] broke my heart.
> I did it with a heavy heart.

In contrast to the bodily "symptoms", discussed in section 2.10, the bodily images presently under discussion combine similes (LIKE) with a counterfactual (AS IF) mode of thinking, roughly along the following lines: X feels like a person who thinks [Y] and who feels because of this as if Z was happening (or: has happened) in their body. For example, a person who says "I was boiling inside (with rage)" does not think that something was actually boiling inside their body, or that if some water were actually boiling inside their body they would feel like they are feeling now. And if one says that something "broke my heart" one doesn't really mean that one feels as one would if one's heart were ruptured. Rather, one is consciously using an image which seems intuitively effective and which can be counted upon to be understood as an image, not literally. Using NSM, this can be represented as follows:

> *She was boiling inside (with rage)* ⇒
> she felt something because she thought something
> I say: something was boiling inside her
> I say this not because I think it is true
> I say this because I want to say how she felt

> *She did it with a heavy heart* ⇒
> when she was doing it
> she felt something because she thought something
> I say: her heart was heavy
> I say this not because I think it is true
> I say this because I want to say how she felt

The phrase "I say" in these explications (e.g. "something was boiling inside her") does not imply that I think that what I say is true; and in fact there is an implicit message there that what I say is only a figure of speech.

Some more examples from Polish:

> *Polish*
> serce    mi      pęka        (z bólu)
> heart    to-me   is-breaking  (from pain)
> "I experience painful emotions as if my heart were breaking"

> serce    mi      się    ściska       (żalu)
> heart    to me   REFL   is-squeezing  (from intense regret)
> "I experience painful emotions, as if my heart were being squeezed"

> serce    mi      się    kraje
> heart    to-me   REFL.  is-cutting
> "I experience painful emotions, as if my heart were being cut to pieces"

Figurative expressions of this kind often encode, in addition to the images, non-metaphorical semantic components. For example, each of the Polish expressions cited above is associated with different thoughts and feelings, as suggested by different collocations that each of them typically enters: the Polish heart (*serce*) *pęka z bólu* "is breaking from [something like] pain", *ściska się z żalu* "is being squeezed from [something like] regret", and *kraje się* "is being cut into pieces" not "from something" but typically "at the sight of something" (*na widok* . . . ). Each figurative expression, then, includes, in addition to the image, its own cognitive scenario. Here are some examples from Polish literature, cited by the *Dictionary of the Polish Language* (*SJP* 1958–69), and supplied here with NSM explications:

> Trzeba się rozstać, choć serce pęka.
> We have to part although one's heart is breaking ⇒

> [I] feel something because [I] think something
>    sometimes a person thinks:
>    "something very bad is happening to me
>    I don't want this to be happening
>    I want to do something because of this
>    I can't do anything
>    I will not be able to live after this"
>    when this person thinks this this person feels something very
>       bad
> I feel something like this because I think something like this

> Serce ściskało mi się, gdym opuszczał okolicę, w której urodziłem się i wzrosłem.
> "My heart was being squeezed as I was leaving the places where I had been born and where I had grown up."⇒

> I felt something because I thought something
>    sometimes a person thinks:
>    "something very bad happened
>    I don't want things like this to happen
>    I can't think: I want to do something because of this
>    I know I can't do anything"
>    when this person thinks this this person feels something bad
> I felt something like this
> because I thought something like this

> Aż się serce kraje jak się na ten sponiewierany naród patrzy.
> "[My] heart is being cut to pieces when [I] look at these poor humiliated people."⇒

> I feel something because I think something
>    sometimes a person thinks about someone else:
>    "something very bad is happening to this person
>    I don't want things like this to happen

> I want to do something because of this
> I can't do anything"
> when this person thinks this this person feels something very
>     bad
> I feel something like this because I think something like this

As these explications show, in the case of *pęka* "is breaking" the very bad thing has to be happening to me personally; in the case of *się kraje* "is being cut to pieces" it is normally happening to someone else, and in the case of *się ściska* "is being squeezed" it can be either. In addition, *pęka* implies the notion that "I won't be able to live after this" (reminiscent of *despair*, cf. chapter 2), and *ściska się* typically refers to events thought of as past (even if it is immediate past), whereas *pęka* and *kraje się* typically refer to events viewed as on-going.

English expressions like *with a heavy heart* or *heart-broken*, in addition to bodily images, also encode certain cognitive scenarios. For example, *a heavy heart* implies the following thought (in addition to feelings and bodily images):

> I will now do something
> I don't want to do it
> I know I have to do it
> I know: someone will feel something bad because of this
> I don't want this to happen
> I can't do anything else

The expression *heart-broken* implies, in addition to feelings and bodily images, the following thought:

> something very bad happened to me
> before it happened, I thought that some very good things
>     would happen
> I wanted these good things to happen
> I did many things because of this
> now I know: these good things will not happen

In addition, the image suggests that the person in question can't think of or want other good things (for some time).

I will adduce some examples from a few other languages, this time, however, without detailed discussion or explications.

Mbula (Austronesian; Bugenhagen 1990: 205; Bugenhagen's glosses):

| Expression | Gloss |
|---|---|
| *kete- (i)malmal* | "angry" (lit. "liver fight") |
| *kete- (i)bayou* | "very angry" (lit. "liver hot") |
| *kete-(i)beleu* | "uncontrollably angry" (lit. "liver swirl") |
| *kete-pitpit* | "get excited too quickly" (lit. "liver jumps") |
| *kete- ikam keN* | "startled" (lit. "liver does snapping") |
| *kete- biibi* | "too slow" (lit. "liver is big") |
| *kete- kutkut* | "anxious" (lit. "liver beats") |
| *kete- iluumu* | "at peace" (lit. "liver cool") |
| *kete- pas* | "out of breath" or "lose one's temper" (lit. "liver removes") |
| *kete- paNana* | "calm, unmoved, long-suffering" (lit. "liver is rock-like") |
| *kete- ise* | "aroused' (lit. "liver goes up") |
| *kete- isu* | "take a rest" (lit. "liver goes down") |
| *kete- pakpak* | "very angry" (lit. "liver is sour") |

For Chinese, Chun (1997) offers the following examples and comments:

1. *chang duan* "broken intestine"

"This expression is used to describe that someone is in great grief, misery or sadness. One can say "someone is crying like *chang duan*'."

2. *xin ru dao ge* "heart is like cut by a knife"

"This expression is used to describe that one is in a very painful situation because of sadness, grief, or misery."

3. *wu zhang ju lie* "five organs all broken"

"This expression is used to describe that one is in great anger and that therefore his or her internal organs are all broken."

4. *xin ji ru fen* "one's heart is like burning"

"This expression describes that one is in great anxiety like fire burning."

5. *xia po dan* "gallbladder is broken from fear"

"One's gallbladder is often linked with courage by the Chinese. If one is very courageous or brave, he or she is said to be *hen you dan liang* (have much gallbladder). On the contrary, if one is terrified badly, then he or she is said to be *xia po dan* (gallbladder broken from fear)".

Finally, for Kayardild (an Australian language) Evans (1994: 212) offers the expressions *mildalatha bardaka* "feel grief-stricken", which means literally "cut through one's stomach"; and *bardaka warriliija* "feel uneasy", which means literally "stomach causes itself to go away". (For additional examples from other languages, see Taylor and Mbense 1998; Palmer and Brown 1998; Reh 1998; Mikołajczuk 1998.)

## 2.13 The grammar of "emotions"

It seems likely that all languages draw some grammatical distinctions in the area of emotions, thus reflecting different perspectives on feelings, available to speakers within one culture. Roughly speaking, different constructions may present a feeling as "involuntary" or as "uncontrollable", or as "overwhelming" and "irresistible", or as "active" and in some sense "voluntary", and so on. It is too early to say whether any such perspectives on "emotions" are universal, but it does seem eminently plausible that speakers of any language have more than one mode for conceptualizing "emotions".

To illustrate; in English, the predominant way of describing "emotions" is by means of adjectives and quasi-participles:

> He was angry/sad/happy/afraid.
> She was worried/disgusted/surprised/amazed/ashamed.

These adjectives and quasi-participles present the experiencer's "emotion" as a state. In some cases, however, there is also a verbal mode of expression, which implies a more active attitude on the part of the experiencer:

> She worried/grieved/rejoiced (archaic).

What this "active" attitude means is that the experiencer is thinking certain thoughts for some time and thus is, as it were, generating certain feelings in himself or herself (a process which – though not necessarily voluntary – in principle could be stopped):

> X was thinking something for some time
> because of this, X felt something (Y) for some time

In other languages distinctions of this kind play a much greater role than they do in English. For example, Russian grammar includes the following three constructions for the description of something akin to "sadness" (see Wierzbicka 1992a and 1995a; for similar examples from Polish, see chapter 6):

(1) On          byl            grusten.
    he-NOM      was-MASC       sad-MASC

(2) Emu         bylo           grustno.
    he-DAT      (it)was-NEUT   sad(ADV)-NEUT

(3) On          grustil.
    he-NOM      sad(VERB)-PAST.MASC

All these sentences can be roughly glossed as "he was sad", but in fact they differ in meaning. In particular, sentence (2) implies that the sadness was involuntary and was, so to speak, "happening to the experiencer", whereas (3) implies active involvement by the experiencer and suggests that he was bringing about his own sadness by thinking certain thoughts (and also that he was somehow displaying it). The reality of these semantic differences is manifested in further grammatical facts, such as, for example, that the verb *grustit'* (infinitive), in contrast to the adjective *grusten* and the adverb *grustno*, takes the preposition *o* (comparable to the English *about*), characteristic of verbs of active thinking:

(4) On dumal o nej.
    "He was thinking about her."

(5) On grustil o nej.
    "He was 'saddening-himself' about her."
    "He was making himself sad by thinking about her."

(6) *On byl grusten o nej.
    "He was sad about her."

(7) *Emu bylo grustno o nej.
    "He experienced sadness about her."

Another grammatical construction, which can be illustrated from English but which has more elaborated analogues in Russian, allows speakers of English to talk of some feelings as overwhelming. In English, this is done by means of a noun with the preposition *in*, which suggests a container image. For example, one can say in English "She was in panic/in despair/in ecstasy/in agony", though not *"She was in fear/in joy/in sadness" (cf. Wierzbicka 1986b). In Russian, feelings perceived as overwhelming can also be described by means of a noun combined with the preposition *v* "in/into", but further related distinctions are drawn by means of accompanying verbs. Thus, in her study of several Russian prepositional constructions used for talking about feelings, Mostovaja (1998) shows that one construction (*on pogruzilsja v X* lit. "he sank into X") implies that the experience lasted for a long time, another (*on prišel v X* lit. "he came into X") implies a short-term feeling which is both intense and externally manifested, and yet another (*on vpal v X*, lit. "he fell into X"), implies that the emotion in question is perceived as "bad".

Finally, for the Austronesian language Mbula, Bugenhagen (1990) lists as many as five different "experiential constructions" (in addition to "body images"), each suggesting a different conceptualization of emotions. For example, *moto* (roughly, "fear") can be reported in the following three constructions, among others (s stands for "subject", PSR, for possessor, and NMZ, for nominalization):

(8) N-io   aŋ-moto.
    1s     1s-fear
    "I am afraid."

(9) Kuli-ŋ      i-moto.
    skin-1s.PSR  3s-fear
    "Something makes me feel uneasy."
    (lit. "something frightens my skin")

(10) Moto-ŋa-na        i-kam      yo.
     fear-NMZ-3s.PSR    3s-do/get  1s.ACC
     "I was terrified."
     (lit. "fear got me")

(For numerous further illustrations, see e.g. Bugenhagen 1990; Ameka 1990b; Wierzbicka 1992a; Reh 1998.)

What such grammatical facts suggest is that in all cultures people conceive of "emotions" as being experienced in many different ways, especially in relation to human will. In some "emotions", the experiencer can conceive of herself in a more or less agentive role, as a person in charge of her feelings, whereas in others, the experiencer perceives herself as someone to whom something happens, independently of, or even against, her will. This flexibility in the interpretation of "emotions" may well be another emotional universal.

## 3 Conclusion

Since all languages appear to have a word for the concept "feel", we can assume that this concept is an integral part of the universal folk model of a person, that is, that in all cultures people attribute feelings to other people, as well as to themselves (cf. D'Andrade 1987, 1995). Furthermore, evidence suggests that in all cultures people distinguish linguistically (and in particular, lexically) between different kinds of feelings. Apparently, in all languages some feelings are lexically linked with thoughts (in the form of words comparable in their over-all semantic structure to English words like *angry, afraid,* or *ashamed*). It seems likely, too, that in all languages there are some words linking feelings with the body, such as *hungry, thirsty,* and *pain* or *hurt* in English.

In all languages there also seem to be ways of speaking that link feelings based on thoughts with events or processes involving the body – a fact strikingly consistent with the emphasis placed by many scholars, especially psychologists, on the biological aspect of "emotions". First of all, these ways of speaking suggest that some externally observable bodily behaviours (in particular, facial behaviours) are seen universally as voluntary or semi-voluntary modes of expressing and communicating cognitively based feelings (e.g. "cry/weep" and "smile/laugh"). Second, they suggest that some visible and/or audible (that is, externally observable) bodily events and processes may be seen, universally, as involuntary symptoms of cognitively based feelings (such as, for example, *blush* in English). Third, all languages also appear to have conventional bodily images, that is, expressions referring to imaginary events and processes taking place inside the body, used as a basis for describing the subjective experience of feelings assumed to be based on thoughts (such as *my heart sank* in English).

It also appears that the main universal mode for describing cognitively based feelings is in terms of a comparison, that is, via LIKE, and that in this, the main human strategy for talking about feelings is analogous to the main human strategy for talking about colours. If *gold* (adjective) means, essentially, "looking like gold", and *blue,* "looking like the sky (when one can see the sun) or like the sea (seen from afar)", so *afraid* means, roughly, "feeling like a person does who thinks: something bad can happen to me, I don't want it to happen". Expressions based on bodily images such as *heart-broken* involve, in addition, saying that something happened inside the person's body (e.g. their heart broke) and implying that one says this not because one thinks it is true but because one needs a peg on which the expression "he/she felt like this" can be hung.

While internal bodily images focus on the subjective aspect of feelings and on their possible links with essentially unknowable processes going on inside the body, full cognitive scenarios often point to social and moral concerns, and to aspects of interpersonal interaction. For example, they reflect concerns about "bad things happening to someone", or about "good things happening to someone else (and not to me)", about "someone doing something bad", about "someone wanting to do good things for someone else", or about "other people thinking something bad about me".

This mode of discourse, referring to feelings but linking them with evaluative and "people-oriented" cognitive scenarios, is of course consistent with the emphasis of anthropologists such as Lutz (1988) or White (1992) on the social, interpersonal, and moral character of discourse about "emotions" in many non-Western societies; and on the culture-specific nature of modern Western (especially Anglo-American) "therapeutic" discourse, with its focus on introspection into one's subjective internal states, rather than on social and moral concerns (cf. also Stearns and Stearns 1988).

Feelings are subjective, and they appear to be universally thought of as related in some cases to what is happening in the body; but they are also often thought of as based on certain recurrent thoughts – cognitive scenarios shaped by the particular culture.

Since in common human experience the content of feeling-provoking thoughts influences the actual feeling, one can legitimately say that not only "emotion-concepts" but feelings themselves are also influenced by culture. Since, furthermore, in common human experience cognitively based feelings often trigger or influence bodily feelings, it makes sense to suggest that bodily feelings, too (and perhaps even some bodily processes associated with them), may be indirectly influenced by culture.

There is no real conflict between the view that human feelings can be "embodied" and have a biological dimension and the view that they are "socially constructed" and have a cultural dimension. There is also no real conflict between a recognition of cross-cultural differences in the area of "emotions" and a recognition of similarities.

Clearly, the ways of thinking and talking about feelings in different cultures and societies (and also different epochs; cf. e.g. Stearns and Stearns 1986, 1988a) exhibit considerable diversity; but neither can there be any doubt about the existence of commonalities and indeed universals. The problem is how to sort out the culture-specific from the universal; how to comprehend the former through the latter; and, also, how to develop some understanding of the universal by sifting through a wide range of languages and cultures rather than by absolutizing modes of understanding derived exclusively from one's own language. For all this, I have claimed, we need a well-founded *tertium comparationis*; and such a *tertium comparationis* is provided by the mini-language of universal human concepts, derived from empirical cross-linguistic investigations.

# Notes

## 1: Introduction

1 In a similar vein, Needham (1981: 99) states: "I take it to be true that what we think of as our real lives is characteristically an account of our feelings."

2 It has often been said that some cultures do not draw a sharp line between the concepts THINK and FEEL, and that they may not even have separate words for these two concepts (cf. e.g. Lutz 1988; Lynch 1990; Wikan 1990). But it is one thing for a culture to treat the phenomena of "thinking" and "feeling" as closely related, and quite another not to make a distinction between them at all. To my knowledge, cross-linguistic investigations focussed on the concepts of THINK and FEEL have so far failed to produce a single example of a language which wouldn't have a word for FEEL, distinct from the word for THINK (cf. Goddard and Wierzbicka (eds.) 1994). To take some languages where the contrary has been asserted: in Hindi, the word for FEEL is *mahsus* (Richard Barz, personal communication), and in Balinese, *asa* (Adrian Clynes, personal communication). The Ifaluk word for FEEL appears to be *niferash* (also "insides"), whereas the word *nunuwan*, glossed by Lutz as "think/feel", can be regarded as an exponent of THINK (see Sohn and Tawerilmang 1976; for further discussion cf. Wierzbicka 1992a: 187; see also chapter 7).

3 V. Apresjan (1997) has raised a doubt as to whether the explication of *toska* proposed in my *Semantics, Culture and Cognition* (1992a) would be sufficient to distinguish *toska* from, for example, *unynie* (another Russian word for something like deep melancholy). I will point out, therefore, that the component of "wanting something to happen" (linking *toska* with *yearning*) is absent from *unynie*, as it is absent from the English *depression*. This is why *toska* can occur in collocations like *toska po rodine* lit. "toska after homeland", which implies that one *wants* to be in one's homeland (and knows that one can't), whereas there can be no *\*unynie po rodine*. When one is in the state of *unynie*, one is, so to speak, in a black hole, past all wanting, yearning, longing. (For detailed discussion of *unynie*, see Uryson 1997.)

At the same time, I entirely agree with Apresjan's suggestion that explications based on cognitive scenarios should be supplemented with a study of metaphors associated with individual words. In fact, her observations concerning the metaphors characteristic of *toska* (in contrast to *unynie*) support the explication based on a cognitive scenario; e.g. *toska soset* lit. "*toska* is sucking" (as if something were sucking at one's heart) suggests that something in one *wants* something. In the black hole of *unynie* no such inner sense of wanting is left, so the metaphor would not be appropriate. An analogy from English: one can be *consumed by envy, consumed by ambition, consumed by passion* or *consumed by worry*, but not *\*consumed by depression*, because *envy, ambition, passion,* and *worry* all imply that one wants something to happen (or not to happen), whereas *depression* implies that one is already past wanting.

4  In my own work the idea that "emotion concepts" can be defined via cognitive scenarios was first developed and illustrated in *Semantic Primitives* (Wierzbicka 1972). A similar idea was put forward, independently, by Lidija Iordanskaja (1970, 1974). For a different, and highly original approach to the semantic analysis of "emotion concepts", see Apresjan and Apresjan (1993).

5  *Guilt* in the factual sense (with no reference to feelings) has an equivalent in the Russian word *vina*, but *guilt* has also a second, "emotional", sense, whereas *vina* does not. For example, if one wanted to say in Russian that someone was "tormented by guilt" one would have to use the expression *čuvstvo viny* "a feeling of guilt", not just the word *vina*.

6  The anthropologist Marshall Sahlins (1994: 379) wrote recently, with apparent exasperation, that "If culture must be conceived as always and only changing, lest one commit the mortal sin of essentialism, then there can be no such thing as identity, or even sanity, let alone continuity." By venturing to say anything about "Anglo culture", or "Russian culture", I, too, am courting the danger of being accused of the "mortal sin of essentialism". But everyday words such as *upset* in English provide incontrovertible evidence of certain wide-spread and relatively enduring attitudes and assumptions, with which every speaker of a language (in this case, English) will be familiar. Facts of this kind give substance to constructs such as "Anglo culture" or "Russian culture", and illustrate their usefulness. Obviously, however, such constructs do not stand for bound, monolithic, and immutable "entities".

7  To say that French doesn't have a word corresponding to *mood* is not to imply that French is "lacking" something that English has, but rather to note that the two languages draw different lexical and conceptual distinctions. The word *mood* can be translated into French, depending on the context, as *humeur, disposition, état d'âme, atmosphère,* or *ambiance,* but none of these words corresponds exactly to the English *mood*. Thus, while the word *humeur* can be used in the collocations *bonne humeur* and *mauvaise humeur* ("good *humour*" and "bad *humour*"), comparable to *good mood* and *bad mood*, it would normally not be used in collocations corresponding to, for example, *serious mood, reflective mood, festive mood, triumphant mood, strange mood, sad mood, happy mood,* and so on. It is clear, then, that while *humeur* overlaps in meaning with *mood*, it does not coincide with it. If a French psychologist decided to draw a theoretical distinction on the basis of the French words *émotion* and *humeur,* it would not be the same distinction which Ekman draws on the basis of the English words *emotion* and *mood*.

8  The concept of *bird* is included in the meaning of *swallow* or *parrot* and the concept of *tree* in the meaning of *oak* or *maple*: semantically, a *swallow* or a *parrot* is "a kind of bird", just as an *oak* or a *maple* is "a kind of tree"; but *sadness* is, semantically, no more "a kind of emotion" than a *knife* is "a kind

of weapon" or "a kind of cutlery" (for detailed discussion, see Wierzbicka 1984, 1985b, and 1988a; see also D'Andrade 1995).

9  Solomon (1995: 278) rightly questions the "common theory (if it deserves to be called a 'theory') [that] 'emotion' (or its equivalents in other languages) is the name of a family or genus, and [that] the particular emotions (anger, fear, love, . . . etc.) are various species of emotion". He clearly assumes, however, that the English word *emotion* does have equivalents in other languages, and he sees no problem with describing "anger", "fear", or "love" as "particular emotions" – a phrasing which actually begs the question of what the relationship is between "emotion" on the one hand and "anger", "fear", or "love" on the other.

10  All the Malay examples adduced in this chapter have been provided by Cliff Goddard (personal communication). See also Goddard 1996a and 1997b.

11  For example, Pinker (1997: 366–7) declares: "The common remark that a language does or doesn't have a word for an emotion means little. New emotion words catch on quickly, without tortuous definitions; they come from other languages (*ennui, angst, naches, amok*) . . . I have never heard a foreign emotion word whose meaning was not instantly recognizable." This suggests that the author's range of cultural experience has never exposed him to "false friends", i.e. words "recognized instantly", but wrongly, by people who rely on their own language in interpreting words of a language that they don't know. (For detailed discussion of the German concept *Angst* and the differences between *Angst* and the English *angst*, see chapter 3).

12  These publications include, amongst others, the following: Bogusławski 1966, 1970; Goddard 1990, 1991a, 1995, 1996a, 1997b; Harkins 1990a and b, 1996; Harkins and Wierzbicka 1997; Hasada 1996, 1998; Mostovaja 1998; Travis 1998; Wierzbicka 1992a, b, and c, 1994a and d, 1995b, c, and e and articles in Wierzbicka 1990e.

13  Many elements listed in the tables below have variants (or "allolexes"), such as *I* and *me* or *where* and *place* in English. In most cases, these variants have not been included in the version of the tables included in this chapter. In some cases, the same word can be regarded as an exponent of two different primitives, e.g. in the Malay table ADA$_1$ and ADA$_2$ are listed as lexical exponents of "existence" and "possession", respectively. Such homophonous elements can be distinguished in terms of their grammatical frames; for example (roughly speaking) ADA$_1$ is intransitive and ADA$_2$ is transitive.

14  The table of universal semantic primitives (presented here in three versions) constitutes a highly condensed exposition of the results of extensive crosslinguistic investigations. A full understanding of it requires some degree of familiarity with the theory that underlies it, as well as the extensive empirical work of which it is a distillation. In particular, it requires some understanding of theoretical concepts such as "polysemy", "allolexy", "syntactic valency", and "canonical sentences". For detailed explanations, see Wierzbicka 1996a and Goddard 1998.

## 2: Defining emotion concepts

1  When used in combination with the word *now*, the expression *has happened* can be regarded as a variant of *happened*. (Semantically, *something has happened*

*now* is equivalent to *something happened now* and the former sounds more natural in ordinary English than the latter.)

### 3: German "Angst"

1 "Das war die Epoche, in der Millionen von Deutschen einfach sagten 'Ich habe Angst', ohne auch nur zu versuchen, Beschaffenheit und Ursache dieser Angst zu präzisieren" (Nuss 1993: 193).

2 "So gab es nach der Euphorie der fünfziger und sechziger Jahre eine Zeit, in der die Deutschen *Angst* vor allem Möglichen hatten: vor der Kernkraft, den Ölscheichs, der Arbeitlosigkeit, den Japanern, den Raketen, vor der Umweltverschmutzung, dem Polizeistaat, der Zukunft . . . Jedesmal, wenn eine Bedrohung überwunden war, tauchte eine andere auf und nistete sich in ihrem Geist ein" (Nuss 1993: 193).

3 Auf dem Boden der Unsicherheit gedeiht die Angst. Je mehr die Deutschen mit Ungewißheiten konfrontiert sind, desto mehr Gründe entdecken sie, sich Sorgen zu machen. Das Angstgefühl breitet sich auf diese Weise immer weiter aus und erzeugt bei manchen einen permanenten Angstzustand. Er wird durch tausend Kleinigkeiten genährt, die nach und nach zu einer ständigen Bedrohung anschwellen, gegen die anzukämpfen unmöglich wird . . .

Für einen Deutschen drücken die unendliche Stille, die Lenz erstickt, und das Grausen, das Woyzeck empfindet, auf eindrucksvolle Weise die namenlose *Angst* aus, die jedes menschliche Wesen empfindet und die man nie vollständig in den Griff bekommen kann. Sie ist allgegenwärtig, weil alles im Grunde genommen eine Gefahr darstellt und der Mensch nirgendwo wirklich in Sicherheit ist. Der Deutsche fürchtet weniger die physische Gefahr (er ist von Natur aus mutig) und die vielfältigen Wechselfälle des Lebens . . . als das Unbekannte. Nicht zu wissen, was geschehen wird, sich nicht darüber im klaren sein, mit welchem Problem man sich befassen muß, denjenigen nicht zu kennen, den man als Gegner haben wird, macht ihm sehr viel mehr *Angst* als eine wirkliche Gefahr" (Nuss 1993: 188–89).

4 "Die Bedrohung, die einzig 'furchtbar' sein kann und die in der Furcht entdeckt wird, kommt immer von innerweltlichem Seienden her . . . *Das Wovor der Angst ist das In-der-Welt-sein als solches.* Wie unterscheidet sich phänomenal das, wovor die Angst sich ängstet, von dem, wovor die Furcht sich fürchtet? Das Wovor der Angst ist kein innerweltliches Seiendes. Daher kann es damit wesenhaft keine Bewandtnis haben. Die Bedrohung hat nicht den Charakter einer bestimmten Abträglichkeit, die das Bedrohte in der bestimmten Hinsicht auf ein besonderes faktisches Seinkönnen trifft. Das Wovor der Angst ist völlig unbestimmt. Diese Unbestimmtheit läßt nicht nur faktisch unentschieden, welches innerweltliche Seiende droht, sondern besagt, daß überhaupt das innerweltliche Seiende nicht 'relevant' ist. Nichts von dem, was innerhalb der Welt zuhanden und vorhanden ist, fungiert als das, wovor die Angst sich ängstet. Die innerweltlich entdeckte Bewandtnisganzheit des Zuhandenen und Vorhandenen ist als solche überhaupt ohne Belang. Sie sinkt in sich zusammen. Die Welt hat den Charakter völliger Unbedeutsamkeit. In der Angst begegnet nicht dieses oder jenes, mit dem es als Bedrohlichem eine Bewandtnis haben könnte . . .

Die Angst ist nicht nur Angst vor . . . sondern als Befindlichkeit zugleich

*Angst um* . . . Worum die Angst sich abängstet, ist nicht eine *bestimmte* Seinsart und Möglichkeit des Daseins. Die Bedrohung ist ja selbst unbestimmt und vermag daher nicht auf dieses oder jenes faktisch konkrete Seinkönnen bedrohend einzudringen. Worum sich die Angst ängstet, ist das In-der-Welt-sein selbst" (Heidegger 1953[1926]: 186–87).

5  "Wenn ein Kind einsam in dunkler Nacht durch den Wald gehen muß, fürchtet es sich, auch wenn man ihm noch so überzeugend bewiesen hat, daß überhaupt nichts sei, wovor es sich zu fürchten brauche. Im Augenblick, wo es allein in der Finsternis ist und so Einsamkeit radikal erfährt, steht Furcht auf, die eigentliche Furcht des Menschen, die nicht Furcht vor etwas, sondern Furcht an sich ist. Die Furcht vor etwas Bestimmtem ist im Grunde harmlos, sie kann gebannt werden, indem man den betreffenden Gegenstand wegnimmt. Wenn jemand sich beispielsweise vor einem bissigen Hund fürchtet, kann man die Sache schnell bereinigen, indem man den Hund an die Kette nimmt. Hier stoßen wir auf etwas viel Tieferes: daß der Mensch da, wo er in letzte Einsamkeit gerät, sich fürchtet, nicht vor etwas Bestimmtem, das man wegbeweisen könnte; er erfährt vielmehr die Furcht der Einsamkeit, die Unheimlichkeit und Ausgesetztheit seines eigenen Wesens, die nicht rational überwindbar ist" (Ratinger 1968: 246).

6  In quotes from early German sources, the original spelling and punctuation (i.e. lower case for nouns) has been retained.

7  "'Peurs particulières': c'est-à-dire 'peurs nommées'. Ici, peut devenir opératoire au niveau collectif la distinction que la psychiatrie a maintenant établie au plan individuel entre peur et angoisse, jadis confondues par la psychologie classique. Car il s'agit de deux pôles autour desquels gravitent des mots et des faits psychiques à la fois parents et différents. La crainte, l'épouvante, la frayeur, la terreur appartiennent plutôt la peur; l'inquiétude, l'anxiété, la mélancolie plutôt l'angoisse. La première porte sur le connu, la seconde sur l'inconnu.

La peur a un objet déterminé auquel on peut faire face. L'angoisse n'en a pas et est vécue comme une attente douloureuse devant un danger d'autant plus redoutable qu'il n'est pas clairement identifié: elle est un sentiment global d'insécurité. Aussi est-elle plus difficile à supporter que la peur . . . Parce qu'il est impossible de conserver son équilibre interne en affrontant longtemps une angoisse flottante, infinie et indéfinissable, il est nécessaire à l'homme de la transformer et de la fragmenter en des peurs précises de quelque chose ou de quelqu'un. 'L'esprit humain fabrique en permanence la peur' pour éviter une angoisse morbide qui aboutirait à l'abolition du moi" (Delumeau 1978: 15–16).

8  "Ein Werk von der Sprachgewalt der Lutherbibel aber, das in einer Zeit sich ausbreitender Lesekunst in Abertausenden von Exemplaren in allen Teilen Deutschlands, auch den katholischen, nicht nur gelesen, sondern weithin auch auswendig gelernt wurde, konnte im Verein mit der Sprache seiner Sendschreiben, Reden und Lieder schließlich festere Grundlagen für eine die ganze Nation umspannende Gemeinsprache legen, als es den Kanzlei- oder den Druckersprachen . . . hätte gelingen können" (Bach 1965: 259–60).

9  das nhd [neuhochdeutsche] *angst*, mit dem wir den begriff von muthlosigkeit, furcht zu verbinden pflegen, entspricht dem alten *angest* durchaus nicht, oder nur zufällig. *angest*, bedeutet den zustand, in dem man sich von not und gefahr umringt sieht, selbst auch dann, wenn man mit der größten herzhaftigkeit gegen sie angeht, oder sie gefaßt erträgt. Die helden in der

Nibelungen haben *angest* genug, aber sie haben keine angst" (Benecke 1854: vol. I, p. 43).

10 "Beneckes behaupteter unterschied in der bedeutung des mhd [mittelehochdeutschen] angest und nhd. *Angst*... übertreibt; warum sollte nicht auch heute den mutigsten krieger manches *ängsten*, ohne dass ihn die geringste feigheit anwandelt?... *angst* is nicht bloss mutlosigkeit, sondern quälende sorge, zweifelnder, beengender zustand überhaupt... (Grimm and Grimm 1854, vol. I, p. 358).

11 "Das Jüngste Gericht wird nicht an einen fernen Punkt auf der Zeitachse gerückt, sondern ist eigene, unmittelbare Gegenwart. Das eigene Gewissen ist die Hölle. Gericht, Zorn, Sünde und Tod sind zugleich gegenwärtig... Wenn wir das Gewissen fühlen, dann fühlen wir die Hölle und meinen, wir seien ewig verloren" (p. 54).

"Es wurde... darauf hingewiesen, daß im bösen Gewissen die Hölle, das Eschaton selbst, in dieses Leben hineinrückt, und zwar so, daß die ohnmächtigen Flüche, die zu Gott emporgesandt werden, nur der Ausdruck letzter Gottesferne und völliger Verzweiflung sind. Hier wird durchlitten, was es heißt, ferne zu sein von seinem Angesicht, und eben das hat der angefochtene Luther vor seinem reformatorischen Durchbruch mit aller Schwere erfahren. Die Grenzen zum Eschaton sind geöffnet. Gottes ewiges Gericht wird hier und heute durchlitten" (Asendorf 1967: 59–60).

12 "Mehr als eine Woche lang bin ich in Tod und Hölle hin und her geworfen, am ganzen Leibe fühl ich mich geschlagen, mir zittern noch alle Glieder. Fast habe ich Christus völlig verloren, umhergetrieben von Fluten und Stürmen der Verzweiflung und Lästerung gegen Gott. Wegen der Fürbitte der Gläubigen hat Gott dann aber angefangen, sich über mich zu erbarmen und meine Seele aus dem Grund der Hölle gerissen" (Luther; quoted in Oberman 1983: 335).

13 "Es war nicht die Begegnung mit dem Tod, die ihn so in Angst und Schrecken versetzt hatte. Körperlich erholt Luther sich schnell, wie er berichtet. Was er mit dem Ausbruch der Krankheit als Überfall des Teufels erfuhr, sollte mit zunehmender Gesundung erst voll in Gang kommen. Es ist auch weiterhin so, daß ihn kein Zweifel über die evangelische Wahrheit plagt. Was ihn ängstigte, ist die Frage, ob er selber in ihr bestehen kann" (Oberman 1983: 335).

14 "Die neue Freiheit mußte in ihm ein tiefes Gefühl der Unsicherheit und Ohnmacht, des Zweifels, der Verlassenheit und Angst wecken" (Fromm 1980b: 254).

15 "' 'Ich bin gewiß!' – Ist das ein Satz aus unseren Tagen? Läßt sich heute so sprechen, wie Paulus einst geschrieben hat? Gewißheit scheint sich seltener finden zu lassen, und sie zu suchen mühsamer. Aber wer könnte wirklich auf Gewißheit verzichten? Gewiß zu sein: seiner selbst, seiner Sache, eines anderen Menschen – und vor allem: des eigenen Glaubens –, das ist lebensnotwendig. In Ungewißheit läßt sich nicht leben. Schon die belanglosen Ungewißheiten das Alltags sind schwer zu ertragen. Nicht selten machen sie krank und lassen darin anschaulich werden, wie der Mensch unter ihnen leidet.

Ungewißheit in den Grundfragen des Lebens bedroht das Leben selbst" (Rössler 1979: 6).

16 "Durch solche Traumbilder entsteht für die Deutschen eine Stätte der Geborgenheit, in der man, wie im Schoße der Familie, den Wechselfällen

und Gefahren des Lebens nicht mehr ausgesetzt ist. Das Schlimmste, was einem Deutschen daher passieren kann, ist, seine *Heimat* zu verlieren. Dann hat er den Eindruck, seiner Seele beraubt zu werden" (Nuss 1993: 178).

17 "Im täglichen Leben wird deutlich, welch unaufhörlichen Kampf die Deutschen unbewußt führen, um ihre latenten *Ängste* abzubauen. Materiell wie psychisch haben sie das Bedürfnis, in einem sicheren Rahmen zu leben". (Nuss 1993: 195).

18 "Für Deutsche ist es unerläßlich, *Ordnung* zu haben und in einer Welt zu leben, in der *Ordnung* herrscht. In der Tat ist nur die *Ordnung* imstande, den inneren Frieden zu sichern. Damit der Kopf ordentlich funktionieren und die Seele sich frei fühlen kann, muß der Körper in einem geordneten Rahmen leben. Der Deutsche kann es nicht ausstehen, wenn er sich nicht "zurechtfindet" – in seinen Sachen wie in seinen Gedanken, im Beruf wie in seinem Gefühlsleben. Er liebt klare Verhältnisse. Er möchte wissen, woran er ist und wie es weitergehen soll. Er ist ein Gewohnheitstier und möchte alles genau geregelt sehen. Das Unbekannte belastet, ja erschreckt ihn. Er hat das Bedürfnis, das Terrain, auf dem er sich bewegt, zu erforschen und abzustecken. Wenn das einmal geschehen ist, fühlt er sich in Sicherheit". (Nuss 1993: 123).

## 4: Reading human faces

1 Cf. also Izard's (1994: 297) statement: "Russell's (1993) review also shows that we probably have not yet determined the exact number or best names of emotions with universal expressions". The assumption that there is "an exact number of emotions with universal expressions" and that the problem consists in finding "the best names" for them, misses the point of the critique.

2 The change of paradigm that Mandler sees as being already under way can't, of course, be expected to occur instantly, given that the old paradigm had already penetrated into undergraduate textbooks, where it was presented as an established truth (cf. Fridlund 1997: 238). Facts such as that, for example, in the research done with the Fore and Dani people in Papua fear was not distinguished from surprise, nor anger from disgust (Fridlund 1994: 245) are glossed over in such presentations, as are also the methodological problems involved in the attempts to test the "universality hypothesis".

3 Arguably, when a message is expressed verbally, its underlying semantic structure includes the component "I say", that is, the full meaning of a sentence like "I feel (something) good now" can be spelled out as "I say: I feel something good now". A facial message, which is conveyed by what I *do*, not by what I *say*, would not include such a component. (For extensive discussions of the component "I say" see Wierzbicka 1987, 1991).

4 If a facial gesture such as a smile or raised eyebrows occurs by itself, rather than as accompaniment of speech, and if it is combined with eye contact with another person, it can be interpreted as including an additional component directed at that other person: "I want you to know this". For example, by smiling at someone while not speaking (but maintaining eye contact) I may be conveying not only the message "I feel something good now" but also "I want you to know this". The interaction between facial gestures, eye contact, and absence of speech requires further investigation.

5 Presumably, a much wider range of messages can be conveyed by means of

intonation. In everyday life people talk readily about a "reproachful tone of voice", a "sarcastic tone of voice", a "disapproving tone of voice", an "imploring tone of voice", and so on. How exactly such different "tones" are identified by ordinary people is a matter for future investigation. It seems clear, however, that here, too, the messages conveyed have a first-person present-tense format, and include components such as "I think you did something bad", "I want you to do something good for me", "I know you don't have to do it". Raising and falling intonation can be linked with messages such as "I want to know this" (e.g. in questions) and "I know this" (in unqualified statements), but generally speaking the semantics of intonation, like the semantics of facial behaviour, is a field still waiting to be developed. (Cf. Bolinger 1986, 1989; Deakin 1981.)

6 Darwin (1955[1872]: 257) described the wrinkling of the nose as a side effect of the strong retraction of the upper lip characteristic of the movement around the mouth preparatory to the act of vomiting. Arguably, however, the wrinkling of the nose and the apparent preparations of the mouth for vomiting can be seen as two distinct symbolic gestures, both implying that "I feel something bad now", and also that "I think this is bad", "I don't want to know about this", and "I cannot not know about it now".

7 The hypothesis that specific semantic components, or configurations of components, can be linked with individual facial gestures does not preclude, needless to say, the possibility that certain combinations of components, too, may in some cultures (if not universally) have an identifiable meaning richer than the sum of the meanings of the individual gestures. Nick Enfield's observation (personal communication) that, for example, in Lao (South-East Asia) people describe certain facial configurations as, literally, "a rotten face" is suggestive in this respect. In any case, combinations such as "raised eyebrows, open mouth" (in English often linked with the word *surprise*), or "corners of the mouth down, lowered eyelids" (in English often linked with the word *sadness*) are likely to be seen as meaningful "molecules" in many cultures.

8 Exact measurement of the facial behaviour may of course be useful for scientific purposes, as the applied research presented in Ekman and Rosenberg 1997 shows. The results of such measurements, however, must be distinguished from the kind of information which "ordinary people" convey by means of their facial behaviour to other "ordinary people".

9 The awareness of a link between movement "above the eyes" and thinking may or may not be universal and it needs to be investigated cross-culturally. Some circumstantial evidence on this point comes from linguistic facts. For example, in the Austronesian language Petats the word for forehead is "*baku ni hatatei*", which glosses literally as "head for thinking". "*Baku ni hatatei*" refers specifically to the forehead, although apparently it may also cover the inside of the head, i.e. "brain" (Claire Bowern, personal communication).

10 Nick Enfield (personal communication) has pointed out to me that the woman in photograph C could maintain her drawn-together eyebrows throughout the operation of removing the rotten meat, in which case the proposed formula would seem not to fit (the woman could in fact be doing what she both wants and doesn't want to do). While I agree with this observation I would note that if the gesture is maintained throughout the operation its pragmatic interpretation may change from "I want to remove this thing – I know I'm not doing it now", to "I want to drop this rotten thing

– I know I'm not doing it now". In both cases there is a "discrepancy" between what one wants to do and what one is actually doing (the woman appears to be aware that she is not doing what she wants to do).

11 In fact, (as suggested to me by Cliff Goddard, personal communication) we usually raise our eyebrows if we want to see more of "what is above us" (just try to see something on the ceiling and the chances are that you will find yourself raising your eyebrows). Cf. also Ekman's (1989: 157) reference to "increasing the superior visual field", quoted earlier.

### 5: Russian emotional expression

1 For a detailed semantic analysis of *duša* see Wierzbicka 1992a; and of *drug, amae*, and *omoiyari*, see Wierzbicka 1997a; for a fuller analysis of *omoiyari*, see also Travis 1997.

2 I owe this observation to Mary Besemeres (personal communication).

3 English has of course the expression *to tear one's hair out*, but Russian has a similar expression, too.

4 One English expression which doesn't have a Russian counterpart is *one's heart in one's mouth*. The more literary expression *his heart was in his boots* has its counterpart in the much more colloquial *ego duša ušla v pjatki* lit. "his heart went into his heels".

5 For a theory of "cultural scripts", stating cultural norms in a natural semantic metalanguage based on universal human concepts see, e.g. Goddard 1997a, 1998; Goddard and Wierzbicka 1994, 1997; Wierzbicka 1994b, c, and d, 1996b and c. See also chapter 6.

### 6: Polish and Anglo-American emotional scripts

1 As Goddard (1997a: 199) put it,

> it is important to acknowledge that cultural scripts are not necessarily "binding" on individuals. Cultural norms may be followed by some of the people all of the time, and by all of the people some of the time, but they are certainly not followed by all of the people all of the time. Whether or not they are being followed in behavioural terms, however, cultural norms are always in the background as an interpretive framework against which people make sense of and access other people's behaviours.

2 The phrase "to feel something good/bad towards someone" should be regarded as an abbreviation for a more complex structure "to feel something good (bad) when [one] thinks about someone".

3 Shore (1996: 53) draws a distinction between "abstract global models" and "more concrete and particular instantiations of those models", and he calls the former "foundational schemas". More general scripts like the one listed here as Polish script 3 can be regarded as examples of such "foundational schemas".

4 Barańczak's perception of the differences between the Polish and Anglo-American cultural norms discussed in this passage has found a poetic expression in his poem titled "Small Talk"; see Barańczak 1989:63.

5 The distinction between "cultural models" and "cultural scripts" employed here is not cast in concrete. As suggested earlier (see, e.g. Wierzbicka 1994b, c, and d; Goddard 1997a), the exact formats of "cultural scripts" (and/or models) most appropriate for different cultures require further investiga-

tion. For example, Goddard (1997a: 199) argues that "Malay cultural scripts lend themselves to formulations in terms of what is 'good' or 'not good' to say or do rather than in terms of what people 'can' or 'cannot' say or do". On the other hand, for Japanese culture the scripts formulated in terms of what one "can" or "cannot" say or do seem often more appropriate (cf. Wierzbicka 1996c). At this stage in the development of the theory of cultural scripts the formats used in current descriptive work must be regarded as exploratory.

6 The frequencies of these words and their derivational families given in the frequency dictionary of modern Polish (based on half a million running words; Kurcz et al. 1990) are as follows:

| | |
|---|---|
| zdenerwowany | 27 |
| zmartwiony | 37 |
| wściekły | 13 |
| przykro | 46 |

This can be compared with the total of 34 for the family of *gniewać się* "be angry". For *zły*, which means also "bad", no frequency could be established, but it is interesting to note that the derived noun *złość* has a higher frequency (15) than the noun *gniew* (7), which is the closest Polish equivalent of *anger*.

7 For a well documented study of the links between emotion, culture, and non-verbal communication see Hasada 1996.

8 For a detailed study of bicultural literature as a source of insight into emotion and culture see Besemeres forthcoming.

# References

Alcott, Louisa May 1975[1846], in Moffat and Painter, pp. 28–33.
Althaus, Paul 1966, *The Theology of Martin Luther* (translated by Robert C. Schultz), Philadelphia: Fortress.
*Althochdeutsches Wörterbuch* 1968, see Blum et al.
Amal'rik, Andrej 1982, *Zapiski Dissidenta*, Ann Arbor: Ardis.
Ameka, Felix 1990a, How discourse particles mean: the case of the Ewe "terminal" particles, *Journal of African Languages and Linguistics* 12(2): 143–70.
  1990b, The grammatical packaging of experiences in Ewe: a study in the semantics of syntax, *Australian Journal of Linguistics* (Special issue on the semantics of emotions) 10(2): 139–81.
  (ed.) 1992, *Journal of Pragmatics* (Special issue on Interjections) 18(2/3).
  1994, Ewe, in Goddard and Wierzbicka, pp. 57–86.
Apresjan, Jurij D. 1992[1974], *Lexical Semantics*, Anna Arbor: Karoma.
  (ed.) 1997, *Novyj Ob'jasnitel'nyj Slovar' Sinonimov Russkogo Jazyka. A New Explanatory Dictionary of Synonyms of the Russian Language*, Moskva: Škola Jazyki Russkoj Kul'tury.
Apresjan, Jurij D., and Valentina Apresjan 1993, Metafora v semantičeskom predstavlenii emocij (Metaphor in the semantic representation of emotions), *Voprosy Jazykoznanija* 3: 27–35.
Apresjan, Jurij D., and A. I. Rozenman 1979, *Anglo-Russkij Sinonimičeskij Slovar'* (An English–Russian Dictionary of Synonyms), Moscow: Russkij Jazyk.
Apresjan, Valentina 1997, "Fear" and "pity" in Russian and English from a lexicographical perspective, *International Journal of Lexicography* 10(2): 85–111.
Asendorf, Ulrich 1967, *Eschatologie bei Luther*, Göttingen: Vandenhoeck and Ruprecht.
Asquith, Pamela 1984, The inevitability and utility of anthropomorphism in description of primate behaviour, in Harré and Reynolds, pp. 138–76.
Athanasiadou, Angeliki and Elżbieta Tabakowska (eds.) 1998, *Speaking of Emotions: Conceptualisation and expression*, Berlin: Mouton de Gruyter.
Austin, J. L. 1962, *How to Do Things with Words*, Oxford: Clarendon.
Averill, James R. 1980, On the paucity of positive emotions, in K. R. Blankstein, P. Pliner, and J. Polivy, *Advances in the Study of Communication and Affect*, vol 6: *Assessment and modification of emotional behaviour*, New York: Plenum, pp. 7–45.
Averill, James R., and Thomas A. More 1993, Happiness, in Lewis and Haviland, pp. 617–30.
Bach, Adolf 1965, *Geschichte der Deutschen Sprache*, Heidelberg: Quelle and

Meyer.

Bally, Charles 1926, L'expression des idées de sphère personnelle et de solidarité dans les langues Indo-Européennes, in F. Fankhauser and J. Jud (eds.), *Festschrift Louis Gauchat*, Aarau: Verlag Sauerländer, pp. 68–78. (Translated into English by Christine Béal and Hilary Chappell, in Hilary Chappell and William McGregor (eds.), pp. 31–61.)

Barańczak, Stanisław 1989, *The Weight of the Body*, Chicago: Chicago Press
    1990, *Breathing Under Water and Other East European Essays*, Cambridge, Mass.: Harvard University Press.

Bauer, Raymond, Alex Inkeles, and Clyde Kluckhohn 1956, *How the Soviet System Works*, Cambridge, Mass.: Harvard University Press.

Bavelas, Janet B., and Nicole Chovil 1997, Faces in dialogue, in Russell and Fernández-Dols 1976, pp. 334–48.

Becker, Ernest 1962, *The Birth and Death of Meaning*, New York: Free Press of Glencoe.

Bellah, Robert N., Richard Madsen, William M. Sullivan, Ann Swidler, and Steven M. Tipton (eds.) 1985, *Habits of the Heart: Individualism and commitment in American life*, Berkeley: University of California Press.

Benecke, Georg Friedrich 1854, see Müller 1963.

Berlin, Brent, and Paul Kay 1969, *Basic Colour Terms: their universality and evolution*, Berkeley: University of California Press.

Besemeres, Mary, forthcoming, The semiotic memoir: language and self in cross-linguistic autobiography.

Bevan, E. Dean 1971, *A Concordance to the Plays and Prefaces of Bernard Shaw*, Detroit: Gale Research.

Birch, Charles 1995, *Feelings*, Sydney: University of New South Wales Press.

Bloomfield, Morton Wilfred, 1967[1952], *The Seven Deadly Sins: an introduction to the history of a religious concept, with special reference to medieval English literature*, East Lansing, Mich.: Michigan State University Press.

Blum, Siegfried, T. Frings, H. Götz, S. Habermann, E. Karg-Gasterstädt, G. Müller, E. Ulbricht, and G. Wolfrum (eds.) 1968, *Althochdeutsches Wörterbuch*, Berlin: Akademie Verlag.

Boas, Franz 1966[1911], Introduction to *Handbook of American Indian Languages*, Lincoln: University of Nebraska Press.

Bogusławski, Andrzej 1966, *Semantyczne Pojęcie Liczebnika*, Wrocław: Ossolineum.
    1970, On semantic primitives and meaningfulness, in R. J. A. Greimas, R. Jakobson, M. R. Mayenowa, and S. Żołkiewski (eds.), *Signs, Language and Culture*, The Hague: Mouton, pp. 143–52. Reprinted in Bogusławski 1994 pp. 49–57.
    1994, *Word Matters – Sprawy słowa*, Warsaw: Veda.

Bolinger, Dwight 1986, *Intonation and its Parts: Melody in spoken English*, Stanford: Stanford University Press.
    1989, *Intonation and its Uses: Melody in grammar and discourse*, Stanford: Stanford University Press.

Bond, Michael (ed.) 1997, *Working at the Interface of Cultures: Eighteen lives in social science*, London: Routledge.

Bourdieu, P. 1977, *Outline of a Theory of Practice*, Cambridge: Cambridge University Press.

Bradbury, Malcolm 1975, *The History Man*, London: Arrow.

Braithwaite, John 1989, *Crime, Shame and Reintegration*, Cambridge, Sydney:

320    References

Cambridge University Press.
Brontë, Charlotte 1971[1847], *Jane Eyre*, New York: Norton.
Bruner, Jerome 1990, *Acts of Meaning*, Cambridge, Mass.: Harvard University Press.
Bugenhagen, Robert 1990, Experiential constructions in Mangap-Mbula, *Australian Journal of Linguistics* (Special issue on the semantics of emotions) 10(2): 183–215.
  1994, The exponents of semantic primitives in Mangap-Mbula, in Goddard and Wierzbicka, pp. 87–108.
Cacioppo, J. T., G. G. Berntson, and D. J. Klein 1992, What is an emotion? The role of somatovisceral afference, with special emphasis on somatovisceral "illusions", *Review of Personality and Social Psychology* 14: 63–8.
Callanan, Maggie and Patricia Kelley 1993, *Final Gifts: Understanding the special awareness, needs, and communications of the dying*, New York: Bantam.
Camras, Linda A. 1992, Expressive development and basic emotions, *Cognition and Emotion*, 6(3/4): 269–84.
Cann, Ronald 1993, *Formal Semantics*, Cambridge: Cambridge University Press.
Capote, Truman 1967, *In Cold Blood: A true account of a multiple murder and its consequences*, London: Penguin.
Chambers, W. Walker, and John R. Wilkie 1970, *A Short History of the German Language*, London: Methuen.
Chappell, Hilary 1986, The passive of bodily effect in Chinese, *Studies in Language* 10(2): 271–96.
  1991, Strategies for the assertion of obviousness and disagreement in Mandarin: a semantic study of the modal particle *me*, *Australian Journal of Linguistics* 11: 39–65.
  1994, Mandarin semantic primitives, in Goddard and Wierzbicka, pp. 109–48.
Chappell, Hilary, and William McGregor (eds.) 1996, *The Grammar of Inalienability: A typological perspective on body-part terms and the part-whole relation*, Berlin: Mouton de Gruyter.
Chestnut, Mary Boykin 1975[1865], in Moffat and Painter, pp. 270–87.
Chierchia, Gennaro, and Sally McConnell-Ginet 1990, *Meaning and Grammar: An introduction to semantics*, Cambridge, Mass.: MIT Press.
Chovil, Nicole 1997, Facing others: a social communicative perspective on facial displays, In Russell and Fernández-Dols, 1997b, pp. 321–33.
Chun, Lilias 1997, Bodily metaphors in Mandarin, unpublished ms., Australian National University, Canberra.
Claessen, Ina Elizabeth 1995, Vater unser, gib mir meine tägliche Pflege . . ., in Pausch and Pausch, pp. 32–8.
Clajus, Johannes 1578, *Grammatica Germanicae linguae ex bibliis Lutheri Germanicis et aliis eius libris collecta*, Leipzig. (Reprinted 1973, Hildesheim: G. Olms.)
Conklin, Harold 1955, Hanunóo color categories, *Southwestern Journal of Anthropology* 1: 339–44.
Coulter, J. 1986, Affect and social context: emotion definition as a social task, in Harré 1986b, pp. 20–134.
Couturat, Louis (ed.) 1903, *Opuscules et Fragments Inédits de Leibniz*, Paris: Presses Universitaires de France. (Reprinted 1961, Hildesheim: Georg Olms.)
Csordas, Thomas J. 1990, The 1988 Sterling Award Essay: Embodiment as a

paradigm for anthropology, *Ethos* 18: 5–47.

1993, *The Sacred Self: Cultural phenomenology of a charismatic world*, Berkeley: University of California Press.

Cüceloglu, D. M. 1970, Perception of facial expression in three different cultures, *Ergonomics* 13: 93–100.

D'Andrade, Roy 1987, A folk model of the mind, in Holland and Quinn, pp. 112–50.

1995, *The Development of Cognitive Anthropology*, Cambridge and New York: Cambridge University Press.

Dalbiez, Roland 1974, *L'Angoisse de Luther*, Paris: Téqui.

Darnell, Regna 1994, Comments on Wolf's "Perilous ideas: race, culture and people", *Current Anthropology* 35(1): 7–8.

Darwin, Charles 1955[1872], *The Expression of Emotions in Man and Animals*, New York: Philosophical Library.

de Tocqueville, Alexis 1953[1835–40], *Democracy in America* (Translated by Henry Reeve; Edited by Phillips Bradley), New York: Alfred A. Knopf.

Deakin, Greg 1981, Indirect speech acts and intonation, MA thesis, Australian National University.

Delumeau, J. 1978, *La Peur en Occident (XIVᵉ–XVIIIᵉ siècles). Une cité assiégée*, Paris: Librairie Arthème; Fayard. (German translation by Monika Hübner "Angst im Abendland Die Geschichte kollektiver Ängste im Europa des 14 bis 18 Jahrhunderts".)

1990, *Sin and Fear: The emergence of a Western guilt culture, 13th–18th centuries* (translated by Eric Nicholson), New York: St Martin's Press.

Demidenko, Helen (Helen Darville) 1994, *The Hand that Signed the Paper*, St Leonards, N.S.W: Allen and Unwin.

Descartes, René 1931[1701], The search after truth by the light of nature, in *The Philosophical Works of Descartes* (Translated by Elizabeth S. Haldane and G. R. T. Ross), vol I. Cambridge University Press, pp. 305–27.

*Die Bibel: die gute Nachricht in heutigem Deutsch* 1982, Stuttgart: Deutsche Bibelgesellschaft.

Dietz, P. 1870, *Wörterbuch zu Dr Martin Luthers deutschen Schriften*, Leipzig.

Dimmendaal, Gerrit 1995, Studying lexical-semantic fields in language: nature versus nurture, or Where does culture come in these days?, *Frankfurter Afrikanistische Blätter* 7: 1–29.

Drosdowski, Günther (ed.) 1981, *Duden Das große Wörterbuch der deutschen Sprache* 6 vols. Mannheim: Duden.

(ed.) 1993, *Duden Das große Wörterbuch der deutschen Sprache* 8 vols. Mannheim: Duden.

Duden 1972, see Müller.

1981, see Drosdowski.

1993, see Drosdowski.

Durham, Michael 1995, *Miracles of Mary*, Mowbray: Fount.

Eibl-Eiblesfelt, I. 1972, Similarities and differences between cultures in expressive movements, in R. A. Hinde (ed.), *Nonverbal Communication*, Cambridge: Cambridge University Press, pp. 297–311.

Ekman, Paul 1972, Universal and cultural differences in facial expressions of emotions, in J. K. Cole (ed.), *Nebraska Symposium on Motivation 1971*, Lincoln: University of Nebraska Press, pp. 207–93.

1973, *Darwin and Facial Expression: A century of research in review*, New York: Academic.

1975, The universal smile: face muscles talk every language, *Psychology Today* September: 35–9.

1980, *The Face of Man: Expressions of universal emotions in a New Guinea village*, New York: Garland STPM.

1984, Expression and the nature of emotion, in K. R. Scherer and Paul Ekman (eds.), *Approaches to Emotion*, Hillsdale, N. J.: Erlbaum, pp. 329–43.

1989, The argument and evidence about universals in facial expressions of emotion, in H. Wagner and A. Manstead (eds.), *Handbook of Social Psychophysiology*, Chichester: John Wiley and Sons, pp. 143–64.

1992a, An argument for basic emotions, *Cognition and Emotion* (Special issue on basic emotions) 6(3/4): 169–200.

1992b. Are there basic emotions?, *Psychological Review* 99(3): 550–3.

1993, Facial expression and emotion, *American Psychologist* 48: 384–92.

1994a, Strong evidence for universals in facial expressions: a reply to Russell's mistaken critique, *Psychological Bulletin* 115(1): 102–41.

1994b, All emotions are basic, in Ekman and Davidson, pp. 15–19

Ekman, Paul, and R. J. Davidson (eds.) 1994, *The Nature of Emotion: Fundamental questions*, Oxford: Oxford University Press.

Ekman, Paul, and W. V. Friesen 1971, Constants across cultures in the face and emotion, *Journal of Personality and Social Psychology* 17: 124–29.

1975, *Unmasking the Face: A guide to recognizing emotions from facial clues*, New Jersey: Prentice Hall. (Reprinted, Palo Alto, Calif.: Consulting Psychologists Press, 1984.)

1986, A new pan-cultural expression of emotion, *Motivation and Emotion* 10: 159–68.

Ekman, Paul, and Erika Rosenberg (eds.) 1997, *What the Face Reveals*, New York: Oxford University Press.

Elias, Norbert 1978, *Über den Prozess der Zivilisation* (*The Civilizing Process*) (translated by Edmund Jephcott), Oxford: Blackwell.

Enfield, Nick forthcoming, The syntax of Natural Semantic Metalanguage expressions in Lao, in Goddard and Wierzbicka.

Erikson, Erik E. 1958, *Young Man Luther: A study in psychoanalysis and history*, London: Faber and Faber.

Evans, Nicholas 1992, *Kayardild Dictionary and Thesaurus*, Department of Linguistics and Language Studies, University of Melbourne.

1994, Kayardild, in Goddard and Wierzbicka, pp. 203–28.

Falla, Paul, Marcus Wheeler, Boris Unbegaun, and Colin Howlett 1992, *The Oxford Russian Dictionary*, Oxford: Oxford University Press.

Fedotov, Georgij 1981[1938], *Rossija i Svoboda Sbornik Statej*, New York: Chalidze.

Fehr, B., and James A. Russell 1984, The concept of emotion viewed from a prototype perspective, *Journal of Experimental Psychology: General* 13: 464–86.

Feinstein, David, and Peg Elliott Mayo 1993, *Mortal Acts: Eighteen empowering rituals for confronting death*, San Francisco: Harper.

Feldman-Barrett, Lisa 1998, The future of emotion research, *The Affect Scientist* 12(2): 6–8.

*Flügel's Complete Dictionary of the German and English Language* (3rd edition) 1845, edited by C. A. Feiling and A. Heinmann, London: Whittaker.

French, Lucia, and Katherine Nelson 1985, *Young Children's Knowledge of Relational Terms: Some ifs, ors and buts*, New York: Springer Verlag.

Freud, Sigmund 1963[1917], Anxiety, in J. Strachey (ed. and transl.) *The Standard Edition of the Complete Psychological Writings of Sigmund Freud*, vol XVI, London: Hogarth, pp. 392–411.

Fridlund, Alan J. 1994, *Human Facial Expression: An evolutionary view*, San Diego: Academic Press.

1997, The new ethology of human facial expressions, in Russell and Fernández-Dols 1997b, pp. 103–29.

Friedrich, Paul 1997, Dialogue in lyric narrative, in Michael Macovski (ed.), *Dialogue and Critical Discourse: Language, culture, critical theory*, New York: Oxford University Press, pp. 79–98.

Frijda, N. H. 1969, Recognition of emotions, in L. Berkowitz (ed.), *Advances in Experimental Social Psychology 4*, New York: Academic, pp. 167–223.

1986, *The Emotions*, New York: Cambridge University Press.

Frisch, Max 1969, *Homo Faber*, Hamburg: Rowohlt.

Fromm, Erich 1980a[1941], *The Fear of Freedom*, London: Routledge and Kegan Paul.

1980b, *Gesamtausgabe* (Collected works), vol I, Stuttgart: Deutsche Verlags-Anstalt.

Gaylin, Willard 1979, *Feelings: Our vital signs*, Boston: G. K. Hall.

Geertz, Clifford 1973, Thick Description: Toward an interpretive theory of culture, in Clifford Geertz, *Interpretation of cultures*, New York: Basic, pp. 3–30.

1976, *The Religion of Java*, Chicago: University of Chicago Press.

1984[1974], From the Native's point of view: on the nature of anthropological understanding, in Richard Shweder and Robert LeVine (eds.), *Culture Theory: Essays on mind, self and emotion*, Cambridge: Cambridge University Press, pp. 123–36.

*GENT* 1979, *Greek–English New Testament*, Stuttgart: Deutsche Bibelgesellschaft.

Gerber, Eleanor Ruth 1985, Rage and obligation: Samoan emotions in conflict, in White and Kirkpatrick, pp. 121–67.

Ginsburg, G. P. 1997, Faces: an epilogue and reconceptualization, in Russell and Fernández-Dols, pp. 349–82.

Glaser, Elizabeth 1991, *Absence of Angels*, New York: Berkeley.

Glasgow, Kathleen 1994, *Burarra Gun-nartpa Dictionary (with English finder list)*, Darwin: Summer Institute of Linguistics.

Goddard, Cliff 1989, Issues in Natural Semantic Metalanguage, *Quaderni di Semantica* 10(1): 51–64.

1990, The lexical semantics of "good feelings" in Yankunytjatjara, *Australian Journal of Linguistics* 10 (2): 257–92.

1991a, Anger in the Western Desert – A case study in the cross-cultural semantics of emotion, *Man* 26: 602–19.

1991b, Testing the translatability of semantic primitives into an Australian Aboriginal language, *Anthropological Linguistics* 33(1): 31–56.

1994, Lexical primitives in Yankunytjatjara, in Goddard and Wierzbicka, pp. 229–62.

1995, Conceptual and cultural issues in emotion research, *Culture and Psychology* 1(2): 289–98.

1996a, The "social emotions" of Malay (Bahasa Melayu), *Ethos* 24(3): 426–64.

1996b, Cross-linguistic research on metaphor, *Language and Communication* 16(2): 145–51.

1997a, Cultural values and "cultural scripts" of Malay (Bahasa Melayu),

324    *References*

*Journal of Pragmatics* 27(2): 183–201.

1997b, Contrastive semantics and cultural psychology: "Surprise" in Malay and English, *Culture and Psychology* 3(2): 153–81.

1998, *Semantic Analysis: A practical introduction*, Oxford: Oxford University Press.

forthcoming a, Universal units in the lexicon, in M. Haspelmath, E. König, W. Oesterreicher, and W. Raible (eds.), *Language Typology and Language Universals*, Berlin: de Gruyter.

forthcoming b, Ethnosyntax, ethnosemantics, ethnopragmatics, in Nick Enfield (ed.), *Ethnosyntax*.

Goddard, Cliff, and Anna Wierzbicka (eds.) 1994, *Semantic and Lexical Universals – Theory and empirical findings*, Amsterdam: John Benjamins.

1997, Discourse and culture, in Teun A. van Dijk (ed.), *Discourse as Social Interaction* (vol. II of *Discourse Studies: A multidisciplinary introduction*), London: Sage, pp. 231–59.

(eds.) forthcoming, *Meaning and Universal Grammar: Theory and empirical findings*.

*Goethe Wörterbuch* 1966, Stuttgart/Berlin/Köln/Mainz: W. Kohlhammer Verlag. (Hrsg. von der Deutschen Akademie der Wissenschaften zu Berlin.)

Goffman, Erving 1958, *Presentation of Self in Everyday Life*, Edinburgh: University of Edinburgh Press.

1967, Embarrassment and social organization, in Erving Goffman, *Interaction Ritual: Essays in face-to-face behavior*, Garden City, N.Y.: Doubleday, pp. 47–95.

Goodenough, Ward 1994, Toward a working theory of culture, in Robert Borofsky (ed.), *Assessing Cultural Anthropology*, New York: McGraw-Hill, pp. 262–75.

Gorer, Geoffrey 1949, Some aspects of the psychology of the people of Great Russia, *The American Slavic and East European Review* 8(3): 155–66.

Grimm, Jacob 1882[1822], "Vorrede" to *Deutsche Grammatik* (2nd edition), Göttingen. W. Scherer (ed.), Hildesheim: G. Olms, 1967–71, 5 vols. (Documenta linguistica Grammatiken des 19 Jahrhunderts. Bde 3–4 edited by G. Roethe and E. Schroder.)

Grimm, Jacob, and Wilhelm Grimm 1854, *Deutsches Wörterbuch*, Leipzig: Verlag von S. Hirzel.

Hahnemann, Christina 1995, Gespräche mit Gott – bitten, danken, in Pausch and Pausch, pp. 58–64.

Hale, Ken 1994, Preliminary observations on lexical and semantic primitives in the Misumalpan languages of Nicaragua, in Goddard and Wierzbicka, pp. 263–83.

Hall, Edward T. 1990, *The Hidden Dimension*, New York: Doubleday.

Hanks, W. F. 1996, *Language and Communicative Practices*, Boulder: Westview.

Harder, Arne 1995, Ich bin kein Atheist – ich bin noch auf der Suche, in Pausch and Pausch, pp. 64–70.

Harkins, Jean 1990a, Shame and shyness in the Aboriginal classroom: a case for "practical semantics", *Australian Journal of Linguistics* 10: 293–306.

1990b, Review of A. Ortony, G. L. Clore, and A. Collins, *The Cognitive Structure of Emotions* (Cambridge Unversity Press, 1988), *Australian Journal of Linguistics* 10: 277–387.

1995, Desire in language and thought: a study in cross-cultural semantics, Ph.D. thesis, Australian National University.

1996, Linguistic and cultural differences in the concept of shame, in David Parker and Rosamund Dalziell (eds.), *Shame and the Modern Self*, Melbourne: Australian Scholarly Publishing, pp. 84–96.

Harkins, Jean, and Anna Wierzbicka 1997, Language: a key issue in emotion research, *Innovation in Social Sciences Research* 10(4): 319–31.

(eds.) forthcoming, *Cross-cultural Semantics of Emotions*.

Harkins, Jean, and David P. Wilkins 1994, Mparntwe Arrernte and the search for lexical universals, in Goddard and Wierzbicka, pp. 285–310.

*Harrap's German and English Dictionary* 1963, see Jones.

Harré, Rom 1986a, An outline of the social constructionist viewpoint, in Harré, 1986b, pp. 2–14.

(ed.) 1986b, *The Social Construction of Emotion*, Oxford: Basil Blackwell.

1990, Embarrassment: a conceptual analysis, in R. A. Crozier (ed.), *Shyness and Embarrassment*, Cambridge: Cambridge University Press, pp. 181–204.

Harré, Rom, and Vernon Reynolds (eds.) 1984, *The Meaning of Primate Signals*, Cambridge: Cambridge University Press.

Harris, Paul 1989, *Children and Emotion: The development of psychological understanding*, Oxford: Basil Blackwell.

1995, Developmental constraints on emotion categories, in Russell et al., pp. 353–72.

Harris, Roy 1984, Comment, in Harré and Reynolds, p. 174.

Hasada, Rie 1997, Some aspects of Japanese cultural ethos embedded in non-verbal communicative behaviour, in F. Poyatos (ed.), *Nonverbal Communication and Translation*, Amsterdam: John Benjamins, pp. 83–103.

1997, Conditionals and counterfactuals in Japanese, *Language Sciences* 19(3): 277–88.

1998, Sound symbolic emotion words in Japanese, in Athanasiadou and Tabakowska, pp. 83–98.

Heidegger, Martin 1953[1926], *Sein und Zeit*, Tübingen: Niemeyer.

1962[1926], *Being and Time* (translated by John Macquarrie and Edward Robinson), London: SCM.

Henderson, John, and Veronica Dobson 1994, *Eastern and Central Arrernte to English Dictionary* (Arandic Languages Dictionaries Program), Alice Springs: I. A. D.

Hentig, Hartmut von 1996, Pflicht und Neigung, in Hartmut von Hentig (ed.), *Deutschland in Kleinen Geschichten*, München: Deutscher Taschenbuch Verlag, pp. 59–62.

Hiatt, L. R. 1978, *Australian Aboriginal Concepts*, Canberra: Australian Institute of Aboriginal Studies.

Hill, Deborah 1994, Longgu, in Goddard and Wierzbicka, pp. 311–29.

Hochschild, Arlie Russell 1983, *The Managed Heart: Commercialization of human feeling*, Berkeley: University of California Press.

Hoffman, Eva 1989, *Lost in Translation – A life in a new language*, New York: Dutton.

Holland, Dorothy, and Naomi Quinn (eds.) 1987, *Cultural Models in Language and Thought*, Cambridge: Cambridge University Press.

Howell, Signe 1981, Rules not words, in Paul Heelas and Andrew Lock (eds.), *Indigenous Psychologies: The anthropology of the self*, London: Academic, pp. 133–43.

1982, *Chewong Myths and Legends*, Kuala Lumpur: Art Printing Works.

1984, *Society and Cosmos: Chewong of Peninsula Malaysia*, Singapore and

Oxford: Oxford University Press.

forthcoming, A timid liver: the moral force of Chewong embodied emotionality, in R. H. Bornes and H. Murphy (eds.), *The Anthropology of Fear*, Cambridge: Cambridge University Press.

Humboldt, Carl Wilhelm von 1903–36, *Wilhelm von Humboldts Werke*, 17 vols. (ed. Albert Leitzmann), Berlin: B. Behr.

Iordanskaja, Lidija 1970, Popytka leksikografičeskogo tolkovanija gruppy russkix slov so značeniem čuvstva, *Mašinnyj Perevod i Prikladnaja Lingvistika*, vyp 13: 3–34.

1974, Tentative lexicographic definitions for a group of Russian words denoting emotions, in V. J. Rozencvejg (ed.), *Machine Translation and Applied Linguistics*, Frankfurt: Athenäum, vol. II: 88–117. (Russian version published 1970.)

1986, Russian expressions denoting physical symptoms of emotions, *Lingua* 69: 245–82.

Iordanskaja, Lidija, and Igor Mel'čuk 1990, The semantics of two emotion verbs in Russian: *bojat'sja* ("to be afraid") and *nadejat'sja* ("to hope"), *Australian Journal of Linguistics* 10(2): 307–57.

Iordanskaja, Lidija, and Slava Paperno 1996, *The Russian–English Collocational Dictionary of the Human Body (RECDHB)*, Columbus, Ohio: Slavica.

Izard, Carroll E. 1971, *The Face of Emotion*, New York: Appleton-Century-Croft.

1977, *Human Emotions*, New York: Plenum.

1984, Emotion–cognition relationships and human development, in C. Izard, J. Kagan, and R. Zajonc (eds.), *Emotions, Cognition and Behaviour*, Cambridge: Cambridge University Press, pp. 17–37.

1991, *The Psychology of Emotions*, New York: Plenum.

1992, Basic emotions, relations among emotions and emotion–cognition relations, *Psychological Review* 99(3): 561–5.

1994, Innate and universal facial expressions: evidence from development and cross-cultural research, *Psychological Bulletin* 115(2): 288–99.

1997, Emotions and facial expressions: a perspective from differential emotions theory, in Russell and Fernández-Dols 1997b, pp. 57–77.

Jaeger, Hans 1971, *Heidegger und die Sprache*, Bern and München: Francke Verlag.

James, William 1890, *The Principles of Psychology*, vol. II, New York: Macmillan.

Jamison, Kay Redfield 1997, *An Unquiet Mind: A memoir of moods and madness*, London: Picador.

Jenkins, Janis 1994, Culture, emotion, and psychopathology, in Kitayama and Markus, pp. 307–35.

Johnson, Mark 1987, *The Body in the Mind*, Chicago: University of Chicago Press.

Johnson-Laird, Philip, and Keith Oatley 1989, The language of emotions: an analysis of a semantic field, *Cognition and Emotion* 3: 81–123.

Jones, Trevor (ed.) 1963, *German and English Dictionary*, London: Harrap.

Keesing, Roger 1994, Radical cultural difference: anthropology's myth?, in Pütz, pp. 3–23.

Keller, R. E. 1978, *The German Language*, London and Boston: Faber.

Kemble, Frances Anne 1975[1839], in Moffat and Painter, pp. 255–69.

Kemper, T. D. 1987, How many emotions are there? Wedding the social and the autonomic components, *American Journal of Sociology* 93: 263–89.

Kierkegaard, Søren 1980, *The Concept of Anxiety* (translated by Reidar Thomte and Albert B. Anderson), New Jersey: Princeton University Press.

Kitayama, Shinobu, and Hazel Rose Markus 1992, Construal of the self as cultural frame: implications for internationalizing psychology, paper for symposium on Internationalization and Higher Education, University of Michigan, 6–8 May 1992.

Kitayama, Shinobu, and Hazel Rose Markus (eds.) 1994, *Emotion and Culture: Empirical studies of mutual influence*, Washington, D. C.: American Psychological Association.

Klemperer, Victor 1996, *Ich will Zeugnis ablegen bis zum letzten: Tagebücher 1933–1941*, Berlin: Aufbau.

Klos Sokol, Laura 1997, *Shortcuts to Poland*, Warszawa: Wydawnictwo IPS.

Kraut, R. E., and R. E. Johnston 1979, Social and emotional messages of smiling: an ethological approach, *Journal of Personality and Social Psychology* 37: 1539–53.

Kurcz, Ida, Andrzej Lewicki, Jadwiga Sambor, Krzysztof Szafran, and Jerzy Worończak 1990, *Słownik Frekwencyjny Polszczyzny Współczesnej*, Kraków: Polska Akademia Nauk.

La Bible, 1988, *Traduction œcuménique de la Bible*, Paris: Alliance Biblique Universelle and Le Cerf.

Lakoff, George 1987, *Women, Fire, and Dangerous Things: What categories reveal about the mind*, Chicago : University of Chicago Press.

Lakoff, George, and Mark Johnson 1980, *Metaphors We Live By*, Chicago: University of Chicago Press.

*Langenscheidts Großwörterbuch Deutsch als Fremdsprache* 1993, Berlin: Langenscheidt.

Lazarus, Richard 1991, *Emotion and Adaptation*, New York: Oxford University Press.

1995, Vexing research problems inherent in cognitive–mediational theories of emotion and some solutions, *Psychological Inquiry* 6(3): 183–96.

*LDOTEL* 1984, *Longman Dictionary of the English Language*, edited by Heather Gay, Brian O'Kill, Katherine Seed, and Janet Whitcut, London: Longman.

Leavitt, John 1996, Meaning and feeling in the anthropology of emotions, *American Ethnologist* 23(3): 514–39.

Lebra, Takie S. 1976, *Japanese Patterns of Behavior*, Honolulu: University Press of Hawaii.

Leech, Geoffrey N. 1983, *Principles of Pragmatics*, London: Longman.

L'Engle, Madeleine 1989, Foreword to C. S. Lewis, *A Grief Observed*.

Levine, Nancy 1981, Perspectives on love: morality and affect in Nyinba interpersonal relations, in Adrian Mayer (ed.), *Culture and Morality*, New York: Academic, pp. 106–25.

Levontina, I. B., and Anna A. Zaliznjak forthcoming, Human emotions viewed through the Russian language, in Harkins and Wierzbicka.

Levy, Robert I. 1973, *Tahitians: Mind and experience in the Society Islands*, Chicago: University of Chicago Press.

1984, Emotion, knowing and culture, in Shweder and LeVine, pp. 214–37.

Lewis, C. S. 1989, *A Grief Observed*, San Francisco: Harper and Row.

Lewis, Michael 1995, Embarrassment: the emotion of self-exposure and evaluation, in Price Tangney and Fisher, pp. 190–218.

Lewis, Michael, and Jeanette M. Haviland (eds.) 1993, *Handbook of Emotions*, New York: Guilford.

Lodge, David 1996, *Therapy*, Harmondsworth: Penguin.

Logan, Sarah 1998, The changing meaning of English emotion terms, B.A.

thesis, Australian National University.

Lucy, John A. 1997, The linguistics of "color", in C. L. Hardin and Luisa Maffi (eds.), *Color Categories in Thought and Language*, Cambridge: Cambridge University Press, pp. 320–46.

Luther, [Martin], *NT*, 1964a, *Das Neue Testament unseres Herrn und Heilandes Jesus Christus, nach der Übersetzung Martin Luthers*, Stuttgart: Württembergische Bibelanstalt.

1964b, *D. Martin Luthers Werke, Die Deutsche Bibel. Graz: Akademische Druck- und Verlagsanstalt.*

*Lutheran Hymn Book* 1961, Adelaide: the Lutheran Publishing Co.

Lutz, Catherine 1985, Ethnopsychology compared to what? Explaining behaviour and consciousness among the Ifaluk, in White and Kirkpatrick, pp. 35–79.

1986, Emotion, thought and estrangement: emotion as a cultural category, *Cultural Anthropology* 1: 287–309.

1987, Goals, events and understanding in Ifaluk emotion theory, in Holland and Quinn, pp. 290–312.

1988, *Unnatural Emotions: Everyday sentiments on a Micronesian atoll and their challenge to Western theory*, Chicago: University of Chicago Press.

1990, Engendered emotion: gender, power and the rhetoric of emotional control in American discourse, in Catherine Lutz and Lila Abu-Lughod (eds.), *Language and the Politics of Emotion*, Cambridge: Cambridge University Press, pp. 69–91.

1995, Need, nurturance, and the emotions on a Pacific atoll, in Marks, Ames, and Solomon, pp. 235–52.

Lynch, Owen M. 1990, The social construction of emotion in India, in Owen M. Lynch (ed.), *Divine Passions: The social construction of emotion in India*, Berkeley: University of California Press, pp. 3–34.

Malcolm, Norman 1966, *Ludwig Wittgenstein: A memoir*, London: Oxford University Press.

Malouf, David 1983, *Fly Away Peter*, Ringwood, Vic.: Penguin.

Mandler, G. 1975, *Mind and Emotion*, New York: John Wiley and Sons.

1997, Foreword, in Russell and Fernández-Dols 1997b, pp. vii–x.

Marks, Joel 1995, Emotions in Western thought: some backgound for a comparative dialogue, in Marks, Ames, and Solomon, pp. 1–38.

Marks, Joel, Roger T. Ames, and Robert Solomon (eds.) 1995, *Emotions in Asian Thought: A dialogue in comparative philosophy*, Albany, N. Y.: State University of New York Press.

Matsumoto, David 1996, *Unmasking Japan: Myths and realities about the emotions of the Japanese*, Stanford: Stanford University Press.

Matsumoto, David, and P. Ekman 1988, *Japanese and Caucasian Facial Expressions of Emotion (JACFEE)*, slide set and brochure, available from first author, San Francisco State University.

Melanchton, Philip (1963), Epistolarum Lib. X 1546, in C. G. Bretschneider (ed.), *Corpus Reformatorum*, Frankfurt am Main: Minerva.

Mel'čuk, Igor 1995, *Glaza Maši Golubye* vs *Glaza u Maši Golubye*: choosing between two Russian constructions in the domain of body parts, in Igor Mel'čuk, *The Russian Language in the Meaning – Text Perspective*, Moscow and Vienna: Škola Jazyki Russkoj Kul'tury, pp. 135–64.

Mel'čuk, Igor, Nadia Arbatchewsky-Jumarie, Louise Dagenais, Léo Elnitsky, Lidija Iordanskaja, Marie-Noëlle Lefebvre, and Suzanne Mantha 1988,

*Dictionnaire Explicatif et Combinatoire du Français Contemporain II*, Montréal: Presses de l'Université de Montréal (Recherches lexico-sémantiques II).

Mel'čuk, Igor, Nadia Arbatchewsky-Jumarie, Léo Elnitsky, Lidija Iordanskaja, and Adèle Lessard 1984, *Dictionnaire Explicatif et Combinatoire du Français Contemporain I*, Montréal: Presses de l'Université de Montréal (Recherches lexico-sémantiques I).

Mel'čuk, Igor, Nadia Arbatchewsky-Jumarie, Lidija Iordanskaja, and Suzanne Mantha 1992, *Dictionnaire Explicatif et Combinatoire du Français Contemporain III*, Montréal: Presses de l'Université de Montréal (Recherches lexico-sémantiques III).

Mel'čuk, Igor, and Alexander Zholkovsky 1984, *Tolkovo-kombinatornyj Slovar' Sovremennogo Russkogo Jazyka (Explanatory Combinatorial Dictionary of Modern Russian)*, Vienna: Wiener Slawistischer Almanach (Sonderband 14).

Messinger, Daniel S., Alan Fogel, and K. Laurie Dickson, 1997, A dynamic systems approach to infant facial action, in Russell and Fernández-Dols 1997b, pp. 205–26.

Mikołajczuk, Agnieszka 1998, The metonymic and metaphorical conceptualisation of *anger* in Polish, in Athanasiadou and Tabakowska, pp. 153–90.

Miller, William Ian 1993, *Humiliation: And other essays on honor, social discomfort, and violence*, Ithaca: Cornell University Press.

Moffat, Mary Jane, and Charlotte Painter (eds.) 1975, *Revelations: Diaries of women*, New York: Bantam.

Mori, Kyoko 1997, *Polite Lies: On being a woman caught between two cultures*, New York: Holt.

Mosse, Walter M. 1955, *A Theological German Vocabulary: German theological key words illustrated in quotations from Martin Luther's Bible and the Revised Standard Edition*, New York: Macmillan.

Mostovaja, Anna 1998, On emotions that one can "immerse into", "fall into" and "come to": the semantics of a few Russian prepositional constructions, in Athanasiadou and Tabakowska, pp. 295–330.

Moynihan, Martin 1976, *The New World Primates: Adaptive radiation and the evolution of social behavior, languages, and intelligence*, Princeton, N. J.: Princeton University Press.

Müller, Wilhelm (ed.) 1963, *Mittelhochdeutsches Wörterbuch mit Benutzung des Nachlasses von Georg Friedrich Benecke*, Hildesheim: Georg Olms.

Müller, Wolfgang (ed.) 1972, *Duden Sinn- und sachverwandte Wörter und Wendungen*, Mannheim/Wien/Zürich: Duden.

Myers, David, and Ed Diener 1995, Who is happy? *Psychological Science* 6, 10–19.

Myers, Fred 1986, *Pintupi Country, Pintupi Self: Sentiment, place and politics among Western Desert Aborigines*, Washington, D.C.: Smithsonian.

Nabokov, Vladimir 1957, *Pnin*, London: Heinemann.

Nathanson, Donald L. 1992, *Shame and Pride*, New York: W. W. Norton.

NEB 1970, *New English Bible: The New Testament* (2nd edition), Cambridge: Oxford University Press and Cambridge University Press.

Needham, Rodney 1981, *Circumstantial Deliveries*, Berkeley: University of California Press.

NGÜ(L) 1989, *Das Evangelium nach Lukas, Neue Genfer Übersetzung*, Genf: Genfer Bibelgesellschaft.

NGÜ(M) 1989, *Das Evangelium nach Matthäus, Neue Genfer Übersetzung*, Genf: Genfer Bibelgesellschaft.

NKJV 1982, *Holy Bible: New King James Version*, Canberra: Bible Society.

Noll, Ingrid 1993, *Der Hahn ist Tot*, Zürich: Diogenes.

*NTL* 1985, *Novum Testamentum Latine*, Stuttgart: Deutsche Bibelgesellschaft.

Nuss, Bernard 1993, *Das Faust Syndrom Ein Versuch über die Mentalität der Deutschen*, Bonn: Bouvier.

Oatley, K, and J. M. Jenkins 1996, *Understanding Emotion*, Cambridge: Cambridge University Press.

Oberman, Heiko A. 1983, *Luther: Mensch zwischen Gott and Teufel*, Berlin: Severin und Siedler.

Ochs, Elinor 1986, From feelings to grammar: a Samoan case study, in Bambi Schiefflin and Elinor Ochs (eds.), *Language Socialization across Cultures*, Cambridge: Cambridge University Press, pp. 251–72.

  1988, *Culture and Language Development: Language acquisition and language socialization in a Samoan village*, Cambridge: Cambridge University Press.

*OED* 1993[1933], *Oxford English Dictionary* (2nd edition), Oxford: Clarendon.

Onishi, Masayuki 1994, Semantic primitives in Japanese, in Goddard and Wierzbicka, pp. 361–85.

  1997, The grammar of mental predicates in Japanese, *Language Sciences* 19(3): 219–33.

Ortony, Andrew, Gerald Clore, and Allan Collins 1988, *The Cognitive Structure of Emotions*, Cambridge: Cambridge University Press.

Ortony, Andrew, and Terence Turner 1990, What's basic about basic emotions? *Psychological Review* 97: 315–31.

Osmond, Meredith 1997, The prepositions we use in the construal of emotion: why do we say "fed up with" but "sick and tired of"?, in Susanne Niemeier and René Dirven (eds.), *The Language of Emotions: Conceptualization, expression, and theoretical foundation*, Amsterdam and Philadelphia: John Benjamins, pp. 111–33.

Oxford Russian Dictionary 1992, see Falla et al..

Palmer, Gary B., and Rick Brown 1998, The ideology of honour, respect, and emotion in Tagalog, in Athanasiadou and Tabakowska, pp 331–57.

Panksepp, J. 1982, Toward a general psychobiological theory of emotions, *Behavioural and Brain Sciences* 5: 407–67.

Parkin, David 1996, Language is the essence of culture in Tim Ingold (ed.), *Key Debates in Anthropology*, London and New York: Routledge, pp. 154–58.

Parrott, W. Gerrod 1991, The emotional experiences of envy and jealousy, in Salovey, pp. 3–30.

Pausch, A., and J. Pausch (eds.) 1995, *Kraft in den Schwachen*, Mainz: Matthias-Grünewald.

Peck, Stephen Rogers 1987, *Atlas of Facial Expression*, New York: Oxford University Press.

Peeters, Bert 1994, Semantic and lexical universals in French, in Goddard and Wierzbicka, pp. 423–44.

  1997, The syntax of time and space primitives in French, *Language Sciences* 19(3): 235–44.

Peirce, Charles 1932, Speculative grammar, in *Collected Papers of C. S. Peirce*, vol. II, Cambridge, Mass.: Harvard University Press.

Pendergrast, Mark 1998, *Victims of Memory: Incest accusations and shattered lives*, London: Harper Collins.

Phillips, Catherine (ed.) 1986, *Gerard Manley Hopkins*, Oxford: Oxford University Press.

Pinker, Steven 1994, *The Language Instinct*. New York: William Morrow.

1997, *How the Mind Works*, New York: Norton.

Plessner, Helmuth 1970[1961], *Laughing and Crying: A Study of the limits of human behaviour* (Translated by James S. Churchill and Marjorie Grene), Evanston: Northwestern University Press.

Plutchik, Robert 1994, *The Psychology and Biology of Emotion*, New York: Harper Collins College.

Polack, W. G. 1942, *The Handbook to the Lutheran Hymnal*, Saint Louis, Mo.: Concordia Publishing House.

Pope, L. K., and C. A. Smith 1994, On the distinct meanings of smiles and frowns, *Cognition and Emotion*, 8: 65–72.

Price Tangney, June, and Kurt W. Fischer (eds.) 1995, *Self-conscious Emotions: The psychology of shame, guilt, embarrassment, and pride*, New York: Guilford.

Provine, Robert R. 1997, Yawns, laughs, smiles, tickles and talking: naturalistic and laboratory studies of facial action and social communication, In Russell and Fernández-Dols 1997b, pp. 158–75.

Pütz, Martin (ed.) 1994, *Language Contact and Language Conflict*, Amsterdam and Philadelphia: John Benjamins.

Rabinow, Paul, and William M. Sullivan (eds.) 1979, *Interpretive Social Science: A reader*, Berkeley: University Of California Press.

Ratinger, Joseph 1968, *Einführung in das Christentum*, München: Kösel.

*RECDHB* 1996, see Iordanskaja and Paperno.

Reh, Mechthild 1998, The language of emotion: an analysis of Dholuo on the basis of Grace Ogot's novel *Miaha*, In Athanasiadou and Tabakowska (eds.), pp 375–408.

Reichmann, Oskar 1989, *Frühneuhochdeutsches Wörterbuch*, Berlin: de Gruyter.

Renwick, George W. 1980, *InterAct: Guidelines for Australians and North Americans*, Yarmouth, Maine: Intercultural.

Ricks, Christopher 1974, *Keats and Embarrassment*, Oxford: Clarendon.

Ricoeur, Paul 1981, Metaphor and the central problem of hermeneutics, in John B. Thompson (ed.), *Hermeneutics and the Human Sciences: Essays on language, action, and interpretation*, Cambridge: Cambridge University Press, pp. 165–81.

Rieschild, Verna 1996, Lebanese–Arabic Discourse: Adult interaction with young children (with reference to Australian–English situations) Ph.D thesis, Australian National University.

Rosaldo, Michelle Z. 1980, *Knowledge and Passion: Ilongot notions of self and social life*, Cambridge: Cambridge University Press.

1984, Towards an anthropology of self and feeling, In Shweder and LeVine, pp. 137–57.

Rosaldo, Renato 1978, The rhetoric of control: Ilongots viewed as natural bandits and wild Indians, in B. Babcock (ed.), *The Reversible World: Symbolic inversion in art and society*, Ithaca, N.Y.: Cornell University Press, pp. 240–57.

Rössler, Dietrich 1979, *Vergewisserung: 22 Beispiele christlicher Rede*, Stuttgart and Berlin: Kreuz Verlag.

Rumsay, Alan forthcoming, Ku Waru ethnosyntax and theories of culture, in Nick Enfield (ed.) *Ethnosyntax*.

Ruoff, Arno (ed.) 1981, *Häufigkeitswörterbuch gesprochener Sprache*, Tübingen: Max Niemeyer Verlag.

Russell, James A. 1991, Culture and the categorization of emotion, *Psychological Bulletin* 110: 426–50.

1993, Forced-choice response format in the study of facial expression? *Motivation and Emotion* 17: 41–51.

1994, Is there universal recognition of emotion from facial expression? A review of the cross-cultural studies, *Psychological Bulletin* 115(1): 102–41.

1995, Facial expressions of emotion: what lies beyond minimal universality? *Psychological Bulletin* 118(3): 379–91.

1997, Reading emotions from and into faces: resurrecting a dimensional-contextual perspective, in Russell and Fernández-Dols 1997b, pp. 295–320.

Russell, James A., José Miguel Fernández-Dols, Antony Manstead, and J. C. Wellenkamp (eds.) 1995, *Everyday Conceptions of Emotion: An introduction to the psychology, anthropology, and linguistics of emotion*, Dordrecht and Boston: Kluwer Academic.

Russell, James A., and José Miguel Fernández-Dols 1997a, What does a facial expression mean? in Russell and Fernández-Dols 1997b, pp. 3–30.

Russell, James A., and José Miguel Fernández-Dols (eds.) 1997b, *The Psychology of Facial Expression*, Cambridge: Cambridge University Press.

Russell, James, and Michelle Yik 1996, Emotion among the Chinese, in Michael Bond (ed.) *The Handbook of Chinese Psychology*, Hong Kong: Oxford University Press, pp. 166–88.

Sahlins, Marshall 1994, Goodbye to tristes tropes: ethnography in the context of modern world history, in Robert Borofsky (ed.), *Assessing Cultural Anthropology*, New York: McGraw-Hill. [Reprinted from *Journal of Modern History* 1993(65): 1–25 Chicago: University of Chicago Press.]

Salinger, J. D. 1964, *Nine Stories*, New York: Bantam.

Salovey, Peter (ed.) 1991, *The Psychology of Jealousy and Envy*, New York: Guilford.

Sapir, Edward 1949[1929], The status of linguistics as a science, in David Mandelbaum (ed.), *Selected Writings of Edward Sapir in Language, Culture and Personality*, Berkeley: University of California Press, pp. 160–66.

Sartre, Jean-Paul 1948. *The Emotions: Outline of a theory* (translated by B. Frechtman), New York: Philosophical Library.

Saunders, B. A. C., and J. Van Brakel 1996, Are there nontrivial constraints on colour categorization? *Behavioural and Brain Sciences* 20(2): 167–79.

Schachter, R., and J. E. Singer 1962, Cognitive, social and physiological determinants of emotional state, *Psychological Review* 69: 379–99.

Scheff, Thomas 1990, *Microsociology: Discourse, emotion and social structures*, Chicago: University of Chicago Press.

Scherer, K. R. 1984, On the nature and function of emotion: a component process approach, in Scherer and Ekman, pp. 293–317.

1992, What does facial expression express? In K. T. Strongman (ed.), *International Review of Studies of Emotion* 2: 139–65.

Scherer, K. R., and P. Ekman (eds.) 1984, *Approaches to Emotion*, Hillsdale, N.J.: Erlbaum.

Schwanitz, Dietrich 1995, *Der Campus*, Frankfurt: Eichborn.

Shaver, P., J. Schwartz, D. Kirston and C. O'Connor 1987, Emotion knowledge: further exploration of a prototype approach, *Journal of Personality and Social Behaviour* 52: 1061–86.

Shore, Bradd 1996, *Culture in Mind: Cognition, culture, and the problem of meaning*, New York: Oxford University Press.

Shweder, Richard 1985, Menstrual pollution, soul loss, and the comparative study of emotions, in Arthur Kleinman and Byron Good (eds.), *Culture and*

*Depression: Studies in the anthropology and cross-cultural psychiatry of affect and disorder*, Berkeley: University of California Press, pp. 182–215.

1990, Cultural psychology: What is it?, in Stigler, Shweder, and Herdt, pp. 1–43.

1994, You're not sick, you're just in love: emotion as an interpretive system, in Ekman and Davidson, pp. 32–44.

Shweder, Richard A. and Robert A. LeVine (eds.) 1984, *Culture Theory: Essays on mind, self, and emotion*, Cambridge: Cambridge University Press.

Simonds, Paul E. 1974, *The Social Primates*, New York: Harper and Row.

*SJP* 1958–69, Słownik Języka Polskiego (*Dictionary of the Polish Language*) ed. W. Doroszewski, 11 vols., Warsaw: PWN.

Smedslund, Jan 1992, Are Frijda's "Laws of Emotion" empirical? *Cognition and Emotion* 6(6): 435–56.

Smith, Craig A. 1989, Dimensions of appraisal and physiological response in emotion, *Journal of Personality and Social Psychology* 56: 339–53.

Smith, Craig A., and Heather S. Scott 1997, A componential approach to the meaning of facial expressions, in Russell and Fernández-Dols 1997b, pp. 229–54.

Smith, Manuel J. 1975, *When I say no, I feel guilty: How to cope – using the skills of systematic assertive therapy*, New York: Bantam.

Smith, Richard H. 1991, Envy and the sense of injustice. in Salovey, pp. 79–99.

Snodgrass, J. 1992, Judgement of feeling states from facial behavior: a bottom-up approach, unpublished doctoral dissertation, University of British Columbia.

Sohn, Ho-min, and Anthony F. Tawerilmang 1976, *Woleaian–English Dictionary*, Honolulu: University Press Of Hawaii.

Solomon, Robert C. 1976, *The Passions*, Garden City, N.Y.: Anchor.

1984, Getting angry: the Jamesian theory of emotion in anthropology, in Shweder and LeVine, pp. 238–55.

1995, The cross-cultural comparison of emotion, in Marks, Ames, and Solomon, pp. 253–308.

1997, Toward a politics of emotion, paper presented at conference on Emotion in Social Life and Social Theory, Australian National University, 9–11 July 1997.

Sommers, Shula 1984, Adults evaluating their emotions: a cross-cultural perspective, in C. Z. Malatesta and C. E. Izard (eds.), *Emotion in Adult Development*, Beverley Hills, Calif.: Sage, pp. 319–38.

Spevack, Marvin 1968, *A Complete and Systematic Concordance to the Works of Shakespeare*, Hildesheim: George Olms.

Spufford, Margaret 1996, *Celebration: A story of suffering and joy*, Mowbray: Fount.

Stanisławski, Jan 1969, *Wielki Słownik Polsko-Angielski*, Warsaw: Wiedza Powszechna.

Stearns, Carol Z. 1993, Sadness, in Lewis and Haviland, pp. 547–61.

Stearns, Carol Z., and Peter N. Stearns 1986, *Anger: The struggle for emotional control in America's history*, Chicago: University of Chicago Press.

1988a, Introduction, in Stearns and Stearns 1988b, pp. 1–21.

(eds.) 1988b, *Emotion and Social Change*, New York: Holmes and Meier.

Stearns, Peter N. 1994, *American Cool: Constructing a twentieth-century emotional style*, New York: New York University Press.

Stein, Nancy L., Tom Trabasso, and Maria Liwag 1993, The representation and organisation of emotion experience: unfolding the emotion episode, in Lewis and Haviland, pp. pp. 279–300.

Steiner, George 1992, *After Babel* (2nd edition), Oxford; Oxford University Press.

Stern, Gustaf 1965[1932], *Meaning and Change of Meaning with special reference to the English language*, Bloomington: Indiana University Press.

Stevenson, Burton 1949, *Stevenson's Book of Quotations, Classical and Modern*, London: Cassell.

Stigler, James W., Richard A. Shweder, and Gilbert Herdt (eds.) 1990, *Cultural Psychology: Essays on comparative human development*, Cambridge: Cambridge University Press.

Taylor, Charles 1979[1971], Interpretation and the sciences of man, in Rabinow and Sullivan, pp. 25–72.

Taylor, Gabriele 1985, *Pride, Shame and Guilt: Emotions of self-assessment*, Oxford: Clarendon.

Taylor, John, and Thandi G. Mbense 1998, Red dogs and rotten mealies: how Zulus talk about anger, in Athanasiadou and Tabakowska, pp. 191–226.

Thayne, David, and Kinuko Suzuki 1996, *Amerikajin no kokoro ga wakaru Eikaiwa*, Tokyo: Nariundo.

Tillich, Paul 1957, *Systematic Theology*, vol. II: *Existence and The Christ*, Chicago: University of Chicago Press.

Tolstoy, Leo 1970[1918], *Anna Karenina* (The Maude Translation), New York: W. W. Norton.

Tomasello, Michael (ed.) 1998, *The New Psychology of Language: Cognitive and functional approaches to language structure*, New Jersey: Lawrence Erlbaum.

Tomasello, Michael, and Joseph Call 1997, *Primate Cognition*, New York: Oxford University Press.

Tomkins, S. S. 1987, Shame, in D. L. Nathanson (ed.), *The Many Faces of Shame*, New York: Guilford, pp. 133–61

Travis, Catherine 1997, *Kind, considerate, thoughtful*: a semantic analysis, *Lexikos* 7: 130–52. (AFRILEX-reeks/series 7).

1998, Omoiyari as a core Japanese value: Japanese-style empathy?, in Athanasiadou and Tabakowska, pp. 55–82.

Tuite, Kevin 1998, Why historical anthropologists need the philologist: theories of variation and change in language and culture, paper presented at the Australian National University, Linguistic Typology Seminar Series, 4 June, 1998.

Uryson, Elena 1997, "Toska", in Apresjan, pp. 441–5.

Van Brakel, Jaap 1993, The plasticity of categories: the case of color, *British Journal for the Philosophy of Science* 44: 103–35.

1994, Emotions: a cross-cultural perspective on forms of life, in W. M. Wentworth and J. Ryan (eds.), *Social Perspectives on Emotion II*, Greenwich: JAI, pp. 179–237.

von Klappenbach, Ruth, and Wolfgang Steinitz (eds.) 1964–77, *Wörterbuch der Deutschen Gegenwartssprache*, Berlin: Akademie-Verlag.

Wace, Nigel 1981, Public attitudes towards uninvited plants, seminar paper presented to the Australian National University Linguistics Society, 10 September, 1981.

Wallerstein, Immanuel 1994, Comments on Wolf's "Perilous ideas: race, culture and people", *Current Anthropology* 35(1): 9–10.

Wanning, E. 1991, *Culture Shock! USA*, Singapore: Time.

*WDG* 1964–77 (*Wörterbuch der Deutschen Gegenwartssprache*), see von Klappenbach, and Steinitz.

White, Geoffrey 1992, Ethnopsychology, in Theodore Schwartz, Geoffrey White and Catherine A. Lutz (eds.), *New Directions in Psychological Anthropology*, Cambridge: Cambridge University Press, pp. 21–45.

1993, Emotions inside out: the anthropology of affect, in Lewis and Haviland, pp. 29–40.

White, Geoffrey, and John Kirkpatrick (eds.) 1985, *Person, Self, and Experience: Exploring Pacific ethnopsychologies*, Berkeley, Calif.: University of California Press.

Wierzbicka, Anna 1972, *Semantic Primitives*, Frankfurt am Main: Athenäum (Linguistische Forschungen, 22).

1973, The semantic structure of words for emotions, In Roman Jakobson, C. H. van Schooneveld, and Dean S. Worth (eds.), *Slavic Poetics: Essays in honor of Kiril Taranovsky*, The Hague: Mouton, pp. 499–505.

1979, Ethnosyntax and the philosophy of grammar, *Studies in Language* 3(3): 313–83.

1980, *Lingua Mentalis: The semantics of natural language*, Sydney: Academic.

1984, *Apples* are not a "kind of fruit": the semantics of human categorization, *American Ethnologist* 11(2): 313–28.

1985a, *Lexicography and Conceptual Analysis*, Ann Arbor: Karoma.

1985b, Cups and mugs: lexicography and conceptual analysis, *Australian Journal of Linguistics* 4(2): 205–55.

1986a, Human emotions: universal or culture-specific? *American Anthropologist* 88(3): 584–94.

1986b, Metaphors linguists live by. Lakoff and Johnson contra Aristotle, (Review of George Lakoff and Mark Johnson 1980, *Metaphors we live by*, Chicago: University of Chicago Press), *Papers in Linguistics* 19(2): 287–313.

1987, *English Speech Act Verbs: A semantic dictionary*, Sydney: Academic.

1988a, *The Semantics of Grammar*, Amsterdam: John Benjamins.

1988b, Emotions across cultures: similarities and differences (A rejoinder to Kolenda), *American Anthropologist* 90(4): 982–3.

1989, Soul and mind: linguistic evidence for ethnopsychology and cultural history, *American Anthropologist* 91(1): 41–58.

1990a, *Duša* (≈ soul), *toska* (≈ yearning), *sud'ba* (≈ fate): three key concepts in Russian language and Russian culture, in Zygmunt Saloni (ed.), *Metody Formalne w Opisie Języków Słowiańskich (Formal methods in the description of Slavic languages)*, Białystok: Białystok University Press, pp. 13–32.

1990b, Kul'turno-obuslovlennye scenarii i ix kognitivnyj status [Cultural scripts and their cognitive status], In *Jazyk i Struktura Znanija*, Moscow: Akademija Nauk, pp. 63–85.

1990c, The meaning of color terms: semantics, culture and cognition. *Cognitive Linguistics* 1(1): 99–150.

1990d, The semantics of emotion: *fear* and its relatives in English, *Australian Journal of Linguistics* (Special issue on the semantics of emotions) 10(2): 359–75.

(ed.) 1990e, *Australian Journal of Linguistics* 10(2) (Special issue on the semantics of emotions).

1991, *Cross-cultural Pragmatics: The semantics of human interaction*, Berlin: Mouton de Gruyter.

1992a, *Semantics, Culture and Cognition: Universal human concepts in culture-specific configurations*, New York: Oxford University Press.

1992b, Defining emotion concepts, *Cognitive Science* 16: 539–81.

1992c, Talking about emotions: semantics, culture and cognition, *Cognition and Emotion* (Special issue on basic emotions) 6(3/4): 285–319.

1993a, A conceptual basis for cultural psychology, *Ethos* 21(2): 205–31.

1993b, Reading human faces: emotion components and universal semantics, *Pragmatics and Cognition* 1(1): 1–23.

1994a, Cognitive domains and the structure of the lexicon: the case of emotions, in Lawrence A. Hirschfeld and Susan A. Gelman (eds.), *Mapping the Mind: Domain specificity in cognition and culture*, Cambridge: Cambridge University Press, pp. 431–52.

1994b, "Cultural Scripts": a new approach to the study of cross-cultural communication, in Pütz, pp. 69–87.

1994c, "Cultural Scripts": a semantic approach to cultural analysis and cross-cultural communication, *Pragmatics and Language Learning*, Monograph Series 5: 1–24.

1994d, Emotion, language and "cultural scripts", in Kitayama and Markus, pp. 130–98.

1995a, Adjectives vs verbs: the iconicity of part-of-speech membership, in M. Landsberg (ed.), *Syntactic Iconicity and Linguistic Freezes*, Berlin: de Gruyter, pp. 223–45.

1995b, Emotion and facial expression: a semantic perspective, *Culture and Psychology* 1: 227–58.

1995c, Everyday conceptions of emotion: a semantic perspective, in Russell et al., pp. 17–47.

1995d, Kisses, handshakes, bows: the semantics of nonverbal communication, *Semiotica* 103(3/4): 207–52.

1995e, Lexicon as a key to history, culture, and society: "Homeland" and "Fatherland" in German, Polish and Russian, in René Dirven and Johan Vanparys (eds.), *Current Approaches to the Lexicon*, Frankfurt: Peter Lang Verlag, pp. 103–55.

1995f, The relevance of language to the study of emotions – a commentary on Lazarus, *Psychological Inquiry* 6(3): 248–52.

1996a, *Semantics: Primes and Universals*, Oxford: Oxford University Press.

1996b, Contrastive sociolinguistics and the theory of "Cultural Scripts': Chinese vs. English, in Marlis Hellinger and Ulrich Ammon (eds.), *Contrastive Sociolinguistics*, Berlin: Mouton de Gruyter, pp. 313–44.

1996c, Japanese Cultural Scripts: cultural psychology and "cultural grammar", *Ethos* 24(3): 527–55.

1997a, *Understanding Cultures through their Key Words: English, Russian, Polish, German, Japanese*, New York: Oxford University Press.

1997b, The double life of a bilingual: a cross-cultural perspective, in Michael Bond (ed.), *Working at the Interface of Cultures: Eighteen lives in social science* London: Routledge, pp. 113–25.

1998a, German cultural scripts: public signs as a key to social attitudes and cultural values, *Discourse and Society* 9(2): 265–306.

1998b, "Sadness" and "Anger" in Russian: the non-universality of the so-called "basic human emotions", in Athanasiadou and Tabakowska, pp. 3–28.

forthcoming a, A culturally salient Polish emotion: Przykro ['pshickro], in W. Gerrod Parrott and Rom Harré (eds.), Special issue of *World Psychology*.

forthcoming b, "Universals of colour" from a linguistic point of view: a commentary on Saunders and Van Brakel, *Behavioural and Brain Sciences*.

forthcoming c, *Cultural scripts: theory and case-studies*.

Wikan, Unni 1990, *Managing Turbulent Hearts: A Balinese formula for living*, Chicago: University of Chicago Press.

Wilkins, David 1986, Particles/clitics for criticism and complaint in Mparntwe Arrernte (Aranda), *Journal of Pragmatics* 10(5): 575–96.

1992, Interjections as deictics, in Ameka, pp. 119–57.

Wittgenstein, Ludwig 1967, *Zettel* (edited by G. E. M. Anscombe and G. H. von Wright; translated by G. E. M. Anscombe), Oxford: Basil Blackwell.

1988[1922], *Tractatus Logico-Philosophicus* (translated by C. K. Ogden), London: Routledge.

Wolf, Eric R. 1994, Perilous ideas: race, culture and people, *Current Anthropology* 35(1): 1–7.

Wolfenstein, Martha 1975, The emergence of fun morality, in James P. Spradley and Michael A. Rynkiewich (eds.), *The Nacirema*, Boston: Little, Brown and Co, pp. 394–402.

Wolfson Nessa 1983, An empirically based analysis of complimenting in American English, in N. Wolfson and E. Judd (eds.), *Sociolinguistics and Language Acquisition*, Rowley: Newbury House, pp. 82–95.

Wordsworth, Dorothy 1975[1802], in Moffat and Painter, pp. 178–92.

Wuthnow, Robert, James Davison Hunter, Albert Bergesen, and Edith Kurzweil 1984, *Cultural Analysis: The work of Peter L. Berger, Mary Douglas, Michel Foucault and Jürgen Habermas*, Boston and London: Routledge and Kegan Paul.

Zaliznjak, Anna 1992, Investigations in the semantics of inner state predicates, *Slavistische Beiträge* B 298, München: Otto Sagner Verlag.

Zaliznjak, Anna, and Irena Levontina 1996, Otraženie Nacional'nogo Xaraktera v Leksike Russkogo Jazyka – Razmyšlenija po povodu knigi: Anna Wierzbicka *Semantics, Culture and Cognition* (The reflection of Russian national character in the lexicon of the Russian language: Reflections on Anna Wierzbicka's book *Semantics, Culture and Cognition*), *Russian Linguistics* 20: 237–64.

# Index

## DATE DUE

| | | | |
|---|---|---|---|
| | | | |
| | | | |
| | | | |
| | | | |
| | | | |
| | | | |
| | | | |
| | | | |
| | | | |
| | | | |
| | | | |
| | | | |
| | | | |
| | | | |
| | | | |
| | | | |
| | | | |
| GAYLORD | | | PRINTED IN U.S.A |